CURRICULUM DEVELOPMENT

Curriculum Development
A Guide to Practice

Jon Wiles
University of Montana

Joseph Bondi, Jr.
University of South Florida

CHARLES E. MERRILL PUBLISHING COMPANY
A Bell & Howell Company
Columbus   Toronto   London   Sydney

Published by
CHARLES E. MERRILL PUBLISHING COMPANY
A Bell and Howell Company
Columbus, Ohio 43216

This book was set in Helvetica.
The production editors were Elizabeth A. Martin and Laura Wallencheck
    Gustafson.
The cover was prepared by Larry Hamill.

Library of Congress Catalog Card Number: 78-61609

International Standard Book Number: 0-675-08315-X

Printed in the United States of America

    5 6 7 8 9 10/ 85 84 83 82

This book is dedicated to our families: Margaret, Amy, and Michael Wiles, and Patsy, Pam, Beth, and Brad Bondi. It is also dedicated to the faculty of the College of Education at The University of Florida for encouraging us to be contributors to the exciting field of professional education.

Contents

Preface

The primary objective of this book is to give both the student of curriculum and the practicing educator a comprehensive understanding of curriculum development. It has been written for those who are responsible for the design and development of school programs in the United States.

Curriculum development as a process is generally a flow from theory to practice. Part One, Curriculum Perspectives, addresses various theoretical concerns of curriculum planning. Part Two, Curriculum Procedures, focuses on activities that carry theory into practice. Part Three, Curriculum Practice, promotes understanding of what presently exists and what may develop in school settings.

The authors believe that successful curriculum development is the result of effective leadership. Such leadership begins with clear purpose; therefore, early chapters of the book are written in a style that will help the readers examine their personal beliefs about education. In addition to clarified values and goals, the curriculum leader must also be able to analyze school environments, understand basic curriculum development processes, and conduct successful practice. These objectives are the basis for later chapters.

Activities at the conclusion of each chapter help the readers in this progression of understanding. Part One activities are designed to assist the reader in conceptualization. Part Two activities are participatory in nature. Part Three activities encourage both insight and creativity in curriculum planning.

J.W.W.

J.C.B.

part one

Curriculum Perspectives

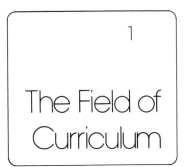

1

The Field of Curriculum

The field of curriculum stands on the threshold of becoming ordered. Although there is presently no comprehensive conceptual system, single theory of development, widely accepted set of designs, or common vocabulary, there have been significant advances in the field during the past three decades. These changes contribute to curriculum's developing structure.

Recent years have witnessed major alterations and refinement of the term *curriculum*. Useful methodologies have been developed to derive goals and objectives for educational planning. Strategies and techniques have evolved for the implementation and assessment of educational programs. Identification of roles and responsibilities is emerging through practice. In short, curriculum is rapidly moving toward professionalism as an area of inquiry.

HISTORICAL PERSPECTIVES

Although an exact date for the origin of the field of curriculum has never been pinpointed in its literature, the most logical point of departure are the meetings of the "great committees" on education in the 1890s. Even though these meetings to "reorganize education" preceded the first book addressed to the study of curriculum by three full decades, it was during these sessions that the first true curriculum questions in the United States were debated.[1]

Prior to 1890 in America there was little questioning of the purpose or organization of formal educational institutions. The nontraditional forms of education, such as the kindergartens and academies, coexisted with the dominant school form without confrontation or even widespread consideration. Schools were regularly believed to be places where students became knowledgeable in content areas, thereby increasing the literacy of the society.

During the last decade of the nineteenth century, however, greater attention was given to alternate forms of education. Ideas about the ultimate goals of education, the substance of an education, and the proper methodology of an education began to clash. The debate was touched off in 1888 during a speech delivered by Charles W. Eliot, President of Harvard University, before the National Education Association. The speech (entitled "Can School Programs Be Shortened and Enriched?") stirred considerable interest and resulted in the appointment of three major committees to study the question.* Although these committees never seriously considered anything but the reorganization of the existing educational structures, the scrutiny of educational systems was initiated. Questions raised at these meetings formed the foundation for the emergence of the field of curriculum— an area of inquiry concerned with the conceptualization, design, implementation, and evaluation of educational programs.

However, social conditions rather than organized inquiry encouraged the early development of curriculum as a specialized area of education. The period from 1890 to 1930 was a formative one in the United States, and as the country changed so did the schools.† Many influences altered the form and substance of public education. As public education developed and became the complex institution it is today, curriculum as a field of inquiry emerged to study and order the changes.

---

* Following Eliot's presentation, the National Education Association formed three major study groups: The Committee of Ten on Secondary Studies, The Committee of Fifteen on Elementary Education, and The Committee on College Entrance Requirements. A fourth committee from the NEA Division of Superintendence, The Committee on Economy of Time in Education, also met during this period to discuss related issues.

† Indicative of the pressures placed on schools by social change during this period was the dramatic increase in secondary enrollment. From 202,000 secondary students in 1890, enrollment increased to four million students by 1924. These developments had the effect of placing "order" in school planning as a high priority and solidified traditional educational approaches in an otherwise fluid period of national development.

Of particular importance during this period was the growth of the field of psychology in America. Early studies, such as those of Hall, promoted understanding of learning and human development which found application in schools.[2] Psychological inquiry also spawned the first generation of American educational theorists. These theorists, such as Dewey, Kilpatrick, Rugg, and Counts, greatly stimulated thinking about the educational process in America and planted pedagogical seeds which are still bearing fruit in the last quarter of the twentieth century.

From that period until the present, social forces have continued to stimulate thinking about schools and to alter the parameters of curricular concern. Depressions, wars, fluctuations in economic prosperity, emerging social expectations, political priorities, technological advancements, and other forces have expanded the horizons of educational planning. The definition of curriculum, as well as the boundaries of its concerns as a field of inquiry, is best understood in light of those societal changes. It is readily apparent that the definition of curriculum has been undergoing immense change during the past fifty years.

AN EVOLVING DEFINITION

The first modern use of the term *curriculum* appeared in the United States around 1820, although the term itself was used in Scotland as early as the seventeenth century. In the United States, curriculum was originally defined as a course of study or training; a product. Curriculum was equated with the content of textbooks, course outlines, teacher guides, or other finished artifacts of study. This oldest conception of curriculum remained in general usage in the United States until approximately 1930 and is still representative of the lay public's understanding of the term. Such a "classic" definition of curriculum is also representative of the most conservative philosophies of education as seen in the following statements:

> The curriculum should consist of permanent studies—the rules of grammar, reading, rhetoric and logic, and mathematics (for the elementary and secondary school), and the greatest books of the western world (beginning at the secondary level of schooling).[3]

> The curriculum must consist essentially of disciplined study in five great areas: (1) command of mother tongue and the systematic study of grammar, literature, and writing, (2) mathematics, (3) sciences, (4) history, (5) foreign language.[4]

> The curriculum should consist entirely of knowledge which comes from the disciplines. . . . Education should be conceived as a guided recapitulation of the process of inquiry which gave rise to the fruitful bodies of organized knowledge comprising the established disciplines.[5]

Identifying the curriculum as a finished product or static body of knowledge caused curriculum planners great difficulty in the early part of this century. This was a time of great expansion in knowledge, and many modern areas of study were being established. In addition, the pairing of knowledge bases, such as sociology and psychology, was creating new ways of using this information. To identify which knowledge was essential knowledge became an increasingly difficult task.

Further, the population to be educated in public schools changed significantly during this formative period. Whereas in 1890 most secondary students had been in college preparatory programs, by 1930 they came from a more general population and the school took on a greater socializing function. Basic skills such as mastering English, for example, took precedence over more classic learning. Even so, educational planners continued to define the curriculum as an essential body of knowledge, and the program of the school became less relevant to the needs of those in attendance.

The definition of curriculum began to stretch to fit the growing distance between the planned curriculum and the experiences that were actually encountered. The established breaking point with the traditional "product" definition came in 1935 when Caswell and Campbell acknowledged the socializing function of the schooling process: "The curriculum is composed of all the experiences children have under the guidance of the teacher."[6]

Other modern writers have followed Caswell and Campbell in defining the curriculum as experiences:

> A sequence of potential experiences is set up in the school for the purpose of disciplining children and youth in group ways of thinking and acting. This set of experiences is referred to as the curriculum.[7]

> The curriculum is now generally considered to be all of the experiences that learners have under the auspices of the school.[8]

By the mid-1950s, it became increasingly evident that schools had a tremendous influence on students' lives. Some of those influences were structured, while others occurred due to the congregation of youth. It was recognized that students also had experiences not planned by the school. During this period, definitions were dominated by those aspects of the curriculum that were planned, as opposed to simply the content or general experiences of students.

> The curriculum is all of the learning of students which is planned by and directed by the school to attain its educational goals.[9]

> A curriculum is a plan for learning.[10]

> We define curriculum as a plan for providing sets of learning opportunities to achieve broad goals and related specific objectives for an identifiable population served by a single school center.[11]

Finally, into the 1960s and early 1970s there was a rising interest in the performance of educational programs. This focus, often referred to as "accountability," pushed the definition of curriculum toward an emphasis on results and ends:

> Curriculum is concerned not with what students will do in the learning situation, but with what they will learn as a consequence of what they do. Curriculum is concerned with results.[12]

> (Curriculum is) the planned and guided learning experiences and intended outcomes, formulated through systematic reconstruction of knowledge and experience, under the auspices of the school, for the learners' continuous and willful growth in personal-social competence.[13]

While the definition of curriculum has been altered in response to social forces and expectations for the school, the process of curriculum development has remained constant. Through analysis, design, implementation, and evaluation, curriculum developers set goals, plan experiences, select content, and assess outcomes of school programs. These constant processes have contributed to the emergence of principles of curriculum planning.

EMERGING PRINCIPLES

The principles that exist in the field of curriculum have evolved primarily from practice rather than from deductive logic. This unusual condition results from the philosophical nature of curriculum thinking. As Taba has observed, "What is considered the domain of curriculum thinking depends (of course) on how one defines curriculum."[14]

Although curriculum development efforts in the United States are not highly ordered, due in large part to our decentralized educational system, it would be grossly inaccurate to characterize curriculum as having no guiding principles. Indeed, they do exist!

The focus of most curricular principles is specific rather than global. As Tanner and Tanner have recently noted, "In the absence of a holistic conception of curriculum, the focus is on piecemeal and mechanical functions . . . the main thrust in curriculum development and reform over the years has been directed at microcurricular problems to the neglect of macrocurricular problems."[15]

Principles of curriculum have evolved as "core" procedures rather than theoretical guidelines. Maccia has called this the "proxiological approach" to theorizing as opposed to a more philosophical or theoretical approach.[16] The cause for this evolution of principles is a combination of the absence of systematic thinking about curriculum planning; the vulnerability of curriculum planning to social, political, and economic forces; and the constantly changing priorities of education in the United States.

Because of this situation, identification of curricular principles is difficult. Taba describes the almost unmanageable condition of curriculum approaches in this way:

> Decisions leading to change in curriculum organization have been made largely by pressure, by hunches, or in terms of expediency instead of being based on clearcut theoretical considerations or tested knowledge. The scope of curriculum has been extended vastly without an adequate consideration of the consequence of this extension on sequence or cumulative learning. . . . The fact that these perplexities underlying curriculum change have not been studied adequately may account for the proliferation of approaches to curriculum making.[17]

Prior to the 1960s, curriculum development was oriented toward producing school programs. In developing courses of study, curriculum specialists sought to refine school programs by seeking new ways of implementing essential topic areas and by undating old programs to keep them in tune with changing times. This rather static role for curriculum developers resulted from the evolution of both theoretical constructs and operational procedures over a long period of time.

An early observation by John Dewey that "the fundamental factors in the educative process are 1) the learner, 2) the society, and 3) organized subject matter"[18] set the stage for defining curriculum parameters. Bode, an early curriculum theorist and student of Dewey, renewed this theme in 1931 when he wrote, " . . . the difference in curriculum aims stems from three points of view: 1) the standpoint of subject-matter specialists, 2) the standpoint of the practical man and, 3) the interests of the learner."[19]

By 1945 these three general concerns were finding acceptance in most curriculum literature. Taba, for instance, discussed the three sources of data in curriculum planning as 1) the study of society, 2) studies of learners, and 3) studies of subject matter content.[20] By the early 1960s Taba had further refined the study of society to mean "cultural demands . . . a reflection of the changing social milieu of the school."[21]

Gaining acceptance as a fourth important planning base for curriculum in the mid-1950s and early 1960s was the study of learning itself. Studies from various schools of psychology and the advent of sophisticated technology in school settings raised new possibilities and choices for educators who were planning programs.

Although these four major concerns of curriculum planners have been challenged by Schwab and others,[22] they remain today the points of origin for most analysis, design, and evaluation of school programs. The importance of these planning bases as organizers for thinking about educational programs is thoroughly summarized by Hilda Taba:

> . . . semantics aside, these variations in the conception of the function of education are not idle or theoretical arguments. They have defi-

nite concrete implications for the shape of educational programs, especially the curriculum. . . . If one believes that the chief function of education is to transmit the perennial truths, one cannot but strive toward a uniform curriculum and teaching. Efforts to develop thinking take a different shape depending on whether the major function of education is seen as fostering creative thinking and problem solving or as following the rational forms of thinking established in our classical tradition. As such, differences in these concepts naturally determine what are considered the 'essentials' and what the dispensable frills in education.[23]

Paralleling the conceptual "mapping out" of the field of curriculum concerns was the evolution of operational procedures. Early curriculum development focused on subject content, which was a mechanical and rather simple operational technique developed in the 1920s and continued as the dominant operational concern until the early 1960s. Writing in the 1926 National Society for the Study of Education Yearbook, Harold Rugg outlined the operational tasks of curriculum development as a three-step process: 1) determine the fundamental objectives, 2) select activities and other materials of instruction, and 3) discover the most effective organization and placement of this instruction.[24]

By 1950, the technique of "inventory, organize, and present" had reached refinement in Tyler's widely read four-step analysis:

1. What educational purposes shall the school seek to attain?
2. What educational experiences can be provided that are likely to attain those purposes?
3. How can these educational experiences be effectively organized?
4. How can we determine whether these purposes are being attained?[25]

Tyler introduced a "system of thinking" about the curriculum development process by including an evaluation step. This analysis of the learning cycle in schools illuminated the comprehensiveness of planning activity and gave birth to notable refinements such as taxonomies of learning and systems thinking about curriculum development.[26,27] Tyler also rekindled a fifty-year-old effort to develop manageable behavioral objectives in education.[28]

The ordering of the development procedure also encouraged a mechanistic approach to curriculum development. Such approaches, long practiced in schools, are thoroughly represented in curriculum literature through various definitions:

Curriculum development . . . it is basically a plan of structuring the environment to coordinate in an orderly manner the elements of time, space, materials, equipment and personnel.[29]

The function of curriculum development is to research, design, and engineer the working relationships of the curricular elements that will be employed during the instructional phase in order to achieve desired outcomes.[30]

Perhaps the most refined version of Tyler's procedure for developing school curriculum was outlined by Taba in 1962. Seven major steps of curriculum development were identified:

1. diagnosis of needs
2. formulation of objectives
3. selection of content
4. organization of content
5. selection of learning experiences
6. organization of learning experiences
7. determination of what to evaluate and means of doing it

Within each step, substeps were provided which identified criteria for action. For example, in the selection of learning experiences it is important that the curriculum developer consider the following:

1. validity and significance of content
2. consistency with social reality
3. balance of breadth and depth of experiences
4. provision for a wide range of objectives
5. learnability-adaptability of the experience to life of student
6. appropriateness to needs and interests of learners[31]

Although we could provide other examples of traditional curriculum development, it should be clear by this time that a fairly standard procedure for developing curricula was taught and practiced between 1920 and 1960 in the United States. This procedure reflected the historical dominance of subject matter content, the increasingly technical nature of curriculum development due to the bureaucratization of major school systems and educational agencies, and the preponderance of the Anglo-Saxon culture in the United States during the period.

Perhaps the whole concept of curriculum development prior to around 1960 was summarized by Alexander in a 1971 speech:

Certainly, a review of the plans made and implemented today and yesterday leaves no doubt that the dominant assumption of past curriculum planning has been the goal of subject matter mastery through a subject curriculum, almost inextricably tied to a closed school and graded school ladder, to a marking system that rewards successful achievement of fixed content and penalizes unsuccessful achievement, to an instructional organization based on fixed classes in the subjects and a time table for them.[32]

Even though there was and continues to be considerable reinforcement for the so-called substantive dimension of curriculum development in terms of operating procedures, it is interesting to note that the dichotomy between curriculum theory and curriculum practice has widened since the early 1960s. Although the operational focus carried out in school environments has been directed toward the refinement of activity steps, the theoretical dimension of curriculum has expanded immensely as study of theoretical constructs has become more sophisticated.

A growing body of social problems and issues, a more complete knowledge about human development, an increased understanding of learning, and a geometric expansion of knowledge base have all contributed to an expanded theory perspective. These new perceptions have altered thinking about the role of education and opened new concerns for curriculum planning.

PROBLEMS AND ISSUES IN CURRICULUM

The massive changes in the American society that occurred during the 1960s contributed significantly to the complexity of curricular concerns. An increased sophistication in recognizing the role of formal education in societal development underscored the many choices and decisions to be made by educational planners. Those choices reflected substantial problems and issues that have been inherent in the field of curriculum since its inception. Issues relating to the role, mission, and direction of curriculum development are worthy of review.

In considering the role of curriculum developers, there has emerged a concern for both the scope and the direction of activity. The important intersection of theory and practice during the instructional phase of learning has expanded planning concerns beyond the areas of material construction and revision. In its literature, the various areas of concern and influence in curriculum planning are referred to as *domains*. At least five such domains presently affect curriculum planning: philosophy-values, instructional systems, materials development, supervision of instruction, and teacher training. These domains influence the analysis, implementation, maintenance, regulation, and perpetuation of educational programs.

With so many interrelated theatres of activity, the role of curriculum development is multi-faceted. A long-term trend toward a "generalist" orientation as a curriculum role has proven ineffective given the increased specialization of concerns in practice.

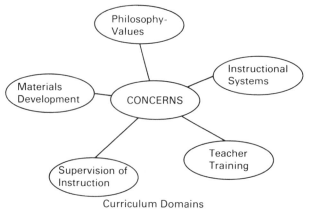

Curriculum Domains

Figure 1.1
Curriculum Domains

Perhaps more critical as an issue for curriculum developers in terms of role, however, is the greater question of curriculum's relationship to education in general. Here, great differences of opinion exist regarding whether curriculum developers should provide direct leadership to the field of education or assume a more subordinated helping posture. The extremes on this question are reflected in the following statements:

> Curriculum planning lies at the heart of educational planning—dealing with the definition of educational ends and the engineering of means for achieving them.[33]

> Curriculum theory should be a subordinate of total educational theory.[34]

Arguments for which of the above role definitions is most suitable for curriculum workers are complex. The argument for an assisting technical role is that curriculum theory and practice have traditionally been far apart. So-called "blue sky" curriculum designs rarely achieve fruitful application in the real world of schools. If curriculum developers are to be useful, so the argument goes, they must meet the real needs of education. This can be done best by maintaining a "tractive" or static orientation, being specific in operations and serving where needed.

Arguments which hold that curriculum developers should provide leadership by being both dynamic and intellectual, and by achieving a global orientation to education, are multiple. Bruce Joyce provides the strongest argument against the traditional posture:

> In the past, educational planners have been technically weak (unable often to clarify ends or engineer means) and morally or technically unable to bring about a humanistic revolution in education . . . curricu-

lum workers have defined themselves as helpers, not leaders, letting the community and teachers make decisions and then assisting in the implementation of those decisions.

> By focusing on schools and teachers in schools, curriculum is being forced to operate within the parameters of the institution . . . by far the most paralyzing effect of the assumptive world in which the curriculum specialist lives is that it tends to filter out all ideas which might improve education but which fit awkwardly into the school pattern.[35]

Because of the traditional orientation, say those calling for an active role for the curriculum specialist, for example, the field of curriculum has continued to speak the language of sequence, prerequisites, academic achievement, and mastery. Learning theories that do not fit the existing school program, or are not seen as feasible in terms of current teacher practices, are neglected.

The perception of a curriculum specialist as a thinker, designer, leader, and projectionist goes back to the writings of Dewey, Counts, and other progressives of the early twentieth century. George Counts, for instance, observed that "the goals of education must be determined by philosophical and analytical concepts of the good life."[36]

Among those perceiving curriculum development as a dynamic operation there is a great fear that the gravitational pull of bureaucracy in education has won out. With each consolidation of schools, with each new piece of legislation, with each new regulation, the school becomes more closed to change, more self-perpetuating and product-oriented. This trend is in direct conflict with the desire of some curriculum theorists to see education as a process. Berman, for instance, calls for a process-oriented person who has opportunities in school to plan for the future; a planning that involves process skills and competencies. Such "communicating, loving, decision-making, knowing, organizing, creating, and valuing" persons will never evolve without strong curriculum leadership.[37]

Finally, it is worth noting that these differences in the perception of the role of the curriculum specialist reflect a differing time-image point of reference. Those seeing curriculum work as a support function are generally concerned with the here-and-now of the present. Those who seek a more dynamic role for curriculum development are more concerned with what schools can become. These role expectations illuminate the great philosophical range among curriculum developers.

Like the role of the curriculum worker, the mission or end sought by those acting in program development capacities is not certain. The pluralistic nature of the American society, the magnetic pull of futurism, and the inability of school leaders to control change in educational environments have all contributed to this condition.

In retrospect, the classic statement of educational goals issued by the Commission on the Reorganization of Secondary Education in 1918 seems both vague and unusable as a guide for local curriculum planning. Set forth as national ideals for education, these so-called Seven Cardinal Principles called for schools to address the following areas in program development:

Health
Command of Fundamental Processes
Worthy Home Membership
Vocational Competence
Effective Citizenship
Worthy Use of Leisure
Ethical Character

Two observations can be made about these goals. First, they have functioned over a fifty-year span to direct the thoughts of school planners to the general purposes of public education. It is interesting to note that even today the Seven Cardinal Principles continue to be cherished for that role.* On the other hand, it can be observed that such goals reflect a much simpler time in our country; a time when the population of the United States was less informed and a great deal less involved in the events of the day. In 1914, for instance, 70 percent of all schools were one-room schools. The absence of effective mass media meant that school programs were not closely scrutinized. The official business of running educational systems was left to a small and rather homogenous slice of the American population. Communication about goals of educating, when such communication existed, was poor.

Today, in contrast, the American public is fairly well informed about the activities of schools, and programs are reviewed by many interested parties in society. General goals for education, such as the Seven Cardinal Principles, can no longer satisfy all people, and curriculum planners are faced with a continually changing mosaic of social priorities and expectations for schools. To some extent, as Taba points out, the above condition is the product of a democratic society:

> In a complex culture with a pluralistic value system, it is difficult to establish a single central function for any agency. It is more difficult to determine the function of a school in a democracy than in a totalitarian society where a small power group decides both what society should be and what role the schools shall play in it.[38]

The problem of mission for curriculum developers is that if there is no social consensus about the ends that schools should seek, then it

---

* A distinguished panel of scholars and educators, headed by Dr. Harold G. Shane, recently gave strong reaffirmation to the Seven Cardinal Principles as appropriate guidelines for the future. For greater detail see Harold G. Shane, "The Seven Cardinal Principles Revised, A Bicentennial Project" *Today's Education* 65, September-October 1976, pp. 57–72.

is not possible to proceed with the development of educational programs. Given this logistical dilemma, curriculum workers may strike out to advocate their own priorities for schools, or they may adopt the role of technician and busy themselves with the maintenance of existing programs of study.

Another issue in dealing with the mission of curriculum work has been futuristic thinking and its implications for school planners. In an age where miracles such as moon landings, computer technology, and solar energy are realities, educational planners are drawn to study the future as a source of input for planning school experiences. Individual educators, commissions, White House panels, and other reputable agencies have done this during the past two decades; and many studies have called for drastic overhaul of our present educational structure.*

Based on a growing body of knowledge about learning, knowledge laced with new understandings about the effects of environment, media, and stimulation patterns, planners face a choice: to stay with traditional programs, to modify traditional programs, or to strike out in new directions to redesign education in order to accommodate futuristic thinking. For many curriculum planners, the dissonance between what they know about the potential of education and what they do in planning on a day-to-day basis is distressing. In the absence of social mandate, curriculum planners must work within the dictates of their own consciences and the political realities of their immediate environments in "blueprinting" the programs of future citizens.

A final problem for curriculum planners in terms of mission and the implementation of school programs is the flow of change in educational environments. To a degree greater than most educational planners like to admit, changes occur in school settings in spite of planning. Macdonald summarizes the difficulty this way:

> The development of the curriculum in the American public schools has been primarily an accident. A description of what curriculum exists is essentially a political and/or ethical document rather than a scientific or technical one. It is a statement which indicates the outcomes of a very complex interaction of groups, pressures, and events which are most often sociopolitical in motivation and which result in decisions about what ought to be.[39]

The uneven and sometimes unpredictable flow of change in school environments is the result of increased public attention to education, media coverage, political activism, legal assessments of educational activity, and the discovery of education as a business market. All of these forces, and others, have led to a decrease in the control over change experienced by school planners. This condition, to a large ex-

---

* For a treatment of this subject see Alvin Toffler, *Future Shock* (New York: Random House, 1970), and *Learning for Tomorrow; The Role of the Future in Education* (New York: Random House, 1974).

tent, is the result of increased federal funding in education which has resulted in the stimulation of these ever-present forces.

The funding of National Science Foundation projects in the late 1950s and Great Society programs in the early 1960s placed the federal government in the role of chief stimulator of curriculum change, and shifted the focus of school program development beyond the immediate realm of the local school district and the curriculum specialist. Almost overnight, program development in schools was being led by university professors, textbook publishers, newly formed educational corporations, and grant writers from all segments and sectors of education. Again, Macdonald summarizes:

> . . . the prospect of publishing a whole new series of textbooks for all subjects to sell for the use of every child in each classroom in each school in the land offered more than a minimal stimulus for development.[40]

The absence of a systematic means of developing, reviewing, and selecting curricula on a national basis has contributed to the unclear mission of the curriculum worker. Despite strong convictions and development skills, the professional curriculum worker is only one of many forces vying for the control of change in the educational environment.

Still another area of uncertainty in curriculum work lies in the realm of planning. Here, the type of planning that succeeds, the effect of environmental conditions on planning, and the ever-present gap between theory and practice affect curriculum development.

There has been a tremendous amount of superficial change in schools in the last three decades. Slogans, innovative practices, and labels are plentiful, but few examples of major program alteration are evidenced. Such a condition reflects the absence of clear educational philosophy in schools and a basic propensity of educators to reject present realities for hoped-for eventualities. [In short, it is easier to plan change in schools by disrupting traditional programs rather than by constructing new curriculum designs.]

Another factor related to planning is the effect of social, political, and economic stress in the society at large. When operating under such stress, educational planning often leaves the control of curriculum workers as Goodlad observes:

> In periods of unusual political, economic, or social stress, curriculum change is likely to be more counter-cyclical in relation to the past, to occur rapidly, and to be led by persons not identified with earlier curriculum change, or, for that matter, with the schools.[41]

Increasingly, social pressures in America are constant phenomena, and the disruption of educational planning a regular occurrence.

A final problem related to curricular planning involves the blending of theory and practice. In this area there is a dual dilemma of plans being either too theoretical to be accepted by practicing educators, or being wholly without design or support from research. Taba observes:

> A gap between theory and practice exists at both ends of curriculum development: theoretical designs of curricula are developed with meager foundations in experimentation and practice, and implementation is carried on without sufficient understanding of theory.[42]

For the curriculum specialist, couching plans for school programs in the correct language, establishing the link of theory to previous practices, and providing an overall outline for curriculum change remain problems to be overcome in planning.

SUMMARY

The field of curriculum development appears to be on the threshold of becoming an ordered discipline of inquiry. To the degree that curriculum is defined, methodologies and strategies developed, and roles and responsibilities clarified, curriculum workers can be effective in their tasks. Before a new era of educational planning can evolve, however, certain conditions which presently impede planning efforts must be eliminated.

Historically, the definition of curriculum, the focus of curricular activity, and the procedures for developing school programs have been in flux. Specific issues related to the roles, mission, and direction of curriculum planning have remained unsolved and, as such, contribute to the largely undefined nature of the field. In many cases, those issues are general education issues beyond the operational control of practitioners and theoreticians alike.

Notes

1. Franklin Bobbit, *The Curriculum* (Boston: Houghton-Mifflin Company, 1918).
2. G. Stanley Hall, "The Contents of Children's Minds on Entering School," *Pedagogical Seminary* 1 (1891): 139–73.
3. Robert Hutchins, *The Higher Learning in America* (New Haven, Conn.: Yale University Press, 1936), p. 82.
4. Arthur Bestor, *The Restoration of Learning* (New York: Alfred A. Knopf, Inc., 1956), pp. 48–49.

5. Phillip H. Phenix, "The Disciplines as Curriculum Content," in A. Harry Passow, ed., *Curriculum Crossroads* (New York: Teachers College Press, 1962), p. 64.
6. Hollis L. Caswell and Doak S. Campbell, *Curriculum Development* (New York: American Book Company, 1935), p. 66.
7. B. Othanel Smith, William O. Stanley, and J. Harlen Shores, *Fundamentals of Curriculum Development* (New York: Harcourt, Brace, Jovanovich, Inc., 1957), p. 3.
8. Ronald Doll, *Curriculum Improvement,* 2nd ed. (Boston: Allyn and Bacon, 1970).
9. Ralph W. Tyler, "The Curriculum Then and Now," in proceedings of the 1956 Conference on Testing Problems, (Princeton, New Jersey: Educational Testing Service, 1957), p. 79.
10. Hilda Taba, *Curriculum Development: Theory and Practice* (New York: Harcourt, Brace, Jovanovich, Inc., 1962), p. 11.
11. J. Galen Saylor and William M. Alexander, *Curriculum Planning for Schools* (New York: Holt, Rinehart, Winston, 1974), p. 6.
12. Mauritz Johnson, "Appropriate Research Directions in Curriculum and Instruction," *Curriculum Theory Network* 6 (Winter 1970–71): 25.
13. Daniel Tanner and Laurel Tanner, *Curriculum Development: Theory into Practice* (New York: Macmillan Publishing Co., 1975), p. 45.
14. Taba, *Curriculum Development: Theory and Practice,* p. 9.
15. Tanner and Tanner, *Curriculum Development: Theory into Practice,* preface.
16. Elizabeth S. Maccia, "Curriculum Theory and Policy," a paper presented at American Education Research Association, Chicago, 1965.
17. Taba, *Curriculum Development: Theory and Practice,* pp. 383–84.
18. John Dewey, *The Child and the Curriculum* (Chicago: University of Chicago Press, 1902), p. 4.
19. Boyd H. Bode, "Education at the Crossroads," *Progressive Education* 8, pp. 543–44.
20. Hilda Taba, "General Techniques of Curriculum Planning," American Education in the Postwar Period, *44th Yearbook,* Part I, National Society for the Study of Education, (Chicago: University of Chicago Press, 1945), p. 85.
21. Taba, *Curriculum Development: Theory and Practice,* p. 10.
22. Joseph Schwab, *The Practical: A Language for Curriculum,* (Washington, D.C.: National Education Association, Center for the Study of Instruction, 1970).
23. Taba, *Curriculum Development: Theory and Practice,* p. 30.
24. Harold Rugg, "Curriculum-Making: Past and Present," *26th Yearbook,* Part I, National Society for the Study of Education (Chicago: University of Chicago Press, 1926), p. 22.
25. Ralph W. Tyler, *Basic Principles of Curriculum and Instruction* (Chicago: University of Chicago Press, 1949).
26. Benjamin S. Bloom, *Taxonomy of Educational Objectives, Handbook I: Cognitive Domain* (New York, David McKay, Inc., 1956) and David R. Krathwohl, Benjamin S. Bloom, and Bertram M. Masia, *Taxonomy of Educational Objectives, Handbook II: Affective Domain* (New York, David McKay, Inc., 1964).

27. Kathryn V. Feyereisen, A. John Fiorino, and Alene T. Nowak, *Supervision and Curriculum Renewal: A Systems Approach* (New York: Appleton-Century-Crofts, 1970).
28. Robert F. Mager, *Goal Analysis* (Belmont, California: Fearon Publishers, 1972).
29. Feyereisen, *Supervision and Curriculum Renewal,* p. 204.
30. A. Dean Havenstein, *Curriculum Planning for Behavioral Development* (Worthington, Ohio, Charles A. Jones, p. 6. 1975).
31. Taba, *Curriculum Development: Theory and Practice,* p. 12.
32. William M. Alexander, "Curriculum Planning As It Should Be," an address to Association for Supervision and Curriculum Development Conference, Chicago, October 29, 1971.
33. Bruce Joyce, "The Curriculum Worker of the Future," *The Curriculum: Retrospect and Prospect,* 71st Yearbook, National Society for the Study of Education, Part I (Chicago: University of Chicago Press, 1971), p. 307.
34. George Beauchamp, *Curriculum Theory* (Wilmette, Kagg Press, Illinois: 1968).
35. Joyce, "The Curriculum Worker of the Future."
36. George Counts, "The Curriculum: Retrospect and Prospect," 71st Yearbook, Part I, National Society for the Study of Education (Chicago: University of Chicago Press, 1971) p. 10.
37. Louise Berman, *New Priorities in the Curriculum* (Columbus, Ohio: Charles Merrill Publishing Co., 1968).
38. Taba, *Curriculum Development: Theory and Practice,* p. 16.
39. James B. Macdonald, "Curriculum Development in Relation to Social and Intellectual Systems," *The Curriculum: Retrospect and Prospect* 71st Yearbook, National Society for the Study of Education (Chicago: University of Chicago Press, 1971), p. 95.
40. Macdonald, "The Curriculum: Retrospect and Prospect," p. 96.
41. John I. Goodlad, "The Changing American School," *66th Yearbook,* National Society for the Study of Education (Chicago: University of Chicago Press, 1966), p. 32.
42. Taba, *Curriculum Development: Theory and Practice,* p. 441.

Suggested Learning Activities

1. Develop a time line of major events which have influenced education and altered the definition of the term *curriculum.*

2. In your own words, state some major principles of curriculum development. Do these principles suggest a utilitarian definition of curriculum?

3. Outline methods by which curriculum workers might best overcome the dissonance between what is known about learning and the way in which learning occurs in most schools.

Books to Review

Bobbit, Franklin. *The Curriculum.* Boston: Houghton-Mifflin Company, 1918.

Caswell, Hollis and Campbell, Doak. *Curriculum Development.* New York: American Book Company, 1935.

Saylor, Galen and Alexander, William. *Planning Curriculum for Schools.* New York: Holt, Rinehart, and Winston, Inc., 1974.

Schwab, Joseph. *The Practical: A Language For Curriculum.* Washington, D.C., NEA, 1970.

Silberman, Charles E., *Crisis in the Classroom.* New York: Random House, Inc., 1970.

Taba, Hilda. *Curriculum Development: Theory and Practice.* New York: Harcourt, Brace, Jovanovich, Inc., 1962.

2

Keys to Successful Curriculum Development

Contemporary students of curriculum rarely appreciate the degree to which the field of study has been altered in a short thirty-year period. As recently as 1950, curriculum development efforts were focused on the mechanics of program improvement, leaving equally important theoretical concerns to a handful of university-based scholars. The kinds of research endeavors, information systems, and massive curriculum projects so familiar to us today were unknown.

The heavy financial support given to all areas of education as a result of Sputnik I radically altered both the focus and the scope of curriculum study. Such funding stimulated in-depth study of school environments, curriculum organization, and development activity by allowing educators to specialize in their inquiries. In-depth inquiry revealed the area of curriculum to be a complex construct, with political, economic, legal, and interpersonal dimensions previously unexplored.

The results of in-depth curriculum study, in turn, altered the understandings educators had about such critical variables as the school environment, the role of the curriculum worker, the types of problems most commonly confronted, and the types of skills needed by the curriculum worker. Collectively, the findings of organized inquiry during the past three decades, and the reaction of the field to such information, provide the student of curriculum development with keys to successful practice.

ENVIRONMENTAL FACTORS

As curriculum study became more sophisticated, the ability of curriculum specialists to be specific in references to curriculum activity increased. Rather than speaking of curriculum tasks as a group, it became possible to speak of precise tasks of curriculum associated with levels of functioning.

Five levels of curriculum activity are now regularly identified by writers of curriculum study: classroom, school, district, state, and national. At the classroom level, curriculum tasks that may be of concern are teacher lesson plans, cognitive and affective learning objectives, and instructional patterns and strategies. At the school building level, curriculum tasks might include program coordination, staffing, inservice activities, and curriculum committee work. District level concerns include vertical articulation (coordination) among school levels, primary resource allocation, and work with community and school boards. At the state level, curriculum tasks might reflect coordination of educational institutions, materials and textbook adoption, work with special interest groups, and legislative and legal activities. Finally, at the national level, curriculum tasks include work with congressional committees, legal court actions, interaction with associations and national education societies, and the implementation of Federal priorities through project work.

In short, as the study of curriculum became specialized, the "layer" effect of curriculum tasks became visible. Such understandings led curriculum workers to develop models and outlines that represented for them the way such practice environments were interrelated. Figure 2.1 illustrates one of these outlines.

In addition to an understanding of the importance of the level at which curriculum tasks were performed, locale was also found to affect role perception. Historically, the curriculum specialist has been portrayed as a lone practitioner holding down a central position with multiple roles and responsibilities. This portrait reflects rural America of the early twentieth century, and is increasingly inaccurate due to the mobility and population patterns of our society.

Certainly, in many of the more than 18,000 school districts of the United States there are curriculum workers who function alone and with multiple responsibilities. But such a pattern is diminishing, and it has taken organized inquiry to reveal this important occurrence. The social consolidation of our society over a thirty-year period has resulted in major concentrations of people, resources, problems, issues, and actions. These changes have placed the curriculum worker in a vastly different kind of work environment. The "typical" curriculum workers today are as often members of a large and highly interdependent team as they are lone generalists. In Joyce's words, "the curriculum worker has become bureaucratized."[1] This effect of environment is important, for each identified area of activity in curriculum development calls for a different and often specific orientation, set of skills, and knowledge.

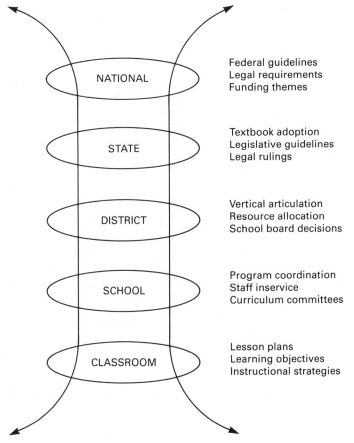

NATIONAL — Federal guidelines / Legal requirements / Funding themes

STATE — Textbook adoption / Legislative guidelines / Legal rulings

DISTRICT — Vertical articulation / Resource allocation / School board decisions

SCHOOL — Program coordination / Staff inservice / Curriculum committees

CLASSROOM — Lesson plans / Learning objectives / Instructional strategies

Figure 2.1
Curriculum Planning Levels

If the curriculum worker performs in one of the more rural and isolated areas of the country, his professional efforts will probably be directed toward the refinement of existing programs, and the interpretation of outside influences such as funded programs and legal mandates. Odds are good that such a functionary will be promoted within the system, and will work closely with only a handful of persons on a regular basis. The day-to-day tasks of a rural curriculum worker will be varied, and the power of his actions will be both direct and influential. Interpersonal skills, rather than knowledge of curriculum, will present the most significant on-the-job asset or liability. *

If, on the other hand, the curriculum specialist is located with the bureaucratic structure of a large urban school district, his role may be significantly altered. The urban curriculum worker may be responsible for a highly specialized function of curriculum development, such as research or directing early childhood programs. He may also be hired according to competence in a highly specialized function such as finance or grantsmanship. He may work with few or many persons each day, and his technical expertise may seem to be more important to his success than human relations.

An understanding of the work environment, and of the relationship between the tasks to be performed and the skills needed to succeed at the task, is essential to overcome barriers which have retarded curriculum development efforts. Such an understanding of the effects of environment on curriculum activity must be preceded by understanding the general changes which have occurred since the early 1950s. Some of these trends are summarized by the Brookings Institute in Table 2.1.

Not only is the general school environment presently more open to lay participation and influence in many school districts, but performance expectations for school officials have increased. These shifts in public awareness and understanding of curriculum activities have forced an alteration in both the roles and methods of practitioners. Some of the changes in curriculum practice seem to be:

> From a primary concern with content per se to a concern with the direction of school development efforts
>
> From a posture of program maintenance to a role of goal-seeking and definition exploration
>
> From a concern with general issues and problems to a concern with highly specific issues and problems
>
> From activity concerned with refinement and updating to activity concerned with design and engineering
>
> From an efficiency orientation to an effectiveness orientation

In many cases curriculum workers are now being asked to perform the dual role of architect and engineer in school planning. This expanded role is made difficult by the lack of clear expectations for on-the-job performance, by consistent problems related to the general organization of most school districts, and by the increasing demand for both interpersonal and organizational skills on the part of the practitioner.

---

* For an analysis of the characteristics of curriculum specialists see Ione Perry, *A Role Study: The County Level Supervisor in Florida,* Department of Education, State of Florida, 1968.

Table 2.1
Changes in the Educational Environment Since 1950

Distinguishing Feature	Traditional System	Reformed System
Center of control	Professional monopoly	The public (community)
Role of parents and organizations	For public relations, to interpret the school in the community	To participate as an active agent in matters substantive to the educational process
Bureaucracy	Centralized authority, limiting flexibility and initiative to the professional at the school level.	Decentralized decision making allowing for maximum lay and professional initiative with central authority concentrating on technical assistance
Educational objectives	Emphasis on grade level performance, basic skills, cognitive achievement	Emphasis on both cognitive and affective development, humanistic oriented objectives
Test of professional efficiency	Emphasis on credentials	Emphasis on performance

Henry Levin, ed., *Community Control of Schools* (Brookings Institute, Washington, D.C., 1970), p. 46.

ROLE PERCEPTIONS

As curriculum has evolved as a field of study, the role expectation for curriculum specialists has become more complex. The breadth of the field, due to the number of planning variables in school environments, has made an exact role definition elusive. As Frymier and Hawn observed in 1970, " . . . curriculum is an area of inquiry so broad and so involved that no one person knows very much." Commenting on the absence of meaningful role definition, the same authors could be only apologetic: "The role of the curriculum worker often appears ambiguous. This may be due to conditions such as the relative newness of the position, the confusion as to whether they are operating in a line of staff relationship, and the fact that they have not had any special preparation for their assignment."[2]

The professional organization in education to which most individuals in curriculum roles belong, the Association for Supervision and Curriculum Development (ASCD), describes the role of a curriculum director: "Used in the broadest sense to indicate persons who, either through working with teachers at the classroom level, or through working with supervisors, principals, or others at the central office level, contribute to the improvement of teaching and/or the implementation and development of curriculum."[3]

At the practice level, curriculum specialists generally perceive their role to be one of four general patterns: content expert, advisor and consultant, facilitator and catalyst, or advocate. Understandings of the scope and meaning of their role affect such perceptions.

Content Expert

Historically, curriculum workers in school systems were promoted through the ranks and generally served as department heads and subject area coordinators. For this reason, many curriculum specialists even today view their roles in terms of the content organization of the schools and address themselves primarily to activities relating to the development of materials and media. By restricting their role to that of subject area specialist or expert, the modern curriculum worker withdraws his or her influence from many other important and related areas of concern. Such a role posture, for instance, would insure a junior and unequal status in district planning efforts, the identification of staff development needs, or resource allocation decisions.

Advisor and Consultant

The role of advisor and consultant insures a wide scope of responsibilities and influence for the curriculum worker. This posture is primarily passive in its orientation and fully accepts the "staff" relationship with other leaders in the district. Since the advising role allows the curriculum worker to intersect the school system in areas where he or she can contribute, it is a politically safe position and often is dominated by activity in "clean" areas where conflict will not occur.

Facilitator and Catalyst

A third role found among curriculum workers draws heavily from the human relations movement in education during the 1950s. Here, the curriculum specialist is seen as a catalyst; a facilitator of persons, processes, and resources. The key to understanding this posture is that the curriculum specialist is often the only person in the school system with the mobility and task pattern to see the "big picture." Such a role perception allows the curriculum worker to bring people and resources together and make activities productive. In the jargon of management theory, the curriculum specialist coordinates, integrates, and maintains the sequential pattern in the work flow.

Advocate

A more recent role of the curriculum development expert is that of advocate of educational needs. Unlike the facilitator, this role envisions the curriculum specialist as being fully involved in the decision-making activities of the district, and leans more in the direction of a partnership with the administration, as opposed to acceptance of a staff relationship.

While the role of advocate appreciates the need for sound human relations and for adequacy in planning and management, there is also an acknowledgment that education and particularly the development of curriculum is a highly politicized process. Experiences during the cultural awareness movements of the 1960s, in responding to teacher unionization demands, and in fights over community control of schools have led curriculum workers to this belief. In short, it is perceived that it is better to be an activist than to submit to external pressures which often usurp the leadership role. Such a role perception sees the curriculum specialist as simply one force among many that can influence the process of curriculum development, regardless of which role he adopts.

CONSISTENT ON-THE-JOB PROBLEMS

There are a number of conditions in the work environment and organization of schools which regularly limit the effectiveness of the curriculum worker, regardless of role perceptions. Unchecked, these conditions often neutralize the efforts of the specialist. At the same time, an understanding of such conditions can provide additional keys to successful practice.

Environmental Conditions

The political, moral, economic, and legal variables which characterize the "open" system of education in the United States pose a serious challenge to structured change in education. The curriculum specialist must be aware of these variables, must react to them, and must attempt to shape them to desired ends. Educational environments are political, in many cases, because the goals for educational programming are unclear. There is an ever-present moral dimension in school planning because of the tremendous influence of education upon the shape of the society's future. An economic sphere exists because education is our nation's second most costly operation. Legal ramifications indicate the shifting nature of this environment and the force of leading priorities.

These environmental and organizational conditions come to the curriculum worker in the form of school elections, bond issues, pressure groups, court decisions, and other public and semipublic forums. To the degree that curriculum specialists understand these events, and relate them to curricular planning and objectives, they can be effective in their roles. If these kinds of events are not anticipated or understood, curriculum leaders will be in constant conflict with the environment around them.

Organizational Conditions

In addition to environmental concerns, there are internal problems that plague most curriculum specialists. Although organizational conditions vary from one job to another, it is possible to identify examples of internal problems. Some of them are:

> The absence of clear goals
> Unpredictable entry of power sources from outside
> A consistent dependence on "money" as the moving force
> Structural line and staff relationships in the district
> The absence of "systems" thinking in problem-solving
> An operational orientation to the present rather than future
> Decentralized decision making and policy implementation
> The absence of evaluative feedback in policy renewal
> An incomplete linkage to vital research
> Inadequate training and understaffing of personnel
> Administrative turnover
> Lack of authority in program development
> An overreliance on administrative arrangements for change
> Responsibility for decisions without adequate guidelines
> A lack of functional training in basic planning skills

In most school districts, curriculum directors appear in a staff role on organizational charts that describe administrative relationships. This means that curriculum specialists have basic responsibilities without clear authority. Often, curricular decisions will affect other dimensions of school organization such as legal, financial, and personnel. Curriculum workers must maintain lines of communication with all such offices and campaign for support of desired objectives. In many school districts, administrative policy and instructional activity are dictated by administrative concerns, rather than by curriculum goals.

Related to the act of "borrowing" authority from administrators is a continual reliance on administrative action to implement curriculum change. Designing school structures, procuring materials and staff, informing the public, and activating programs are all beyond the immediate control of the curriculum specialist.

Curriculum personnel are also regularly faced with the task of making crucial value-laden decisions without supporting evidence or visible support. Deciding where programmatic emphasis should be, making recommendations for change, and calming curricular conflict among the "actors" are all tasks undertaken by curriculum personnel.

Finally, most mechanical actions taken by curriculum specialists are done without the benefit of formal training. Curriculum positions, due to the span of responsibility, and the fluidity of the environment are in constant need of being updated. Today's concern may be the writing of a grant proposal, while tomorrow's may be the interpretation of the latest educational innovation. The skills required for these tasks are learned "while doing."

Because of the nebulous quality of the role, the overload of responsibility, the lack of clear mandates, the situational authority, the congestion of the work environment, and the propensity of the position to attract odd jobs, many curriculum specialists fail to be effective. Their daily routine consists of fragmented, knee-jerk reactions to small crises, rather than an effort to coordinate the total curriculum of the school district. They fail to grasp, in a sense, the keys of successful practice. Such a response causes a leadership vacuum in school planning which intensifies the already turbulent environment of an open system of education.

THE DEMAND FOR SKILLS

There is a tremendous need for both strong interpersonal skills and organizational skills in curriculum development. While the processes of curriculum development will always be changing as it strives to sort beliefs and values into meaningful programs of education, the predominant need is to make such a process orderly and somewhat predictable. There must be diagnostic tools which will allow for an analysis of complex variables. There must be planning skills which will allow for the engagement and management of thoughts and practices. Criteria must be developed which will enable an assessment of relative progress in the attainment of goals. But, most essential, there must be the development of both a theory of curriculum development and a strategy for bringing such development into being.

SUMMARY

It is clear that the tremendous changes experienced by the American society over the past thirty years have greatly altered the school environments in which curriculum development occurs. Scholarly inquiry, encouraged by the infusion of Federal funding during the 1960s and 1970s, has revealed the complexity of such environments.

Understanding the problems faced by curriculum workers can provide clues regarding what might comprise successful practice. Changing school environments suggest different role perceptions, strategies, and skills needed by curriculum specialists. To the degree that curriculum personnel are aware of real conditions and needs, they can prepare themselves for more effective roles regardless of their position.

Notes

1. Bruce Joyce, *Leadership For Improving Instruction,* 1960 Yearbook, Association for Supervision and Curriculum Development, (Washington, D.C. 1960), p. 70.
2. Jack R. Frymier and Horace C. Hawn, *Curriculum Improvement for Better Schools* (Charles A. Jones Publishing Company, Worthington, Ohio, 1970), p. 25.
3. R. Leeper, ed., "Role of the Supervisor and Curriculum Developer in a Climate of Change," 1960 Yearbook, Association for Supervision and Curriculum Development, (Washington, D.C., 1965), p. 2.

Suggested Learning Activities

1. Using a school with which you are familiar, identify active curriculum development relating to classroom, school, district, state, and national levels.

2. Define the role that you feel is most appropriate for a curriculum specialist in today's schools.

Books to Review

Lewis, Arthur, and Miel, Alice. *Supervision for Improved Instruction.* Belmont, California: Wadsworth Publishing Company, Inc., 1972.

Mosher, Ralph, and Purpel, David. *Supervision: The Reluctant Profession.* Boston: Houghton-Mifflin Company, 1972.

Oliver, Albert. *Curriculum Improvement: A Guide to Problems, Principles, and Procedures.* New York: Dodd, Mead & Company, 1977.

3

An Analysis of the Development Process

The conceptualization of educational programs is often a pure act, undisturbed by shifting environmental variables. By contrast, the development of programs in a school setting is often a complex political phenomenon. Attempts to systematically organize cultural beliefs, values, and expressive symbols into meaningful patterns of activity are difficult due to the dynamic nature of schools.

American public education is administered by officials who are under constant pressure from local political and social forces. Of all of society's institutions, the school is probably the most yielding to the demands for change by outside forces. Rarely are such forces comprehensive in their demands, and only sometimes are such demands motivated by educational concerns.

The primary task of any educational development effort is to achieve a state of stability in its actions; an ability to realize purposeful change. Such a ideal condition is in stark contrast to a more common pattern of instability in curriculum development. Such disorganization reflects the failure of curriculum leadership to accommodate the changing balance of values in society or to advance any desired objectives.

Accordingly, curriculum development becomes the act of pursuing change in a purposeful manner. It is composed of planning, implementing, and evaluating educational change in a systematic and logical manner. Such a procedure includes a variety of subactivities such as clarifying values, setting goals, designing programs, promoting positive human interaction, applying and managing resources, making assessments, and redesigning outcomes. In a comprehensive sense, the job of curriculum development is most often managerial in nature, the primary objective being the coordination of activity to achieve desired ends. Adequate behaviors for such a task are often situationally defined by the environment in which they are applied.

Curriculum development is the advocating of change, the moving from the present condition to a more desirable one. Such a posture accepts change as a given, and treats curriculum improvement as a dynamic activity. The question is not whether change is desired, but rather the type of change desired. Thus, curriculum development is seen as a process; a continuum of events.

Within such an orientation, it is initially important to recognize three approaches to change; a rational or educative approach, a power or coercive approach, and a normative or valuing approach. Ultimately, these approaches suggest both strategies and behaviors for curriculum workers.

The rational or educative approach seeks to promote curricular change by providing information and assistance that will bring a desired response from those being informed. Familiarity with low achievement test scores in reading, for instance, might lead to a decision to redesign a reading program.

The coercive, or power, approach seeks to promote curricular change by exerting force or pressure. New mandated regulations for teacher accountability, for instance, might be used to force in-depth instructional evaluation in classrooms.

The normative or valuing approach seeks to promote curricular change by assisting in the realignment of personal values and beliefs. The integration of schools, for instance, might be best approached by training school personnel in human relations and ethnic understanding.

The importance of perceiving curriculum development as requiring change, and seeing such change as an approach to working with people, is critical. Curriculum development is often people development. Additionally, because curriculum improvement is often linked to factors which are not logically educational concerns, such as taxes, there is a need to view curriculum development comprehensively. Such a long view of improvement activities will allow curriculum planners to develop change strategies which will circumvent or neutralize obstacles in the environment. Strategies in curriculum development efforts are often a combination of the three approaches to change; a combination based on an understanding of the real environment for change.

Beyond an orientation to the development process, strategies are required. Once curriculum specialists have an accurate perception of the key factors which can influence planning, they can select maneuvers that will support the acheivement of goals. Through strategies the curriculum specialist gains power; defined by Goldhammer and Shils as "the extent to which he can influence the behavior of others in accordance with his own intentions."[1]

We have already observed that curriculum workers have rarely been given the authority to insure their responsibilities. Such a condition reflects the "residual" role of curriculum development in many school districts. Such a professional posture undoubtedly makes school program development more difficult since the application of ideas in school settings calls for action more than advice.

To overcome this static posture and to become more effective in promoting desirable programs in schools, curriculum leaders must be activists who engineer educational improvements. To be leaders in public school settings, curriculum specialists must be both directed toward change and capable of designing and employing strategies to bring about desired change.

ORGANIZING FOR DEVELOPMENT

The promotion of purposeful change requires organization. Where possible, goals must be clear, barriers identified and neutralized, relevant resources pressed into action, and objectives achieved at acceptable levels of programming, managing, and assessing.

Analyzing

Often in curriculum development activities there is an absence of philosophic consensus which detracts from the spirit and efficiency of the development effort. Because the goals of public education are multiple and ever-changing, maintaining philosophic consensus is difficult. The process of clarifying values and setting goals, because of its regularity, can be perceived as both time-consuming and redundant. Yet, without such a basic operation, curriculum development remains largely unstructured and directionless. Without clear communication about the destination of development activities, relationships such as those alluded to in *Alice in Wonderland* are both possible and probable:

Alice: "Will you tell me, please, which way I ought to go from here?"
Cat: "That depends a good deal on where you want to get to."
Alice: "I don't much care where . . . "
Cat: "Then it doesn't matter which way you go."
Alice: "So long as I get somewhere . . . "
Cat: "Oh, you're sure to do that if only you walk long enough."[2]

In order to make clear and correct decisions in planning curriculum development, the situation must be analyzed and the ultimate goals identified. Organizing development must be rationalized in terms of objectives.

Planning

Once the intentions of curriculum change are clear, relevant data about the desired changed must be gathered and reviewed. Some data useful to curriculum planning are primary and can be used over again to give perspective to planning. Examples of such data are: philosophy statements, formal objectives, school district policies, socio-economic data about the community, student achievement data, district research reports, knowledge of school district resources and fiscal capacity, information about instructional staff, and the previous history of related changes in the district.

Other kinds of planning data may be specific or situational to the planning effort. Examples of such ad hoc data are: the philosophy of the chief school officer and school board, the degree of involvement of parents and community in school affairs, the strength of the teacher professional groups, the degree of novelty of the proposed change, and the timing of the change in relation to the cyclical nature of the school year.

The assessment of planning data pays dividends in two ways. First, such a process reduces the possibility of direct confrontation between the programs of the school and the support environment in which all schools operate. Second, the continual assessment of planning data enables curriculum leaders to refine operational strategies to increase the impact of resources on problem areas.

Feyereisen and associates, more than other curriculum theorists, view the planning process as a system.[3] The achievement of philosophic consensus and the assessment of planning data are perceived in tandem, with data being selected on the basis of the objectives being pursued. This viewpoint of Feyereisen is important because most school districts suffer from excessive information rather than a scarcity of planning data. The intentions of the curriculum planner would thus serve to filter the data gathering and analysis process.

The third component of organization for curriculum development concerns programming or designing the desired change. To an extent, such behavior is model building, because the planner must accurately perceive the environment and anticipate how the change should occur.

For years writers in the field of curriculum have tried to create a model of how the curriculum development process proceeds. The best-known author of such a process was Hilda Taba who outlined seven major steps:

1. Diagnosis of need
2. Formulation of objectives
3. Selection of content
4. Organization of content
5. Selection of learning experiences
6. Organization of learning experiences
7. Determination of what to evaluate and of the ways and means of doing it[4]

Modern lists of these steps differ from Taba's in that they see curriculum as a more comprehensive process which may or may not be tied to a content product. In the following example, for instance, Feyereisen presents curriculum development as a problem-solving action chain:

1. Identification of the problem
2. Diagnosis of the problem
3. Search for alternative solutions
4. Selection of the best solution
5. Ratification of the solution by the organization
6. Authorization of the solution
7. Use of the solution on a trial basis
8. Preparation for adoption of the solution
9. Adoption of the solution
10. Direction and guidance of staff
11. Evaluation of effectiveness[5]

The broader focus of the Feyereisen description reflects a growing concern in curriculum development with planning for change in school environments from a macro-perspective. Curriculum development is increasingly a process with systemic concerns.

Many other conceptualizations of the curriculum development process exist. In Table 3.1, Wiles outlines stages of development for an intermediate school moving toward the middle school philosophy and program.

Table 3.1
Developmental Staging

	Present Condition Stage 1	Awareness Stage Stage 2	Experimentation Stage Stage 3	Adoption Stage Stage 4	Desired Condition Stage 5
The School Philosophy	Either no formal statement or a written document on file in the school office.	School staff share beliefs, look for consensus, restate philosophy and objectives in terms of expected behavior.	Staff begins use of goals as guide to evaluating school practices. Begin to involve students and community in planning.	Philosophy and goals used to shape the program. Formal mechanism established to monitor program and decision making.	Philosophy a living document. Guides daily decision. The program a tool for achieving desired educational ends.
			THE LEARNING ENVIRONMENT		
Use of the Building	Only uniform instructional spaces. Little use of the building spaces for educational purposes.	Some deviation from traditional spaces utilization (classroom learning center). Possibly a complete demonstration class for bright ideas.	Limited building conversions (knock out walls). Begin to identify unused spaces. Planning for large learning spaces.	Development of a comprehensive plan for use of grounds and building. Total remodeling of spaces.	Tailor-made learning environment—all spaces used to educate. Building facilitates the learning intention.
Use of Materials	Classrooms are dominated by a grade-level text. Library with a limited offering. Used as a study hall for large groups.	Use of multi-level texts within classroom. Materials selected after an analysis of student achievement levels. Supplemental resources made available to students.	Diverse materials developed for the students. Resource centers established. Cross-discipline selection of materials. More multi-media used. Some independent study.	Materials purchasing policies re-aligned. Common learning areas established as resource centers. More self-directed study built in.	Diversified materials. Something for each student. Integrated subject materials. Portable curriculum units (on carts). Heavy multi-media. Active learning centers.

Use of Community	Little or no access to school. Information about programs scanty. Trust low.	Some school program ties to community. Token access via PTA and media. School perceived as island in neighborhood.	Preliminary uses of community as learning environment. Identification of nearby resources. Use of building for community functions.	Regular interchange between school and community. Systematic communication. A network of services and resources established.	School programs outwardly oriented. Community seen as a teaching resource. Systematic ties with services and resources around school.

INSTRUCTIONAL ORGANIZATION

Staffing Patterns	Building teachers isolated in self-contained classrooms. Little or no lateral communication or planning present.	Limited sharing of resources. Some division of labor and small-scale cooperation in teaching. Informal communication about student progress.	Regular cooperative planning sessions. Some curricular integration via themes. Students rotate through subect areas. Problems of cooperation identified.	Interdepartmental organization. Use of common planning time. Administrative support such as in scheduling. Use of philosophy as curricular decision-making criteria.	Teaching staff a "team" working toward common ends. Staff patterns reflect instructional intentions. Administration in support of curricular design. Coursework integrated for students.
Teaching Strategy	Some variety but lecture and teacher-dominated Q-A session the norm. Homework used to promote day-to-day continuity.	Observation of other teaching models. Skill development via workshops. An identification of staff strengths and weaknesses. Some new patterns.	Building level experiments by willing staff members. "Modeling" of ideas. On-site consultant help made available for skill development.	School day divided according to the teaching strategy employed. Faculty evaluation of the effectiveness of new ways after a trial period.	Great variety of methods used in teaching, uses of media, dealing with students. The curricular plans determine strategy.

Table 3.1—*continued*

	Present Condition Stage 1—*continued*	Awareness Stage Stage 2—*continued*	Experimentation Stage Stage 3—*continued*	Adoption Stage Stage 4—*continued*	Desired Condition Stage 5—*continued*
Staff Development	Staff development is global, rarely used to attack local needs and problems. Occurs as needed.	Staff identifies in-service needs and priorities. Philosophy assists in this process. Local staff skills and strengths are recognized.	Staff development re-aligned to serve needs of teachers. Opportunities for personal growth are made available.	Formal procedures for directing staff development to needs established. Staff development seen as problem-solving mechanism.	Staff development an on-going process using available resources. An attempt to close theory practice gaps.
			ADMINISTRATIVE CONDITIONS		
Organization of Students	Uniform patterns. One teacher, 30 students in six rows of five in each row in each period of each school day.	Understanding that organization of students should match curricular intentions. Some initial variation of group sizes in classroom.	Limited organization to facilitate the grouping of the students. Begin use of aides and parents to increase organizational flexibility.	Full administrative support for a reorganization of students. Building restructured where necessary. An increase in planning for effectiveness.	Group sizes vary according to the activity planned. Full support given to eliminate any problem areas.
Report of Student Progress	"Progress" is defined narrowly. Letter grades or simple numerals represent student learning in the subject areas.	Recognition of broader growth goals for students. Use of philosophy to evaluate the existing practices.	Experimentation with supplemental reporting procedures. Involvement of student and parents in the process.	Development of a diverse and comprehensive reporting procedure for student progress.	Descriptive medium used to monitor individual student progress. Broadly focused evaluation. Team of teacher, student, and parents involved.
Rules and Regulations	High degree of regimentation. Many rules, most inherited over the years. The emphasis on the enforcement and on control.	Staff and students identify essential rules. Regulations matched against the school philosophy.	Rules and regulations streamlined. Used as a teaching device about life outside of school. Increased student self-control.	Greater use of student and staff input into the regulation of the school environment. Rewards built-in for desirable performance.	Moving toward minimal regulation and an increased student self-control. Regulations a positive teaching device.

ROLES OF PARTICIPANTS

Discipline	Reactive pattern ranging from verbal admonishment to paddling and expulsion. Recurring offenders.	Staff analysis of school policies. Shift of emphasis to causes of the problems. Some brainstorming of possible solutions.	Establishment of a hierarchy of discipline activity. Begin implementing preventive strategies.	Design of curriculum programs to deter discipline problems. High intensity program for regular offenders.	Program of the school eliminates most sources of discipline problems. The procedure for residual problems clear to all.
Student Roles	Passive recipient of knowledge. Instruction is geared to average student. Reactive communication with the teacher.	Investigation of new student roles by teacher. Limited hierarchy of trust established in the classroom. Needs and interests of student investigated.	Ground rules for increased student independence set. Student involvement in planning. Role of student connected to philosophy of the school.	Periodic staff review of student roles. Roles linked to school-wide rules and regulations. Philosophy guides role possibilities.	Students involved in planning and conducting the program. Increased independence *and* responsibility. Use of "contracts" to maintain new understandings.
Teacher Roles	Defined by the subjects taught. Perceived as the source of all knowledge. Other roles peripheral.	Perceiving roles suggested by the philosophy. Roles accepted at verbal level. Limited experimentation with new roles.	Investigation of new roles—trying on new relationship. Goal-setting for individual teacher. Skill development through in-service.	Administrative reorganization for role support. A sharpened planning and action skills needed to serve the student according to the philosophy.	Teacher role is defined by student needs. Teacher the organizer of the learning activities. Teacher talents used more effectively.
Principal Roles	Solely responsible for school operation. The "boss." Enforcer of all rules. The linkage to all outside information and resources.	Awareness of role limitations. An awareness of real leadership potential. A setting of role priorities.	Limited sharing of decision-making in area of curriculum. Limited joint planning with the faculty. Review of existing policy according to the philosophy.	Role perception changes to manager of resources. Emphasis on development (active) rather than on order (static). Increase in curriculum leadership functions.	An instructional leader. Administrative acts support the curriculum program. Philosophy guiding decision-making. Built-in monitoring system for evaluating building level progress.

From "Developmental Staging—In Pursuit of Comprehensive Curriculum Planning" by Jon Wiles, *Middle School Journal* 6 (September 1975): 7–10. Used by permission.

In a sense, the programming stage of organization develops a road map by which change can be anticipated and followed. In Table 3.2, a comprehensive road map for curriculum development is given, generalized to fit school settings:

Table 3.2
An Outline for Curriculum Development

Operation	Focus	Activity	Resource Base
Analyze	Clarify values Set goals	Identify purposes Set parameters Outline program Select content Order content	Environmental forces Information sources
Design	Establishing programs	Develop lessons Select materials Choose instruction strategy Establish management pattern	Knowing about the learning process
Implement	Training for interaction	Integrate learning Individualizing instruction	Knowledge of human development
	Application and management of resources	Delivery systems, grouping, space, time, focus of learning, climate, personnel roles	Change theory Knowledge of the act of learning
Evaluate	Assessment	Evaluative criteria Student and teacher assessment	All of the above

---

Managing

Beyond goal-setting, planning, and designing curriculum change is a management stage of organization. Here, the design is set into motion and monitored. The activation of planning as a management function is developed more fully in chapter 8.

Assessing

Finally, in all curriculum development efforts, there is an assessment component. The priorities and objectives which have been planned and implemented are evaluated. When necessary, corrections and rethinking of goals can result from such assessment. Organization for curriculum development, as shown in Figure 3.1, takes on a cyclical pattern:

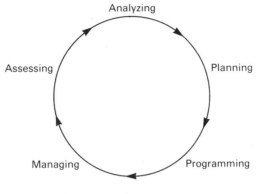

Figure 3.1
Common Strategies for Development

Curriculum development in a school setting always represents a compromise between the orderly progression toward new objectives and the promotion of organizational stability. The degree of curricular activity must be manageable if order is to be maintained in the system. On the other hand, curriculum change must be forceful if desired progress is to be achieved. Such a blend requires both a sensitivity to the environment in which change is occurring and an appropriate curriculum development strategy.

Over the years, a number of curriculum development strategies have become common in school environments. These strategies are designed to alter the educational organization, the people within the educational organization, or the way in which activity occurs in the educational organization. Four such strategies are the renewal strategy, the human resources strategy, the evaluation strategy, and an environmental strategy.

The main idea behind renewal, or master planning strategy, is to analyze goals, programs, fiscal expenditures, staff development efforts, and evaluation procedures for their contribution to identified ends. Such a process usually begins with an effort to clarify goals, and uses the products of such analysis as the criteria to assess other functions within the system. Using objectives to analyze budget, decision-making patterns, resource allocation, purchasing patterns, existing instructional materials, personnel policies and other substantive items will often reveal areas in need of attention.

The second curriculum development strategy is to emphasize the development of human resources. This approach is based on the belief that curriculum development will occur naturally if barriers to communication and interaction are minimized or removed. A human relations approach to curriculum improvement might address activities toward conditions such as the following:

People use words that have different meanings
Members of groups have different values
Different perceptions of the problem are held
Emphasis is put on status
Words are used to prevent thinking
There is a lack of acceptance of diversity
Feelings of superiority are held
Vested interests interfere
An obvious attempt to sell something is made[6]

The human resources strategy sees people as the operational connectors between components of the school system, and tries to encourage interaction as a means to improved performance.

A third curriculum development strategy is an evaluation approach. Here, programs and activities are placed in experimental or research perspectives, with a strong emphasis on results. Human and organizational activity is reviewed in terms of relative progress toward goals, rather than absolute ends or conditions. This evaluation approach is characterized by practices such as zero-based budgeting, management-by-objectives, and personnel assessments based on growth rather than set criteria.

A final approach to curriculum improvement might be called environmental. This strategy seeks to stimulate the surrounding environment of a setting through a constant bombardment of ideas, activities, and opportunities for change. Incentive programs, model programs, extensive staff development opportunities, and a low-risk posture for experimentation characterize this approach.

Individually, or in combination, these strategies represent "themes" which encourage new patterns of activity or behavior in school settings. Whether a systems, human resources, evaluation, or environmental approach is employed depends both on the objectives of the planners and the conditions of the school setting. The choice of strategy would be instrumental in determining a medium to use in implementing the approach.

DEVELOPMENT MEDIUMS

The activation of ideas and goals in schools occurs through a number of mediums which serve as organizers for progress. The choice of the correct medium for curriculum development should be a logical extension of the desired objective and the strategy for change.

Common mediums for the "systems" approach to curriculum improvement include school surveys, needs assessments, a citizen or lay study council, and other such general reviews of the status quo.

The main objective of *school surveys* is to provide basic information about the organization of the school system as well as to reveal glaring deficiencies in the school program. In most districts, states, and regions, surveys are conducted on a regular five or ten year cycle and are the basis of accreditation.

Needs assessments, like surveys, review a wide range of concerns. Unlike the survey, needs assessments are addressed to more qualitative variables and seek to identify areas in need of development. Student attitudes and home life conditions, for instance, may suggest a special program to supplement the regular curriculum being experienced by the student.

Lay study councils are employed by curriculum planners as a means of increasing public participation in school affairs, to increase vital public feedback, to educate the public as the school district moves toward a new program and to provide a forum for the exploration of diverse ideas. Lay study groups and councils usually serve on an ad hoc or temporary basis until policy is formalized. When such groups are called councils, they generally work on a continual basis in identified areas such as textbook committees, community coordination, or regulations review boards.

Human Resources Approach

Within the human resources approach to curriculum improvement are a number of mediums which encourage communication and interaction. Examples would be workshops, retreats, networks and leagues of schools, teacher centers, and supervisory processes which focus on the analysis of classroom interaction.

Although *workshops and retreats* are often used to stimulate school personnel by introducing new ideas, they also serve as socializing functions which help overcome the physical and mental isolation experienced by many teachers. By being brought into proximity with other educators who perform similar tasks, teachers have an opportunity to compare practices and share ideas. Such initial communication often leads to meaningful curriculum improvement in classrooms.

Collaborative ventures such as *networks and leagues of schools* are also regularly used to promote human interaction in school settings. The concept of bringing together people who have like interests and needs often results in the formation of a cadre of teachers or administrators who launch and develop curricular ideas.

In many school districts a *teacher center* is the location where school personnel meet regularly. Such centers are characterized by location, a facilitating staff, relevant instructional materials, and broad assistance in curriculum improvement activities. Teacher centers are designed to promote human interaction in ways directed toward curriculum improvement.

Curriculum development is sometimes promoted through the *supervision of classroom teachers.* When supervision is clinical, or focused on the analysis of interaction rather than set criteria, a message is sent which tells teachers that the concern is with improvement rather than perfection. Interaction analysis can also be used effectively to emphasize the importance of the human dimension in teaching and learning. *

Evaluation Approach

The evaluation strategy for curriculum improvement seeks to illuminate the results of school planning and activity. Such an approach is characterized by such mediums as task-focused consultation, action research, and performance contracting.

One method of emphasizing desired results in school planning is *periodic consultation* in relation to specific tasks. A specialist from either within or outside the school system meets with those individuals who are responsible for task accomplishment to assess progress toward goals. The consultant provides an objective review of progress in relation to goals, and suggests ways to improve the procedures leading to task attainment.

Action research is a means of testing new procedures or programs against intended outcomes by providing an analysis of the activity over a period of time. If such analysis bears out the desired results the procedure or program is endorsed or adopted. If monitoring the activity fails to endorse the procedure, the activity is restructured.

The *performance contract,* utilized heavily by school districts during the late 1960s and early 1970s, seeks to relate the continuation of programs and practices to anticipated results. Often, such contracts set achievement targets with attainment dates. Rewards and penalties are attached to the attainment or failure of the activity. Performance contracts stretch curriculum development projects toward desired ends.

Environmental Approach

Environmental curriculum improvement strategies seek to stimulate change through the alteration of perceptions of those in the system.

---

* See the works of Ned Flanders or Richard Ober for a thorough treatment of direct interaction analysis techniques. This topic is the major theme of chapter 17.

This set of strategies is characterized by pilot programs, "lighthouse" schools, alternative programs, and the introduction of external sources of information.

Pilot programs, unlike action research efforts, introduce new concepts and practices into a school district with minimal expectations for results or outcomes. Such programs are usually of short duration, are heavily publicized, and feature unique or futuristic ideas or practices. The main contribution of pilot programs to curriculum change is their power of demonstration and the posing of alternative means of achieving desired ends.

Lighthouse schools and programs are similar to pilot programs in that they present new ideas to practitioners in schools. The lighthouse concept differs from the pilot program in that it generally is comprehensive in scope and fully supported by existing resources; it is a permanent component of the system. The value of the lighthouse program is to introduce the possibility of programs, practices, and procedures which, if given priority support, could succeed throughout the district.

Alternative programs, such as magnet schools, attempt to induce change by satisfying the needs of specific populations thought ready to change. Once a pattern of changing is established, other populations may follow the lead by demanding their own alternatives to the status quo.

A final medium for approaching curriculum improvement through altering the environment is the use of *external sources of information* for study. Speakers, consultants, teacher exchanges, material displays, conferences, and other such "bombardment" techniques can be used to implant ideas or support desired changes.

CURRICULUM TASKS AND ROLES

As desired curriculum change is being pursued through the employment of strategies and the selection of mediums, curriculum specialists must also make decisions about the types of tasks and roles they will utilize. The behaviors available to curriculum workers are many, and where they place emphasis in their daily work may equal in importance the actual tasks they perform.

Curriculum Tasks

Curriculum tasks may be broken into two major groups: those that maintain the system and those that facilitate change in the system. Examples of regular tasks performed by curriculum personnel that maintain or reinforce existing programs are:

Setting priorities among curricular alternatives
Keeping records of activities and decisions

Developing and utilizing evaluation systems
Coordinating activities related to school programs

Other tasks performed by the curriculum specialist do not refine existing programs, but rather encourage change. Examples of such tasks are:

Supporting research and experimentation
Identifying alternative courses of action
Opening and maintaining communication channels
Introducing novel ideas to the system

The selective application of such tasks, and the emphasis given to either maintenance or the facilitation of change is important to overall curriculum development efforts.

Curriculum Roles

Like tasks, an element of choice exists in terms of the roles to be played by the curriculum specialist. By assuming certain roles, performing certain functions, and behaving in specific ways, the curriculum leader can place emphasis on activities. The behavior of the specialist can be active or passive, direct or indirect, according to the kind of activity involved and the outcome desired. Often, the curriculum worker will "zoom in" to initiate an "action-chain"* and then withdraw into a passive posture after a momentum for change has been attained.

Ronald Havelock and associates at the University of Michigan have spent considerable time and effort in the analysis of such roles and behaviors.† They see the promotion of change in school environments as a series of problem-solving interventions which weave together overall activity. Interventions, according to Havelock, are selected with consideration of where they fit into the macro problem-solving phases, the particular strategies being used, and the role of the change agent. For Havelock, the critical concept is that the micro problem-solving efforts (strategies, roles) must be carried out within the larger scale improvement effort. Failure to heed such insight quickly leads to inappropriate behavior or irrelevant action by the curriculum developer.

Like curriculum strategies, mediums, and tasks, the roles must be selected in relation to the desired ends. Among behaviors commonly employed by curriculum specialists are:

---

* Action chains are "if-then" behaviors observable in everyday life (Hello, how are you? Fine, and you?) For an in-depth treatment of the effects of such chains see Edward Hall's, *The Silent Language.*

† For a thorough treatment of this area see Ronald Havelock's *A Guide to Innovation in Education,* Institute of Social Research, (University of Michigan, 1970).

managing	producing
storing	legitimizing
reporting	diagnosing
evaluating	telling
valuing	planning
deciding	retrieving
inventing	validating
judging	listening

Such behaviors are usually enacted through regular functions performed by curriculum specialists on a day-to-day basis. Examples of such functions might be: identification of concerns (listening, diagnosing, storing, reporting), diagnosing situations (evaluating, judging, deciding), considering alternative actions (retrieving, planning, managing) and directing changes (producing, legitimizing, telling, validating).

The impact of the curriculum specialist's functioning is often determined by the role assumed. Roles are critical due to their influence on the human systems found in school settings. Havelock and associates identify numerous roles commonly found in schools during curriculum development activity:

expert	advisor	retriever
linker	manager	advocate
counselor	trainer	data collector
diagnoser	modeler	referrer
instructor	observer	confrontor
demonstrator	evaluator	analyzer

SOME DESIRED CONDITIONS

In its totality, curriculum development is a process of promoting desired change through purposeful activity. The desired condition is a state of stability where environmental and situational variables are controlled or accounted for, and where activity is coordinated and managed toward attainable goals. The means by which such a process succeeds is most often determined by the correct assessment of the situation, the adoption of the appropriate strategy for promoting change, and the assumption of functions and roles by the curriculum leader which support the advancement of critical activities.

In pursuing a state of stability in curriculum development, there are a number of questions which should be asked to assess the conditions. These following questions suggest characteristics of a purposeful curriculum development program:

1. Is the curriculum development process visible and predictable? As program development moves toward specified goals, an important objective is to manage events to the extent that critical variables can be identified and controlled if necessary to influence the outcome.
2. Is the curriculum development process efficient? A goal of any curriculum improvement effort is to achieve maximum results for the energy and resources expended. Critical resources, particularly human resources, should only be utilized when they directly contribute to desired outcomes.
3. Is there a control of momentum in the curriculum change? Every change in curriculum is a flow of events characterized by direction, speed, and magnitude. A change under curriculum management indicates clear objectives, intensive planning, and reliable evaluation.
4. Is the curriculum development process consistent? Any development effort should maintain a consistency in action so that one effort does not negate another. Such consistency reflects a regular appraisal of the relation of actions to overall objectives.
5. Is the curriculum development process effective? The ideal condition would find a close match between uses of personnel, resources, and the type of environment in which change is being promoted. In the final analysis, can it be said that the outcome of the effort matches the end originally sought?

These five questions form the foundation of an evaluation of any curriculum development effort. They underscore the main goal of any improvement effort and make curriculum development an orderly process despite the disorder typically encountered in school environments.

SUMMARY

Curriculum development, as a process, is complex. There are numerous levels of activity in curriculum improvement and, due to the political nature of change in schools, the translation of values into meaningful programs is a slow and difficult process.

In the broadest sense, curriculum development is a process that promotes change in schools. The primary task for a curriculum developer is to achieve a state of stability in school environments so that change is pursued in a purposeful manner.

Curriculum developers must recognize the value questions that are inherent in educational change. Strategies for changing school programs must be appropriate to the school environment if the curriculum worker is to be influential. The selection of strategies, development mediums, and roles should follow logically from the identification of goals for change.

Notes

1. Herbert Goldhammer and Edward Shils, "Types of Power and Status," *American Journal of Sociology* 45, September 1939, p. 171.
2. Lewis Carroll [pseud.], Charles Dodgson, *Alice's Adventures in Wonderland* (London: Macmillan & Co., 1932).
3. Kathryn V. Feyereisen, A. John Fiorino and Alene T. Nowak, *Supervision and Curriculum Renewal: A Systems Approach* (New York: Appleton-Century-Crofts, 1970).
4. Hilda Taba, *Curriculum Development: Theory and Practice,* p. 12.
5. Feyereisen, *Supervision and Curriculum Renewal,* p. 61.
6. Kimball Wiles, *Supervision For Better Schools* (Prentice-Hall: Englewood Cliffs, New Jersey, 1956), p. 64.

Suggested Learning Activities

1. Using Havelock's lists of behaviors and roles, develop two job descriptions. Have one job description be for a curriculum specialist who is expected to promote change. Have the other job description be for a curriculum specialist who is expected to maintain the existing program.
2. Select five strategies and five mediums outlined by the authors as means to promote curriculum change. What are the advantages of these techniques? What are the disadvantages?

Books to Review

Association for Supervision and Curriculum Development. *Role of the Supervisor and Curriculum Director in a Climate of Change,* 1965 Yearbook. Washington, D.C.: The Association, 1965.

Doll, Ronald. *Curriculum Improvement: Decision-Making and Process.* Boston: Allyn and Bacon, Inc., 1970.

Miel, Alice. *Changing the Curriculum. A Social Process.* New York: Appleton-Century-Croft, 1946.

Unruh, Adolph and Turner, Harold. *Supervision for Change and Innovation.* Boston: Houghton-Mifflin Company, 1970.

Wiles, Kimball. *Supervision for Better Schools.* Englewood Cliffs, New Jersey: Prentice-Hall, Inc., 1967.

4

Foundations of Curriculum Planning

During this century educational planners have been faced with a growing number of choices in constructing school programs. These choices result from increasing knowledge about the ways in which people develop and learn. To be effective as planners, those who are responsible for curriculum development must become familiar with and put into effective order, extensive data about growth and learning.

Our increased knowledge of the learning process is a result of both experience and organized inquiry. From a historical perspective, it is difficult to ascertain whether beliefs about learning preceded or resulted from critical inquiry. What is clear is that there have been certain issues in American education that have encouraged resolution through both demonstrated practice and basic research. These issues have encouraged the collection and ordering of primary data in a number of well-defined areas, and these areas form the foundations of curriculum planning.

ISSUES THAT STIMULATE INQUIRY

The latter half of the nineteenth century and the first quarter of the twentieth century were a time during which American education was bombarded by new thoughts and findings relevant to the process of school planning. Basic sources of data came from educational thought and practices in Europe, from experimental programs, and from the early efforts of the field of psychology in this country. By 1925, this influx of ideas had fragmented American education into schools of thought that held very different premises about the purpose and procedures of education.

Major differences of opinion about planning educational programs revolve around these primary questions: Education for what? Education for whom? Education by what means? What is the role of the formal education programs and to what ends are they to be directed? Who is to be served by these programs, and should their focus be broad or narrow? How are these programs to be designed and what is the best way to promote effective learning? The scope of these and other such foundational questions are demonstrated by a list of unknowns compiled by Briggs over fifty years ago:

1. What are the desired ends of education?
2. What is the good life?
3. To what extent shall education modify the character and actions of future citizens?
4. For what ends are the schools responsible?
5. What subject areas are most vital in attaining these ends?
6. What should be the content of these subject arrangements?
7. How should the material be organized?
8. What is the responsibility of each level of schooling?
9. What is the relative importance of each course of study?
10. How much time should be allotted for each subject?
11. How long should education be continued at public expense?
12. What is the optimum length of the school day? School year?
13. What is the optimum work load for each pupil?
14. What are the most probable future needs of the pupil?[1]

Questions such as those posed by Briggs encouraged debate, inquiry, and experimentation in school environments. These activities began to produce information that educational planners could use to defend school practices. This information also suggested considerable changes in the form of schooling, as observed by Tanner and Tanner:

> The need for a radically new conception of curriculum was the inevitable result of a number of forces—changes in our conception of knowledge, particularly scientific knowledge; changes in our knowledge of the learning process as a result of the child-study movement; and the need to link formal school studies with the life of the learner and the changing demands of the larger social scene.[2]

It can be observed that the field of curriculum as a specialized area of education has developed in an effort to study these questions and translate what is known about these concerns into viable school programs. Four major areas of study have become recognized: social forces affecting schools, treatments of knowledge, human growth and development, and learning as a process. These four areas comprise the basic foundations of curriculum planning.

Social Forces

There has been an unprecedented amount of change in the United States during the twentieth century. Revolutionary changes have occurred in the ways in which we live as the result of advancements in transportation, communication, and manufacturing. In a single lifetime an agrarian culture has been transformed into a highly mobile, complex, urban society.

The relationship of this nation's education system to these changes is a dynamic one. Public education in this country is an open system, susceptible to all currents of political, economic, and cultural change. Public education also possesses a unique historical role in our nation as the adaptive mechanism for change. If change is to occur in an orderly manner, the school is generally perceived to be the correct vehicle for such controlled change.

Adapting to changes in the social milieu, and assuming the responsibility for leading orderly change in the society, has placed great stress on the American school. Communication mediums and changing social values serve as prime examples of social forces that have had an impact on school planning.

At the beginning of the twentieth century, communication was fairly primitive by today's standards. There was a great dependence, of course, on the printed page. The telegraph existed, the telephone was in infant stages of development, and motion pictures were a promising medium. Mass communication, however, was both scarce and inefficient. Communication, such as the result of a presidential election, took considerable time to disseminate. Three mass communication devices appeared within a fifty-year period to alter this pattern: radio, television, and the computer.

Radio was the first communication medium to broaden the scope of the organized knowledge that had previously been in the domain of schools. Large amounts of information could be distributed quickly, and by mid-century could be broadcast to other countries.

> The effect of radio on expansion of nonrelated and non-applied knowledge is analogous to the distribution of seed by a grass spreader, creating in effect a 'carpet of knowledge' by cultivating a lawn so thick that single blades became indistinguishable. Regarding the interrelationships between segments of knowledge, the nuances and vagaries of the unusual become entwined with the simplicity and ordinariness of the mundane. Prospectives of knowledge are clouded and often obfuscated

entirely by their lack of definition.³ Conjecture becomes fact because, as McLuhan has so aptly stated, 'the medium is the message.'⁴

Television added another means by which we gained information and was even more influential in one respect. Beaming into 97 percent of all homes an average of six-and-one-half hours daily by 1970, this medium influenced the values and standards of American society. In *Crisis in the Classroom,* Silberman observes:

> Television has taken over the mythic role in our culture; soap operas, situation comedies, Westerns, melodramas, et al., are folk stories or myths that convey or reinforce the values of the society. . . . The trouble is that television does not enable its audience to see things the way they really are. On the contrary, while more current and realistic than schools, television nonetheless presents a partial and, in important ways, distorted view of contemporary society.⁵

By the late 1970s, concern for controlling the impact of television, particularly as a medium affecting the thoughts and perceptions of children, was intense. Congressional hearings, campaigns by parent-teacher organizations and criticism by members of the television industry were common.* A line from a widely acclaimed movie, *Network,* summarizes the impact of television as a communication medium:

> This tube can make or break presidents, popes, prime ministers. This tube is the most awesome goddamned force in the whole godless world. And woe is us if it ever falls into the hands of the wrong people!⁶

A third communication innovation of the twentieth century that had a major effect on both society and schools was the *computer.* Although the impact of the computer was perhaps more subtle than that of either radio or television, due to its inaccessibility and mystique for the average citizen, the implications of computer usage are more powerful.

> Thirty years ago the comical product of the 'mad cap' scientists' nocturnal devisements, today computer science is as much a part of our lives as our favorite breakfast cereal, and with every day that passes encroaches ever so more fitfully into the domain of human life, human decisions, and human behavior.

> Partly akin to the television in its mechanical wizardry, whereas the television indoctrinates, the computer coerces us into action through its assumed infallibility in making decisions and plotting paths of action necessary to our living in comfort. While the computer habituates the

---

* For an unusually thorough treatment of this problem see *The National Elementary Principal* 56, 3, Jan./Feb., 1977.

pinnacle of man's intellectual genius, it is likewise the jailer who holds the key to our intellectual freedom. With his peice-by-piece orientation to information and knowledge application, man is, quite simply, presented with an unchallengeable opponent in the computer. The variance in speed in processing knowledge posits man in the impossible position of receiving computation as *fait accompli* from the computerized savant. In creating the computer, man has performed the heretofore-thought impossible task of devising a being superior to himself in intellectual capacity, a being who can theoretically 'outthink' all men combined, a being who in fact is a god.[7]

In terms of data processing and the generation of cross-referenced knowledge, and in terms of the transmission of such information across long distances at rapid speeds and in major volumes, the computer has presented a challenge.

These three communications mediums have greatly influenced our society. We have become accustomed to satellite-aided direct-dial communication, instantaneous news updating, and machine-monitoring of our complex communications needs. These mediums have also had a significant impact on the way school planners have thought about the role of the school.

A century ago, schooling was almost exclusively a knowledge-focused activity. Students and teachers interacted to master intellectual essentials such as Virgil's *Aeneid,* Xenophon's *Anabasis,* orthography, and Latin prose. Today, because of advances in communication capabilities, some fundamental issues about schooling have been revised. If, for instance, knowledge is being generated and disseminated at a pace beyond our capacity to absorb it, what is the point of stressing the mastery of essential data in schools? Or, if there is too much to be known today, what essential knowledge should all of our children possess? Or, if radio and television are currently functioning as the disseminators of fundamental information about the society in which we live, a function once the exclusive preserve of the schools, what should be the role of the formal educating medium?

Another force that acts upon schools and the planning of school programs is the ever-changing value structure of our society. Primary concerns for educational planners are the assessment of social values, the identification of comprehensive values, and the development of educational programs in which values are relevant to the time.

The twentieth century has seen massive changes in both personal and social value structures in the United States. Such changes have resulted from the interaction of economic, social, political, and technological forces over a period of time. Contrasting two time periods twenty years apart, such as 1950 and 1970, indicates the scale of value alteration within a generation.

In 1950, the United States was in a process of renewal following World War II. There was a desire to return to simpler, more normal times, and the American people looked to social institutions for structure in their lives. The family, the church, the government, the law—all were respected without question. In 1950, people held strong beliefs in the work ethic, pursued materialism relentlessly, and saw formal education as the means to a better life. Religion, patriotism, tradition, privacy, and conformity were cherished. There was a high degree of predictability in everyday life.

By 1970, only twenty years later, the American society had undergone tremendous changes. Two wars, a space race, the racial integration of the society, a host of technological triumphs, and a major redefinition of the role of the individual in society had altered the face of America. Gone was the blind allegiance to social institutions, replaced by a basic cynicism about government, church, and other social agencies. Gone was the dedication to the work ethic and the foundational belief in formal schooling as the means to the "good life." Gone was the ready acceptance of tradition, patriotism, conformity, and roles. Gone, in many cases, was the predictability of everyday existence.

Replacing the primary values of 1950 was a set of beliefs which held individuality in esteem, defended the rights of persons and groups, accepted a broader pattern of behavior and moral codes, sought the preservation of natural resources, honored good health, and recognized mobility and temporary relationships as normal.

The contrasts in these two societies, 1950 and 1970, are remarkable. Alvin Toffler, first proposing the theme of his later best-selling book, *Future Shock,* described the conditions as the "dizzying disorientation brought on by the premature arrival of the future."[8] Other well-known observers attempted to describe the changes along traditional lines of social science inquiry such as anthropology, sociology, or economics.* Few authors were successful in capturing the scope of the changes that had occurred, or the meaning of such changes.

School planners during this twenty-year period were deluged with data input and projections of changes. Schools were criticized for being obsolete, discriminatory, irrelevant, and unresponsive during the short twenty-year period. Major questions were asked for which there were few ready answers:

What is the purpose of formal education in the United States?

What are the priorities of the school? Its goals and objectives?

What dominant values does the school support and promote?

Who does the school serve through its programs?

How does the school make decisions about its programs?

How does the school keep abreast of the change?

During the period from 1950 to 1970 there was evidence that the schools were changing. What emerged was an institution that was attempting to serve a plural culture and in doing so adopted a multifaceted role. The school was maintaining its historic role as a pres-

---

* See the writings of Margaret Mead, Charles Reich, and Kenneth Boulding.

ervation mechanism: identifying and passing on to the next generation the history, heritage, habits, and achievements perceived to be most valuable. The school was also in the position of meeting societal needs. A policy to integrate society serves as an example. Finally, the school was seeking to react to massive value changes by constructing programs that had immediate utility for individuals. A considerable amount of educational legislation, financing, program development, and innovation can be explained by the attempts of school planners to meet the changing value expectations of society.

In serving the past, the present, and the future simultaneously, educational planners were confronted with major value decisions concerning the role of schooling. Is the school's primary function to be the preservation of society, to assist in meeting pressing social needs, or to design the future society? These three purposes for the school presented curriculum designers with potential value screens through which they would sift input data.

Treatment of Knowledge

The kinds of societal changes outlined in the previous section had an important effect on curriculum planning. Organized information was more plentiful and accessible, but its proliferation also made it less manageable. Value-laden decisions that might govern the selection, organization, relevance, presentation, and evaluation of information were difficult, if not impossible, to make. Arno Bellack, writing in the midst of curriculum reforms of the early 1960s, outlined the planner's dilemma:

> In current debates about what should be taught in schools, the 'conventional wisdom' long honored in pedagogical circles about the nature of knowledge and the role of knowledge in the curriculum is being called into question. The enemy of conventional wisdom, Professor Galbraith (the originator of that felicitous term) tells us, is the march of events. The fatal blow comes when conventional ideas fail to deal with new conditions and problems to which obsolescence has made them inapplicable. The march of events in the world at large that is placing new demands on the schools, and in the world of scholarship that is making new knowledge in great quantities, is forcing us to reexamine our ideas about the nature of knowledge and its place in the instructional program.[9]

The scope of information available to scholars, and to school children, was immense. Estimates of the rate at which organized knowledge doubled its volume ranged from every seven years in the mid-1960s to every two years by the mid-1970s. Traditional curriculum tasks such as reviewing and updating the subject content became unmanageable.

Related to the problems of scope and volume of organized knowledge was one of organization. Cases of knowledge overload were plentiful, conjuring visions of a nation choking on the proliferation of its own wisdom:

> The American crisis, then, seems clearly to be related to an inability to act. It is not that we do not will action but that we are unable to act, unable to put existing knowledge to use. The machinery of our society no longer works or we no longer know how to make it work.[10]

Educational planners, in general, reacted to the glut of data that related to traditional school subjects by refocusing on the structure of information rather than on information itself. One of the best-known leaders of this reorganization movement was Jerome Bruner. Bruner rationalized the shift away from mastery of essential data to the study of representative data structures in this way:

> Teachers ask me about the 'new curricula' as though they were some special magic potion. They are nothing of the sort. The new curricula are based on the fact that knowledge has an internal connectedness, a meaningfulness, and that for facts to be appreciated and understood and remembered, they must be fitted into that internal meaningful context.[11]

Another problem related to the organization of knowledge sources for the school curriculum was the advent of "new" fields of knowledge created from crossing standard disciplines of study. Knowledge in the sciences, such as biochemistry, and in the social sciences, such as demography, gave rise to new structures of organization. The incorporation and management of such new areas posed difficult problems for school planners due to the compactness of traditional knowledge organizations.

With the dramatic increase in the volume of knowledge, and the corresponding questions of how to meaningfully organize it, came even more pressing inquiries about the purpose of knowledge in organized learning. Although challenges to the knowledge-based curriculum weren't novel, the regularity with which educators questioned the traditional motif of educating in public schools during this period was surprising. Defining education in a new way, Earl Kelley wrote:

> The only man who is educated is the man who has learned how to learn; the man who has learned how to adapt and change; the man who has realized that no knowledge is secure, that only the process of seeking knowledge gives the basis for security.[12]

Futurist Toffler, in assessing the onrush of the knowledge explosion as it related to the role of schooling, observed:

> Instead of assuming that every subject taught today is taught for a rea-
> son, we should begin from the reverse premise: nothing should be in-
> cluded in the required curriculum unless it can be strongly justified in
> terms of the future. If this means scrapping a substantial part of the for-
> mal curriculum, so be it.[13]

The reaction of educational planners to the problem of organization of knowledge was to place emphasis on the identification of goals and objectives of educating, which would serve as guidelines for content selection. This orientation placed knowledge in a new and different role in educational planning:

> The education received in school is not meant to perpetuate an aca-
> demic discipline, prepare students for college, or train bricklayers.
> All these things may be accomplished, but its chief mission is to pro-
> duce graduates who are capable of becoming active, participating, con-
> tributing members of society. To achieve this goal the individual must
> learn to live with himself and others and must have a system of values
> to guide him. Therefore, if this is the ultimate purpose of education, we
> must start by defining the needs of the individual, the nature and needs
> of society, and the system of values from which we can derive the ob-
> jectives of the curriculum.
> The means should not determine the ends. For example, if the areas of
> knowledge are used to determine the objectives, they will in all proba-
> bility prejudice the objectives. In addition, the inclusion of a variable
> such as knowledge areas would also predestine the content, curricular
> organization, scope, and sequence variables. . . . [14]

Another consideration for educational planners that related to treat-
ments of knowledge was the way in which individual learners reacted to information. In particular, research efforts studying the effects of attitude, emotion, and feelings toward learning (affect), and the process of information manipulation, storage, and retrieval (cognition), linked reception and retention of learning with readiness and attitudes toward learning. The question of form of knowledge thus became a concern.

Mario Fantini, widely recognized advocate of change in urban educational environments, stated the relationship this way:

> Although educators have hinted at the relationship between affect and
> cognition, the functional linkage is seldom made. Too often, the school
> severely limits the relationship between the two with its definition of af-
> fect. It considers affect only in terms of play, interests, classroom cli-
> mate, readiness, teacher-pupil interaction, motivation, and the like, all
> of which it can use to induce the child to accept prescribed academic
> content.
>
> Yet it is obvious that knowing something cognitively does not always
> result in behavior that follows on that knowing. This is because knowl-

edge alone cannot influence total behavior. Moreover, all kinds of knowledge are not equally influential. The missing ingredient in this equation seems to be knowledge that is related to the affective or emotional world of the learner.

What most often prompts action or behavior is a feeling or emotion about something rather than knowledge per se. It may be that 'knowing about' can prompt feeling, but it is feeling that generates behavior. Unless knowledge relates to feeling, it is unlikely to affect behavior appreciably.[15]

Closely related to the relationship of affect and knowledge were two other concerns of educational planners, language usage and the medium of delivery. When curriculum planners attempted to bring knowledge to the schools, they had to deal with school populations that represented many cultures. This situation meant that planners were confronted with both nonstandard English and a problem in communication.

Communication is a funny business. There isn't as much of it going on as most people think. Many feel that it consists in saying things in the presence of others. Not so. It consists not in saying things but in having things heard. Beautiful English speeches delivered to monolingual Arabs are not beautiful speeches. You have to speak the language of the audience—of the whom in the who-says-what-to-whom communications diagram. Sometimes the language is lexical (Chinese, Japanese, Portuguese), sometimes it is regional or personal (125th Street-ese, Holden Caufield-ese, anybodyese). It has little to do with words and much to do with understanding the audience. . . .[16]

In addition to language patterns and word usage, planners discovered the medium of delivery to have special effect on the interpretation and utilization of knowledge. McLuhan, in particular, opened the eyes of planners to the effects of electronic communication, describing information delivery systems in such terms as "hot," "cool," and "slick." In its extreme form, according to McLuhan, the medium can be both the "message" and the "massage."[17] *How* knowledge is delivered may be more important than *what* knowledge is delivered.

A final input that affected the planning of knowledge utilization in schools was the advent of serious forecasting of the future. As educators reviewed past utilization of knowledge and studied the present knowledge explosion, the wisdom of continuing with a content-dominated curriculum was questioned. After all, facts, by definition, were phenomena of the past and present rather than of the future. In some respects traditional knowledge placed blinders on our ability to escape the pull of the present and open our minds to the real possibilities of the future. The call for creative, nonlinear thinking presented an interesting challenge.

Related to a futuristic treatment of knowledge was the concept of programming. In viewing school curriculums it becomes clear that the knowledge taught to children programs their ability to meet the future. If education's image of the future is inaccurate, or if the knowledge given our students does not prepare them for the future, then the schools have betrayed those they teach.

In summary, the questions raised in assessing organized knowledge as a planning foundation are significant: What is to be taught? What should be the role of organized knowledge? What is the relative importance of knowledge bodies? What is the correct organization of information? What is the best form for bringing knowledge to students? All of these questions must be addressed by educational planners.

Human Growth and Development

A third foundational consideration important to educational planners has been the growing body of information related to human development. These data have been critical in such regular school activities as placement and retention, counseling, and planning curricular content and activities. Knowledge about human development has also provided the impetus for the development of a host of new programs in schools such as early childhood education, special education, compensatory education, and middle school education. Perhaps most important, our understandings about patterns of growth and development have caused educators to perceive formal educational planning from the perspective of the individual student.

Contributions to our understanding of human development have been gradual throughout this century. Early growth and development studies, such as those by psychologist G. Stanley Hall, provided important input to educational planners and resulted in new educational programs such as the junior high school. More recent developments, such as the contributions of sociologist Robert Havighurst, psychologist B.F. Skinner, and educator Paul Torrance have suggested new avenues for educating contemporary children.*

As information about human development has accumulated, various schools of thought have emerged in an effort to organize the data. These interpretations of our knowledge about human growth provide the basis for the difference in learning theories found among educators. Such differences can most clearly be understood in relation to several basic issues related to human development.

One issue revolves around the question of what constitutes normal development. Record keeping on the physical maturation of school

---

* See Robert J. Havighurst, *Developmental Tasks and Education* (1972), B.F. Skinner, *Beyond Freedom and Dignity* (1974), and E. Paul Torrance, *Guiding Creative Talent* (1962).

children over extended periods has made available to educators fairly predictable ranges of growth for chronological age. It appears, in general, that children in the United States are achieving physical maturation at an ever earlier age. Such findings are attributed to better health and nutritional care during childhood.

Our knowledge of intellectual, social, and emotional development during the school-age years is considerably less precise. However, organized inquiry has developed significant studies that guide our present decision making about development-related factors in these areas.

In the area of intelligence, considerable documentation exists regarding student performance on intelligence measuring devices such as the Stanford-Binet Scale. Little concrete evidence exists, however, to support hypotheses about intellect or intellectual capacity. What we currently operate with are models of how people are believed to develop and normal ranges of development in the capacity to think.

Without question, the dominant model in this area is one developed by Swiss educator Jean Piaget nearly sixty years ago. Piaget hypothesized four distinct but chronologically successive models of intelligence: (a) sensorimotor, (b) preoperational, (c) concretely operational, and (d) formal operational.* Piaget's model of continual and progressive change in the structure of behavior and thought in children has assisted educators in preparing intellectual experiences in schools.

In the areas of social and emotional development there exists even less precise data about human development, although there has been considerable educational research into these areas over the past thirty years. Studies such as Project Talent,[18] Robert Havighurst's "Growing Up in River City,"[19] and James Coleman's study of equality of educational opportunity[20] have provided planners with documented long-term studies of the social development of certain populations. Such studies have been supplemented by lists of social concerns such as those developed by Stratemeyer.[21]

Data related to emotional development has been compiled by the National Institute of Health and other health-related agencies. At best, our vision of what constitutes normal emotional development is a rough estimate.

For educational planners, the question of normal development is largely unresolved, particularly in areas of expectation relating to such questions as capacity and creativity. Our data base regarding human development grows daily.

Another issue relating to human development is whether such growth can be or should be controlled or accelerated. Primary re-

---

* For treatment of this subject see Richard M. Gorman, *Discovering Piaget: A Guide for Teachers* (Columbus, Ohio: Charles E. Merrill Publishing Co., 1972).

search with infants and children by White and associates[22] suggests that development can indeed be accelerated through both experience and environment. The work of behaviorist B.F. Skinner,* on the other hand, is conclusive in its demonstration that behavior can be shaped. These two options leave the curriculum developer with significant value decisions about both the anticipated outcome of an education and the more mechanical aspects of planning learning experiences.

Two final issues are indicative of the many planning considerations which relate to foundational data in human development. First, there is the mind-boggling question of the type of person schools should create. All developmental theorists agree that human growth is, to some degree, malleable. Medical research and practice suggest that a bright future is in store for the manipulation of gene pools, the alteration of chromosomes to overcome heredity, and the transplantation of artificial organs. Diet and direct stimulation of mind and body seem capable of uncovering talents and developing more fully functioning individuals. Experience with thought control and extrasensory perception, as well as studies in deprivation,† would suggest that human growth can be purposefully expanded or stunted. Schools appear to be increasingly in the unique position of defining and controlling human development.

Perhaps even more interesting for planners is the question, "What is the role of affect in education?" Here the command of basic human emotions seems perfectly possible. The works of Kohlberg and Mayer suggest that our understanding of moral development in students has only begun.[23]

Issues such as the definition of normal growth, the means by which we promote growth and development, the type of growth we seek, and our growing understanding of affective development in human beings make the study of human development a necessary foundation for school planning.

Learning as a Process

New understandings of human development, new perspectives of the role of knowledge in learning, and new social values related to the schooling process have meant that a variety of learning approaches have become fashionable and acceptable in schools. Specifically, school planners must incorporate the following givens into their design of educational programs: biological basis of development can be altered, physical maturation can be retarded or accelerated, intel-

---

* See the application of Skinnerian psychology in *Beyond Freedom and Dignity* (New York: Vintage Books, 1971).

† Lucian Malson, *Wolf Children and the Problem of Human Nature* (New York: Monthly Review Press, 1972).

lectual growth can be stimulated, social and emotional behavior can be accelerated and expanded, and cultural influences on learning can be controlled or encouraged. These givens, taken collectively, suggest that schools can promote multiple types of learning and development for students. The learning theory and the learning approach selected by the planner are functions of the desired goals for growth.*

At the philosophical level, a topic to be treated more fully in the following chapter, educators differ considerably regarding the type of development schools should promote. Three major approaches to learning have evolved: a behavioral approach, an approach incorporating drive theories, and an environmental approach. While each of these basic approaches to learning have numerous identifiable subtheories, they are presented here, in this form, to indicate the range of learning theory which exists among school planners.

The *behavioral approach* is characterized by an external perspective of the learning process, viewing learning as a product of teacher behavior. Under this approach to learning, educational planners and teachers who deliver such plans study the student to ascertain existing patterns of behavior and then structure specific learning experiences to encourage desired patterns of behavior.

Armed with terms such as *conditioning* (repetitive response), *reinforcement* (strengthening behavior through supportive action), *extinction* (withdrawing reinforcement), and *transfer* (connecting behavior with response), the behavioral learning theorist seeks to shape the student to a predetermined form. Common school practices under this learning approach are fixed curriculums, didactic (question-answer) formats, and programmed progression through materials. Perhaps the most interesting and controversial use of this learning approach in schools today is in the practice of behavior modification.

Behavior modification is a simple cause-effect programming of observable behavior. The procedure uses a four-step technique: identifying the problem, recording baseline data, installing a system to alter behavior, and evaluating the new condition. As an external system of behavior control, behavior modification is not concerned with the attitudes or motivations of students under such a system, but rather with the results of the modification system. According to this learning approach, behavior that is rewarded will continue while behavior that goes unrewarded will extinguish.†

A second learning theory is the *need-structured approach,* which is concerned with the needs and drives of students and seeks to use

---

* For example, see T.D. Yawkey and S.B. Silvern, "Evaluating Instructional Goals of Developmental Programs in Early Childhood Education," *Education* 96 (1975), pp. 36–39.

† For a complete description of this technique see Clifford K. Madsen and Charles H. Madsen, Jr., "What is Behavior Modification," *Instructor* 81, 2 (October, 1971), pp. 48–49.

such natural motivational energy to promote learning. Teachers will often analyze and utilize the interests and needs of students as instructional vehicles when following this approach.

Key terms used with the needs/drives approach are *readiness, identification, imitation,* and *modeling.* Taking a cue from Freudian psychology, this theory orders the curriculum to coordinate with developmental readiness. Students learn through pursuit of unfulfilled needs, often modeling behaviors of others or developing predictable identification patterns.

Drive theories rely heavily on findings of human growth and development in planning curricular activities. This set of theories is dependent on student growth in planning school experiences.

The *environmental approach* to learning is concerned with the restructuring of the learning environment or the students' perceptions so that they may be free to develop. Unlike the static definition of growth presented by the behavioral approach or the dependent theories of need-structured approaches, the environmental approach is dynamic in nature. It acknowledges human diversity, believes in human potential, and promotes both uniqueness and creativity in individuals.

The basis of the environmental approach is the belief that behavior is a function of perception, and that human perceptions are the result of both experiences and understandings. When students have positive experiences that are self-enhancing, their perception and understanding of themselves and the world around them is altered. These new perceptions, in turn, allow for additional growth experiences. Student potential for development, under this learning approach, is limitless.

These three primary approaches to the structuring of learning in schools, approaches which might be labeled "push," "pull," and "restructure," are very different in their assumptions about people and possibilities for human development. They differ, for instance, in their beliefs about human potential. They differ in terms of their vantage point in describing learning (external vs. internal). They differ in their beliefs about the source of academic motivation.

To select any one of these approaches to learning would mean that basic classroom considerations such as the design of learning spaces, the choice of materials, and the roles of participants would have a distinct form. The learning theory of the planner is crucial to decision-making and projection. As such, learning as a process represents a strong fourth planning foundation.

The area of educational foundations is highly complex. It is an effort to bring order to a rapidly changing world that has an increasing number of relevant variables. Throughout the treatment of foundations of curriculum planning, there is an element of choice: which input to select, which data to validate, which decisions to make.

Joseph Schwab, in his book *The Practical: A Language for Curriculum,*[24] observes that to some extent a study of educational foundations is an inadequate approach for planning. This, he states, is so because even upon finding the most current and useful data the planner must still make value decisions concerning its application. This observation points to a more difficult task in curriculum planning which is the translation of data into plans and the activation of that planning.

Ultimately, the choices and decisions related to the selection, activation, and evaluation of educational designs are normative matters. Before educational planners can be effective and consistent in their work they must understand their personal belief systems and formulate a philosophy of education that complements that system. The following chapter introduces some established philosophies of education and assists you in determining your priorities for schools.

SUMMARY

Educational planners have been forced to assimilate and organize extensive data related to the development of school programs. Key issues about the purpose of schooling have led to the ordering of such data into four major areas: social forces, treatments of knowledge, human growth and development, and learning as a process. These four areas serve as primary organizers for the foundations of curriculum planning.

Our growing knowledge in these areas suggests that curriculum planning is increasingly normative in nature; there are value-laden decisions to be made about crucial issues that affect school programs. To be able to make such choices, curriculum planners must understand their own beliefs and form them into a consistent philosophy of education.

Notes

1. Thomas H. Briggs, *Curriculum Problems* (New York: Macmillan Company, 1926).
2. Daniel Tanner and Laurel N. Tanner, *Curriculum Development: Theory Into Practice* (New York: Macmillan Publishing Company, 1975), pp. 9–10.
3. Jon Wiles and John Reed, "Quest: Education for a Technocratic Existence," (Unpublished manuscript, 1975), p. 58.
4. Marshall McLuhan and Quentin Fiore, *The Medium is the Message* (New York: Bantam Books, 1967).
5. Charles Silberman, *Crisis in the Classroom,* (New York: Random House, 1970), pp. 33–34.
6. Paddy Chayefsky, *Network,* released by United Artists, 1977.

7. Wiles and Reed, "Quest," pp. 61–2.
8. Alvin Toffler, "The Future as a Way of Life," *Horizons* 10, (Summer, 1965), p. 109.
9. Arno A. Bellack, "Conceptions of Knowledge: Their Significance for Curriculum" in William Jenkins, ed., *The Nature of Knowledge: Implications for the Education of Teachers* (Milwaukee, Wisconsin: University of Wisconsin—Milwaukee, 1962), p. 42.
10. Charles A. Reich, abstract from "The Greening of America," *New Yorker,* (September 26, 1970), pp. 43–4.
11. Jerome S. Bruner, "Structures in Learning" *NEA Journal,* 52, (March, 1963), p. 26.
12. Earl C. Kelley, *Education For What Is Real* (New York: Harper Publishing, 1947).
13. Alvin Toffler, *Future Shock* (New York: Random House, 1970).
14. Kathryn V. Feyereisen, A. John Fiorino, and Arlene T. Nowak, *Supervision and Curriculum Renewal: A Systems Approach* (New York: Appleton-Century-Croft, 1970), p. 138.
15. Mario Fantini, "Reducing the Behavior Gap," *National Education Association Journal* 57, (January, 1968), pp. 23–24.
16. John M. Culkin, "A Schoolman's Guide to Marshall McLuhan," *Saturday Review,* 50, 11, (March 18, 1967), p. 71.
17. Marshall McLuhan, and Quentin Fiore, "The Medium is the Message."
18. John C. Flanagan, *The Identification, Development, and Utilization of Human Talents: The American High School Student,* Cooperative Research Project No. 635 (University of Pittsburgh, 1964).
19. Robert J. Havighurst, et al., *Growing Up In River City* (New York: J. Wiley and Sons, 1962).
20. Frederick Mosteller and Daniel P. Moynihan, eds., *On Equality of Educational Opportunity* (New York: Vintage Books, 1972).
21. Florence B. Stratemeyer et al., *Developing A Curriculum for Modern Living* (New York: Teachers College, Columbia University, 1947), p. 155.
22. Burton L. White et al., *Experience and Environment: Major Influences on the Development of the Young Child* 1, Childhood Series, (Englewood Cliffs: Prentice-Hall, Inc., 1973).
23. Lawrence Kohlberg and Rochelle Mayer, "Development as an Aim of Education," *Harvard Educational Review* 42, (November, 1972), pp. 452–53.
24. Joseph Schwab, *The Practical: A Language for Curriculum* (Washington, D.C.: National Education Association, 1970).

Suggested Learning Activities

1. Identify recent developments in our understanding of curriculum foundations that have implications for schools of the future.

2. Prepare a one-page reaction to data presented in this chapter for each of the bases of curriculum planning: social forces, utilization of knowledge, human growth and development, and learning as a process.

Books to Review

Hass, Glen. *Curriculum Planning: A New Approach,* 2nd ed. Boston: Allyn and Bacon, 1977.

Havighurst, R. and Neugarten, B. *Society and Education,* 3rd ed. Boston: Allyn and Bacon, 1967.

Unruh, Glenys. *Responsive Curriculum Development: Theory and Action.* Berkeley, California: McCutchan Publishing Company, 1975.

Zais, Robert S. *Curriculum: Principles and Foundations.* New York: Thomas Y. Crowell Publishing, 1976.

5

The Role of Philosophy in Curriculum Development

At the heart of purposeful activity in curriculum development is an educational philosophy that guides action. To John Dewey, this philosophy was a general theory of education. One of Dewey's students, Boyd Bode, envisioned this type of philosophy to be "a source of reflective consideration." A contemporary educator, Ralph Tyler, has likened educational philosophy to a "screen for selecting educational objectives." It is clear that educational philosophies serve numerous functions: to clarify objectives and activities in schools, to guide strategies for curriculum changes, to suggest learning theories, and to define the roles of persons engaged in curriculum improvement.

In this book, curriculum development has been given an active definition: it is a leadership function. Curriculum specialists must know what they favor, having in mind a best possible form of education. Curriculum leaders must also be able to organize and manage the activities that improve school programs. Curriculum workers must be able to recommend their programs effectively to classroom teachers. It has been demonstrated that the classroom teacher is the final decision-maker in terms of the curriculum experienced by students.*

---

* A classic study of the impact of teachers on curriculum improvement efforts is Goodlad, Klein, and associates, *Looking Behind the Classroom Door* (Worthington, Ohio: Charles A. Jones Publishing, 1970).

In arriving at an educational philosophy, curriculum specialists are forced to make value-laden choices. It is clear that there are many ways to operate schools, and curriculum decisions ultimately reflect differing beliefs and values about the nature and capacity of man. If curriculum specialists are aware of the range of beliefs about education, and if they have solidified their professional values, they will be better able to make consistent everyday decisions.

The need for a curriculum leader to have a strong philosophy of education has become increasingly obvious over the past thirty years because of the degree of change in schools. Public education has seen wave after wave of innovation, reform, new themes, and other signals of dissatisfaction with the status quo. Indicative of the calls for reformation of the schools is the following statement issued by the President's Advisory Committee on Science:

> When school was short, and merely a supplement to the main activities of growing up, the form mattered little. But school has expanded to fill time that other activities once occupied, without substituting for them. . . . Every society must somehow solve the problem of transforming children into adults, for its very survival depends on that solution. In every society there is established some kind of institutional setting within which the transformation is to occur, in directions predicated by societal goals and values. . . . In our view, the institutional framework for maturation in the United States is in need of serious examination. The school system, as it now exists, offers an incomplete context for the accomplishment of many important facets of maturation.[1]

Although it is certain that there is a desire for change in public education today, there is no strong mandate for the direction of such change in the United States. In the absence of centralized public planning and policy formation, local school boards rely on input from pressure groups, expert opinion, and various forces in the societal flow. Often, decisions about school programs are made in an isolated, piecemeal fashion, without serious consideration of the pattern of decision making. When goals are unclear, when there is no public concensus on value-laden decisions, or when curriculum specialists are unable to clearly articulate positions on controversial issues, then schools slip into the all-too-common pattern of reactive thinking and action.

The reactive curriculum strategy that emerges from a decision-making vacuum is characterized by numerous false starts in planning, innovations for the sake of innovations, and programs that are contradictory. The absence of direction often results in a curriculum that includes nearly everything but which accomplishes little. Given the public nature of American education, the dynamic nature of public school decision-making forums, and the dependence of school boards and superintendents on curriculum specialists for direction, the beliefs and values of the curriculum leader must be clear.

THE SEARCH FOR A PHILOSOPHICAL ATTITUDE

Although there has been a steady interest in educational philosophies for nearly a century, the use of philosophical attitudes in planning school programs has been severely limited in the United States. With the exception of the "progressive" schools of the 1920s and 1930s, few educational programs have emerged that reflect strong philosophical understanding and commitment. As McClure has stated:

> With depressingly few exceptions, curriculum design until the 1950's was a process of layering society's new knowledge on top of the hodge-podge accumulation of society's old knowledge and arranging for feeding it, in prescribed time units, to students who may or may not have found it relevant to their own lives.[2]

The dependence of school leaders on public acquiescence for the development of school programs explains, in large part, the absence of philosophic consistency and the standardization of school programs over time. Without public demand for or approval of change, often interpreted in the public forum as no opposition, elected school leaders have failed to press for more distinct school programs.

Equally, the mandate of public education to serve all learners has acted to restrict the specification of educational ends and the development of tailored programs. The role of the schools as the assimilator of diverse cultures, from the turn of the century until the mid-1960s, contributed to the general nature of public school education.

Another factor in the absence of educational specificity in programs has been the lack of strong curriculum leadership at state and local levels. With the exception of university-based theorists, few curriculum specialists have had an understanding of philosophy, the clarity of vision, and the technical skills to direct school programs toward consistently meaningful activity. Although this condition is rapidly improving due to the greatly increased number of persons trained in curriculum development, the presence of a highly skilled curriculum leader often separates the successful school district from the mediocre school district.

The development of a clear and consistent set of beliefs about the purpose of education requires considerable thought, for there is a great amount of information to consider and strong arguments for the many philosophical positions which have developed. Perhaps the most important point to be made for the reader is to underscore Saylor and Alexander's observation that schooling is always a "moral enterprise":

> A society establishes and supports schools for certain purposes; it seeks to achieve certain ends or attain desired outcomes. Efforts of adults to direct the experiences of young people in a formal institution such as the school constitutes preferences for certain human ends and values.

> Schooling is a moral venture, one that necessitates choosing values among innumerable possibilities. These choices constitute the starting point in curriculum planning.[3]

To illustrate the diversity of beliefs about the purpose of formal education and approaches to educating, consider the two following statements by Robert Hutchins and A.S. Neill. These statements are representative of two established educational philosophies, *perennialism* and *existentialism*. First Hutchins:

> The ideal education is not an ad hoc education, not an education directed to immediate needs; it is not a specialized education, or a preprofessional education; it is not a utilitarian education. It is an education calculated to develop the mind.

> I have old-fashioned prejudices in favor of the three R's and the liberal arts, in favor of trying to understand the greatest works that the human race has produced. I believe that these are permanent necessities, the intellectual tools that are needed to understand the ideas and ideals of our world.[4]

Now Neill:

> Well, we set out to make a school in which we should allow children to be themselves. In order to do this, we had to renounce all discipline, all direction, all suggestion, all moral training. . . . All it required was what we had—a complete belief in the child as a good, not evil being. For almost forty years, this belief in the goodness of the child has never wavered; it rather has become a final faith. My view is that a child is innately wise and realistic. If left to himself without adult suggestions of any kind, he will develop as far as he is capable of developing.[5]

Such differences of opinion about the purpose and means of educating are extreme, but they illustrate the range of choices to be made by curriculum planners. These statements also indicate the trends of education which various philosophies favor. The perennialists who favor a highly controlled curriculum, strict discipline, and uniform treatment for students can easily identify with trends such as "back to the basics," "accountability," or "performance contracts." The existentialists who see a nonschool environment for personal growth, an environment with highly individualized activities, can identify with "alternative programs," "student rights" movements, and other nonstandard choices.

CRITICAL QUESTIONS TO BE ANSWERED

Each curriculum planner must face and answer some difficult questions about the purpose and organization of schooling. The answers to such questions are critical to school planning, and establish the criteria for future decision-making and action. As Saylor and Alexander state the condition, it is one of defining responsibility:

> In selecting the basic goals which the school should seek to serve from among the sum total of ends for which people strive the curriculum planner faces the major issue: In the total process of human development what parts or aspects should the school accept responsibility for guiding?[6]

Tanner and Tanner suggest that three major ends for schooling have been suggested repeatedly in the past:

> Throughout the twentieth century educational opionion and practice have been sharply divided as to whether the dominant source and influence for curriculum development should be the body of organized scholarship (the specialties and divisions of academic knowledge), the learner (the immature developing being), or society (contemporary adult life).[7]

Whether the specialists in curriculum relate to the knowledge of the past and present, or tie their philosophies to the present and future needs of the learner and society is critical. This decision determines whether curriculum developers will define their roles in terms of restructuring or refining the existing system of education.

Most often, curriculum development in schools is a mechanical, static function because the content base is accepted as the main criterion for curriculum work:

> In the absence of reflective consideration of what constitutes the good man leading to the good life in the good society, the curriculum tends to be regarded as a mechanical means of developing the necessary skills of young people in conformance with the pervading demands of the larger social scene. Under such circumstances, the school does not need to bring into question the existing social situation, nor does it need to enable pupils to examine through reflective thinking possible alternative solutions to social problems. Instead, the school is merely expected to do the bidding of whatever powers and forces are most dominant in the larger society at any given time.[8]

When the curriculum planner accepts the needs of learners as criteria for developing school programs, such as in early childhood or middle school curriculums, then the purpose of formal public education is altered. The same is true if social reform, such as in the alternative school programs of the 1960s, is chosen as the criterion. In accepting an alteration of the perceived purpose of schooling, curriculum developers cross over into an advocacy role as they attempt to restructure the existing curriculum as opposed to the traditional role of mechanical refinement. Their effectiveness in such a role is often determined by the clarity of the objectives they work toward.

A number of primary questions override the value choices of all major educational philosophies: What is education for? What kind of citizens and what kind of a society do we want? What methods of instruction or classroom organization must we provide to produce these desired ends?

McNeil poses eight questions that are useful in developing the philosophical assumptions needed to screen educational objectives:

1. Is the purpose of school to change, adapt to, or accept the social order?
2. What can a school do better than any other agency or institution?
3. What objectives should be common to all?
4. Should objectives stress cooperation or competition?
5. Should objectives deal with controversial issues, or only those things for which there is established knowledge?
6. Should attitudes be taught? Fundamental skills? Problem-solving strategies?
7. Should teachers emphasize subject matter or try to create behavior outside of school?
8. Should objectives be based on the needs of the local community? Society in general? Expressed needs of students?[9]

THE STRUGGLE TO BE A DECISIVE LEADER

While few educators would deny the importance of a philosophy in directing activity, few school districts or teachers relish discussions on the topic. Even well-known educators have confessed a dislike for such discourse:

> It is well to rid oneself of this business of "aims of education." Discussions on this subject are among the dullest and most fruitless of human pursuits.[10]

> A sense of distasteful weariness overtakes me whenever I hear someone discussing educational goals and philosophy.[11]

Part of the problem with discussing educational philosophies in earnest, in the past, has been the pervasiveness of the subject-dominated curriculum in American schools. This problem has been further compounded by "expert opinion" on the topic by college professors who, being products of the system, possess monumental conflict-of-interest in rendering such opinion. In school districts where inquiry into the purpose of educating has been quickly followed by retrenchment of the subject-matter curriculum, there has been little payoff in conducting philosophical discussions. But, where inquiry into educational purpose is honest, open, and leads to meaningful change, philosophical discussions are among the most exciting endeavors.

Charles Silberman, in his book *Crisis in the Classroom,* expresses the meaning of philosophical understandings for the learning programs of the school.

> What educators must realize, moreover, is that how they teach and how they act may be more important than what they teach. The way we do things, that is to say, shapes values more directly and more effectively than the way we talk about them. Certainly administrative procedures like automatic promotion, homogeneous grouping, racial segregation, or selective admission to higher education affect "citizenship education" more profoundly than does the social studies curriculum. And children are taught a host of lessons about values, ethics, morality, character, and conduct every day of the week, less by the conduct of the curriculum than by the way schools are organized, the ways teachers and parents behave, the way they talk to children and each other, the kinds of behavior they approve or reward and the kinds they disapprove and punish. These lessons are far more powerful than verbalizations that accompany them and that they frequently controvert.[12]

Two major benefits can be derived from an exploration of philosophical attitudes. First, major problem areas and inconsistencies in the school program can be identified:

> Many contemporary educational principles and practices are something of a hodgepodge rooted in premises about the nature of man and his relationship with his physical-social environment that frequently are incompatible with one another.[13]

Second, areas of common ground among those responsible for educational leadership can be discovered. Common values which overlap individual beliefs form the most fertile ground for curricular collaboration and the development of successful projects and programs.

Before curriculum specialists can work with parents, teachers, administrators, and other educators to explore educational values, they must complete an examination of their own attitudes. During this process, the curriculum worker is seeking to identify a value structure which can organize and relate the many aspects of planning.

To clarify the values and beliefs that will tie together curriculum organization, instructional procedures, learning roles, materials selection, and other components of school planning, curriculum leaders must identify themes that seem true to them. While this process may be time-consuming, the investment is necessary. Curriculum leaders, in order to be both decisive and effective in their roles, must combat the urge to ignore the value implications of the job or reduce all arguments to "thoughtful uncertainty."

DETERMINANTS OF AN EDUCATIONAL PHILOSOPHY

Major philosophies of life and education have traditionally been defined by three criteria: What is good? What is true? What is real? Individual perceptions of goodness, truth, and reality differ considerably, and an analysis of these questions reveals unique patterns of response. When such responses are categorized and labeled, they become formal philosophies.

In the language of philosophy, goodness is referred to as *axiology,* truth as *epistemology,* and reality as *ontology.* Axiological questions deal primarily with values, and in a school context philosophical arguments are concerned with the ultimate source of values to be taught. Questions of an epistemological nature in a school context are directed toward the mediums of learning or the best means of seeking truth. Ontological questions, in search of reality, are most often concerned with the substance of learning or content of study. Thus, the standard philosophic inquiries concerning goodness, truth, and reality are translated into questions concerning the source, medium, and form of learning in a school environment.

These queries are not simple, for there are many ways to select ideas, translate them into instructional patterns, and package them into curriculum programs. Those possibilities are forever increasing as our knowledge of the world becomes more sophisticated. Essential questions arise, questions that must be answered prior to planning learning experiences for students. Why do schools exist? What should be taught? What is the role of the teacher and the student? How does the school deal with change?

FIVE EDUCATIONAL PHILOSOPHIES

There are many kinds of educational philosophies, but for the sake of simplicity it is possible to extract five distinct ones. These five philosophies are perennialism, idealism, realism, experimentalism, and existentialism. Collectively, these philosophies represent a broad spectrum of thought about what schools should be and do. Educators holding these philosophies would create very different schools for students to attend and learn in. In the following section, each of these standard philosophies is discussed in terms of their postures on axiological, epistemological, and ontological questions.

Perennialism

The most conservative, traditional, or inflexible of the five philosophies is perennialism, a philosophy drawing heavily from classical definitions of education. Perennialists believe that education, like human nature, is a constant. Since the distinguishing characteristic of humans is the ability to reason, education should focus on developing rationality. Education, for the perennialist, is a preparation for life, and students should be taught the world's permanencies through structured study.

For the perennialist, reality is a world of reason. Such truths are revealed to us through study and sometimes through divine acts. Goodness is to be found in rationality itself. Perennialists would favor a curriculum of subjects and doctrine, taught through highly disciplined drill and behavior control. Schools for the perennialist exist primarily to reveal reason by teaching eternal truths. The teacher interprets and tells. The student is a passive recipient. Since truth is eternal, all change in the immediate school environment is largely superficial.

Idealism

Idealism is a philosophy that espouses the wisdom of men and women that has been refined. Reality is seen as a world within a person's mind. Truth is to be found in the consistency of ideas. Goodness is an ideal state, something to be strived for.

Idealism would favor schools teaching subjects of the mind, such as is found in most public school classrooms. Teachers, for the idealist, would be models of ideal behavior.

Idealists would see the function of schools as being to sharpen intellectual processes, to present the wisdom of the ages, and to present models of behavior which are exemplary. Students in such schools would have a somewhat passive role, receiving and memorizing the reporting of the teacher. Change in the school program would generally be considered an intrusion on the orderly process of educating.

Realism

For the realist, the world is as it is, and the job of schools would be to teach students about the world. Goodness, for the realist, would be found in the laws of nature and the order of the physical world. Truth would be the simple correspondence of observation.

The realist would favor a school dominated by subjects of the here-and-now world, such as math and science. Students would be taught factual information for mastery. The teacher would impart knowledge of this reality to students or display such reality for observation and study. Classrooms would be highly ordered and disciplined, like nature, and the students would be passive participants in the study of things. Changes in school would be perceived as a natural evolution toward a perfection of order.

Experimentalism

For the experimentalist, the world is an ever-changing place. Reality is what is actually experienced. Truth is what presently functions. Goodness is what is accepted by public test. Unlike the perennialist, idealist, and realist, the experimentalist openly accepts change and continually seeks to discover new ways to expand and improve society.

The experimentalist would favor a school with heavy emphasis on social subjects and experiences. Learning would occur through a problem-solving or inquiry format. Teachers would aid learners or consult with learners who would be actively involved in discovering and experiencing the world in which they live. Such an education program would focus on value development, but in terms of group consequences.

Existentialism

The existentialist sees the world as one personal subjectivity, where goodness, truth, and reality are individually defined. Reality is a world of existing, truth subjectively chosen, and goodness a matter of freedom.

For existentialists, schools, if they existed at all, would be places that assisted students in knowing themselves and learning of their place in society. If subject matter existed, it would be matter of interpretation such as the arts, ethics, or philosophy. Teacher-student interaction would center around assisting students in their personal learning journeys. Change in school environments would be embraced as both a natural and necessary phenomenon.

The five standard philosophies are compared in Table 5.1 in terms of attitudes on significant questions.

It should be noted by the reader that few educators hold a pure version of any of these philosophies, for schools are complex places with many forces vying for prominence. These schools of thought have evolved as distinctive forms of philosophy following the examination of beliefs on pertinent issues. When an educator chooses not to adopt a single philosophy, or blends philosophies for experience, or selectively applies educational philosophies in practice, it is called an *eclectic* position. Most classrooms and public schools come closest to an eclectic stance, applying philosophic preferences as conditions demand.

Whatever the educator's philosophy or beliefs about schools, and each of the five philosophies presented here are legitimate beliefs, it is critical that these values be clarified and understood in terms of their implications. To this end, the reader is invited to participate in a self-assessment that has been developed to show preferences on

Table 5.1
Five Major Educational Philosophies

	Perennialism	Idealism	Realism	Experimentalism	Existentialism
Reality Ontology	A world of reason and God	A world of the mind	A world of things	A world of experience	A world of existing
Truth (Knowledge) Epistemology	Reason and revelation	Consistency of ideas	Correspondence and sensation (as we see it)	What works What is	Personal, subjective choice
Goodness Axiology	Rationality	Imitation of ideal self, person to be emulated	Laws of nature	The public test	Freedom
Teaching Reality	Disciplinary subjects and doctrine	Subject of the mind—literary, philosophical, religious	Subjects of physical world—math, science	Subject matter of social experiences—social studies	Subject matter of choice—art, ethics, philosophy
Teaching Truth	Discipline of the mind via drill	Teaching ideas via lecture, discussion	Teaching for mastery, of information—demonstrate, recite	Problem-solving, project method	Arousing personal responses—questioning

	Perennialism	Idealism	Realism	Experimentalism	Existentialism
Teaching Goodness (Values)	Disciplining behavior (to reason)	Imitating heroes and other exemplars	Training in rules of conduct	Making group decisions in light of consequences	Awakening self to responsibility
Why Schools Exist	To reveal reason and God's will	To sharpen the mind and intellectual processes	To reveal the order of the world and universe	To discover and expand the society we live in to share experiences	To aid children in knowing themselves and their place in society
What Should Be Taught	External truths	Wisdom of the ages	Laws of physical reality	Group inquiry into social problems and social sciences, method and subject together	Unregimented topic areas
Role of the Teacher	Interprets, tells	Reports, person to be emulated	Displays, imparts knowledge	Aids, consultant	Questions, assists student in personal journey
Role of the Student	Passive reception	Receives, memorizes	Manipulates, passive participation	Active participation, contributes	Determines own rule
School's Attitude Toward Change	Truth is eternal, no real change	Truth to be preserved, anti-change	Always coming toward perfection, orderly change	Change is ever-present, a process	Change is necessary at all times

value-laden educational questions. Scoring instructions are found at the conclusion of the chapter.*

PHILOSOPHY PREFERENCE ASSESSMENT

Directions: For each item below, respond according to the strength of your belief. A one (1) indicates strong disagreement, a five (5) strong agreement. Use a separate sheet of paper.

1. Ideal teachers are constant questioners.
2. Schools exist for societal improvement.
3. Teaching should center around the inquiry technique.
4. Demonstration and recitation are essential components for learning.
5. Students should always be permitted to determine their own rules in the educational process.
6. Reality is spiritual and rational.
7. Curriculum should be based on the laws of natural science.
8. The teacher should be a strong authority figure in the classroom.
9. The student is a receiver of knowledge.
10. Ideal teachers interpret knowledge.
11. Lecture-discussion is the most effective teaching technique.
12. Institutions should seek avenues towards self-improvement through an orderly process.
13. Schools are obligated to teach moral truths.
14. School programs should focus on social problems and issues.
15. Institutions exist to preserve and strengthen spiritual and social values.
16. Subjective opinion reveals truth.
17. Teachers are seen as facilitators of learning.
18. Schools should be educational "smorgasbords."
19. Memorization is the key to process skills.
20. Reality consists of objects.
21. Schools exist to foster the intellectual process.
22. Schools foster an orderly means for change.
23. There are essential skills everyone must learn.
24. Teaching by subject area is the most effective approach.
25. Students should play an active part in program design and evaluation.
26. A functioning member of society follows rules of conduct.
27. Reality is rational.

---

* The authors wish to thank former students Bill Suggs and Sidney Mitchell for suggesting a similar assessment instrument.

28. Schools should reflect the society they serve.
29. The teacher should set an example for the students.
30. The most effective learning does not take place in a highly structured, strictly disciplined environment.
31. The curriculum should be based on unchanging spiritual truths.
32. The most effective learning is nonstructured.
33. Truth is a constant expressed through ideas.
34. Drill and factual knowledge are important components of any learning environment.
35. Societal consensus determines morality.
36. Knowledge is gained primarily through the senses.
37. There are essential pieces of knowledge that everyone should know.
38. The school exists to facilitate self-awareness.
39. Change is an ever-present process.
40. Truths are best taught through the inquiry process.

THE MEANING OF PHILOSOPHY IN CURRICULUM

A philosophy, the clarification of beliefs about the purpose and goals of education, is essential to curriculum development. Without direction, school programs meander, become targets for social pressure, or operate in a state of programmatic contradiction. The development of a philosophy of education is a prerequisite to assuming a leadership function in school program development.

Curriculum specialists can assist others with whom they work in the clarification of their beliefs and goals. This can be done in three basic ways:

1. Others can be asked to review existing statements of philosophy or related documents and restate them in terms of desired changes.
2. Others can be asked to transfer their own personal philosophy of living into a school context, setting goals for school from general life goals.
3. Others can be asked to look for patterns in current behavior in society that might suggest goals for schools.

Methods that can be used to help others achieve goal clarity and consistency include writing personal goal statements, assigning priorities to various items, surveying existing documents, and analyzing school programs.

As curriculum specialists clarify their own beliefs about the purpose of education and assist others in finding their value systems, the odds for meaningful curriculum development increase. Shared values can form the bond of commitment to change. The time spent in assessing group philosophies has significant payoff in areas such as continuity in school programs and articulation among school levels, developing relationships and roles among school faculties, the selection of learning activities and materials, evaluation of school programs, and the redesign of basic curriculum offerings.

Most important, however, is the connection of philosophy to leadership and decision making in education. To be decisive leaders, and consistent decision makers, the curriculum specialists must know their values and those of the persons around them.

SUMMARY

Educational philosophies are the heart of purposeful activity in curriculum development. Philosophies serve as value screens for decision-making. Because educators today are confronted by multiple choices, it is vital that the curriculum specialists understand their own values and beliefs about schooling.

Numerous educational philosophies exist, reflecting a wide range of choice concerning the role and organization of educational institutions. Critical questions about schools and their operation can be used to determine educational philosophic postures. In this chapter, five major educational philosophies were presented along with a philosophy assessment inventory to assist the readers in their responses to key questions about schools.

The authors believe that in order to be a decisive leader, curriculum specialists must be aware of their own values. Understanding the value structure of others with whom they work will enable curriculum developers to seek out the most promising areas for curriculum improvement.

Notes

1. *Youth: Transition To Adulthood,* A report of the President's Advisory Commission on Science, 1973.
2. Robert M. McClure, "The Reforms of the Fifties and Sixties: A Historical Look at the Near Past," *The Curriculum: Retrospect and Prospect* National Society for the Study of Education, 1971, p. 51.
3. Galen Saylor and William M. Alexander, *Planning Curriculum for Schools* (New York: Holt, Rinehart, Winston, 1974), pp. 144–45.

4. Robert Hutchins, *On Education* (Santa Barbara, California: Center for the Study of Democratic Institutions, 1963), p. 18.
5. A.S. Neill, *Summerhill* (New York: Hart Publishing Company, 1960), p. 4.
6. Saylor and Alexander, *Planning Curriculum For Schools,* p. 146.
7. Daniel Tanner and Laurel N. Tanner, *Curriculum Development: Theory Into Practice* (New York: Macmillan Publishing Company, 1975), p. 95.
8. Tanner and Tanner, *Curriculum Development: Theory into Practice,* p. 64.
9. John D. McNeil, *Designing Curriculum: Self-Instructional Modules* (Boston: Little, Brown and Company, 1976), pp. 91–92.
10. Martin Mayer, *The Schools* (New York: Harper & Row Publishers, 1961).
11. James B. Conant, as reported in *Crisis in the Classroom* (New York: Random House, 1970).
12. Charles E. Silberman, *Crisis in the Classroom* (New York: Random House, 1970), p. 9.
13. Morris L. Bigge, *Learning Theories for Teachers* (New York: Harper and Row, 1971), viii.

Suggested Learning Activities

1. Using the philosophy assessment inventory found in this chapter, analyze your beliefs about the roles of schools. If your profile does not correspond to what you think you believe, explain this discrepancy.

2. Using a public school with which you are familiar, attempt to identify the dominant philosophy of education using a questionnaire developed from the list of questions found in the philosophy assessment inventory.

PHILOSOPHY ASSESSMENT SCORING

The following sets of test questions relate to the five standard philosophies of education:

Perennialist—6, 8, 10, 13, 15, 31, 34, 37
Idealist—9, 11, 19, 21, 24, 27, 29, 33
Realist—4, 7, 12, 20, 22, 23, 26, 28
Experimentalist—2, 3, 14, 17, 25, 35, 39, 40
Existentialist—1, 5, 16, 18, 30, 32, 36, 38

Scoring Steps

1. Taking these questions by set, multiply each question by the value of the answer given (i.e., strongly disagree = 1). Total

the numerical value of the set. In a single set of numbers, the total should fall between 8 (all 1s) and 40 (all 5s).
2. Divide the total score for each set by five (Example: 40/5 = 8).
3. Plot the scores on the graph shown in Figure 5.1.

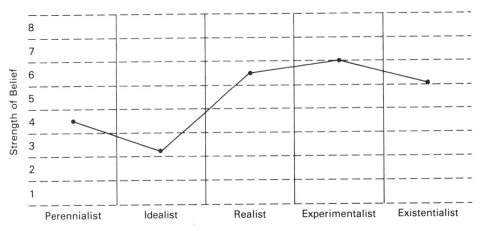

Figure 5.1

Interpretation

Having scored and plotted your responses on the grid provided, you now have a profile which is distinctive to your own beliefs about schools. It can be noted that some patterns are common and therefore subject to interpretation. The pattern already on the grid, for instance, is a composite response by over 800 students, both graduate and undergraduate, at two universities.

Pattern #1—If your profile on the response grid is basically flat, reflecting approximately the same score for each set of questions, an inability to discriminate in terms of preference is indicated.

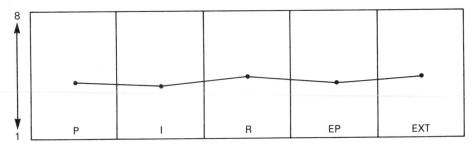

Pattern #2—If your pattern is generally a slanting line across the grid, then you show a strong structured or nonstructured orientation in your reported beliefs about schools.

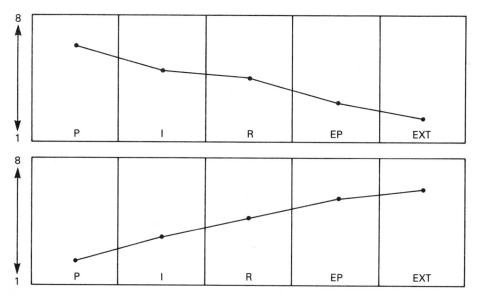

Pattern #3—If your pattern appears as a bimodal or trimodal distribution, (two or three peaks), it indicates indecisiveness on crucial issues and suggests the need for further clarification. The closer the peaks (adjacent sets) the less contradiction in the responses.

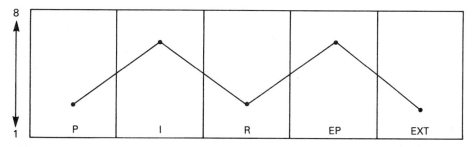

Pattern #4—If the pattern appears U-shaped, as in either of the pictures below, a significant amount of value inconsistency is indicated. Such a response would suggest strong beliefs in very different and divergent systems.

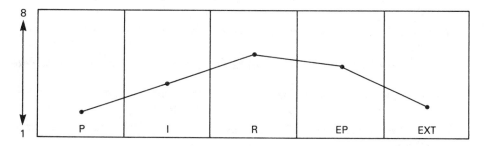

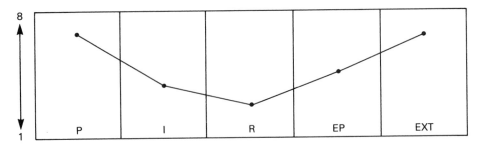

Pattern #5—Finally a pattern which is simply a flowing curve without sharp peaks and valleys may suggest either an eclectic philosophy, or a person only beginning to study his or her own philosophy.

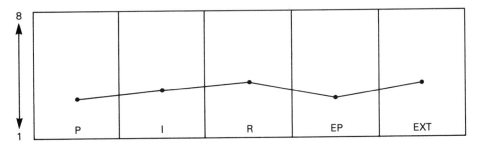

Books to Review

Bigge, Morris. *Learning Theories for Teachers.* New York: Harper & Row Publishers, 1971.

Bode, Boyd. *Modern Educational Theories.* New York: Macmillan Publishing Company, 1927.

Dewey, John. *Democracy and Education.* New York: Macmillan Publishing Company, 1916.

Ehlers, Henry. *Crucial Issues in Education,* 6th ed. New York: Holt Rinehart and Winston, Inc., 1977.

Guttchen, Robert and Bandman, Bertram. *Philosophical Essays on Curriculum.* New York: J.P. Lippincott Company, 1969.

Kneller, George. *Existentialism and Education.* New York: John Wiley and Sons, Inc., 1958.

Peddiwell, J. [pseud.] *The Saber-Tooth Curriculum.* New York: McGraw-Hill Book Company, 1939.

Phenix, Philip. *Realms of Meaning.* New York: McGraw-Hill Book Company, 1964.

6

Leadership in Curriculum Development

Leadership represents a critical element in the curriculum development process. Without strong leadership in instructional improvement, values and goals are not clarified, plans are not drawn, and activities are not implemented. Leadership is the intangible driving force in planned educational change. Despite its importance, leadership remains one of the least understood concepts in educational program development.

The question of what makes a good leader has interested social scientists for many years. During this century there have been numerous attempts to analyze and define leadership. Such study has evolved through three stages of inquiry: a study of leadership traits, a situational or environmental analysis, and a study of exchange or transaction.

In early studies of leadership, there was an attempt to identify characteristics that were unique to leaders. Although many traits were nominated for uniqueness, no traits withstood objective analysis as absolute predictors of leadership style or capacity. A benchmark in such personality research was the 1933 list developed by Smith and Krueger:

Personality Traits

Knowledge	Initiative
Abundance of physical and nervous energy	Imagination
	Purpose
Enthusiasm	Persistence
Originality	Speed of decision

Social Traits

Tact
Sympathy
Faith in others and self
Prestige
Patience
Ascendance-Submission

Physical Characteristics

Some advantage as to height, weight, and physical attractiveness[1]

Although leadership trait research still continues today, it has been largely abandoned due to lack of productive results. Numerous studies in the area showed little overlap from one investigation to the next.

A 1948 study by Stogdill proved to be an important turning point in research on leadership. Stogdill categorized personal factors associated with leadership under five general headings: capacity, achievement, responsibility, participation, and status. To these five, Stogdill added a sixth: the situation. Stogdill conceptualized leadership as a relationship that exists between persons in a social situation, rather than a singular quality of an individual who serves as a leader. He concluded, "A person does not become a leader by virtue of the possession of some combination of traits, but the pattern of personal characteristics of the leader must bear some relevant relationship to the characteristics, activities, and goals of the followers."[2] With this observation, inquiry into leadership shifted to an environmental analysis.

Stogdill's observation was important to an understanding of what constitutes leadership because it provided a much broader definition of a leader. A leader is a person who, due to a situation, emerges to help a group attain specific goals. Other things being equal, any member of a group who has special abilities can become a leader given the correct situation. On the other hand, when a leader ceases to have the important function of facilitating the attainment of group goals, he or she may cease to function as the leader.

Further research on leadership turned up another important factor in the formula of leadership: the follower. Studies showed that the follower is crucial in determining leadership because it is this person who perceives the leader and the situation and reacts according to what he or she perceives. With the acknowledgment of the importance of the leader's characteristics, the situation in which those characteristics are displayed, and the perceptions of the followers, research on leadership emerged into the exchange stage.

Exchange theory, or transactional analysis, focuses on how leaders initially motivate groups to accept their influence, the processes that underlie the prolonged exertion of that influence, and the ways in which leaders make contributions to the attainment of group goals; in short, how leaders work within groups to establish and maintain influence.

In this chapter, the role of the curriculum leader is explored with emphasis on working with groups to achieve effective decision making. Such an exploration includes inquiry into roles and tasks, organizations, groups, communication patterns, perception, motivation, and a host of other interpersonal variables that contribute to successful leadership performance.

ROLES AND TASKS

Leadership in curriculum development is not a function of title or appointed position. Titles may legitimize formal authority, but they do not insure leadership capacity. Leadership is a function of four complex variables: the character of the leader, the character of the followers, the character of the organization, and the character of the environment.

Leadership in educational organizations is a situational phenomenon. It is determined by the collective perceptions of individuals, is related to group norms, and is influenced by the frequency of interaction among members of the organization. Before leadership can be effective in an open organization such as a school, it must be acknowledged as a group activity.

To some extent, leadership is a product of the leader's vision. The way in which the leader conceives of the group's tasks, and the policies and practices to successfully achieve those ends, defines leadership. In the words of management specialist Douglas McGregor, "The theoretical assumptions management holds about controlling human resources determines the whole character of the enterprise."[3]

The way in which the leader sees the organization and its needs, when formalized, sets the foundation for a theory of leadership. Without such a theory, leadership behaviors will be little more than a series of activities and projects that have little relationship to one another. Most often, conceptions of leadership are developed in terms of what the leader is to be and do, in terms of roles and tasks.

Leadership roles in curriculum development activities are multiple due to the numerous environments in which the curriculum specialist operates and due to the supportive role of most curriculum positions. A monolithic perception of what a curriculum worker is to do is not applicable in most school environments.

Havelock and associates have identified nineteen roles which may be applicable to the work of curriculum development:

Expert—sometimes the consultant is the source of knowledge or skill in an area.

Instructor—the consultant may take the role of instructing about an area of knowledge.

Trainer—a trainer goes beyond instruction in that he helps people master "do it" behavioral skills in performing actions.

Retriever—the retriever brings what is needed to the client system.

Referrer—the referrer sends the client system to a source where it can find what it needs.

Linker—the linker provides a bridge to parties, or parts of a system, that need to be in contact.

Demonstrator—the demonstrator shows the client system how something is done, but does not necessarily show him how to do it for himself.

Modeler—the modeler provides an example of how to do, or be, something by evidencing it is his (the consultant's) own behavior.

Advocate—there are times when a consultant can best facilitate an intention by taking the role of advocate for a goal, value, or strategy.

Confronter—when the client system needs to be confronted with awareness of a discrepancy.

Counselor—the role of the counselor generally includes listening, acting as a sounding board, and raising awareness of alternatives. It is a nondirective effort in helping the client think through issues.

Advisor—the advisor role differs from the counselor in being more directive about what the client might do and how to do it.

Observer—the observer comments on the things that exist and how things are being done.

Data Collector—the data collector gathers information about what exists and how things are being done.

Analyzer—the analyzer interprets the meaning of data found in the system.

Diagnoser—the diagnoser uses analyses, data, and observations in determining why things happen the way they do in the system.

Designer—the designer develops action strategies, training programs, and management models for use by the system.

Manager—the manager takes charge of the development process by ordering events to achieve accountability.

Evaluator—the evaluator serves to feed back information that will make the system more effective in its task.[4]

These roles, and others, are all legitimate leadership actions given the correct conditions and needs of followers.

Leadership Tasks

The tasks of curriculum leadership, like roles, are numerous.[5] The exact tasks required to be a leader vary from organization to organization and work situation to work situation. However, some generic tasks are found in most curriculum leadership opportunities.

Developing an Operating Theory

Leaders must be able to conceptualize tasks and communicate the approach to those tasks to others in the organization. The pattern of task identification and response forms the basis of an operating theory.

Developing Organization and a Work Environment

Curriculum tasks are often nonpermanent responses to needs. In such cases, the way in which people, resources, and ideas are organized is left to the leader. An important task is to structure an organization and work environment that can respond to those needs.

Setting Standards

Because curriculum problems often involve diverse groups of individuals with different needs and perceptions, an important task for a curriculum leader is to set standards and other expectations that will affect the resolution of problems. Such standards may include work habits, communication procedures, time limitations, or a host of related planning areas.

Using Authority to Establish an Organizational Climate

Persons assigned to leadership positions generally are able to structure organizations by suggesting changes and initiating policies. One of the most important tasks for a curriculum leader is using such authority to establish a desirable work climate. Such a climate, discussed later in this chapter, is made up of the collective perceptions of persons affected by the structure of the organization.

Establishing Effective Interpersonal Relations

Since leadership is a product of human exchanges or transactions within organizations, it is essential that interpersonal relationships contribute to the attainment of desired ends. The way in which a curriculum leader interacts with others in the organization can assist in the establishment of a pattern of effective interpersonal relationships.

Planning and Initiating Action

The curriculum leader is sometimes the only person with the authority to plan and initiate actions. Deciding when and how to initiate action is a strong leadership activity. Failure to lead planning or initiate action can undermine other leadership functions.

Keeping Communication Channels Open and Functioning

Many times the curriculum leader is in a unique position of being able to communicate with others in an organization when lateral and horizontal communication is limited for most members. The leader can use his or her position to facilitate the matching of persons who need to communicate with one another. The leader can also make changes in communication patterns, where necessary, to insure that such communication channels are functioning.

Personal Tasks

In addition to these organizational tasks, the leader must also master some personal tasks. Chief among these are being able to integrate many diverse roles, being sensitive to other persons' needs and concerns, and being able to integrate the emotional and intellectual dimensions of work-related tasks.

In terms of roles and tasks, then, leadership is a complex pattern of activities and behaviors. Leadership is diffused throughout any group or organization, and many individuals can exert leadership depending on which roles and tasks correspond to group needs at a particular time. To fully understand leadership in this contextual manner, we must look into the human system which is found in any organization.

ORGANIZATIONS

Organizations are, first of all, people. All organizations contain a human system which initiates and determines all activities of the organization. Leaders coordinate such activities, and as long as the organization serves individual and group needs, such leadership will be supported. In the words of Rensis Likert:

> The leadership and other processes of the organization must be such as to ensure a maximum probability that in all interactions and all relationships within the organization, each member, in the light of his background, values, desires, and expectations, will view the experience as supportive and one which builds and maintains his sense of personal worth and importance.[6]

A desired condition in any organization is a high degree of predictability, a coordination of effort, and productivity in terms of desired ends. Such a condition exists in organizations where structures are clear and roles are highly elaborated. In organizations where structures are not always permanent and where roles are largely situational, predictability, coordination, and productivity are achieved by the influence of leadership. Such influence is a transactional process whereby the leader seeks to structure the work group and environment in such a way as to satisfy members of the organization. To the degree that members feel they are being served by the organization, they contribute to the organization and accept the influence of the leader. If members do not feel they are being served by the organization, their behaviors become less predictable, efforts become less coordinated, and productivity declines. In extreme cases, a search for new leadership begins.

GROUPS

An executive decision is only a moment in the total process of the solution to a problem. In order to be effective, leaders must involve and service identifiable groups within an organization. As long as a leader is successful in working for them, individuals and groups will subordinate themselves to both organizational requirements and leadership style. Leadership and followership are reciprocal relationships.

Groups are established for mutual benefit. In the words of Sherif and Sherif, "Groups provide their members with social support and give them feelings of personal worth."[7] As an entity, groups are collections of individuals who join together because of common goals, values, and norms. It is important for leaders to recognize that leadership can only be provided if the leader shares common values with group members.

Another important thing that has been learned about groups through organized research is that groups have greater influence on value formation than other sources of communication.* Leaders who acknowledge groups and seek to influence them through purposeful behavior will be more likely to succeed in organizational matters.

In curriculum planning and development, group work is a common medium for identifying values and constructing plans for programs. The following principles seem to govern group productiveness:

> To become productive as a group, the individuals in question must first become a group in a psychological sense through acquiring the feeling of group belongingness which can come only from a central purpose which they all accept.
>
> If a group is to be productive, its members must have a common definition of the undertaking in which they are to engage.
>
> If a group is to be productive, it must have a task of some real consequence to perform.
>
> If a group is to be productive, its members must feel that something will actually come of what they are expected to do; said differently, its members must not feel that what they are asked to do is simply busywork.
>
> If a group is to be productive, the dissatisfaction of its members with the aspect of the status quo to which the group's undertaking relates must outweigh in their minds whatever threats to their comfort they perceive in the performance of this undertaking.
>
> If a group is to be productive, its members must not be expected or required to attempt undertakings which are beyond their respective capabilities or which are so easy for the individuals in question to perform that they feel no sense of real accomplishment.
>
> If a group is to be productive, decisions as to work planning, assignment, and scheduling must be made, whenever possible, on a shared basis within the group, and through the method of consensus rather than of majority vote; in instances in which these decisions either have already been made by exterior authority or in which they must be made

---

* See Kurt Lewin's classic study of opinion formation during World War II, "Experiments in Social Science," *Harvard Educational Review* 9 (January, 1939), pp. 21–32.

by the group leader alone, the basis for the decisions made must be clearly explained to all members of the group.

If a group is to be productive, each member of the group must clearly understand what he is expected to do and why, accept his role, and feel himself responsible to the group for its accomplishment.

If a group is to be productive, its members must communicate in a common language.

If a group is to be productive, its members must be guided by task-pertinent values which they share in common.

If a group is to be productive, it is usually necessary for its members to be in frequent face-to-face association with one another.

If a group is to be productive, its members must have a common (though not necessarily a talked-about) agreement as to their respective statuses within the group.

If a group is to be productive, each of its members must gain a feeling of individual importance from his personal contributions in performing the work of the group.

If a group is to be productive, the distribution of credit for its accomplishments must be seen as equitable by its members.

If a group is to be productive, it must keep on the beam and not spend time on inconsequential or irrelevant matters.

If a group is to be productive, the way it goes about its work must be seen by its members as contributing to the fulfillment of their respective tissue and social-psychological needs, and, by extension, of those of their dependents (if any) as well.

If a group is to be productive, the status leader must make the actual leadership group-centered, with the leadership role passing freely from member to member.

If a group is to be productive, the task it is to perform must be consistent with the purposes of the other groups to which its members belong.

If a group is to be productive, the satisfactions its members expect to experience from accomplishing the group's task must outweigh in their minds the satisfactions they gain from their membership in the group *per se*.

In order for leaders to know the needs of individuals and groups in an organization, so that they might be attentive to them in their leadership acts, an adequate communication pattern must be established. An understanding of communication in organizations is vital to curriculum development activities since such activity is heavily dependent on human interaction.

COMMUNICATION

Communication patterns in organizations vary tremendously due to a high number of variables which affect such patterns. Curriculum leaders should be aware of such variables, and sensitive to regular causes of poor communication.

From an organizational standpoint, there are three regular causes of faulty communication. First, there is a speaking-listening breakdown. Early communications models, such as those by Ryan, identified an information system which consists of sender-message-receiver.[8] Distortions in the system, called "noise," can be caused by either faulty transmission, the environment, or faulty reception. Speaking-listening breakdowns can be either accidental or purposeful.

Another common cause of poor communication in organizations is an uncommon frame of reference between the sender and receiver. Each of us has certain experiences, knowledge, and values which we use to filter incoming communication. When the frame of reference of the sender and receiver are not alike, communication is likely to be distorted. This is especially important for the curriculum leader to remember when trying to reach groups to which he or she does not belong.

Finally, in organizations, there are a host of environmental barriers which can impede clear communication. An example of such a barrier might be the use of a formal written form of communication in an organization which values face-to-face communication. Other environmental barriers might be timing of communication, distance of communication, or the confidentiality of the communication.

Other communication barriers may be of a personal nature. While there are an almost unlimited number of interpersonal barriers to communication, several are commonly found in organizations working for curriculum improvement. Among these are conflicting belief systems, the effects of previous communication, nonverbal communication, and the method of delivery.

Often in public school curriculum development, committees will be formed to solve problems or formulate policy. These groups are made up of populations as diverse as those found throughout the United States, including individuals with differing beliefs and values. Those values may be exhibited as biases or prejudices. Under such circumstances, the leader must work to bring to the surface such values and direct communication to the task at hand.

Sometimes a pattern of previous communication will serve as a barrier to honest communication in the present. This occurs quite often when a curriculum leader is elevated from the ranks of classroom teachers and previous relationships between the new leader and former teaching mates carry over into the new role. Another version of this same barrier is the initial communication between the leader and groups which causes an impression that dominates later communication.

Very strong personal barriers to clear communications are the accompanying nonverbal signals which are transmitted by the sender and receiver. Facial expressions, gestures, and even body posture can send a message that may or may not be intended.

Finally, the method of delivery can serve as a personal barrier to communication. Some persons have a communication medium, such as the printed word, that they favor over others. The curriculum leader who wants to communicate with others must study patterns of communication to identify the favored medium. Such study will have payoff during times when clear communication is a necessity.

INDIVIDUAL PERCEPTION

The authors would be misleading if the reader were left with the impression that leadership is a residual act which occurs due to interaction among groups of persons in organizations. Although there is a natural flow in organizations regarding roles, communication, and tasks, much of what occurs is caused by what the leader does. The leader, through his or her actions, can alter the way people perceive the organization, how they act, and even the motives for such action. The leader can, in short, create an image and set activities into motion.

During the past forty years a special branch of psychology called phenomenological, or perceptual, psychology has developed with application in all areas of social interaction. Perceptual psychologists hold that all behavior is a product of the perceptual field of the behaver at the moment of action. To deal effectively with others, leaders must be sensitive to and understanding of how things seem to others. The perceptual psychologist would explain behavior in an organization in the following way:

1. All persons act from their own frames of reference.
2. Understanding individual perceptions assists in understanding individual motivation.
3. Individual motivation (behavior) can be altered by changing the perceptual field of the behaver.
4. Perception is the product of vision and experience.

If leaders understand that people behave, at all times, in ways which seem logical to them, a significant portion of behavior that is maladaptive to organizations can be explained and reacted to. In addition, leaders can do a great deal to alter behavior by structuring the kinds of experiences and information that others in the organization are exposed to. *

A determining factor in how leaders see others in the organization is the leader's beliefs about human nature. It is important that each person who holds a leadership position clarify his or her own beliefs about this subject so that leadership behaviors can be fully understood. Valuable tools for accomplishing this are Douglas McGregor's Theory X-Theory Y model and Blake and Mouton's Managerial Grid.

In 1960, McGregor published a book called *The Human Side of Enterprise.* [9] In this book McGregor attempted to examine the reasons underlying the way leaders tried to influence human activity. He perceived leadership thinking and behavior as based on two very different sets of assumptions about people. He called these assumptions Theory X and Theory Y.

THEORY X ASSUMPTIONS

1. The average human being has an inherent dislike of work and will avoid it if possible.
2. Because of this human characteristic of dislike of work, most people must be coerced, controlled, directed, threatened with punishment to get them to put forth adequate effort toward the achievement of organizational objectives.
3. The average human being prefers to be directed, wishes to avoid responsibility, has relatively little ambition, wants security above all.

THEORY Y ASSUMPTIONS

1. The expenditure of physical and mental effort in work is as natural as play or rest.
2. External control and threat of punishment are not the only means for bringing about effort toward organizational objectives. People will exercise self-control in the service of objectives to which they are committed.
3. Commitment to objectives is dependent on rewards associated with their achievement. The most important rewards are those that satisfy needs for self-respect and personal improvement.

---

* For more information about perceptual psychology see Arthur Combs and Donald Snygg, *Individual Behavior: A Perceptual Approach to Behavior* (New York: Harper and Row, 1949).

4. The average human being learns, under proper conditions, not only to accept, but to seek responsibility.
5. The capacity to exercise a relatively high degree of imagination, ingenuity, and creativity in the solution of an organizational problem is widely, not narrowly, distributed in the population.
6. Under the conditions of modern industrial life, the intellectual potentiality of average human beings is only partially utilized.

McGregor's contrasting assumptions about human nature opened the field to analysis of leadership perceptions of workers and the effect of those perceptions on leadership style and activity.

A development paralleling McGregor's formulation of Theory X and Y management was Blake and Mouton's Managerial Grid. The Managerial Grid was conceptually different from the two-factor "good guy," "bad guy" approach of McGregor, and allowed for numerous managerial attitudes. The grid also identified the concerns of each manager according to personal style.[10]

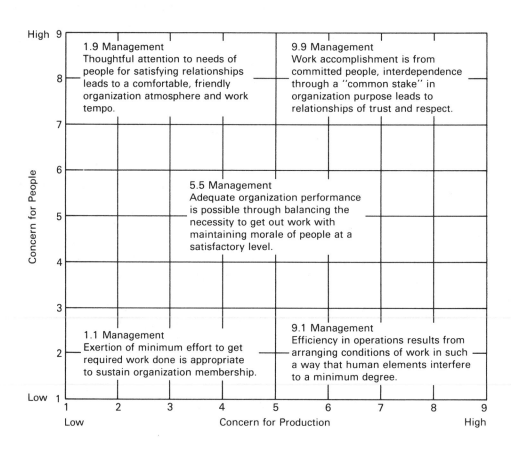

Blake and Mouton describe five primary styles that can be used to describe the grid:

1.1 *Impoverished Management*   Effective production is unobtainable because people are lazy, apathetic and indifferent. Sound and mature relationships are difficult to achieve, because human nature being what it is, conflict is inevitable.

1.9 *Country Club Management*   Production is incidental to lack of conflict and good fellowship.

5.5 *Middle of the Road Management*   Push for production but don't go "All Out," give some but not all. "Be fair but firm."

9.1 *Task Management*   Men are a commodity just as machines. A manager's responsibility is to plan, direct and control the work of those subordinate to him.

9.9 *Team management*   Production is from integration of task and human requirements into a unified system of interplay towards organizational goals.

WHAT IS YOUR STYLE?

The reader is encouraged to reflect for a moment and rank the following paragraphs from most typical (1) to least typical (5):

_____ 1. I accept decisions of others. I go along with opinions, attitudes, and ideas of others to avoid taking sides. When conflict arises, I try to remain neutral or stay out of it. By remaining neutral, I rarely get stirred up. My humor is seen by others as rather pointless.

_____ 2. I place high value on maintaining good relations. I prefer to accept opinions, attitudes, and ideas of others rather than to push my own. I try to avoid generating conflict, but when it does appear, I try to soothe feelings and keep people together. Because of the disturbance a temper flare produces, I strive to keep my emotions under cap. My humor aims at maintaining friendly relations or when strains do arise, it shifts attention away from the serious side.

_____ 3. I place high value on making decisions that stick. I stand up for my ideas, opinions, and attitudes, even though it sometimes results in stepping on toes. When conflict arises I try to cut it off or to win my position. When things are not going right, my temper wells up. My humor is hard hitting.

_____ 4. I search for workable, even though not perfect, decisions. When ideas, opinions, and attitudes different from my own appear, I initiate middle ground positions. When conflict arises I try to be fair but firm and to get an equitable solution. I rarely lose my temper but I tend to be impatient when things are not moving. My humor sells myself or my position.

_____ 5. I place high value on getting sound creative decisions that result in understanding and agreement. I listen for and seek out ideas, opinions, and attitudes different from my own. I have clear convictions but respond to sound ideas by changing my mind. When conflict arises I try to identify reasons for it and to resolve the underlying causes. I rarely lose my temper, even when stirred up. My humor fits the situations and gives perspectives; I retain a sense of humor even under pressure.

Leaders who can understand the behavior of others in an organization, and analyze their own behavior in terms of basic assumptions about human behavior, possess the power to assert influence over the transactional process. Such influence can be most effectively applied in the area of motivation.

MOTIVATION

Research indicates that the success of any form of social influence depends upon altering the ability of others to achieve their goals or satisfy their needs. Leaders in the curriculum development process can have increased success if they keep such research in mind.

In order to exert influence on the process of program development, the leader must have an understanding of the factors that motivate individuals. The work of two social scientists, Abraham Maslow and Frederick Herzberg, provides insight on motivation and points the way to entry into the transactional process.

Maslow theorized that experienced needs are the primary influences on an individual's behavior. When a particular need emerges, it determines the individual's behavior in terms of motivations, priorities, and actions taken.

Maslow placed all human needs into five need systems. He believed that there is a natural process whereby individuals fulfill needs in an ascending order from primitive to sophisticated, and he therefore developed a hierarchical model thought common to all persons. According to this model, people ascend upward toward more complex needs only after successfully fulfilling lower order needs. The needs are, in order of importance, survival, safety, belonging, status, and self actualization.

The value of the Maslow model for understanding individual motivation in an organization is that it sensitizes leaders to the complexity of motives and provides a rough analytic tool for estimating the type of motivation which is appropriate for any individual.

A second major contribution to the understanding of human motivation in organizations has been provided by Frederick Herzberg. Herzberg, following on the work of Maslow and others, stressed that the factors which truly motivate workers are those "growth" experiences which give the worker a sense of personal accomplishment through the challenge of the job itself. For Herzberg, the motivation is to be found in the job itself—in the internal dynamics that the worker experiences in completing a task.

Although it is the job itself that provides satisfaction in work, Herzberg also observed that poor environmental (hygiene) factors can be the source of unhappiness and dissatisfaction in work. In the following list, the Herzberg findings give leadership some variables by which to assess an organization and individual patterns of motivation.[11]

MOTIVATION FACTORS (*Job Content*)	HYGIENE FACTORS (*Job Environment*)
SATISFIERS	DISSATISFIERS
Work Itself	Company Policy & Administration
Achievement	Supervision
Recognition	Working Conditions
Responsibility	Interpersonal Relations
Growth and Advancement	Salary

Collectively, the research on motivation and leadership provides leaders with the beginnings of a way in which they can analyze and intercede in the human dynamics of an organization. Such an injection of leadership into the workings of the organization is a transactional strategy that appears to hold promise for exerting significant influence on organizations.

LEADERSHIP AS A TRANSACTION

In its attempt to exert influence on an organization, leadership has two primary sources of power: official authority and informal influence. Official authority is granted rather than earned, and allows this status leader to lead in some areas of organization. Such areas are generally identifiable and limited in scope.

Overuse of official authority is dangerous because it leads to leader isolation. When a leader begins to feel that official authority means power over others, there is a natural tendency for him to isolate himself from the group he seeks to lead because the leader must feel he is above the group.

The other type of power available to leaders in an organization is informal influence, and such influence is always more powerful than official authority. Because informal influence is earned by activity within the organization, it is natural power. In open organizations, such as schools, informal influence is a necessity if change is to occur.

In this chapter we have seen that leadership is a dependent human condition. To be a leader, in the real sense of the word, a person must be perceived as a leader by those groups that make up an organization. The leader can have an impact on the perceptions of members of an organization by being aware of their needs and structuring the organization so that their needs are met. Specific acts may include selectively applying roles and tasks to problems, encouraging desired communication patterns, changing individual perceptions with information and experience, and tailoring rewards to the motivational levels of members. When viewed collectively, the actions of the leader to influence the organization can be seen as the establishment of an environment that controls transaction.

Research by Litwin and Stringer[12] shows that the development of a transactional climate can be a purposeful activity. In their work, Litwin and Stringer outline a climate theory that consists of the following:

1. Individuals are attracted to work climates that arouse their dominant needs.
2. Such on-the-job climates are made up of experiences and incentives.
3. These climates interact with needs to arouse motivation toward need satisfaction.
4. Climates can mediate between organizational tasks requirements and individual needs—it is the linkage.
5. Climates represent the most powerful leverage point available to managers to bring about change.

Leadership can, by its actions, affect the perceptions of individuals in the organization. The collective perceptions of leadership form a climate that influences change in the organization.

In their research, Litwin and Stringer identified nine organizational variables which can be manipulated to influence the climate of an organization:

1. **Structure**—the feelings that employees have about the constraints in the group, how many rules, regulations, procedures there are; is there an emphasis on red tape and going through channels, or is there a loose and informal atmosphere.
2. **Responsibility**—the feeling of being your own boss; not having to double-check all of your decisions; when you have a job to do, knowing that it is your job.

3. **Reward**—the feeling of being rewarded for a job well done; emphasizing positive rewards rather than punishments; the perceived fairness of the pay and promotion policies.
4. **Risk**—the sense of riskiness and challenge in the job and in the organization; is there an emphasis on taking calculated risks, or is playing it safe the best way to operate.
5. **Warmth**—the feeling of good fellowship that prevails in the work group atmosphere; the emphasis on being well-liked; the prevalence of friendly and informal social groups.
6. **Support**—the perceived helpfulness of the managers and other employees in the group; emphasis on mutual support from above and below.
7. **Standards**—the perceived importance of implicit and explicit goals and performance standards; the emphasis on doing a good job; the challenge represented in personal and group goals.
8. **Conflict**—the feeling that managers and other workers want to hear different opinions; the emphasis placed on getting problems out in the open, rather than smoothing them over or ignoring them.
9. **Identity**—the feeling that you belong to a company and you are a valuable member of a working team; the importance placed on this kind of spirit.

Variables such as these allow the leader to make input into the flow of events and influence the perceptions of individuals and groups that make up the organization. To the degree that such input and influence serves organizational members, a successful transaction will be accomplished and leadership will be strengthened.

SUMMARY

Leadership is a critical element in curriculum planning; it is the intangible driving force of planned educational change. Research suggests that leadership is a mix of leadership characteristics, the situation, and the types of transactions that occur between the leader and other members of an organization.

Studies of transaction in organizations suggest that a knowledge of organizations, groups, communication patterns, individual perception, and human motivation can aid a leader in asserting influence. Specific organizational variables can be manipulated to create a leadership climate.

Notes

1. H.L. Smith and L.M. Krueger, "A Brief Summary of Literature on Leadership," 9, no. 4 (Bloomington: Indiana University, 1933):3–80.
2. R.M. Stogdill, "Personal Factors Associated With Leadership: A Survey of the Literature," *The Journal of Psychology* 25 (1948):64.
3. Douglas McGregor, *The Human Side of Enterprise* (New York: McGraw-Hill Book Company, 1960), p. vii.
4. Ronald G. Havelock and Associates, Institute for Social Research, University of Michigan.
5. For a listing of skills and competencies used in training curriculum workers see Allen Sturges, "Competencies for the Curriculum Worker" in Association for Supervision and Curriculum Development, *Curriculum Leaders: Improving Their Influence* (Washington, D.C., 1976).
6. Rensis Likert, *New Patterns in Management* (New York: McGraw-Hill, 1961), p. 103.
7. M. Sherif and C.W. Sherif, *Reference Groups: Exploration into Conformity and Deviation of Adolescents* (New York: Harper and Row, 1964).
8. Bryce Ryan, "A Study of Technological Diffusion," *Rural Sociology* 13 (September, 1948): 273–85.
9. McGregor, *The Human Side of Enterprise,* pp. 33–57.
10. The Managerial Grid figure from *The Managerial Grid,* by Robert R. Blake and Jane Srygley Mouton, Houston, Gulf Publishing Company, Copyright 1964, page 10. Reproduced by permission.
11. Frederick Herzberg, *Work and the Nature of Man* (Cleveland: World Publishing Company, 1966).
12. George H. Litwin and Robert A. Stringer, Jr., *Motivation and Organizational Climate* (Boston: Division of Research, Harvard University, 1968), pp. 81–82.

Suggested Learning Activities

1. Develop an operational definition of leadership in curriculum development efforts.

2. Outline specific behaviors identified by the authors that would allow curriculum leaders to be more effective in transactions.

3. Using Litwin and Stringer's categories, outline a plan for affecting the climate of a school involved in curriculum development.

Books to Review

Combs, Arthur and Snygg, Donald. *Individual Behavior: A Perceptual Approach to Behavior.* New York: Harper and Row Publishers, 1949.

Havelock, Ronald. *Planning for Innovation Through Dissemination and Utilization of Knowledge.* Institute for Social Research, University of Michigan, 1971.

Homans, George. *The Human Group.* New York: Harcourt, Brace & Co., 1950.

Jacobs, T.O. *Leadership and Exchange in Formal Organizations.* U.S. Office of Naval Research, HumRRO, 1970.

Katz, Daniel and Kahn, Robert. *The Social Psychology of Organizations.* New York: John Wiley & Sons, Inc., 1966.

Litwin, George and Stringer, Robert. *Motivation and Organizational Climate.* Harvard University: Division of Research, Graduate School of Business Administration, 1968.

Speiker, Charles A. *Curriculum Leaders: Improving Their Influence.* Washington, D.C.: Association for Supervision and Curriculum Development, 1976.

7

The Change Process
in Curriculum Development

Curriculum improvement is almost always a case of curriculum change. For this reason, persons preparing for positions of leadership in curriculum should have a clear understanding of the change process in educational environments. There are a number of pressing questions in the area of change that need to be addressed. Among these are:

1. What causes a school to change?
2. Why do innovations nearly always fail in some schools?
3. Why do some schools never attempt to make changes?
4. What factors are significant in making a school either a high risk or a low risk for an innovation attempt?
5. What is the profile of an innovative school?

The answers to such questions as these will not come easily because change in school environments is a highly complex process with an interplay of many multifaceted variables.* Still, a review of

---

* For a complete set of generalizations about the diffusion of innovations see Appendix A of Everett M. Rogers and F. Floyd Shoemaker, *Communication of Innovations: A Cross-Cultural Approach* (New York: Free Press, 1971).

existing literature on change as it interacts with educational environments can greatly increase understanding and make curriculum leaders more effective in their jobs.

RESEARCH ON CHANGE IN SCHOOL ENVIRONMENTS

The study of change in schools, while not new, is being pursued vigor-
ously by researchers. Rogers and Shoemaker observed in 1971: "There
are about three times as many publications on the subject as there
were eight years ago, which means more diffusion research has been
done in the past few years than in the previous thirty years."[1]

Part of the difficulty in studying what is known about change in
schools, then, is the result of the sheer volume of data that is currently being gathered. To clarify the related literature for the reader,
it is useful to separate such data into categories. The following arbi-
trary categories have been devised: types of change, models of
change, strategies of change, barriers to change, and variables affecting change.*

Types of Change

Change is not synonymous with innovation. According to Miles,
change is "any alteration in someone or something."[2] An innovation, by contrast, has unique qualities such as novelty or deliberate-
ness. It is the specific application of change that distinguishes an
innovation from random change. Such a distinction is underscored
by the two types of change identified by Goodson: planned change
and evolutionary change.[3]

Numerous types of change in organizations have been identified.
Bennis, in *Changing Organizations,*[4] identified eight types of change:
planned change, indoctrination, coercive change, technocratic change,
interactional change, socialization change, emulative change, and natural change. Another classification is offered by Guba,[5] who identifies
three types of change: evolutionary (natural change), homeostatic (reactive change), and neomobilistic (planned change).

Models of Change

In addition to types of change, the literature on change contains numerous models that consider the process from a variety of perspec-

---

* The authors wish to thank former research colleague Tim Murphy, Jr. for
his contributions to this section.

tives. Among some of the most interesting to educational planners are those institutional models that reveal how other areas of society approach the concept of planned change. Here are four stereotypic models of other institutions:

Agriculture—uses a *change agent* approach by having county agents go into the field to demonstrate new techniques of farming.

Medical—uses *action research* in approaching change. The diffusion of medical change proceeds from clinical research to development to dissemination.

Business—uses the *incentive approach* of rewards to encourage change. In organizations, sometimes this approach is used to pull persons toward change.

Military—uses *authority* to enforce change. This is a pushing strategy.

Other visible models of change are those dealing with social change in organizations. Bennis proposes three general classes of models:[6]

Equilibrium—aims at tension and conflict resolution.
Organic—emphasizes internal problem solving.
Developmental—aims at interpersonal competence.

The Process Approach

The emphasis in change models that appears to have captured the greatest concern and attention in education has been the process approach. The tremendous advances that the application of systems concepts have produced in science and technology are now being employed in education with promising results.

Kurt Lewin is generally acknowledged to be the intellectual forebearer of process models in change. His three-step change model has become a classic.[7] The process basically involves (1) unfreezing an old pattern, (2) changing to a new one, and (3) refreezing the new pattern. Lewin's model is based on the notion of the opposing forces that create varying amounts of pressure on situations. When forces are equal, the situation does not change. However, by the addition or subtraction of forces the pressure becomes unequal and change occurs.

Another popular model is one that conceptualizes the change process in terms of five stages leading to adoption:[8]

1. awareness
2. interest
3. evaluation
4. trial
5. adoption

Gross, emphasizing the stages of time relative to change, has also proposed a five-step model: antecedent, initiation, implementation, incorporation, and effects.[9]

Another approach to the change process has been offered by Lippitt, Watson, and Wesley in their pioneer work, *The Dynamics of Planned Change.*[10] They focus on the relationship between the change agent and the client system and identify seven stages:

1. the development of a need for change
2. the establishment of a change relationship
3. the diagnosis of the client system's problem
4. the examination of goals and alternative routes of action
5. the transformation of intentions into action
6. the generalization and stabilization of change
7. the achievement of a terminal relationship

Strategies of Change

Another area of research on change in organizations is that of strategy. Chin offers three general headings of change strategies: (1) rational-empirical, (2) normative-reeducative, and (3) power-coercive.[11] The first is based on the assumption that people are rational and that they will follow their rational self-interests once they are revealed to them. The second is founded on different assumptions about human motivation. The rationality of people is not denied; however, behavior is recognized as a socio-cultural phenomenon reinforced by values and attitudes of individuals in the system. The third group of strategies is based on the application of power in some form, political or otherwise.

Guba has developed a typology of strategy on the basis of assumptions made about the adapter of change.[12] These are: (1) value strategy, (2) rational strategy, (3) didactic strategy, (4) psychological strategy, (5) economic strategy, (6) political strategy, and (7) authoritative strategy.

Often mentioned along with strategies in the literature are techniques used for changing. Bennis identifies the following eight traditional techniques of change:[13]

1. exposition and propagation
2. elite corps
3. human relations training
4. scholarly consultation
5. circulation of ideas to the elite
6. staff
7. developmental research
8. action research

Barriers to Change

The barriers to change that are set forth in the literature are innumerable. Many authors telescoping particular segments of the process have identified countless barriers that impede change. Further, such barriers are described with varying amounts of specificity. Most common in the literature are lists of the potential barriers that affect educational change.

Four such lists give an overview of the barriers. Here are eight barriers as compiled by McClelland:

1. Despite rapid social change, forces favoring the status quo in education remain strong as ever.
2. There are no precise goals for educational institutions.
3. There is no established systematic approach in the educational process.
4. Teacher education programs have failed to develop the skills and knowledge needed for innovations.
5. Teachers have failed to develop in themselves the habits of scholarship necessary to stay abreast of the knowledge explosion.
6. Evaluation and revision based on feedback are absent in educational institutions.
7. Many educators are reticent, suspicious, and fearful of change.
8. Complex management and funding problems always cost more than simple divisible problems.[14]

Rogers depicts the barriers in this manner:

1. There is no profit motive for being an innovator in education.
2. There is no corps of change agents in education comparable to extension agents in agriculture.
3. Educational innovations are less clear cut in their advantage over the existing ideas they are to replace.
4. Innovation decisions in education may not be an individual matter and the norms, statuses, and formal structure of the systems affect the process of diffusion.[15]

Guba and Horvat, analyzing the characteristics of educational research, portray these major barriers:

1. Lack of viable alternative solutions to existing educational problems.
2. Lack of understanding of the educational change process.
3. Lack of personnel competent to study the change process, to exercise leadership in designing and mounting change programs, or to implement those programs into action.
4. Lack of tools and strategies through which educational improvements may be offered.[16]

Finally, a study by the Kentucky State Department of Education presented to the Committee on Innovations and Barriers to Educational Change of the Southern States Work Conference offered additional examples of barriers that inhibit the change process:[17]

1. finance
2. restrictive regulations
3. professional personnel
4. leadership
5. school organization
6. college preparatory programs
7. support services
8. school-community relations
9. U.S. Office of Education
10. requirements of external agencies
11. community attitudes
12. research
13. local boards of education
14. lack of comprehensive planning

Even though there are many barriers to change in schools, such resistance may have a functional effect. Klein, for instance, notes that resistance

1. protects the organization against random change, which may be harmful;
2. protects the system from take-over by vested interests; and,
3. may insure that unanticipated consequences of a change be spelled out and thus possibly avoided.[18]

Other Variables

The literature on change in educational environments indicates that there are numerous variables that affect planned change. Human nature is the most influential of those variables. The level at which change is taking place and those who are affected will determine which variables will be involved and how they will be weighted.

Administrative personnel, such as the superintendent, central office staff, and school principals, have tremendous influence on what change occurs and how it occurs. Teachers, students, and parents also influence change. In addition, there are a host of other personalities that interact with the open system of the school.

THE PROMOTION OF PLANNED CHANGE

While the literature on change in educational environments can outline some of the models, strategies, and barriers likely to be encountered, it is not yet sophisticated enough to serve as an absolute guide to practice. It is up to the individual curriculum leader to discover a means of reaching the desired goals.

One of the first realities that must be acknowledged by a curriculum leader is that change is often a political process. It is this political activity that activates the variables in an educational community. If there were no planning and maneuvering within school districts, there would be no change. According to Iannaccone and Lutz, " . . . politics is recognized as probably the single most important question in determining the course, present and future, of American education."[19]

Rather than being perceived as evil or undemocratic, the use of political influence can be seen as a means of altering the rate of change in school settings. Educators who seek the support of those interest groups that coincide in social intent with the school can legitimately do so in the name of better programs of education for children. Intellectual choices in planning are, inevitably, social choices with political implications.

Carlson found that in some communities schools are essentially tame, domesticated organizations controlled by local forces.[20] Under such circumstances, improved school programs cannot occur without an agent of change. As curriculum leaders acknowledge political reality they will be more effective in promoting planned changes.

The second important idea related to change in schools is that resistance to change is not unnatural. Individuals strive to bring order to their world and most change involves the realignment of roles and relationships. In the words of Warren Bennis: "Change will be resisted to the degree that the target has little information or knowledge of the change, has little trust in the source of change, and has little influence in controlling the nature and direction of the change."[21]

The third idea about change in school environments, which is supported by case studies, is that change is not an isolated event. Change in any complex organization involves interrelated events.

An awareness of the political dimensions of change, the natural tendency of individuals to resist change, and the awareness of change as a continuing process suggest that desired change is not a haphazard process but one which is the result of a concerted effort to influence the educational environment. Such influence is most effective when the curriculum leader possesses the concept of the change environment and an organizational structure.

While directing a project concerning the analysis of planned change in Florida schools, one of the authors attempted to develop such a concept in terms of the potential of innovation targets. The result of this effort was a probability chart, shown in Table 7.1, that roughly indicates the degree of readiness for innovation within a school. This construct has proven useful as a way of looking at change in schools.

Curriculum leaders need a structure for promoting planned alterations of the school environment. As Miles has observed: "This review

Table 7.1
Educational Innovations Probability Chart

	Higher Risk				Lower Risk
Source of Innovation	Superimposed from outside	Outside agent brought in	Developed internally with aid	External idea modified	Locally conceived, developed, implemented
Impact of Innovation	Challenges sacrosanct beliefs	Calls for major value shifts	Requires substantial change	Modifies existing values or programs	Does not substantially alter existing values, beliefs or programs
Official Support	Official leaders active opposition	Officials on record as opposing	Officials uncommitted	Officials voice support of change	Enthusiastically supported by the official leaders
Planning of Innovation	Completely external	Most planning external	Planning processes balanced	Most of planning done locally	All planning for change done on local site
Means of Adoption	By superiors	By local leaders	By Reps	By most of the clients	By group consensus
History of Change	History of failures	No accurate records	Some success with innovation	A history of successful innovations	Known as school where things regularly succeed
Possibility of Revision	No turning back	Final evaluation before committee	Periodic evaluations	Possible to abandon at conclusion	Possible to abort the effort at any time

Table 7.1—*continued*

	Higher Risk →			Lower Risk →	
Role of Teachers	Largely bypassed	Minor role	Regular role in implementing	Heavy role in implementation	Primary actor in the classroom effort
Teacher Expectation	Fatalistic	Feel little chance	Willing to give a try	Confident of success	Wildly enthusiastic about chance of success
Work Load Measure	Substantially increased	Heavier but rewarding	Slightly increased	Unchanged	Work load lessened by the innovation
Threat Measure	Definitely threatens some clients	Probably threatening to some	Mild threat resulting from the change	Very remote threat to some	Does not threaten the security or autonomy
Community Factor	Hostile to innovations	Suspicious and uninformed	Indifferent	Ready for a change	Wholeheartedly supports the school

Shade the response in each category which most accurately reflects the condition surrounding the implementation of the middle school. If the "profile" of your school is predominately in the high risk side of the matrix, substantial work must be done to prepare your school for change.

Source: Adapted from Jon Wiles, *Planning Guidelines for Middle School Education* (Dubuque, Iowa: Kendall/Hunt Publishing Co., 1976), p. 30. Used with permission.

of innovative processes shows clearly that innovative attitudes are not enough. Structures which permit design, adaptation, evaluation, trial, and routinization of innovations are essential. Without them, innovative motivation simply leads to 'dithering' quasi-random perturbations of practice."[22]

The long-term goal of any immediate change effort is to construct an institution that becomes capable of updating the renewing of itself as the environment changes. What is called for is the complex interweaving of continuity and change. Such a task is the central theme of John Gardner's book, *Self-Renewal:* "Over the centuries the classic question of social reform has been, 'how can we cure this or that specific ill?' Now we must ask another kind of question. How can we design a system that will continuously reform (renew) itself, beginning with presently specifiable ills and moving on to ills that we cannot now foresee?"[23]

SUMMARY

Because curriculum improvement is almost always a case of curriculum change, persons in positions of leadership in curriculum should have a clear understanding of the change process.

The literature on change is complex and it is expanding at an incredible rate. Such literature tells us that change can be viewed in many ways, and provides models and strategies that are useful in overcoming common barriers to change. The application of such models and strategies would necessarily be a situational phenomenon.

Leaders who wish to actively promote planned change should be aware of the political dimensions of change, understand that resistance to change is normal, and perceive change as a chain of interrelated events rather than an isolated event. Such understandings and perceptions suggest a need for a conceptual framework for viewing change in schools and a plan for structuring change efforts.

A long-term goal is to develop an institution that embraces change as a means to self-renewal.

Notes

1. Everett M. Rogers and F. Floyd Shoemaker, *Communication of Innovations: A Cross-Cultural Approach* (New York: Free Press, 1971), p. xvii.

2. Matthew B. Miles, "Educational Innovation: The Nature of the Problem," *Innovations in Education* (New York: Teachers College Press, 1964).
3. M.R. Goodson, "Models for Effecting Planned Educational Change " (Madison, Wisconsin: Research and Development Center for Training and Re-Education, 1966), ED 010214.
4. Warren G. Bennis, *Changing Organizations* (New York: McGraw Hill Book Company, 1966).
5. Egon Guba, "The Role of Educational Research in Educational Change" (Bloomington, Indiana: National Institute for the Study of Educational Change, 1967), ED 012505.
6. Warren G. Bennis, "A New Role for the Behavioral Sciences: Effecting Organizational Change," *Administrative Science Quarterly* 8 (September, 1963).
7. Kurt Lewin, *Field Theory in Social Science* (New York: Harper-Torch Books, 1951).
8. H. Lionberger, *Adoption of New Ideas and Practices* (Ames, Iowa: State University Press, 1961) and E.M. Rogers, *Diffusion of Innovations* (New York: Free Press, 1962).
9. N. Gross, *An Attempt to Implement a Major Educational Innovation* (Cambridge, Massachusetts: Center for Research and Development on Human Differences, 1968).
10. R. Lippitt, J. Watson, B. Westley, *The Dynamics of Planned Change* (New York: Harcourt, Brace and World, 1958).
11. W. Bennis, K. Benne, R. Chin, *The Planning of Change* (New York: Holt, Rinehart, and Winston, 1969), pp. 34–35.
12. Egon Guba, "Development, Diffusion, Evaluation," paper presented for University Council for Educational Administration, Portland, Oregon, 1967, ED 015534.
13. Bennis, *The Planning of Change,* pp. 67–68.
14. W.A. McClelland, "The Process of Effecting Change" (Washington, D.C.: George Washington University Human Resources Office, 1968).
15. E.M. Rogers, *Innovations: Research Design and Field Studies* (Columbus, Ohio: Research Foundation, Ohio State University, 1965), ED 003120.
16. E. Guba and J. Horvat, "Concluding Note: The Role of Educational Research in Educational Change" (Bloomington, Indiana: National Institute for the Study of Educational Change, 1967), ED 012505.
17. R.L. Winebarger, *The Development of Tentative Strategies for Program Experimentation in Kentucky,* Kentucky State Department of Education, Southern States Work Conference Committee on Innovation, 1972.
18. D. Klein, "Some Notes on the Dynamics of Resistance to Change: The Defender's Role," in G. Watson, ed., *Concepts for Social Change,* COPED, NTL, Washington, D.C., 1967.
19. L. Iannaccone and F. Lutz, *Politics, Power, and Policy: The Governing of Local School Districts* (Columbus, Ohio: Charles E. Merrill Publishing Company, 1970), p. v.
20. R.O. Carlson, "Barriers to Change in Public Schools," in *Change Processes in the Public Schools* (Eugene, Oregon: Center for the Advanced Study of Educational Administration, 1965), pp. 3–8.
21. Bennis, Benne, and Chin, *The Planning of Change.*

22. M. Miles, *The Development of Innovative Climates in Organizations* (Menlo Park, California: Stanford Research Institute, 1969), p. 7.

23. J.W. Gardner, *Self-Renewal: The Individual and the Innovative Society* (New York: Harper and Row, 1964).

Suggested Learning Activities

1. Reviewing the various models presented in this chapter, try to identify what they have in common. In what way do these models differ?

2. Develop a list of potential means by which you might address change in a school that is dedicated to renewal.

Books to Review

Strategy for Curriculum Change. Washington, D.C.: Association for Supervision and Curriculum Development, 1965.

Bennis, W., Benne, K., and Chin, R. *The Planning of Change.* New York: Holt, Rinehart, and Winston, 1969.

Carlson, R. et al. *Change Processes in the Public Schools.* Eugene, Oregon: Center for the Advanced Study of Educational Administration, 1965.

Havelock, Ronald. *Innovation in Education: Strategies and Tactics.* Ann Arbor, Michigan: Institute for Social Research, 1971.

Kirst, Michael. *The Politics of Education at the Local, State, and Federal Levels,* Berkeley, California: McCutchan Publishing, 1970.

Lippitt, R., Watson, J. and Westley, B. *The Dynamics of Planned Change.* New York: Harcourt, Brace & World, Inc., 1958.

Miles, Matthew, *Innovation in Education.* New York: Teachers College Press, Columbia University, 1964.

Roberts, Arthur. *Educational Innovation: Alternatives in Curriculum and Instruction.* Boston: Allyn and Bacon, Inc., 1975.

Rogers, Everett and Shoemaker, F. *Communication of Innovations: A Cross-Cultural Approach.* New York: The Free Press, 1971.

Sarason, Seymour. *The Culture of the School and the Problem of Change.* Boston: Allyn and Bacon, Inc., 1971.

Skeel, Dorothy and Hagan, Owen. *The Process of Curriculum Change.* Pacific Palisades, California: Goodyear Publishing Company, 1971.

Watson, Goodwin (ed). *Change in School Systems.* Cooperative Project for Educational Development, National Training Laboratories, NEA, 1967.

8

Managerial Aspects of Curriculum Development

The area of curriculum, like other major components of the educational system, is rapidly moving in the direction of specialization, institutionalism, and bureaucratic operation. In the future, the effectiveness and efficiency of curriculum development efforts in schools will depend on a number of key functions by curriculum specialists. Among these functions will be the abilities to correctly analyze situations; match personnel, functions, and resources; solve recurring problems; and create desired programs.

As curriculum enters the era of specialization, the role of curriculum workers will have a definable management dimension. As managers, curriculum workers will be mediating between human and material resources. Curriculum workers will, in the words of Sayles,[1] manage the work flow.

THE MANAGEMENT FUNCTION

Historically, curriculum specialists in school systems have held an advisory relationship to the administrative structure. Although curriculum personnel could conduct studies and make suggestions, the activation of programs was left to leaders with formal administrative power. Such a staff relationship has proven to be ineffective in bringing about desired changes in instructional programs due to:

1. the overbearing workload of line administrators,
2. the absence of understanding on the part of line administrators concerning the role of curriculum development, and
3. the emphasis on programs in schools as the "proof" of an accountable system.

In recent years, the role of curriculum specialists has become more active, with the implementation of programs becoming as important as the conceptualization and design of programs. The role of curriculum specialists has become managerial in nature, concerned more with the organization and development of programs than with maintenance of them.

The management of program development implies that the curriculum workers understand the organizations in which they work and possess the skills to promote desired changes. The overall task of the manager becomes one of establishing a predictable process of leadership that enables the organization to meet changing needs.

Over the past twenty years, schools have become more bureaucratic, due primarily to the consolidation of school districts and the growth of unions. Max Weber's classic characteristics of a bureaucratic organization indicate the types of structural changes that have evolved during this period in many districts:

1. fixed jurisdictional areas ordered by rules and regulations
2. principles of hierarchy and levels of graded authority
3. administration based on written documents
4. administration by full-time trained officials
5. administration planned according to comprehensive general policies.[2]

Such changes in schools have led to a division of labor, technical specialization, an emphasis on written communication, high organizational discipline, and specific procedures for work situations. The net effect of the consolidation of educational organization and the drift to bureaucratization has been to diminish the traditional interpersonal role of the curriculum worker.

On the other hand, the growth of unionization in school settings has forced curriculum specialists to adopt new patterns of coordination that bear little resemblance to the customary pattern of human relations. New interpersonal tools that have been developed include advanced consultation, negotiation, exchange of favors, and collusion.

Traditional bureaucratic techniques of management have limitations in school settings. In Sarason's words: "This complexity is more than one person can grasp and experience, especially if one's goal is to do more than deal with organizational charts, job descriptions, and written accounts of what school personnel say they do."[3]

The distinct characteristics of the school, with human variables that often supercede institutional variables, call for a blend of technological and humanitarian management. The curriculum leader must have at his or her command a repertoire of behaviors that can be applied to a wide range of needs.

The requirement for successful curriculum management becomes one of displaying a predictable leadership pattern while maintaining the flexibility to be adaptable to the school organization. To maintain this pattern, the curriculum leader must have a clear perception of the management structure, the management process and the interpersonal skills to deliver finished school programs.

Katz, in an early observation of the role of management, identified three basic skills needed for effective leadership:

1. technical proficiency in specific activities relating to method, process, and procedure
2. human proficiency needed to work effectively as a group member
3. conceptual proficiency to see the enterprise as a whole.[4]

In this chapter, technical and conceptual proficiency will be addressed fully. Interpersonal skills will be discussed in chapter 9.

TECHNIQUES OF MANAGEMENT

Curriculum specialists employ a variety of techniques that allow them to bring order to the work flow in curriculum development. Such techniques are necessary if the day-to-day activities of the curriculum worker are not to become a form of crisis management in meeting budget deadlines, required reports, and other organizational requirements.

Management consultant Peter Drucker has suggested that the first technique to be mastered by anyone serving in a managerial role is the control of time. Without such control, managers find their efforts dissipated and time to be the scarce commodity in their work role. By logging events and analyzing those activities in terms of their productivity, time-wasting activities can be identified and eliminated.

According to Drucker, effective managers concentrate their efforts: "If there is one secret to effectiveness it is concentration. Effective executives do first things first and they do one thing at a time."[5]

Drucker suggests that effective managers know where their time goes, and gear their efforts to results rather than work. They should build on strengths rather than focusing on weaknesses, and concentrate on a few areas where superior performance will produce results.

Beyond the management of time, the curriculum leader must have a method of bringing order to the events relating to idea development, goal setting, decision making, delegation of authority, supervision of activity, and evaluation. Such a method must be clear to others in the organization and yet allow for flexibility. Borrowing from research in the field of management, curriculum leaders can employ goal-setting criteria, management-by-objectives techniques, and progress charts to monitor progress and order events.

Focusing on goals for improvement has been proven to be effective for bringing order to events in an organization. Because organizational goals can be translated into individual goals (see chapter 6), all members of an organization can relate their function to such a broad focus. Making such goals explicit and formal, rather than implicit and assumed, facilitates group coordination and group productivity.

When goals are stated explicitly in an organization such as a school, at least three benefits occur immediately. First, the management of personal, social, and intellectual development becomes easier to direct. Second, such goals assist members of an organization in feeling a sense of momentum and accomplishment since all activities are related to a fixed pattern of achievement. Third, and perhaps most important, a process begins whereby organizational resources are used more effectively in relation to an end product.

The following five criteria can be applied to any set of goals and help the curriculum leader assure their usefulness to the organization.

1. Are the goals realistic? If goals are attainable they possess a quality that allows members of the organization to relate to them in daily work.
2. Are the goals specific? Specific goals imply behaviors that need to be changed.
3. Are the goals related to performance? Goals that are developed in an organizational context suggest patterns of interaction.
4. Are the goals suggestive of involvement? To be effective, goals must be stated in such a way as to allow individuals in the organization to see themselves as being able to achieve the objective.
5. Are the goals observable? Can people in the organization see the results of their efforts and monitor progress toward the desired condition?

Not only does goal clarification allow members of the organization to understand their role in terms of the total operation, it can also aid in activity toward those ends. A technique, known as management-by-objectives, or MBO, has been developed to help leaders assist workers in addressing organizational goals in their daily activities. The management-by-objectives approach is perfectly suited to professional and open organizations like schools.

Management is the art of getting things done by the effective use of people. The corresponding term in education is *supervision.* As a manager or supervisor, the task in most cases is to convert resources, both human and material, into desired results. Using the management-by-objectives method, the leader deemphasizes the methods of accomplishing objectives and focuses heavily on clarifying the goals and attaining the desired results.

The MBO concept rests on the assumptions that:

1. the system to be managed is rational,
2. the goals of the organization can be identified and described through clear communication, and
3. the final product will be contributed to by those who will conduct the activities.

There are a number of principles that must be adhered to if the management-by-objectives approach is to succeed. First, the leader must work with organization members to establish overall organizational objectives that are clear. Second, members of the organization should discuss their function in terms of the relation to these overall objectives. Third, long-range plans must be drawn that are a composite of the planning of groups within the organization. Fourth, such a plan should be stated in terms of the specific results that are expected, including a definite date for completion. Such dates should be clearly defined, measurable where possible, and realistic.

Two derivatives of the MBO approach that have particular promise for application in school environments are a *management-by-total-objectives* plan and an *exemplary profile* model. In the MBTO approach, the units of the organization are asked to develop goals independent of, and prior to, finalization of the overall plan. As each department designs its goals and accomplishments, there is a move away from one-person management. The sub-leaders become responsible for identifying what they believe their units can accomplish. The result is often greater productivity for the total organization.

The exemplary profile model is the version of MBO that seeks to constrain action in rapidly changing organizations or organizations that have multiple needs and problems. In this model, groups or individuals are allowed to select activities from among the many objectives of the organization and approach an exemplary profile. A supervision example of this approach is outlined in the following six steps:

1. During release time within the school day, staff members collectively identify key performance areas in instruction according to the goals of the system in which they work. These areas are then ranked by the staff as to importance.

2. Staff members collectively describe behaviors which, as a composite, indicate the optimal (desired) performance or solution in each area from number one above. The descriptions, as a whole, form an exemplary instructional profile. The profile is disseminated to all persons affected by the supervisory process.

3. At an agreed-upon time, the supervisor observes the instructional performance of the classroom teacher to record and assess the current condition of instruction in each of the teacher-determined areas from number one above. The observation period is followed by a conference between the supervisor and teacher during which an agreement is reached concerning the present realities in each area. The product of the conference is a shared perception of "what is" by both the teacher and supervisor.

4. Viewing the instructional pattern of the classroom teacher as a totality, the supervisor and the teacher conduct a "discrepancy analysis" to identify those areas where performance deviates most from desired conditions. At this point, the behaviors which mediate between the actual and desired state in priority categories are identified.

5. In the priority areas, the teacher, with the assistance of the supervisor, sets improvement goals. The supervisor sets observation goals at the same time. These goals describe anticipated changes in behavior, the evidence of which will be accepted as proof of improvement by both, and the time by which the desired changes will occur.

6. On the date identified in number five above, the supervisor returns to the classroom to observe and verify the progress of instructional improvement. At this time, also, new improvement goals are set. By this means, classroom instruction is continually being upgraded toward the ideal profile with emphasis directed toward the eradication of greatest deficiencies.[6]

There is ample evidence that suggests a payoff in the joint planning approach of management-by-objectives.* Among these advantages are:

1. a greater commitment and desire to contribute from subordinates because they have been fully involved in the formulation of goals for which they are working,

2. a clear picture for all members of the organization about what their role is to be,

---

* As an example, see "When Workers Manage Themselves," *Business Week* (March 20, 1965): 93–4.

3. greater control and coordination within the organization toward goal accomplishment, and
4. an increased capacity for leaders to direct their efforts to assist members through the identification of mutual needs.

TECHNICAL PLANNING AIDS

Beyond working with members of the organization in the identification of goals and the delegation of responsibilities, the leader must be able to organize and coordinate the activities to achieve desired results. To do this in a school environment, curriculum planners must be familiar with technical planning aids that display and monitor progress. Among the many technical aids adopted by educational planners during the past twenty years are the Gantt Chart, various planning checklists, flow charts, and displays.

The *Gantt Chart,* developed by Henry Gantt during World War I, is a linear calendar on which future time is spread horizontally and work to be accomplished is displayed vertically in bar graph fashion. Using the Gantt Chart, planners can view activities in terms of the only constant in planning procedure—time. The Gantt Chart, shown in Table 8.1, is useful in avoiding an overload of organizational activity during any single period of time.

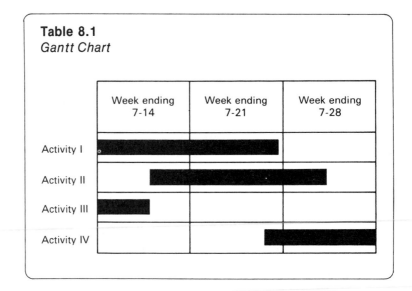

Table 8.1
Gantt Chart

	Week ending 7-14	Week ending 7-21	Week ending 7-28
Activity I	████████	████	
Activity II		████████	████
Activity III	███		
Activity IV			████████

Planning checklists like the one shown in Figure 8.1 are used regularly by curriculum planners as aids for insuring that all responsibilities for projects are fully delineated. Among categories to be considered are goals, activities, tasks, events, and time.

_____NEED ASSESSMENT COMPLETED

> Formal—survey, interview, question-
> naire
> Informal—discussion, belief, etc.
> Directive—necessary mandate
> Other

_____GOALS DEVELOPED
Start Date Established
Target Date Projected
(most likely time)

> Goals Identified
> Goals Synthesized
> Mission Identified
> Mission Clarified
> Mission Accepted

_____MAJOR ACTIVITIES DELINEATED

> All Possible Mission Objectives
> Synthesize All Objectives
> Convert to Product Statements
> Activities (Product Statement) Agreed
>   Upon

_____RESPONSIBILITY CHARTED

> Activities Stated
> Personnel (Human Resources)
>   Identified
> Responsibility Allocated

_____ACTIVITIES ASSIGNED

> Supervision Responsibility Accepted
> Work Accepted

_____TASKS IDENTIFIED

> Work Detailed
> Target Date Set

_____EVENTS DELINEATED

> Work Assigned
> Target Dates Set

_____TIME SCHEDULED

> Event, Task, Activity, Time Combined
> Combined Time and Target Date
>   Compared
> Time Adjusted When Necessary

_____MANUAL COMPLETED AND
DISTRIBUTED

> Mission, Activity, and Task Sheets
>   Collated and Tabbed
> Responsibility Chart Entered
> Manual Duplicated

_____TIME SCHEDULES COMPLETED

> Time Charts Developed
> Time Charts Centrally Posted

Figure 8.1
Planning Checklist

Another technical aid useful to the curriculum planner is the *flow chart*—a display which specifies the scheduled implementation plan.

Such schedules can be simple, as in Figure 8.2, which depicts events and dates over a short period of time, or complex, which includes names, resources, and evaluative criteria.

MAJOR EVENT	STARTING DATE	COMPLETION DATE
Hiring administrative staff (Project Director and secretary)	Notification of Funding Date	August 1
Overall planning	August 1	May 23
Recruiting three lead teachers and two counselors	Notification of Funding Date	August 1
Recruiting 12 teacher aides and 12 student tutors	August 1	August 17
Evaluating and selecting instructional materials	Notification of Funding Date	August
Purchasing instructional materials	August	August 17
Purchasing office supplies	August 1	June 30
Concentrated training of instructional staff	August 20	August 24
In-service training of instructional staff	September 4	May 24
Pretesting of students in program	September 10	September 14
Posttesting of students in program	April 22	April 26
Interim testing of students in program	September	May
Working with parents and community groups	September 17	May 24
Disseminating information about program	August 1	June 29
Developing and implementing instructional program	August 1	May 24
Replicating project activities in other schools within LEA	August	Indefinitely
Demonstrating the project to interested observers and making available staff members as well as materials, equipment, and facilities which are relevant to the project.	January	Indefinitely

Figure 8.2

A final technical planning aid used by curriculum developers to communicate the work flow is the *technical display*. In the one shown in Figure 8.3 on page 130, a middle school program is shown in its various stages of development.

SYSTEMS—THE CONCEPTUAL FRAMEWORK FOR MANAGEMENT

Two recent trends in the field of education, a focus on capacity and increasing role specificity, hold promise that curriculum development may be emerging from the conditions of years gone by. By focusing on capacity, curriculum development concerns itself with performance, outputs or products, efficiency, effectiveness, and consistency. In becoming more role specific, curriculum development is approaching the specialization and functionalism necessary to give the process a system-wide orientation.

The main force driving education to such a specialization is the scope and complexity of schooling. In the decade between 1967 and 1977, for instance, the total amount of money spent on education in the United States doubled from 61.5 billion dollars to 125 billion dollars. During this same period, the program focus of schooling became highly specialized to deal with specific learners. Given these events, educational planning has become more scientific and the rise of a managerial class has evolved from necessity. Without systematized organization, the whole educational process would break down under its own weight.

Over a twenty-year period, educational planners have searched for a conceptual framework to assist in the management of education. Such a construct was found in systems theory and its application to educational environments. Systems analysis has provided personnel in curriculum with a way of viewing the interaction, interdependence, and integration of the planning components in terms of the purpose of the educational organization.

The central idea of a systems analysis approach is that the functional components of an organization are related and that the complex interaction of these components is best understood if treated as a whole. The parts of educational institutions, such as resource needs, training requirements, or budgetary constraints, are related in a causal network; the activities in one affect activities in another. The parts of educational institutions are limited by boundaries, outside of which is an environment. The whole of the system, all of the parts interacting, is more than the sum of the parts due to organization.

Several conditions are prerequisite to a school's being perceived as a system. First, there must be boundaries that are defined by the goal statements. Second, the relationship among the many parts must be

STATE PLAN DOCUMENT WRITING PROCESS FOR MIDDLE SCHOOLS AND MIDDLE CHILDHOOD EDUCATION

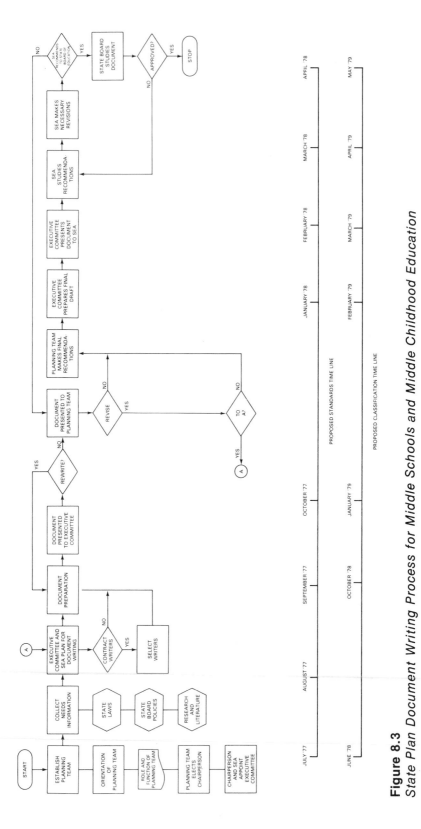

Figure 8.3
State Plan Document Writing Process for Middle Schools and Middle Childhood Education

Source: State Plan for Middle Childhood Education (Charleston: West Virginia Department of Education, Bureau of Learning Systems, Division of Instructional Learning Systems, 1977), Joseph C. Basile, Director.

unified, working toward objectives. Third, the process of interaction must be perceived as an input-output situation. In schools, uneducated children are the measure of input while educated young adults are the common output. Finally, there must be an understanding that the system is in use to maximize the efforts in achieving that output.

By definition, a system is a set of components that are organized to impel action toward the accomplishment of purposes for which the organization exists. Functionally, systems help educational planners identify purposes, make decisions, marshal resources, and evaluate.

In designing a system, planners proceed through five basic steps:

1. A description of the desired end product, uncontaminated by means, is drawn.
2. Objectives are analyzed to find preconditions needed to produce the desired end product.
3. Analysis proceeds downward, describing in greater and greater detail what is to occur.
4. When the smallest components are outlined, the process to produce the desired result is constructed.
5. The process is activated.

Systems are organized by function but managed by product. In managing a system in schools designed for program development, curriculum leaders can arrange and control major transformation components. Among these managerial variables, or manipulative components, are the goals and values of the organization, the structure of the organization, the psychosocial relationships within the organization, and the technological or delivery mediums of the organization. Collectively, these transformation systems allow the designer considerable latitude in managing to achieve desired ends.

In most curriculum systems, the complexity of the related tasks requires that management be done by committees. Such committees are usually called task forces or curriculum councils. Such committees, depending upon their autonomy and delegated powers, consider problems, formulate recommendations, make assignments, and authorize and follow the implementation of programs. In a systems design, the role of such a committee would appear in a form such as that found in Figure 8.4.

THE CURRICULUM COUNCIL

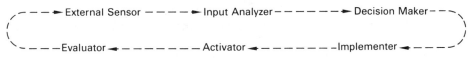

Figure 8.4
The Curriculum Council

In educational systems, there are unusual constraints which sometimes are negotiable but often are beyond the control of the systems designer. Among major constraints are the constant press of time, the inadequacy of planning data and knowledge in critical areas, the scope of educational systems, the interface of educational systems with the outside environment, and existing facilities.

The greatest weakness found in conceptualization of educational planning from a systems analysis perspective is the tendency to establish a *closed system.* A closed system is one that continually refines itself to a state of obsolescence. The constant change in educational technique demands an openness to new ideas and innovation. Educational systems must therefore be constantly reviewed for relevance and functionality.

ORGANIZATION DEVELOPMENT—
A PROCESS FRAMEWORK

While systems thinking can assist the curriculum designer in following the overall work flow, it does not adequately indicate the process by which change occurs in schools. Borrowing once again from social science research, curriculum leaders can use a framework known as *organization development* (OD) to understand the activation of curriculum development.*

Organization development is a strategy for activating change in organizations based on the assumption that it is more productive to change structure than to attempt to change individuals. By focusing on social structure and social interaction, patterns that govern roles and relationships within organizations, OD attempts to integrate individual needs with organizational goals and objectives.

The primary values underlying a program of organization development are:

1. provision of opportunity for each organization member, as well as for the organization as a whole, to develop to full potential,
2. provision of opportunity for people to act as human beings rather than as resources in the productive process,
3. striving to create a work environment in which it is possible to find challenging and exciting work, and the

---

* For a complete coverage of organization development principles, see Richard A. Schmuck and Matthew B. Miles, *Organization Development in Schools* (Palo Alto, California: National Press Books, 1971).

4. provision of opportunity for people in the organization to influence the way in which they engage work.

The terminal goals for a program of organization development are:

1. An open problem-solving climate throughout the organization,
2. decision-making responsibilities located as close to the information source as possible,
3. authority by role supplanted by authority of knowledge and competence,
4. increasing degrees of trust among individuals and groups in the organization,
5. maximized collaborative efforts in daily work,
6. increased feelings of ownership by organization members,
7. management according to relevant objectives rather than past practices, and
8. increasing degrees of self-control and self-direction.

Organization development would allow specific schools to determine for themselves the nature of organizational and programmatic changes that are appropriate and critically needed. Through training in planning, interpersonal skills, small group leadership skills, and other interaction attributes, organization members can begin to move toward self-determined goals and objectives. The tools for change are techniques such as brainstorming, small groups, decision by consensus, setting agendas prior to meetings, and widening the base of decision making. These specific skills are discussed in chapter 9.

In the final analysis, organization development seeks to find the best combination of structures and patterns within a particular setting to elicit full contributions from all members of the organization.

As curriculum leaders employ such conceptual tools as systems analysis and organization development methodology, they approach a strategy for promoting desired change in school programs. Such a strategy is the key to successful curriculum leadership because real progress in helping schools become more effective can only occur through an orderly sequence of planning and execution.

The first step in developing such a plan is to become aware of the fact that the key to opening schools to change does not lie with material objects or personality changes, but rather with the structure of the organization. In Sarason's words:

> It becomes increasingly difficult to become aware that individuals operate in various social settings that have a structure not comprehensible by our existing theories of individual personality. In fact, in many situations, it is likely that one can predict an individual's behavior far better on the basis of knowledge of the social structure and his position in it than on the basis of personality dynamics.[7]

Any real change in an organization is the product of a rearrangement of structure in areas such as power, association, communication, and status. Given the correct combination of structures, the organization will pursue change and improvement in a natural fashion.

Through management, the curriculum leader can assist educational organizations in becoming more effective. Effectiveness is achieved when the organization knows its needs and has the capacity to meet those needs.

SUMMARY

As schools become more bureaucratic and specialized, the managerial aspects of curriculum development become more pronounced. Such a management function implies that curriculum leaders understand organizations, possess a viable strategy for change, and have the skills to promote desired practices in a productive manner.

To be successful as a manager, the curriculum leader must be knowledgeable about the techniques, planning aids, and conceptualizations that will contribute to the accomplishment of desired change. Such management tools are constantly being developed by social scientists and others involved in the study of management.

Recent studies of organizations indicate that a combination of structural management and humanitarian leadership allows organizations such as schools to achieve maximum success in meeting goals. When schools are organized in a manner that allows them to pursue desired results and capitalize on opportunities to meet changing needs, they can be considered effective as organizations.

Notes

1. Leonard R. Sayles, *Managerial Behavior* (New York: McGraw-Hill Book Company, 1964).
2. Max Weber, *The Theory of Social and Economic Organization* (New York: Oxford University Press, 1947).
3. Seymour B. Sarason, *The Culture of the School and the Problem of Change* (Boston: Allyn and Bacon, Inc., 1971), p. 1.
4. Robert L. Katz, "Skills of an Effective Administrator," *Harvard Business Review* (January/February, 1955): 33–42.
5. Peter F. Drucker, *The Effective Executive* (New York: Harper and Row, Publishers, 1966), p. 100.
6. Jon Wiles and Alfred Arth, "Providing Supportive Supervision for Instructional Improvement in the Middle Years," *Kappa Delta Pi Record* (February, 1978).
7. Sarason, *The Culture of the School,* p. 12.

Suggested Learning Activities

1. Spend a working day with a curriculum director or supervisor of instruction in a public school district. Using fifteen-minute observations, determine how well time is managed.

2. Using a flow-chart format such as that found in Figure 8–3, develop a comprehensive plan for upgrading one subject area commonly found in public schools.

3. Plan a strategy for staff development in a school district using an organization development (OD) format. What is the unique feature of this approach?

Books to Review

Drucker, Peter. *The Effective Executive.* New York: Harper & Row, Publishers, 1966.

Feyereisen, K., Fiorino, A., and Nowak, A. *Supervision and Curriculum Renewal: A Systems Approach.* New York: Appleton-Century Crofts, 1970.

Holland, James, et al. *The Analysis of Behavior in Planning Instruction.* Reading, Massachusetts: Addison-Wesley Publishing Company, Inc., 1976.

Landers, Thomas and Myers, Judith. *Essentials of School Management.* Philadelphia: W.B. Saunders Company, 1977.

McGregor, Douglas. *The Human Side of Enterprise.* New York: McGraw-Hill Book Company, 1960.

Schmuck, Richard and Miles, Matthew. *Organization Development in Schools.* Palo Alto, California: National Press Books, 1971.

9

Interpersonal Dimensions of the Development Process

Curriculum development in schools is basically a process in which organization members interact to produce improved school programs. While curriculum planning can produce goals, objectives, syllabi, and evaluation outlines, the quality of such products is determined by the face-to-face interaction of those involved in the curriculum development processes. It is important for those who engage in curriculum leadership to understand and use their knowledge of this interpersonal dimension of the development process.

In chapter 6 the authors developed the idea that leadership in organizations such as schools is a transactional process. Leaders must coordinate individual needs and organizational tasks. While attempting this difficult act, the leader is dependent upon others in the organization. As Kimball Wiles has observed:

> An executive decision is only a moment in the total process of the solution of the problem. It is the final statement of policy that the official leader is asked to administer. The solution begins with a clear definition of the problem, involves analysis of the factors of the situation, is based on procedure formulated by the group, is stated as an official decision, and is implemented by activities agreed upon by the group members as their responsibility in carrying out the decision.[1]

With this statement in mind, it is possible to view the dependence of the curriculum leader in each of the basic steps as shown in Figure 9.1. Because of this dependence and the effect of interaction on the quality of the curriculum development process, curriculum leaders can benefit from an analysis of various interpersonal factors.

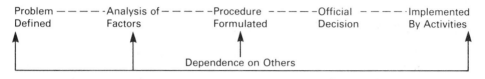

Figure 9.1

Interpersonal relationships in school environments can be thought of as having the following six levels:

1. **Individual**—a personality system that is made up of many parts organized to enable the individual to respond to both internal and external conditions.
2. **Dyad**—a social unit of two individuals who develop patterns of response to each other as well as response to other levels of the human system.
4. **Group**—a small social system of individuals with fairly well-defined purpose, able to respond to itself and to external conditions.
4. **Organization**—a social unit of individuals with clearly defined and specialized functions requiring a disciplined and systematic relationship among members, able to respond to internal needs and external conditions.
5. **Community**—a social unit composed of a large number of individuals who form a variety of interacting sub-parts which are likely to respond more frequently to situations internal to itself.
6. **Society**—a social unit including all previous levels interacting, related by some common norms of political, economic, and cultural coordination that together form an observable identity.

At each of these levels the curriculum specialist is interacting to facilitate the development of school programs. Such interaction is carried out through the following standard development functions:

Human Systems	Functions	Interactions
Individuals	Diagnosing	Perceiving
Dyads	Deciding	Valuing
Groups	Planning	Communicating
Organizations	Managing	Influencing
Communities	Producing	Cooperating
Society	Evaluating	Belonging

Understanding the exact relationship of interaction in curriculum development functions, human systems, and interpersonal relations, is aided by a study of communication in organizations, individual personality theory, small group work, and group leadership.

COMMUNICATION IN ORGANIZATIONS

Communication among individuals in organizations is a delicate art requiring, among other things, self-discipline and a cooperative spirit. Spoken English is a complex language which is full of subtleties. Superimposed on these language patterns are a host of nonverbal clues that can alter the meaning of speech. Add to these dimensions an environmental context, and the result is a communication system that operates at varying levels of effectiveness.

Various social sciences have developed entire languages to describe the intricacies of communication in the American culture. Galloway has provided a model of foci in three such social sciences:[2]

Anthropology	Sociology	Psychology
Cultural behaviors	Role behaviors	Personal behaviors
Acculturation	Interaction	Personality
Implicit meanings	Empathetic meanings	Inferred meanings

Collectively, social science inquiry in the area of interpersonal communication has added immeasurably to our understanding of this complex and important dimension of curriculum improvement.

In any pattern of communication among humans there are at least the following nine elements:

1. What the speaker wants to say
2. What the speaker wants to conceal
3. What the speaker reveals without knowing it
4. What the listener wants or expects to hear
5. What the listener's perception of the speaker will let him hear
6. What the listener's experiences tell him the words mean
7. What the listener wants to conceal
8. What the emotional climate of the situation permits the persons to share
9. What the physical structure of the situation permits the persons to share[3]

Various models have shown communication to be a process of encoding and decoding. A source encodes a message and tries to transmit it to a receiver who tries to receive it and decode the message. Such a transmission between sender and receiver is often distorted by various barriers to communication and by defensive behaviors. Gibb has defined such communication defense:

> Defensive behavior is defined as that behavior which occurs when an individual perceives a threat or anticipates threat in the group. The person who behaves defensively, even though he gives some attention to the common task, devotes an appreciable portion of his energy to defending himself. Besides talking about the topic, he thinks about how he appears to others, how he can be seen more favorably, how he may win, dominate, impress, or escape punishment, and/or how he may avoid or mitigate a perceived or an anticipated attack.[4]

Berlo, in a study of human communication, has identified the following four major predictors of faulty communication that can be used by curriculum leaders to anticipate possible communication breakdown:

1. The amount of competition messages have.
2. The threats to status and ego which are involved.
3. The uncertainty and error in what is expected.
4. The number of links there are in the communication chain.[5]

Other barriers to effective communication among people might include any of the following:

1. People use words and symbols that have differing meanings.
2. People have different perceptions of problems being discussed.
3. Members of communication groups possess different values.
4. People bring to discussions varying levels of feeling or affect.
5. Words are sometimes used to prevent real thinking.
6. A lack of acceptance of diverse opinion is present in some communication.
7. Vested interests can interfere with genuine communication.
8. Feelings of personal insecurity can distort communication.
9. Tendencies to make premature evaluations are a barrier to communication.
10. Negative feelings about situations block effective communication.

In addition to verbal and conscious barriers to effective communication, there are a number of nonverbal and often unconscious obstacles to accurate two-way communication.

During the past fifteen years substantial study has been conducted in the area of nonverbal communication resulting in specialties such as *proximics* (study of personal space) and *kinesics* (body language). Such study suggests that the way in which communication is delivered and the context of communication is as important as what is actually said.

Pioneer work by Hall and Ardrey has provided tremendous insight into the effects of personal space on two-way communication. A major contribution in this area was Hall's observation of communication zones. Stated simply, Hall found that the type of communication must be matched with interpersonal distance to truly communicate. He identified four distances which he called intimate zones, personal zones, social zones, and public zones, and hypothesized that an intimate message, for instance, must be delivered in the intimate zone to be effective. In Hall's words: "Spatial changes give a tone to communication, accent it, and at times even override the spoken word. The flow and shift of distance between people as they interact is part and parcel of the communication process."[6]

Other nonverbal studies have concentrated on signals emitted by postures, expressions, and gestures which usually are transmitted unconsciously but nonetheless send a message.* These studies, known as body language, have revealed cultural patterns which are painfully accurate predictors of the communication intent of the sender.

A final area of study in nonverbal communication is the effect of time on communication. Again, Hall observes: "Time talks. It speaks more plainly than words. The message it conveys comes through loud and clear. Because it is manipulated less consciously, it is subject to less distortion than the spoken language. It can shout the truth where words lie."[7]

Persons in leadership positions should be aware that nonverbal communication that is negative has the following characteristics:

1. There is a discrepancy between verbal intent and nonverbal referents.
2. There is an unresponsiveness to feedback.
3. There is a negative affectivity present.
4. There is inattentiveness to others.

Collectively, awareness of barriers to spoken communication and nonverbal cues can assist leaders in analyzing and improving interpersonal communication in human systems. Further, understanding of individual personalities can provide a means for improving communication.

INDIVIDUAL PERSONALITY

Distinctive and particular individual qualities, known as personality, are a real and vital ingredient of the interpersonal dimension of cur-

---

* For an overview of kinesics, see Julius Fast, *Body Language* (New York: Pocket Books, 1970).

riculum development. These individual patterns of behavior can be viewed as a positive or negative force in an overall attempt to develop school programs. They must be acknowledged by leadership.

Donald Snygg has identified four major ways in which an individual acts to maintain or enhance the self in everyday activity:

1. Change in body state leading to change in the perception of the self
   a. Restoration of the body balance by eating, breathing, elimination, rest, etc.
   b. Blocking off organic sensations of fatigue, pain, or tension indicative of personal inadequacies by use of drugs or alcohol
   c. Elicitation of an organic mobilization and increase in body strength by entering a dangerous or irritating situation: speeding, gambling, etc.
2. Self-reassurance by demonstration of mastery, control, or superiority
   a. Over people: competition leading to victory over worthy opponents, superiority by gossip, practical joking, scapegoating, making gifts
   b. Demonstration of control over material objects: such as creativity, destruction of material things
   c. Accumulation of property, hoarding
3. Reassurance and enhancement by association and identification with respected individuals and groups. Evidence of respect and love by respected persons. Feelings of identity with a great cause, or being part of a great movement.
4. By change of the nonself part of the field which places the self in a less threatened position
   a. By change in the physical environment: travel, moving, redecorating
   b. By daydreaming or fantasy, including that done by professionals: radio, television, theatre, fiction, etc.[8]

Viewing individual behavior and the reflecting personality in terms of a drive for self-enhancement is useful to leaders as an explanation for dysfunctional organizational behavior. It can also provide leaders with an insight concerning how interpersonal communication can be improved. We must be able to see interpersonal communication and the interaction of personalities from the perspective of individual frames of reference.

If we wish to understand the behavior of any one person, it is useful to be aware that how we think of and feel about him may be very unlike how he thinks and feels about himself. The behavior of an individual will always be more a function of his own view than the perception of an external person. The task, then, is to seek to understand how the individual sees himself and his immediate surroundings.

In order to understand another's behavior, we have to be willing to suspend, at least for a while, judgments about him and his behavior. We must be willing to try to understand how he sees himself and his situation, and what needs he is trying to satisfy at the moment. We must try to see him as he perceives himself, not as an outsider sees him. This view of himself and his situation can be called his personal frame of reference. When we observe personal behavior from this perspective, being aware of self-enhancement needs as outlined by Snygg, much of the dysfunctional behavior in organizational settings is understandable. If personality and behavior can be understood, it can be reacted to in ways that will improve interpersonal relations.

Earl Kelley has stated this condition from the position of the role of leadership in organizations:

> The fact that each individual is unique means that each person has something, knows something, which nobody else on earth has or knows. It is, of course, not always easy to bring out this special contribution, but it is there if it can be made to function. This difference is what the individual uses, when he makes his own special contribution to any enterprise. This is the way by which an individual achieves significance.[9]

For curriculum leaders to see individual personalities as a positive force in the development process, they must be accepting of diversity in personality. Not only must leaders be aware that all persons are continually in a search for self-enhancement, but they must also recognize that the idiosyncrasies of personality can strengthen the interaction process. Consider, for instance, the ways in which introverted and extroverted personalities complement each other:

Introverts

live in an inner world
prefer to focus attention on ideas and concepts
are reflective
like to consider every consequence before acting

Extroverts

live in an outer world
prefer to focus attention on people and things
are active
use trial and error with confidence[10]

Studies of personality types in organizations, such as those conducted by Myers and Briggs, suggest that all personalities have preferences and strengths that can contribute to organizational effectiveness.[11] An acceptance of individual personality as a natural ingredient in the interpersonal processes of curriculum development can lead to new insights relative to motivation and organizational interaction.

GROUP WORK

While relationships exist at the dyad, organizational, community, and societal levels, most curriculum development work proceeds at the group level. For this reason, curriculum leaders need to be particularly attentive to group work as a means of promoting better school programs.

Groups can generally be described as two or more people who possess a common objective. As groups interact in pursuit of an objective, their behavior is affected by a number of variables, including: the background of the group, participation patterns, communication patterns, the cohesiveness of the group, the goals of the group, standards affecting the group, procedures affecting the group, and the atmosphere or climate surrounding the group.

Groups perform various tasks that are important to the development of school programs. Among these group tasks are:

1. Initiating activities: suggesting new ideas, defining problems, proposing solutions, reorganizing materials.
2. Coordinating: showing relationships among various ideas or suggestions, pulling ideas together, relating activities of various subgroups.
3. Summarizing: pulling together related data, restating suggestions after discussion.
4. Testing feasibility: examining the practicality or feasibility of ideas, making preevaluation decisions about activities.

Group work in educational environments is often ineffective due to various types of nonfunctional behaviors. Leaders should be aware of some of the more common forms of nonfunctional actions:

1. Being aggressive—showing hostility against the group or some individual, criticizing or blaming others, deflating the status of others.
2. Blocking—interfering with group process by speaking tangentially, citing personal experiences unrelated to the problem, rejecting ideas without consideration.
3. Competing—vying with others to talk most often, produce the best idea, gain favor of the leader.
4. Special pleading—introducing ideas or suggestions that relate to one's own concerns.
5. Seeking recognition—calling attention to oneself by excessive talking, extreme ideas, or unusual behavior.

6. Withdrawing—being indifferent or passive, daydreaming, doodling, whispering to others, physically leaving the discussion.

As a group leader, the curriculum specialist should be able to differentiate between those roles and actions that contribute to group effectiveness and those roles that are basically negative and do not contribute to the effectiveness of the group. The following can be thought of as productive and contributing to group effectiveness:

1. Person brings the discussion back to the point.
2. Person seeks clarification of meaning when ideas expressed are not clear.
3. Person questions and evaluates ideas expressed in objective manner.
4. Person challenges reasoning when the soundness of logic is doubtful.
5. Person introduces new way of thinking about topic.
6. Person makes a summary of points.
7. Person underscores points of agreement or disagreement.
8. Person tries to resolve conflict or differences of opinion.
9. Person introduces facts or relevant information.
10. Person evaluates progress of the group.

Roles that can be thought of as negative or nonproductive are:

1. Person aggressively expresses disapproval of ideas of others.
2. Person attacks the group or the ideas under consideration.
3. Person attempts to reintroduce idea after it has been rejected.
4. Person tries to assert authority by demanding.
5. Person introduces information which is obviously irrelevant.
6. Person tries to invoke sympathy by depreciation of self.
7. Person uses stereotypes to cover own biases and prejudices.
8. Person downgrades the importance of group's role or function.

Sensitivity to such roles allows the group leader to analyze the flow of group work and head off potential distractions to group progress.

GROUP LEADERSHIP

While working with groups, the curriculum leader does not have to restrict his or her role to that of passive observer. It is possible to take steps that will encourage greater group productivity. In any group discussion, the leader has at least six roles which, if pursued, will lead the group toward accomplishment of its objectives. These areas are:

presentation of the topic, the initiation of discussion, guiding the discussion, controlling discussion, preventing side-tracking, and summarizing the discussion.

In presenting the topic to be discussed, the leader should suggest the importance of the problem, place the general purpose of the discussion before the group, suggest a logical pathway for the discussion to follow, and define any ambiguous terms to remove misunderstanding. It is useful, where possible, to relate the current discussion to previous meetings or other convenient reference points.

In initiating the discussion, the leader provides advanced thinking for the group. Major questions to be answered are identified, and relevant facts and figures are cited. A case in point may be drawn for purposes of illustration. In some cases, it may even be useful to purposefully misstate a position to provoke discussion.

The leader's job in guiding the discussion involves keeping the discussion goal-directed, assisting members in expressing themselves through feedback, and providing the transition from one aspect of the discussion to another. In fulfilling this role, the leader may use direct questions, stories, illustrations, or leading questions to maintain the flow of interaction.

In controlling the discussion the leader is concerned with the pace of progress and the involvement of the participants. Among techniques which can be used to keep discussion moving are purposeful negative statements, drawing contrasts between positions of participants, and regularly calling attention to the time remaining.

The discussion leader in a small group can deal with side-tracking in a number of ways. He can restate the original question or problems. He can secure a statement from a reliable group member to head off a rambler. He can request that side issues be postponed until main issues are settled.

Finally, the leader summarizes the discussion. This involves knowing when to terminate discussion and reviewing the high points that have been talked to.

Three situations in particular are troublesome to persons new to leading discussions in small groups; the dead silence, the over-talkative member, and the silent member. Any of these three conditions can sabotage an otherwise fruitful discussion period.

A most anxiety-producing situation is one in which there is a complete absence of participation resulting in an awkward silence among group members. While the natural response in such a situation is to speak to fill the conversational vacuum, the leader must do just the opposite. Silence in discussions sometimes means that real thinking is occurring, and this assumption must be made by the leader. Another common impulse is to seek out a member of the group and prod him or her for a contribution. Such a tactic will surely contribute to less participation. When the silent period is convincingly unproductive, the leader should try an encouraging remark such as, "There must be some different points of view here." Failing response, the leader should turn to the process involved with a comment such as, "Let's see if we can discover what's blocking us."

Another situation that can ruin a group discussion is an over-talkative member. Such a person, if permitted, will monopolize discussion and produce anxiety among group members. The best strategy in such a situation is to intervene after a respectful period of time with a comment such as, "Perhaps we can hear from other members of the group." In the event that the dominating member still doesn't get the message, the leader can initiate an evaluation of the process and draw attention to the fact that a way must be found to gain input from all members.

A final situation that can be awkward occurs when a member of the group is regularly silent. The leader should recognize that some persons are fearful of being put on the spot and will resent being spotlighted. The leader can, however, observe the silent member and look for signals that he or she is ready to participate. If the member seems to be on the verge of speaking, an encouraging glance or nod may be all that is needed.

In cases where the leader becomes convinced that a member's silence is the result of boredom or withdrawing, it may be useful to confront the member away from other group members with a provocative or challenging question. Whether a member should be forced into a discussion, and whether such an act is productive for the entire group, is a matter of judgment and discretion.

Leaders of small groups should regularly evaluate their own performance following a discussion by asking themselves a series of questions such as the following:

1. Did members contribute to the discussion?
2. Did some people do more talking than others?
3. Are the most talkative persons, and the silent ones, sitting together?
4. Do members talk mostly to the leader or to each other?
5. Was there evidence of cliques or interest groups in the discussion?

Group leaders can sometimes retard creative thinking by regulating discussions in nonproductive ways. Among the most common errors in this respect are:

1. A preoccupation with order throughout the discussion.
2. Stressing too often "hard evidence" or factual information.
3. Placing too much emphasis on history or the way things have been done.
4. Using coercive techniques to insure participation.
5. Suggesting that mistakes are not acceptable.

Two skills that are useful for all small group leaders to possess are that of paraphrasing and brainstorming. In paraphrasing, the leader attempts to restate the point of view of another to his satisfaction prior to continuing discussion. This technique is especially useful in argumentative situations, and often sets a pattern which is followed by other group members.

In brainstorming, the leader introduces a technique that frees the group discussion from previous barriers to speaking. Here the leader sets ground rules which include the following: no criticism of others is allowed, the combining of ideas is encouraged, quality ideas are sought, wild ideas are encouraged. In introducing a brainstorming session the leader hopes to have members "spark" each other and have one idea "hitch-hike" upon another. Brainstorming, as a technique, is recommended when discussions continually cover familiar ground and little or no progress toward a solution to problems is forthcoming.

Finally, leaders of small groups should work to become better listeners. Numerous studies have identified poor listening skills as the biggest block to personal communication. Nicholas has identified ten steps to better listening:

1. While listening, concentrate on finding areas of interest that are useful to you.
2. Judge the content of what is said rather than the delivery.
3. Postpone early judgment about what is being said. Such a posture will allow you to remain analytical if you favor what is being said or to keep from being distracted by calculating embarrassing questions should you disagree with the speaker's message.
4. Focus on the central ideas proposed by the speaker. What is the central idea? What are the supporting "planks" or statements?
5. Remain flexible in listening. Think of various ways to remember what is being said.
6. Work hard at listening. Try to direct all conscious attention on the presentation being made.
7. Resist distractions in the environment by making adjustments or by greater concentration.
8. Exercise your mind by regularly listening to technical expository material that you haven't had experience with.
9. Keep your mind open to new ideas by being aware of your own biases and limited experiences.
10. Capitalize on thought speed. Since comprehension speed exceeds speaking speed by about 3:1, the listener must work to keep his concentration. This can be done by anticipating what is to be said, by making mental summaries, by weighing speaker evidence, and by listening between the lines.[12]

SUMMARY

Curriculum development involves considerable human interaction. For this reason, curriculum leaders should understand the interpersonal process and use this knowledge to become more effective in small group activities.

Interpersonal activity occurs at numerous levels within the human system, and is a standard part of most curriculum development activities. Awareness of communication in organizations, individual personality theory, small group work, and leadership functions in small groups can allow the curriculum leader to be more effective in his work.

Communication involves both speech patterns and nonverbal influences. Persons aware of regular barriers to clear communication can address those restraints through various strategies and leadership techniques.

Knowing about individual personality traits, such as the need for self-enhancement, can allow leaders to understand individual behavior and capitalize on human diversity. Seeing individuals as unique can lead to improved organization interaction.

Group work is a regular process through which most curriculum development is conducted. Knowledge of group functions, roles, and barriers to successful group communication can help leaders improve group performance.

Finally, leading successful small group discussions calls for specific analytic and organizational skills. Among these skills are how to direct a discussion and how to be a more effective listener.

Notes

1. Kimball Wiles, *Supervision For Better Schools,* 3rd ed. (Englewood Cliffs, N.J.: Prentice-Hall, Inc., 1967), pp. 39–40.
2. Charles Galloway, speech to the Ohio State Association of Student Teaching, Columbus, Ohio, October, 1968.
3. Wiles, *Supervision for Better Schools,* p. 53.
4. J.R. Gibb, "Defense Level and Influence Potential in Small Groups," in L. Petrullo and B.M. Bass, eds., *Leadership and Interpersonal Behavior* (New York: Holt, Rinehart and Winston, Inc., 1961), p. 66.
5. D. Berlo, "Avoiding Communication Breakdown," BNA Effective Communication film series.
6. Edward T. Hall, *The Silent Language* (New York: Doubleday and Co., Inc., 1959).
7. Hall, *The Silent Language,* p. 1.
8. Donald Snygg, "The Psychological Basis on Human Values," in D. Avila,

W. Purkey, and A. Combs, eds., *The Helping Relationship Sourcebook* (Boston: Allyn and Bacon, Inc., 1971), pp. 184–85.

9. Earl C. Kelley, "Another Look at Individualism," in *The Helping Relationship Sourcebook,* pp. 302–3.

10. Adapted from D. Roberts, C. Fox, and C. Branch, *Investigating the Riddle of Man: A Modular Learning Program* (New York: Prentice-Hall, Inc., 1974).

11. Studies conducted using the Myers-Briggs Type Indicator: Form F. Katherine C. Briggs and Isabel Myers (Gainesville, Florida: University of Florida, 1959).

12. Ralph G. Nicholas, "Listening is a Ten-Part Skill," in *Managing Yourself,* compiled by editors of *Nation's Business.*

Suggested Learning Activities

1. Visit a school classroom or other place where people are interacting. Try to determine if the type of communication you observe is in any way related to the communication distance between participants.

2. State, in your own words, a hypothesis concerning the relationship between human personality and organizational tasks.

3. List ten ground rules for leading a small group discussion. What are some probable areas of difficulty for persons new to this process?

Books to Review

Perceiving, Behaving, Becoming: A New Focus for Education, 1962 Yearbook, Association for Supervision and Curriculum Development. Washington, D.C., 1962.

Cartwright, D. and Zander, A. *Group Dynamics: Research and Theory.* Evanston, Illinois: Row, Peterson Company, 1960.

Hall, Edward. *The Silent Language.* Garden City, New York: Doubleday and Company, Inc., 1959.

Wiles, Kimball. *Supervision for Better Schools.* Englewood Cliffs, New Jersey: Prentice-Hall, Inc., 1967.

10

Instructional Considerations in Curriculum Development

Since curriculum is a plan for learning and objectives determine what learning is important, it follows that good curriculum planning will involve the selection and organization of both content and learning experiences. Instructional considerations in curriculum development require curriculum planners to move beyond a theoretical framework of curriculum to the implementation of curriculum plans at the classroom level. The most significant part of any curriculum plan is the organized classroom plan. Parents see this aspect of curriculum development as the cornerstone of the school. Instructional considerations in curriculum development at the classroom level include teachers making daily decisions about content, grouping, materials, pacing and sequencing of activities, and assessing how well students have learned. Each of these decisions directly affects student learning. This chapter will explore curriculum development as it interfaces with classroom instruction. The selection of curriculum experiences, organizing for instruction, resources for learning, and teaching strategies will be analyzed from a planning perspective. A checklist of curriculum planning considerations at the classroom level will be provided.

SELECTION OF CURRICULUM EXPERIENCES

Selection of curriculum experiences has always been a problem in curriculum development. Today's schools have inherited responsibilities for instruction that go well beyond the basic instruction provided by schools fifty years ago. There is more for students to learn than there is time available in school. Because of the back-to-the-basics movement in recent years, there is less time available for those learning experiences not classified as "basic instruction." Yet the needs of society have made the school assume more of the responsibilities formerly assumed by other institutions. How to reconcile the push for more time for basics and more time for the personal development of children is a major problem facing the modern curriculum leader.

At the classroom level, the push and pull of pressure groups becomes even more critical. Here, the teacher is often faced with a school board mandate to provide a certain number of minutes of reading per day for every child. This is often accompanied by a push for so many class periods a week of mathematics. Many school districts have requirements that certain subjects be taught in certain years in a prescribed manner. Curriculum planners must realize that the classroom teacher must ultimately carry out the instructional program and must have some flexibility in selecting curriculum experiences.

Providing Balance in the Instructional Program

In the past, most curriculum experiences were grouped as "curricular" or "extra-curricular." Furthermore, they were almost universally grouped or described within subject fields. The broadening of the definition of curriculum today has diminished somewhat the distinction between curricular or extra-curricular experiences.

Within a school program all learning experiences can be classified under the following headings:

1. The personal development of the individual
2. Skills for continued learning
3. Education for social competence

The above classification can serve as the basis for planning a school program, and provides direction for instruction at the classroom level. Clear attention can be given to each of the three phases of the school program while still recognizing that the three phases are related.

Using such a classification system, curriculum planners can develop a plan that will provide a great variety of rich learning opportunities in each area. The personal development phase would include exploratory, and enrichment experiences in a broad range of human activities. There can be activities leading to a better understanding of one's self, health and physical activities appropriate to levels of maturity, and various school services that would involve the learner's family and home. The skills for the continued learning phase can include diagnosis of learning needs with cognitive learning experiences so structured that students can master critical skills and progress in an individualized manner. The social competence phase might include courses of study in the sciences and mathematics, social studies, humanities, languages and literature, and the vocational fields.

Although such a classification system would be primarily a check on the scope of the school program, it might also provide teachers with a guide for determining balance in the curriculum as they develop lesson plans or participate in writing curriculum guides. The classroom instructor would also use different means of organizing for instruction as he or she provides learning experiences in the different phases of the curriculum. For instance, there might be more organized group instruction in the social competence phase than in the personal development phase. Group sizes could also vary with respect to the particular phase of the curriculum.

Providing for
Culturally Diverse Students

In selecting curriculum experiences, teachers today must take into consideration the needs of culturally diverse students. Individualizing instruction for culturally and ethnically diverse students does not mean these students are deficient and need individual help to catch up with their fellow students. The burden should not be on the child to adjust to a monocultural school (basically white, Anglo, and middle class in orientation). Rather, school personnel must realize that we live in a poly-cultural society and must develop a sensitivity to the cultural orientations of each child.

Recent authors of texts and articles have emphasized the need to recognize the individuality of children. Ernest Garcia in an ERIC document wrote, "Cultural differences that need the attention and sensitivity of the teacher are going to come with individuals."[1] Teachers need to recognize and accent cultural differences and be able to respond with the types of teacher behaviors designed to install a feeling of pride, not shame, on the part of students.

The Association for Supervision and Curriculum Development Commission on Multicultural Education has suggested all educational content and processes be examined for evidence of realistic treatment of cultural pluralism. They offer the following recommendations:

1. Examine text materials for evidence of racism, classism, sexism, and realistic treatment of cultural pluralism in American society.
2. Develop new curricula for all levels of schooling—curricula that enhance and promote cultural diversity.
3. Provide opportunities to learn about and interact with a variety of ethic groups and cultural experiences.
4. Include the study of concepts from the humanistic and behavioral sciences, which are applicable for understanding human behavior.
5. Organize curricula around universal human concerns, which transcend usual subject-matter disciplines; bring multicultural perspectives to bear in the study of such issues.
6. Broaden the kinds of inquiry used in the school to incorporate and facilitate the learning of more humanistic modes of inquiry.
7. Create school environments that radiate cultural diversity.
8. Maximize the school as a multicultural setting, with the idea of utilizing the positive contributions of all groups to accomplish common tasks and not just to reduce deficiencies for the deprived.
9. Recognize and utilize bilingualism as a positive contribution to the communication process, and include bilingual programs of instruction of monolingual children.
10. Examine rules, norms, and procedures of students and staff with the purpose of facilitating the development of learning strategies and techniques that do not penalize and stigmatize diversity, but rather encourage and prize it.
11. Institute a system of shared governance in the schools, in which all groups can enter equally in the learning and practice of democratic procedures.
12. Organize time, space, personnel, and resources to facilitate the maximum probability and flexibility of alternative experiences for all youngsters.
13. Institute staffing patterns (involving both instructional and noninstructional positions) that reflect our culturally pluralistic and multiracial society.
14. Design and implement preservice and in-service programs to improve staff ability to successfully implement multicultural education.[2]

Rational Selection of Content

Today, the problems of rational selection of content are especially crucial. There is a growing trend to exclude from the curriculum certain courses of study. The M.A.C.O.S. controversy, the banning of certain books in schools, has left educators confused about the criteria by which to decide the content of curriculum.* Many school districts have adopted strict guidelines for the inclusion or exclusion of curriculum content. In an effort to gain acceptance of certain programs of study, school superintendents and Boards of Education have appointed citizens to committees to evaluate content, select textbooks, and perform other duties formerly exclusively the domain of school personnel. It is early yet to see how far this trend will go and whether parents and citizens can make any better selections of content than teachers, administrators, and supervisory personnel. The danger of militant groups taking extreme steps to include or exclude content by influencing textbook selection dictates a strong stand by professional educators to repudiate bigotry and alienation in our society.[3]

Relevancy of Subject Matter

Content should be relevant and significant. To be relevant and significant, content must constantly be examined to see that it reflects not only recent scientific knowledge, but also reflects the social and cultural realities of the times.

In the advanced technological age in which we are living, subject matter in school curricula many times becomes obsolete before it reaches the printed or audiovisual form. Publishers and other producers of school materials are faced with not only the growing body of knowledge itself, but the growing complexity of that knowledge. The minimum level of understanding of mathematics and science that an ordinary person must develop to live comfortably in a technical society has increased dramatically in recent years. What is "basic" today was not even imagined fifty years ago.

Similar problems of significance exist in social studies and language arts. What social studies text can keep up with the changes in government experienced in recent years? What literature book can compete with television for the attention of school children? Certainly, there will be a need for texts that deal with fundamental concepts underlying each of the disciplines. Distinguishing what is fundamental or basic knowledge is not an easy task for curriculum planners. The more fundamental a concept, the greater will be the breadth of application, for the concept is fundamental because it has a broad and powerful applicability. In those districts and states where there is mandated mastery of certain "fundamentals," students run the risk of being exposed to information that will have very little applicability outside the classroom.

---

* M.A.C.O.S.—Man A Course of Study, a social studies curriculum project for upper elementary grades which has been attacked by ultra-conservative elements for its value orientations.

If content is to be useful, it must be in tune with the social and cultural realities of the times. American education tends to be overly responsive to immediate social pressures as evidenced by the emphasis on science and mathematics during the Sputnik era and the current back-to-the-basics movement. Although public education must be responsive to society, taking cues from the demands of an immediate situation sometimes leads to an imbalance of curriculum experiences that poorly prepare students for the future. An example was the increased emphasis on science and mathematics in elementary schools after Sputnik was launched because there was supposedly a shortage of technically trained personnel. By the time elementary-grade youngsters became employable, that shortage no longer existed.

Selecting the curriculum experiences that are critical in developing a future generation that can exist in an ever-shrinking world means the curriculum planner must be in tune with a changing world. Independence has changed to interdependence in today's world. Our curriculum can no longer perpetuate the degree of provincialism and ethnocentricity it has in the past. Understanding our own diverse society is important, but we must also have comparative materials and experiences to understand other cultures as well as our own.

Developing loyalty to democratic human values remains a major task of curriculum planners. The breakdown of the great institutions of our society, most especially the family, has led to an alienation of the individual from the basic sources on which to build a value orientation. Modern technology also tends to influence social institutions in directions that are inimical to democratic human values. The challenge of selecting curriculum experiences for today's curriculum planners is to maintain the balance between intellectual proficiency and intelligent social perspective. It is ironic to note that Hilda Taba vividly pointed this out in 1962 as she discussed the impact of technology on American education.

> Some educators take a simple view of the needs arising from a technological society and combine this view with the traditional concept of education. . . . they believe that a technological society simple requires technically prepared people. . . . that the task of the school is to increase and to improve the training in mathematics and science for everyone. . . .[4]

INSTRUCTIONAL ORGANIZATION IN CURRICULUM DEVELOPMENT

If curriculum development is a plan for learning, learning experiences need to be organized so that they serve the educational objectives of a school. This section will examine some of the ways schools are organized so that instruction can be provided. Classroom organization will also be examined to identify ways of organizing curriculum experiences to make learning more efficient.

Individualizing instruction means a child can truly progress at his or her own rate, that he or she can pursue interests in great depth, and that independence and responsibility for learning are fostered. Often a curriculum is ineffective not because its content is ineffective, but because learning experiences are organized in a way to prevent learning. For years, some schools have operated under the following fallacious assumptions:

1. A classroom group size of 30 to 35 students is the most appropriate for a wide variety of learning experiences.
2. The appropriate amount of time for learning a subject is the same uniform period of length, 40 to 60 minutes in length, 6 or 7 periods a day, for 36 weeks out of a year.
3. All learners are capable of mastering the same subject matter in the same length of time. For example, we give everyone the same test on chapter 7 on Friday. We pass everyone from level one of Spanish to level two when June comes.
4. We assume the same material is appropriate to all members of a group. For example, we give the same assignment to the entire group.
5. We assume once a group is formed the same group composition is equally appropriate for a wide variety of learning activities.
6. We assume the same classroom is equally appropriate for a wide variety of learning activities. Conference rooms are not provided for teacher-pupil conferences. Large group facilities are not provided for mass dissemination of materials. Small group rooms are unavailable for discussion activity, etc.
7. We assume the same teacher is qualified to teach all aspects of his subject for one school year.
8. We assume all students require the same kind of supervision.[5]

Operating on these assumptions we lock students into an educational egg-crate, 25 students to a cubicle, from 8 or 9 A.M. to 3 or 4 P.M., 5 days a week for 12 or 13 years. We stand up in front of the students, talking 90 percent of the time, asking them questions which we have deemed appropriate for their formal education. In short, it might be suggested that our present educational system is designed more for the convenience of teaching than it is for the facilitation of learning.

Schools need to break this lockstep approach to instruction. Rigid class sizes, inflexible classroom facilities, and fixed schedules should be challenged by curriculum planners. Organizing schools for instruction is not an easy task. We need to apply all we know about the nature of knowledge, human growth and development, and learning styles of children in formulating a plan for instructional organization.

Graded vs. Nongraded Instruction

The organizational plan used by a majority of schools is the graded plan. Some schools have dropped the artificial barriers of grades and adopted a nongraded organizational plan. There is more evidence of a nongraded structure in the elementary school, especially in the primary years, than any other school level. In recent years schools have been constructed to accommodate a nongraded structure.

Some schools have implemented ability or achievement grouping within grades. Such an arrangement "nongrades" a curriculum, but allows children of the same age level to remain together. An interesting method of cutting across grade lines has been the grouping of students according to physical or social maturity rather than relying on the single criterion of achievement in subject matter. Some middle schools have implemented physical or social grouping arrangements. Others have used exploratory and enrichment courses as a means of breaking down grade barriers. The criterion for grouping in this arrangement is not age or years in school, but an interest in a particular field of study.

A way of appraising graded and nongraded patterns of organizing for instruction can be seen in Table 10.1 beginning on page 158.

ORGANIZING FOR INDIVIDUALIZED INSTRUCTION

There are very few educational plans that do not have as a major goal the individualization of instruction. Individualized instruction remains, however, largely an unfulfilled goal.[6] The topic of individualization is not a new one, nor has it been ignored in the literature. Indeed, we can go back to the 1925 yearbook of the National Society for the Study of Education (NSSE) and find the title of their yearbook to be *Adapting the Schools to Individual Differences.* NSSE also published a 1962 yearbook entitled *Individualizing Instruction.* The literature and work on which those two volumes drew went back over one hundred years. Our addition to whole-class instruction within a graded framework has been strong and some doubt whether we can ever bring about any other forms of instruction.

Instruction focuses upon the teacher's behaviors and the delivery system being used. Perhaps we should use the term "individualized learning" to illustrate that this is the phenomenon we are trying to influence. All teaching must ultimately be construed in terms of the ef-

Table 10.1
Dimensions of Graded and Nongraded Instruction

Dimension	Graded Pattern	Transitional Pattern (Pseudo-Nongraded)	Nongraded Pattern
1. Grouping (Operational practices and/or factors considered)	1. Age	1. Reading ability	1. Multi-factors
	2. Grade achievement	2. Reading levels	2. Multi-age for diversity
	3. Academic progress in relation to grade standards	3. Homogeneity	3. Intra-class grouping for individual and group needs
	4. Homogeneity in subjects	4. Multi-grade for homogeneity	4. Multi-age skills groups —planned for individual needs
	5. Intelligence quotients	5. Academic progress on basis of level standards	5. Multi-age interest groups—planned for individual interest
		6. Subject groups—planned for homogeneity	6. Interclass grouping—for individual and group needs
2. Pupil progress (Operation practices and/or factors considered)	1. Grade requirements	1. Level requirements	1. Multi-factors
	2. Reading ability	2. Reading ability	2. Collective decision based on extensive data
	3. Group standards	3. Traditional marks	3. Mobility to new organizational block after two or three years (no special promotion period)

4. Annual promotion	4. Modification in marking and reporting narrative reports and/or parent conferences	4. Continuous progress on basis of the individual's potential
5. Marks as reflected on report card	5. Promotion upon completion of level requirements (short periods for some students, longer for others)	
3. Teacher (Operational practices and/or factors considered)		
1. Selects curriculum materials on basis of grade	1. Selects curriculum materials on basis of levels (levels equivalent to grades, example: Level 1-We Read Pictures, etc.)	1. Selects curriculum materials on the basis of individual need, interest, and potential
2. Long-range plans based on books, topics or units required for specific grade	2. Long-range plans based on completion of books, topics, or skills designated for a specific level	2. Identifies concepts, attitudes, and skills which are to be a part of a longitudinal program
3. Groups for instruction on the basis of progress in reading texts (Usually three groups)	3. Groups for instruction on basis of skills to be introduced at a specific level	3. Long- and short-range goals determined by individual potential and proficiency
4. Tends to ignore range of reading ability in content area (same text for all in spelling, science, social studies, health, etc.)	4. Tends to ignore range of reading ability in content areas	4. Encourages open-ended pursuits and in-depth study

Dimension	Graded Pattern	Transitional Pattern	Nongraded Pattern
	5. Gives uniform assignments	5. Gives uniform assignments	5. Frequently plans individual conference sessions, seminars, and small group skill sessions
	6. All pupils exposed to same materials—at different periods during the school year	6. All pupils exposed to same materials. Pacing based on completion of materials planned for specific levels	6. Group membership changes frequently (often from period to period and day to day)
	7. Pupil success equated with grade requirements	7. Pupils' success equated with level requirements	7. Open-ended goals—no super-imposed limitations. Limitations determined by individual in academic potential and level of proficiency
	8. Group progress of primary concern	8. Group progress of primary concern	8. Gives personalized assignments including homework
	9. Teacher success based on coverage of graded materials	9. Increased teacher freedom in the selection of materials	9. Utilizes a variety of materials. Only a few copies of any one instructional source utilized
	10. Sex differences, cultural differences and learning styles ignored	10. Sex differences, cultural differences and learning styles ignored	10. Considers individual differences in all curriculum areas
	11. Considers graded manual, curriculum as the perfect guide to instruction success	11. Increased utilization of multi-level materials	11. Works with individuals over an extended period of time

4. Curriculum content (Operational practices and/or factors considered)		
1. Graded textbooks	1. Graded textbooks with levels	12. Utilizes team learning and cooperative teaching whenever feasible
2. Graded course of study	2. Graded course of study translated into levels	1. Recognition of a body of knowledge in each curriculum area
3. Emphasis upon covering designated content within a specific period	3. Emphasis upon covering content designated for each level	2. Emphasis upon individual potential in regard to mastery of skills
4. Emphasis upon mastering designated skills for each grade	4. Emphasis upon covering content designated for each level	3. Introduction, teaching and refinement of content varies with individual learners
5. Mastery of graded content expected of all pupils	5. Mastery of level requirements expected of all pupils—but at a different rate of progress	4. Curriculum content organized on a continuous and recurring scheme
		5. Introduction, teaching and reteaching of concepts and skills based on analysis and diagnosis
		6. Success and mastery relative—viewed in relation to individual differences
		7. Continuity based on understanding and mastery of skills and concepts at lower proficiency levels

fect of teaching on learning. There is no single instructional approach that can be advocated for all types of learners. Eclectic systems that utilize a number of diverse approaches seem likelier to succeed than systems of limited variety.

The following are assumptions for organizing a school for individualized instruction:

1. The organization of the school should not only encourage but require varied rates of pupil progress.
2. Reporting and marking procedures should convey a clear idea of the pupil's rate of progress with respect to his particular developmental norms and standards.
3. Subject matter—i.e., substantive content—must have meaning for the learner and an importance which he both understands and accepts.
4. Administrative policies that govern pupil progress should not be based on a grade-level concept but on a continuum of cumulative experience along which children and youth move at personalized and uneven rates.
5. Provisions for program enrichment and for related school activities should be developed to encourage willing and psychologically sound participation of children moving toward maturity at diverse and uneven rates.
6. The nature of social activities encouraged by the school should not tend to exclude children who are more or less mature than or "different" from their age mates.
7. Reliance should not yet be placed on any single grouping plan, however ingenious it may appear to be.
8. The instructional staff should be sufficiently large, competent, and diversified to permit every child to be well-known by at least one faculty member-counselor at a given time.
9. Instructional aids should not be allowed to supersede a basic reliance on the human element in the teaching-learning process. Large-group instruction must be counter-balanced by small, close-knit groups and guided individualized experience.

Formal and Informal Approaches
to Individualized Instruction

Attempts at individualization fall into two general categories: *informal* and *formal*. In the informal approach, the teacher attempts to stay alert to the fact that some learners need more time and attention to master a particular skill, concept, or body of knowledge, while other learners need less time and attention. Extra practice is given the slow learner while the faster learner is provided with additional challenges. Teachers will use different resources and teaching strategies to reach students of different abilities. Good teachers have followed those practices for years.

In formal systems of individualized instruction, there is an attempt to provide a unique program of studies for every child. This is accomplished by a sequence of diagnosis, prescription, and evaluation. Pretests are used in the diagnosis stage to identify what a student can do in each learning area. A prescription follows which includes the materials necessary to teach the particular skill. Finally, an evaluation procedure called the posttest is administered. The child works through a rather rigid sequence of activities achieving mastery in one level before moving to the next level.

There are several formal systems that are widely used in today's schools. All are found in elementary schools, although these systems have been modified for use in middle schools and high schools. Formal systems have several advantages in practice. They force a school to define clearly what is to be learned and provide a monitoring process to see that it is done. They also demand that mastery of one unit of work be accomplished before the student moves on to the next unit.

Three formal systems that are widely used in elementary schools are Individually Prescribed Instruction (IPI), Program for Learning in Accordance with Needs (PLAN), and Individually Guided Education (IGE), or the Wisconsin Design. IPI was developed by the University of Pittsburgh and Research for Better Schools. PLAN was developed by the Westinghouse Learning Corporation. PLAN utilizes a computer hookup for assessment and involves a series of teacher-learner units (TLU's).

IGE was developed by the University of Wisconsin and later used by the Institute for Development of Educational Activities (IDEA). IGE is a comprehensive system of organization and management of instruction and learning environments. It represents an alternative to schools organized in either age-graded, self-contained classrooms or in subject-centered departments.[7] A typical IGE school organization is illustrated in Figure 10.1 on page 164.[8]

Along with the advantages of formal systems, there are disadvantages. In comparison with total class instruction, systems like IPI and PLAN reduce the time pupils and teachers are in contact. Students sometimes move from unit to unit or packet of materials to packet of materials without much contact with an adult or other students. Another problem involves the amount of paperwork required in such programs. Unless teacher aides or parent volunteers are available, teachers sometimes are overwhelmed by recordkeeping. PLAN does utilize a computer for this task, but at considerable expense. In IPI and IGE the teacher or aide must keep the records.

It is difficult to determine whether formal or informal systems of individualized instruction result in greater learning on the part of stu-

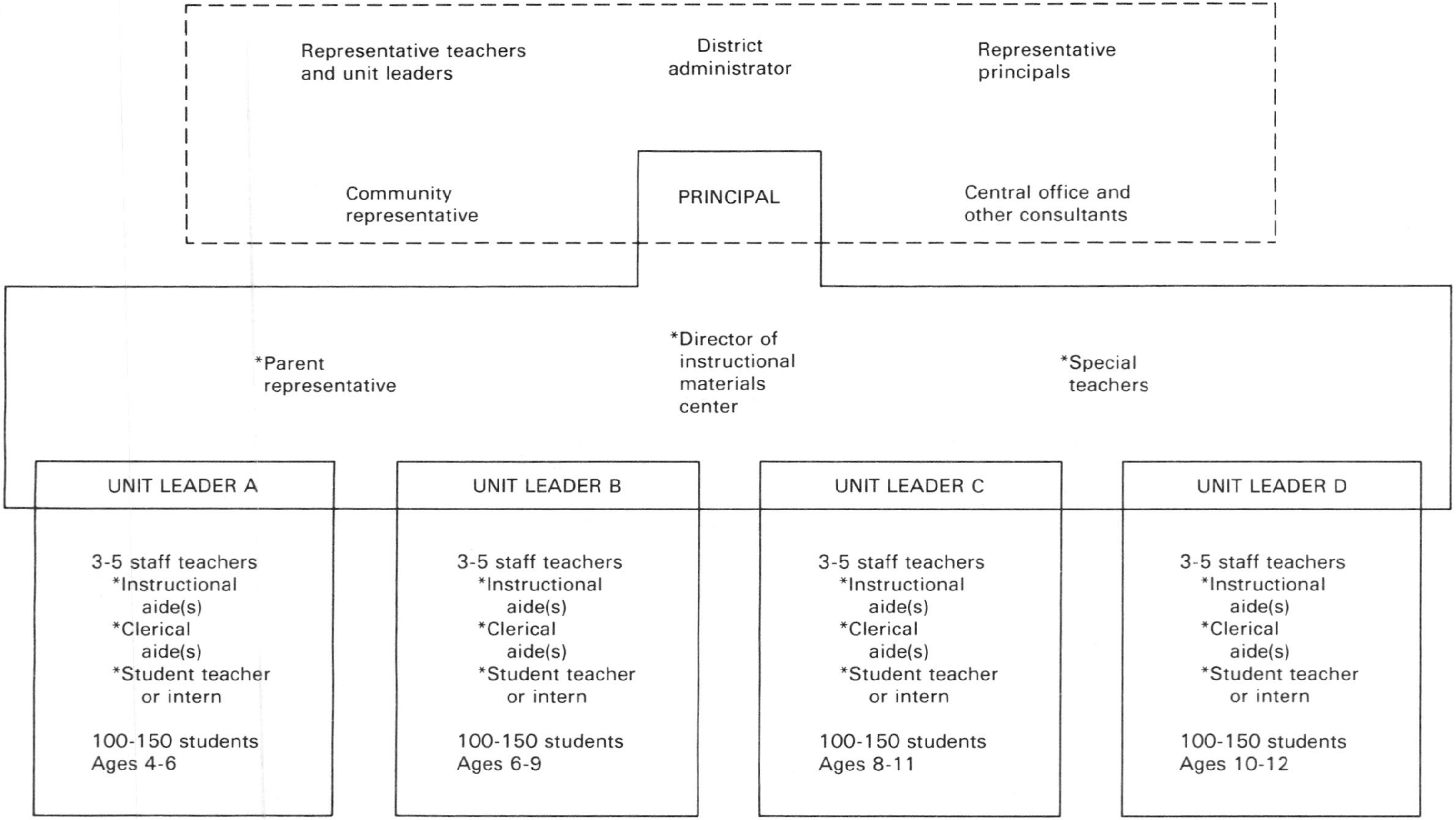

Figure 10.1
Multiunit Organization of IGE School of 400–600 Students

The organizational chart contains the following elements:

Top grouping (dashed box):
- Representative teachers and unit leaders
- District administrator
- Representative principals
- Community representative
- Central office and other consultants

- PRINCIPAL

- *Director of instructional materials center
- *Special teachers
- *Parent representative

UNIT LEADER A
3-5 staff teachers
*Instructional aide(s)
*Clerical aide(s)
*Student teacher or intern
100-150 students
Ages 4-6

UNIT LEADER B
3-5 staff teachers
*Instructional aide(s)
*Clerical aide(s)
*Student teacher or intern
100-150 students
Ages 6-9

UNIT LEADER C
3-5 staff teachers
*Instructional aide(s)
*Clerical aide(s)
*Student teacher or intern
100-150 students
Ages 8-11

UNIT LEADER D
3-5 staff teachers
*Instructional aide(s)
*Clerical aide(s)
*Student teacher or intern
100-150 students
Ages 10-12

dents. It is not guaranteed that individualized instruction, formal or informal, results in greater learning. There are many variables influencing the success of an instructional program, such as the training and support given teachers, the Hawthorne effect, and the enthusiasm of teachers who volunteer for special programs. We should not get so involved with the cult of individualized instruction that we lose sight of the fact that individualizing instruction is a means, not an end, in education.[9]

Scheduling Instructional Groups

A number of formal plans for scheduling instructional groups have been developed over the years. The Trump plan and the nongraded high school are two organizational plans that have influenced the secondary school. The Trump plan advocates variable schedules for individual and class activities. It attacks the traditional class period of 50–60 minutes. Periods of variable length provide for greater flexibility in organizing the instructional program. In variable scheduling, the school day is divided into time frames (modules) of 15–20 minutes each. The grouping of the modules allows for shorter or longer periods of time. The nongraded high school received the most attention from the plan implemented at the Melbourne (Florida) Senior High School.[10] In the Melbourne school, the content and learning units, except for some nonacademic subjects, are divided into five phases rather than into the traditional subject pattern:

Phase One: Subjects designed for students needing special attention in small classes.

Phase Two: Subjects designed for students needing more emphasis on the basic skills.

Phase Three: Materials designed for average ability in the subject matter.

Phase Four: Subject matter designed for capable students seeking education in depth.

Phase Five: Challenging new courses available to students with exceptional ability who are willing to assume responsibility for their own learning and go beyond the requirements of the normal high school.

Phase Six: Nonacademic subjects offered that do not permit student mobility; for example, typing and physical education are upgraded but unphased.

Other plans of scheduling instructional groups such as core instruction, interdisciplinary instruction, and the previously mentioned IGE plan have been applied to elementary, middle, and high schools. Whether instructional groups are scheduled by content, at grade level, or across grade levels, classroom teachers still must be able to schedule instructional groups within a single classroom. Elementary teachers have met with greater success in scheduling within a classroom than high school teachers. Through the use of skill groups, interest groups, and learning centers, elementary teachers have been able to shift groups or the nature of pupil activities. Middle school teachers have adopted many of the elementary techniques of organizing for instruction and have added core arrangements and interdisciplinary units of instruction to provide for even more flexibility. Unfortunately, very few high schools have moved beyond the traditional type of scheduling that requires that all subjects be taught the same length of class time and the same number of days a year.

Homogeneous vs. Heterogeneous Grouping

Homogeneous grouping refers to the practice of assigning students to instructional groups on the basis of their similarity, presumed ability, or achievement. This is sometimes called *tracking.* The major argument in favor of homogeneous grouping is that pupils of equal ability can be taught more efficiently than children of varying abilities. There are many arguments against grouping children homogeneously. They include research data indicating that homgeneous ability grouping tends to sort pupils into somewhat socioeconomic groups, that errors in placement of pupils are often made, and that designated "smart" or "slow" children do not perform any better or worse because of the way they are grouped. Another serious objection is that the process of labeling "slow" children can have serious consequences in their lives, because they accept and ultimately internalize the school's judgment of them.

Heterogeneous grouping allows students of varying abilities, interests, and achievement to interact together in an instructional group. It is interesting to note that parents do not object to homogeneous grouping as long as their children are in a "high" track.

Recent federal court decisions and legislation have resulted in decisions and regulations barring tracking of elementary and secondary students on the basis of ability or sex. Title Nine federal regulations have barred grouping practices based on sex of students. For instance, home economics and industrial arts classes must provide equal opportunity for the enrollment of both boys and girls. Sports programs cannot be limited to just boys. The Federal District Court of Washington, D.C. ruled in 1976 that the practice of ability grouping was unconstitutional because it was discriminatory and resulted in the denial of equal protection of the laws for children from varying racial and socioeconomic backgrounds. That decision and others led many school administrators to reexamine their grouping practices.

RESOURCES FOR LEARNING

Learning resources are not limited to textbooks and traditional teaching materials. Learning resources are now so varied, plentiful, and powerful that they are sometimes confusing to the teacher. The recent extensive application of technology to education has created a critical need to establish criteria for the selection of learning resources. Curriculum planners need to give much consideration to the selection and use of learning resources as more and more commercial materials are produced for schools.

Guidelines for Selection of Learning Resources

Perhaps the most important characteristic to be considered in selecting any resource for learning is its relevancy to the goal-seeking activity involved. The use of an outdated textbook or films without relation to the subject at hand certainly indicates that a teacher has ignored the obvious criterion of relevancy.

A second criterion to be used in the selection of learning resources is accuracy. For years, texts and other materials depicted all children in pictures as white. Sex roles were obvious in those same materials. Recently, a national awareness of cultural pluralism and changing sex roles has caused publishers and other producers of school materials to eliminate sexist and racist types of references in materials. Teachers need to help pupils identify particular biases, such as those used for advertising, and use materials showing different viewpoints.

Resources for learning should be selected that are appropriate to the needs and interests of the learners. Relevant materials are available on almost any topic to fit any level of student ability or maturity. Teachers must select a wide range of resources sufficient to provide for each individual. Student interests, though, do not dictate that only materials of interest to students should be included in the curriculum. The danger of organizing all resources around the current interests and needs of children, except perhaps in the primary grades, has long been recognized. George Counts in the 1926 Yearbook of the National Society for the Study of Education (NSSE) stated, "Nothing should be included in the curriculum merely because it is of interest to the children, but whatsoever is included should be brought into the closest possible relation with their interest."[11]

The Influence of Mass Media

Today's educators are faced with growing evidence that television, radio, and other media now have as much impact on learning as all of the learning resources provided by the school. Students spend as much time in front of the television sets as they do in the classroom. The difficulty of influencing what students listen to or view away from the school has resulted in little or no reaction from curriculum planners. Recently, curriculum planners have begun to view mass media as a resource that can have a positive influence on student learning. Technological advances now make it possible to tape outstanding television programs and replay them with supporting instruction during the school day. Local and national television companies are now providing study guides and other resources to schools to help them utilize taped programs. *Beauty and the Beast,* an outstanding television production, is being shown in schools. Combining viewing that production with a careful analysis of the written story makes a dull literature class come alive. Networks and local affiliates are producing written texts of television programs so students can improve reading skills.

Concern over quality of programming has resulted in a call for schools to provide students with skills for sorting out the messages provided by the media. Unfortunately, because the structure of mass communication requires it to be relevant to all, it ends up being relevant to none. In theory, the function of information is to increase control over our lives. Mass media is often about events so far removed from our lives that there is little or nothing we can do to affect or even verify them. Rather than media helping us feel informed, involved, and in command of our destinies, it often makes up feel helpless or alienated. The challenge then to schools is to work in cooperation with the producers of mass media to turn media into a positive learning resource. Mass communication represents a resource for lifelong learning. Harnessing this resource may be the most important task ahead for curriculum planners.

Human Resources for Learning

Significant curriculum plans give first importance to the role of human resources for learning. Beginning with the classroom teacher, to other school personnel and community people, the potential of human resources is unlimited. Resources sometimes forgotten are pupils themselves. Working in pairs on projects, serving as tutors, or presenting material to the class, students can help carry out many learning activities. Enthusiasm for learning can be greatly increased when students find resources for learning other than the classroom teacher or textbook.

Selecting Appropriate Teaching Strategies

Strategies or methods of teaching include all those techniques, procedures, manipulations, and facilitations of content and learning environments that are performed by teachers. There are seven functions that are of vital importance to effective teaching. Teachers must be able to:

1. identify and separate the contributing elements constituting a given teaching-learning situation
2. conceptualize the relationships between those interacting elements
3. select and plan appropriate instructional strategies
4. develop and sharpen suitable skills in order to translate the selected strategies into practice
5. acquire reliable and meaningful feedback in the form of empirical and objective data
6. evaluate the effectiveness of the selected strategies
7. modify and revise strategies for future improvement.

Preliminary to developing curriculum plans, the teacher must answer the following questions:

Who are my students?
What should they learn?
How should they learn it?
When should they learn it?

Teaching strategies then are preceded by a determination of the characteristics of the learners, including physical and intellectual characteristics, age level, maturity, reading ability, I.Q., and performance evaluations. Other data including attitudes, learning styles, and cultural backgrounds provide valuable clues to teachers and other curriculum planners.

Determining what the student should learn involves establishing criteria for the selection of content. Those criteria include determining whether the content is valid, significant, and consistent with social realities.

While questions of content may be difficult to answer, determining how and when to present content is an easier task if data regarding students form the basis for instructional decisions. Once curriculum planners determine needs and interests of learning, the next step is the selection of appropriate strategies to help achieve stated objectives. Different students do learn at different rates and in different ways. Some methods are more appropriate than others. Some are more effective. The selection of teaching strategies is but one step in a complicated teaching-learning process that begins with a thorough knowledge of the learner.

Popham and Baker have identified a series of instructional activities to promote the learner's attainment of instructional objectives. They include:

1. Appropriate Practice—allowing the learner opportunities to practice the behavior implied by the instructional objective.
2. Knowledge of Results—the teacher allowing a pupil to discover whether his responses are adequate.

3. Analyzing and Sequencing Learner Behaviors—identifying and sequencing learner behaviors to be mastered enroute to the achievement of an educational objective.
4. Perceived Purpose—identifying the methods used to develop a learning set where learners perceive the worth of what they are studying.
5. Evaluation—includes pre-assessment of learner competencies, test-construction, item sampling, and interpretation of student-performance data.[12]

Selecting appropriate teaching strategies then is a key element in the instructional process. Figure 10.2 will help the reader see the relationship of the phase of selecting teaching strategies to other phases of the instructional process.

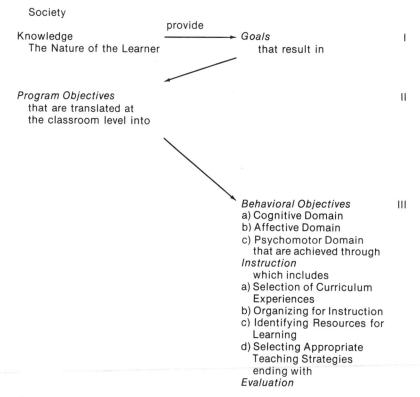

Bases of the Curriculum

Society

Knowledge   provide
The Nature of the Learner   →   *Goals*   I
         that result in

Program Objectives   II
   that are translated at
   the classroom level into

Behavioral Objectives   III
a) Cognitive Domain
b) Affective Domain
c) Psychomotor Domain
   that are achieved through
Instruction
   which includes
a) Selection of Curriculum
   Experiences
b) Organizing for Instruction
c) Identifying Resources for
   Learning
d) Selecting Appropriate
   Teaching Strategies
   ending with
Evaluation

Figure 10.2
A Model of the Instructional Process

Teachers can select from a variety of teaching strategies to present or deliver instruction to students. The options presently available in today's public school classrooms are as follows:

1. **COMPARATIVE ANALYSIS**—A thought process, structured by the teacher, that employs the description, classification, and analysis of more than one system, group, or the like in order to ascertain and evaluate similarities and differences.
2. **CONFERENCE**—A one-to-one interaction between teacher and learner where the individual's needs and problems can be dealt with. Diagnosis, evaluation, and prescription may all be involved.
3. **DEMONSTRATION**—An activity in which the teacher or another person uses examples, experiments, and/or other actual performance to illustrate a principle or show others how to do something.
4. **DIAGNOSIS**—The continuous determination of the nature of learning difficulties and deficiences, used in teaching as a basis for the selection, day by day or moment by moment, of appropriate content and methods of instruction.
5. **DIRECTED OBSERVATION**—Guided observation provided for the purpose of improving the study, understanding, and evaluation of that which is observed.
6. **DISCUSSION**—An activity in which pupils, under teacher and/or pupil direction, exchange points of view concerning a topic, question, or problem to arrive at a decision or conclusion.
7. **DRILL**—An orderly, repetitive learning activity intended to help develop or fix a specific skill or aspect of knowledge.
8. **EXPERIMENTATION**—An activity involving a planned procedure accompanied by control of conditions and/or controlled variation of conditions together with observation of results for the purpose of discovering relationships and evaluating the reasonableness of a specific hypothesis.
9. **FIELD EXPERIENCE**—Educational work experience, sometimes fully paid, acquired by pupils in a practical service situation.
10. **FIELD TRIP**—An educational trip to places where pupils can study the content of instruction directly in its functional setting, e.g., factory, newspaper office, or fire department.
11. **GROUP WORK**—A process in which members of the class, working cooperatively rather than individually, formulate and work toward common objectives under the guidance of one or more leaders.
12. **LABORATORY EXPERIENCE**—Learning activities carried on by pupils in a laboratory designed for individual or group study of a particular subject-matter area, involving the practical application of theory through observation, experimentation, and research, or, in the case of foreign language instruction, involving learning through demonstration, drill,

and practice. This applies also to the study of art and music, although such activity in this instance may be referred to as a studio experience.

13. **LECTURE**—An activity in which the teacher gives an oral presentation of facts or principles, the class frequently being responsible for note-taking. This activity usually involves little or no pupil participation by questioning or discussion.

14. **MANIPULATIVE AND TACTILE ACTIVITY**—Activity by which pupils utilize the movement of various muscles and the sense of touch to develop manipulative and/or perceptual skills.

15. **MODELING AND IMITATION**—An activity frequently used for instruction in speech, in which the pupils listen to and observe a model as a basis upon which to practice and improve their performance.

16. **PROBLEM SOLVING**—A thought process structured by the teacher and employed by the pupils for clearly defining a problem, forming hypothetical solutions, and possibly testing the hypothesis.

17. **PROGRAMMED INSTRUCTION**—Instruction utilizing a workbook or mechanical and/or electronic device which has been programmed by (a) providing instruction in small steps, (b) asking one or more questions about each step in the instruction and providing instant knowledge of whether each answer is right or wrong, and (c) enabling pupils to progress at their own pace.

18. **PROJECT**—A significant, practical unit of activity having educational value, aimed at one or more definite goals of understanding and involving the investigation and solution of problems.

19. **READING**—Gathering information from books, periodicals, encyclopedias, and other printed sources of information, including oral reading and silent reading by individuals.

20. **RECITATION**—Activities devoted to reporting to a class or other group about information acquired through individual study or group work.

21. **ROLE-PLAY**—An activity in which students and/or teacher take on the behavior of a hypothetical or real personality in order to solve a problem and gain insight into a situtation.

22. **SEMINAR**—An activity in which a group of pupils, engaged in research or advanced study, meets under the general direction of one or more staff members for a discussion of problems of mutual interest.

SUMMARY

Instructional considerations in curriculum development include the selection of curriculum experiences, organizing for instruction, identi-

1. A good curriculum provides experiences that are rich and varied and designed for culturally diverse students.
   a) Content is in tune with social and cultural realities of the times.
   b) Subject matter has meaning for the learner and an importance the student accepts and understands.
   c) Classroom activities are arranged to provide a balanced program of learning opportunities.
2. A good curriculum is organized flexibly to serve the educational objectives of the school.
   a) Grouping practices do not discriminate against students because of their sex, race, or socioeconomic status.
   b) Both formal and informal grouping methods are used to promote individualization of instruction.
   c) Variable time allotments and schedules are provided for individual and group activities.
3. A good curriculum utilizes resources that are appropriate to the needs and interests of learners.
   a) Resources are selected that are relevant to the goal-seeking activities involved.
   b) Materials are used that are free from biases of sexism and racism.
   c) Students are provided with necessary skills for sorting out messages provided by mass media.
4. A good curriculum includes appropriate teaching strategies to carry out learning objectives.
   a) Teaching strategies take into consideration characteristics of learners.
   b) Cooperative teaching and planning are encouraged so teachers can share learning resources and special talents.
   c) Classroom practices give attention to the maturity and learning problems of each student.

Figure 10.3

A Checklist of Curriculum Planning Considerations

fying resources for learning, and choosing teaching strategies. Selection of curriculum experiences has to include a balance of activities leading to the personal development of the learner, skill building, and acquisition of knowledge. Materials, subject matter, and activities should promote cultural diversity and be relevant and significant.

There are many ways of organizing for instruction. There are few organizational plans that do not have as a major goal individualization of instruction. Formal and informal approaches to individualized instruction are found in today's schools. Major formal programs include IGE, IPI, and PLAN. Homogeneous and heterogeneous grouping patterns are used in schools. Recent court decisions have attacked homogeneous grouping as being discriminatory against minorities and certain socioeconomic groups.

Resources for learning should be free from biases and appropriate to the interest and needs of learners. The influence of mass media is a subject of much concern to educators.

Teaching strategies are determined by the nature of the learner and the learning objectives established for that learner.

Notes

1. Ernest F. Garcia, "Chicano Cultural Diversity: Implications for Competency Based Teacher Education." ERIC Documents, ED 901375 (May, 1974): 15.
2. A.S.C.D. Multicultural Education Commission, "Encouraging Multicultural Education," *Educational Leadership* 34, No. 4 (January, 1977): 291.
3. Joseph Watras, "The Textbook Dispute in West Virginia: A New Form of Oppression," *Educational Leadership* 33, No. 1 (October, 1975): 21–23.
4. Hilda Taba, *Curriculum Development, Theory and Practice* (New York: Harcourt, Brace and World, Inc., 1962), p. 40.
5. Joseph C. Bondi, Jr., *Developing Middle Schools: A Guidebook* (Wheeling, Illinois: Whitehall Company, Publishers, 1977), p. 87.
6. Robert H. Anderson, "Individualization—The Unfulfilled Goal," *Educational Leadership* 34, No. 5 (February, 1977): 323–24.
7. Herbert Klausmeir, Richard Rossmiller, and Mary Saily, *Individually Guided Elementary Education* (New York: Academic Press, 1977), p. 1.
8. Klausmeir, Rossmiller, Saily, *Individually Guided Elementary Education,* p. 12.
9. George Weber, "The Cult of Individualized Instruction," *Educational Leadership* 34, No. 5 (February, 1977): 326–29.
10. B. Frank Brown, *The Nongraded High School* (Englewood Cliffs, N.J.: Prentice-Hall, Inc., 1963).
11. George S. Counts, "Some Notes on the Foundations of Curriculum Making," in *The Foundations of Curriculum Making.* 26th yearbook, Part II, National Society for the Study of Education (Bloomington, Indiana: Public School Publishers Co., 1926), p. 80.
12. James Popham and Eva Baker, *Planning an Instructional Sequence* (Englewood Cliffs, N.J.: Prentice-Hall, Inc., 1963), pp. 2–3.

Suggested Learning Activities

1. Develop an instructional plan in your own teaching field. Consider the differences it will make if the focus is on (a) content, or (b) student interests.

2. Conduct a panel discussion on the pros and cons of homogeneous and heterogeneous grouping.

3. You are on a curriculum committee to examine formal systems for individualizing instruction such as IGE, IPI, or PLAN. What criteria would you use for appraising such approaches?

4. Summarize the research on nongraded vs. graded instruction.

5. Develop guidelines you would use for the selection of learning resources in your classroom or school.

6. Develop a "television viewing" unit that would help your students identify and analyze the messages provided by that medium.

Books to Review

Berman, Louise and Roderick, Jesse. *Curriculum: Teaching the What, How, and Why of Living.* Columbus, Ohio: Charles E. Merrill Publishing Company, 1977.

Gagne, Robert and Briggs, Leslie. *Principles of Instructional Design.* New York: Holt, Rinehart and Winston, Inc., 1974.

Hass, Glen; Bondi, Joseph; and Wiles, Jon. *Curriculum Planning: A New Approach.* Boston: Allyn and Bacon, Inc., 1974.

Popham, James and Baker, Eva. *Planning an Instructional Sequence.* Englewood Cliffs, New Jersey: Prentice-Hall, Inc., 1970.

_____. *Systematic Instruction.* Englewood Cliffs, New Jersey: Prentice-Hall, Inc., 1970.

Ragan, William and Shepherd, Gene. *Modern Elementary Curriculum,* 5th edition. New York: Holt, Rinehart and Winston, 1977.

Saylor, Galen and Alexander, William. *Curriculum Planning for Modern Schools.* New York: Holt, Rinehart and Winston, Inc., 1966.

Taba, Hilda. *Curriculum Development—Theory and Practice.* New York: Harcourt, Brace, and World, Inc., 1962.

11

Research and Evaluation
in Curriculum Development

Research and evaluation play a unique role in the curriculum development process. Because the study and assessment of educational programs often suggest a discrepancy or need, research and evaluation serve an initiating role in the development of curriculum. There is a natural and cyclical relationship between educational inquiry, curriculum development, and evaluation processes.

Evaluation is a broadly defined term that refers to efforts to assess the effects of educational programs. In most school settings, the use of the term *evaluation* includes research activities, the systematic testing of data, clarifying discrepancies between goals and objectives, and a decision-making function. Common targets of the evaluation process are the appraisal of student outcomes, determining the value of the curriculum, and the assessment of administrative and managerial practices.

Evaluation in schools might best be thought of as the basis for effective decision making about programs experienced by students. Quality programs in schools are dependent on good decision making by school planners. Such decisions result when alternatives are known. Knowing about alternatives calls for valid and reliable information, and the availability of such information depends on a systematic way of providing it. Thus, evaluation can be thought of as the process needed to provide information for decision making in schools.

THE EMERGENCE OF EDUCATIONAL RESEARCH

From a historical standpoint, educational research has come a long way in the past twenty years. Early studies, plagued by methodological problems and inconclusive findings, resulted in criticism both from inside education and from outside groups. Highly respected researchers Campbell and Stanley have commented with regard to experimentation in schools:

> . . . there seems to be two main types of experimentation going on in schools: (1) research "imposed" upon the school by an outsider, who has his own ax to grind and whose goal is not immediate action (change) by the school; and (2) the so-called action researcher who tries to get teachers themselves to be experimenters, using that word quite loosely. The first researcher gets results that may be highly rigorous but not applicable. The latter gets results that may be highly applicable, but probably not "true" because of the extreme lack of rigor in research.[1]

A sample of outside opinion is found in the summary statement of a Rand Corporation study of educational research: "Data used by researchers are, at best, crude measures of what is really happening. Education is an extremely subtle phenomenon. Researchers in education are plagued by the virtual impossibility of measuring those aspects of education they wish to study."[2]

One major problem with early educational research was that it did not clearly address the question, What is to be evaluated? Research in schools was conducted as if in a vacuum, causing the findings of such study to be limited to the context of the inquiry. An exception to this rather myopic focus was a comprehensive study known as the Eight Year Study, or the Thirty Schools Study, conducted during the late 1920s and early 1930s. In this study, the importance of evaluation to curriculum development was demonstrated through the relating of objectives and learning activities.

Another early failure of educational research was to see schools as a social system with feedback functions. Hence, the planning, activating, and assessing functions of curriculum development were seen and enacted in isolation. Evaluation data were not brought to bear on educational programs.

A final difficulty with most educational research prior to the 1960s was the absence of accurate statistical treatment of data gathered. Data gathered in school environments were interpreted by researchers without controls, causing the reliability of many findings to be challenged. The result of this condition was an extremely low credibility for all educational research.

As the entire field of education grew and became specialized, so too did the area of educational research. The emergence of a cadre of trained educational researchers led to improved methodologies, a research language, more accurate statistical treatment of data, and large funded projects. Such an emergence is still occurring and evidence of an emphasis on research in education is all about us.

Perhaps the greatest impetus for an evaluation emphasis throughout education in the 1960s and 1970s, other than funding, has been the legal legitimacy given to the educational researchers. In state after state, educational programs have been mandated by law to be "accountable; to be held responsible for the results they achieve." The landmark bill, California's Stull Bill, set the tone for successive legislation:

> Each school district is required to adopt specific evaluation and assessment guidelines which shall include but not necessarily be limited to (a) the establishment of standards of expected student progress in each area of study and of techniques for the assessment of that progress (b) assessment of certified personnel competence as it relates to the establishment standards. *

Subsequent legal activity in states has led to state-wide accountability plans such as the Standards of Quality enacted in Virginia during the 1970s, and the establishment of minimal graduation competencies such as those found in California and Florida. Almost every school in the nation has been touched by the emergence of "evaluation" in education.

In the 1980s, those persons responsible for developing school programs will share increased responsibility for evaluating school programs. Curriculum leaders will need to be familiar with the many aspects of the evaluation process and possess skills to supervise the revision of existing activities. Among the many evaluative activities, curriculum personnel will have responsibilities in the following areas: establishing evaluation programs, focusing evaluation, designing evaluation systems, assessing educational research, translating research findings into programs, and reporting findings of educational research to others in the school environment.

ESTABLISHING EVALUATION PROGRAMS

Curriculum leaders, in their search to make effective decisions about school programs, will increasingly study available research concern-

---

* California Assembly Bill 293, Ch. 361 Sec. 13403–13489, Education Code, enacted July, 1971.

ing education. Where quality research exists, improved practices for schools will be suggested. In the absence of quality research, curriculum specialists will need to establish evaluation programs which will give them the type of information to make such decisions.

There are some existing guidelines found in most curriculum texts which indicate the type of concerns general to all programs. Saylor and Alexander provide one such list in their "marks of a good curriculum":

1. The program should be systematically planned and systematically evaluated.
2. Learning opportunities should reflect the aims of the school.
3. Balance should be maintained among all of the goals of the school.
4. Continuity among learning experiences should be promoted.
5. Flexibility in the curriculum should be both encouraged and utilized.
6. Each learner should be provided for adequately.[3]

In order to check on such criteria, the curriculum leader needs to establish various evaluation programs and initiate research in numerous areas. Examples of such areas are student performance, staff development patterns, parent-community feedback, policies and regulations, utilization of facilities and resources, design of specific programs, effectiveness of instruction, and administrative procedures. Collectively, research in these and other areas will lead to a comprehensive evaluation program for the school, as illustrated in Figure 11.1.

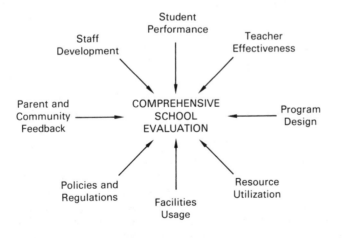

Figure 11.1

In most districts, one of three types of comprehensive evaluation will be conducted on a regular basis: an accreditation visit, a school survey, or a needs assessment. Although they are similar, these three types of comprehensive evaluation differ in important ways.

Accreditation

Accreditation visits occur at regular intervals, every five or ten years, and assess schools according to quantitative criteria. They possess an organizational orientation, and analyze schools in terms of what presently exists. They are comprehensive studies dealing with all aspects of school life. Accreditation teams use established standards to assess programs and make evaluations about what has already occurred in a school.

School Surveys

School surveys, like accreditation visits, view schools externally and look at what has already occurred in the school. They use many of the same standards used by accreditation agencies, but usually evaluate the programs in only those areas identified for analysis. Surveys are conducted when needed, and usually rely heavily on the judgment of a panel of selected experts. School surveys, like accreditation visits, usually have a quantitative orientation and focus heavily on structure.

Needs Assessments

Needs assessments, unlike accreditation visits and school surveys, focus primarily on school programs and their clients. They tend to be prescriptive, as opposed to descriptive, and are often conducted internally by members of the organization under review. Needs assessments are just that; they identify problems and tie suggestions to remediation of those problems.

These three common forms of general evaluation found in schools are contrasted in Table 11.1.

Major comprehensive evaluations are most productively thought of as a problem-identification/problem-solving mechanism. They assist schools in clarification of goals, they gather and analyze evidence of attainment of those goals, they identify discrepancies, and they suggest corrections. As a process, major evaluations are cyclical in nature as shown in Figure 11.2, page 182.

All evaluation efforts should have three basic characteristics: diagnostic, descriptive, and directive. Evaluation studies should help schools assess where they presently are in relation to their goals. Evaluation studies should provide a record of present conditions in a language understandable to all involved. Evaluation efforts should also indicate the ways in which schools should change in order to be more effective in accomplishing their goals. In order for evaluation and research to possess these characteristics, they must be focused. In short, what is to be assessed must be clear.

Table 11.1
School Evaluations

Accreditation	Survey	Needs Assessment
Organizational orientation	Administrative orientation	Programmatic orientation
Concern with structure, organization	Concern with structure and management	Concern with clients and corresponding programs
Analysis of what actually exists (descriptive)	Analysis of what actually exists (descriptive)	Assessment of what should be in existence (prescriptive)
Scheduled	Self-contained	Tied to remediation
Comprehensive	Quasi-comprehensive	Focused on client needs
Validation emphasis	Judgmental	Objective with design

	Data	
Pupil-teacher ratio	Community background	School-community history
Number library books	Administration and organization	Achievement patterns
Statement of purpose	Instructional patterns	Attitudes toward school
Quality of buildings	Finance	Motivation, self-concepts
Financial patterns	Extracurricular	Student interests
Pupil-personnel services		Teacher perceptions
STANDARDS	STANDARDS	PROBLEMS
EXTERNAL	EXTERNAL	INTERNAL
Post-evaluation	Post-evaluation	Pre-evaluation

One question concerning the focus of evaluation is whether it is to address design, process, or product. If, for example, evaluation activity was being conducted in a fourth grade math class, do we hope to learn (1) if the math program is sound in its construction, (2) if the interaction between teacher and students is fostering positive atti-

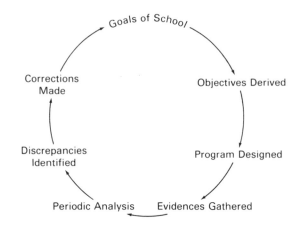

Figure 11.2
Focusing Evaluation

tudes toward math, or (3) if the students score well on achievement tests measuring mathematics skills? Without such focus, it is unlikely that an evaluation program will tell us what we wish to know.

Another question related to the focus of the evaluation effort is whether our inquiry is formative or summative. That is, to use the example above, do we wish to know how the students are doing in math or how they have done in math. If the evaluation is formative in nature, corrections can be made. If the evaluation is summative, the judgment is absolute.

Finally, it is important to know if the intention of the evaluation is really to evaluate or to validate. Do we seek to make a judgment of the relative progress of the fourth graders according to some external criteria, or are we merely "keeping score" of their progress to date?

By focusing evaluation efforts prior to their activation, there is a greater chance that the assessment will have value.

DESIGNING EVALUATION SYSTEMS

In cases where existing patterns of evaluation do not exist, curriculum leaders may be called upon to construct designs that will provide data for decision making. In setting up a design, the curriculum worker will need to decide how the study is to be focused, how the data will be collected, the way information will be organized and analyzed, how the data and findings are to be reported, and the way the evaluation effort is to be administered.

Daniel Stufflebeam has developed an outline or evaluation structure that is general to all types of evaluation:

A. Focusing the Evaluation
   1. Identify the major level(s) of decision-making to be served e.g., local, state, or national.
   2. For each level of decision-making, project the decision situations to be served and describe each one in terms of its locus, focus, timing, and composition of alternatives.
   3. Define criteria for each decision situation by specifying variables for measurement and standards for use in the judgment of alternatives.
   4. Define policies within which the evaluation must operate.
B. Collection of information
   1. Specify the source of the information to be collected.
   2. Specify the instruments and methods for collecting the needed information.
   3. Specify the sampling procedure to be employed.
   4. Specify the conditions and schedule for information collection.
C. Organization of Information
   1. Specify a format for the information which is to be collected.
   2. Specify a means for coding, organizing, storing, and retrieving information.
D. Analysis of Information
   1. Specify the analytical procedures to be employed.
   2. Specify a means for performing the analysis.
E. Reporting of Information
   1. Define the audiences for the evaluation reports.
   2. Specify means for providing information to the audiences.
   3. Specify the format for evaluation reports and/or reporting sessions.
   4. Schedule the reporting information.
F. Administration of the Evaluation
   1. Summarize the evaluation schedule.
   2. Define staff and resource requirements and plans for meeting these requirements.
   3. Specify means for meeting policy requirements for conduct of the evaluation.
   4. Evaluate the potential of the evaluation design for providing information which is valid, reliable, credible, timely, and pervasive.
   5. Specify and schedule means for periodic updating of the evaluation design.
   6. Provide a budget for the total evaluation program.[4]

Another useful resource for curriculum leaders responsible for designing evaluation systems is a classification outline developed by the Phi Delta Kappa National Study Committee on Evaluation. This outline presents the following four types of evaluation commonly found in schools according to their objective, method, and relationship to the decision-making process:

1. Context Evaluation

Objective:	To define the operation context, to identify and assess needs in the context, and to identify and delineate problems underlying the needs.
Method:	By describing individually and in relevant perspectives the major sub-systems of the context; by comparing actual and intended inputs and outputs of the subsystems; and by analyzing possible causes of discrepancies between actualities and intentions.
Relation to DM Process:	For deciding upon the setting to be served, the goals associated with meeting needs and the objectives associated with solving problems, i.e., for planning needed changes.

2. Input Evaluation

Objective:	To identify and assess system capabilities, available input strategies, and designs for implementing strategies.
Method:	By describing and analyzing available human and material resources, solution strategies, and procedural designs for relevance, feasibility, and economy in the course of action to be taken.
Relation to DM Process:	For selecting sources of support, solution strategies, and procedural designs, i.e., for programming change activities.

3. Process Evaluation

Objective:	To identify or predict, in process, defects in procedural design or its implementation, and to maintain a record of procedural events and activities.
Method:	By monitoring the activity's potential procedural barriers and remaining alert to unanticipated ones.
Relation to DM Process:	For implementing and refining the program design and procedure, i.e., for effecting process control.

4. Product Evaluation

Objective:	To relate outcome information to objectives and to context, input, and process information.
Method:	By defining operationally and measuring criteria associated with the objectives, by comparing these measurements with predetermined standards or comparative bases, and by interpreting the outcome in terms of recorded input and process information.
Relation to DM Process:	For deciding to continue, terminate, modify, or refocus a change activity, and for linking the activity to other major phases of the change process, i.e., for evolving change activities.[5]

ASSESSING EDUCATIONAL RESEARCH

Another task for curriculum workers that is related to school evaluation activities is to assess educational research. In some cases such research will be conducted external to the school district while in other cases the research will be "in-house" evaluation. The curriculum specialist should be able to identify good research and be able to assess research reports.

Good research possesses a number of characteristics which, while seemingly obvious, distinguishes it from mediocre research. The following guidelines will assist the review of research efforts:

1. The problem should be clearly stated, be limited, and have contemporary significance. In the proposal the purpose, objectives, hypotheses, and specific questions should be presented concisely. Important terms should be defined.
2. Previous and related studies should be reported, indicating their relationship to the present study.
3. The variables, those which are controlled and those to be manipulated, should be identified.
4. A description of procedures to be used should be clear enough to be replicated. Details such as the duration of the study and the treatments utilized should be spelled out in depth.
5. The groups being studied should be defined in terms of significant characteristics.
6. The report should note the school setting, describing among other things organization, scale of operations, and any special influences.

7. The evaluation instruments should be applicable to the purpose of the study. Growth in self-concept, for instance, is not
   measured by standardized achievement tests in reading. Evidence of validity (is this test the correct one) and reliability
   (measures what it is supposed to) should be given for all evaluation instruments used.
8. Scoring of measures should be done by the most appropriate
   method whether it be means, medians, percentages, quartiles,
   rank or whatever.
9. Results or findings should be clearly stated in the report in a
   prominent location.
10. Limitations on findings, and there usually are limitations,
    should be clearly stated.

In addition to understanding what goes into "good research," the
curriculum specialist may sometimes be asked to assess specific research reports which have application to the schools with which they
work. The following questions will help in such an assessment:

1. *Problem presentation*—Is the question being asked an important one? Will the question being asked add to further understanding? Will the question being asked aid in decision making? Is the problem explained well in light of limitations in the
   research area? Are the concepts presented reasonable and
   testable?
2. *Methodology*—Are the hypotheses stated in a manner which
   will reveal expected differences? Can this research be replicated? Is the sampling adequate and representative? Is the
   study designed to show evidence of causation or correlation?
   Will the results be generalizable to other groups with similar
   characteristics?
3. *Results*—Are the observational categories used relevant to the
   purpose of the study? Are the statistical treatments appropriate to the data presented? Are the reported differences statis-
   tically significant? (Significance at the .01 level of confidence,
   for instance, means that there is only 1 chance in 100 that differences as observed occurred by chance.) Are the results presented in a manner that makes them understandable?
4. *Conclusions*—Are logical inferences drawn from the findings?
   Are inferences of any use to decision making? Are the limitations of the research identified?

It is useful for those considering research to understand conceptually how it is organized and where the major decision points are in research proceedings. The following diagram by Roberts describes those
relationships:

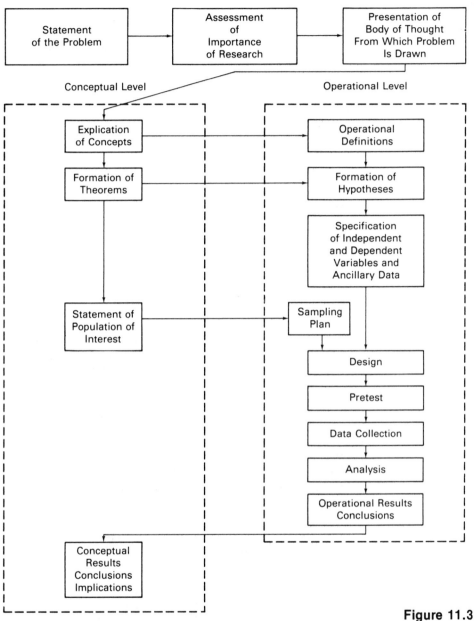

Figure 11.3
Decision Points in Research

TRANSLATING RESEARCH FINDINGS

One of the most difficult tasks facing curriculum specialists is taking research and evaluation reports, which are often technical in nature, and making them understandable to those who can benefit by their findings. In school districts with over 10,000 pupils this function usually is carried out by a research division, but in most of the more than 18,000 school districts in the United States, translation of research is a responsibility of the curriculum director.

The key to an effective translation of research findings is to deliver the information in a style that shows its direct application and in a language that is understandable. Because most classroom teachers are not trained in measurement techniques, jargon must be kept to a minimum.

An example of an effective translation of research is provided by Douglas Brooks who summarized Rosenshine and Furst's hallmark research on teacher performance for classroom teachers in the following manner:

Rosenshine and Furst: Eight studies have been found in which counts of total use of student ideas and / or counts of extended (more than three seconds) use of student ideas were correlated with measures of student achievement. A significant bivariate correlation between teacher use of student ideas and student achievement was not obtained in any study. However, in seven of the eight studies correlations were positive. . . . The consistency of these results suggests that the variable "teacher use of student ideas" appears important enough to warrant more intensive study.[7]

Brooks: Research on the use of student ideas in class, as summarized by Rosenshine and Furst, suggests that the practice may be positively related to student achievement. The following guidelines are recommended for the use of student ideas:

Before instruction:
1. Hold a preclass discussion of ideas not necessarily related to the class topic.

During instruction:
1. Invite ideas from students from time to time
2. Exhibit an accepting non-evaluative behavior
3. Reinforce student ideas when volunteered.

After Instruction
1. Utilize student ideas to alter content or method[8]

If curriculum specialists can generalize from existing research and present such findings to teachers in a language that is understandable and situationally appropriate, research can improve educational practices.

REPORTING FINDINGS

A final task for curriculum workers related to research and evaluation is to summarize such activities in a manner that allows others to understand the role of research in decision making. Usually, such summaries are most effective when the entire scope of research, from objectives to action, is displayed. Table 11.2 is one version of a display.

Table 11.2
Final Evaluation Report Form

Objective	Evaluative Technique Used	Results	Need Indicated	Proposed Action

In column one, list the objectives you have implemented and evaluated in the year. In column two, indicate the evaluative technique (e.g., survey, rating scales, check sheets) used to evaluate each of the objectives. In the column labeled "Results," tally and analyze the results of the evaluations to determine what happened in the implementation of each objective. List briefly the results for each of the objectives. In the fourth column, after comparing the *actual* outcomes with *desired* outcomes, determine discrepancies between the two to get a measure of adequacy and list the needs (if any) for each objective. Indicate in the last column the action you intend to take in regard to each objective implemented and evaluated during the year (e.g., to use as part of a future needs assessment, in public relations, in curriculum development, or in reporting).

SUMMARY

Research and evaluation are processes that seek to assess the effects of educational programs. These processes exist in a natural and cyclical relationship with curriculum development activities. Research and evaluation are most appropriately thought of as a means of providing information for effective decision making in schools.

Educational research has become more sophisticated in recent years due to increased levels of funding, specialization of educational roles, and legal mandates requiring educational accountability.

In most school districts, however, curriculum specialists function to initiate and assess research and evaluation. Among the many activities for which the curriculum worker may be responsible are: establishing evaluation programs, focusing evaluation, designing evaluation systems, assessing educational research, translating research into programs, and reporting research developments to others.

Notes

1. D.T. Campbell and J.C. Stanley, "Experimental and Quasi-Experimental Designs for Research on Teaching in *Handbook of Research on Teaching* (Chicago: Rand-McNally, 1963), p. 191.
2. Harvey Averch, et al., "How Effective is Schooling? A Critical Review and Synthesis of Research Findings" (Santa Monica, Ca.: The Rand Corporation, 1971), p. ix.
3. J. Galen Saylor and William M. Alexander, *Curriculum Planning For Modern Schools* (New York: Holt, Rinehart and Winston, 1966), pp. 243–50.
4. D.L. Stufflebeam, "Toward a Science of Educational Evaluation," *Educational Technology* (July 30, 1968).
5. In *Educational Technology,* July 30, 1968, p. 8.
6. Karlene H. Roberts, "Understanding Research: Some Thoughts on Evaluating Completed Educational Projects," An occasional paper from ERIC at Stanford, 26, ED 032 759.
7. Barak Rosenshine and Norma Furst, "Research on Teacher Performance Criteria" in *Research in Teacher Education: A Symposium,* B.O. Smith (ed.) (Englewood Cliffs, New Jersey: Prentice-Hall, Inc. 1971), p. 49.
8. Douglas Brooks, "Guide for Student Teachers" (University of Texas at Arlington, 1976).

Suggested Learning Activities

1. Describe the relationship between educational research and educational evaluation. Can you reduce this relationship to a model or outline?

2. Differentiate between *formative* and *summative* evaluation. Outline a summative evaluation plan for school children at any level of education.

3. From the library select a recent dissertation which is an experimental study. Write a critical review of the study including these questions: Is the title appropriate? Is the problem clearly defined? Do the conclusions follow from the treatment of data?

4. Using the analysis of the dissertation, try to write a paragraph which would explain the study, in an understandable form, to a classroom teacher.

Books to Review

Glaser, Barney and Strauss, Anselm. *The Discovery of Grounded Theory: Strategies for Qualitative Research.* Chicago: Aldine-Atherton, 1967.

Lien, Arnold, *Measurement and Evaluation of Learning.* Dubuque, Iowa: W.C. Brown Publishers, 1976.

NSSE, *Educational Evaluation: New Roles, New Means.* Chicago: 68th Yearbook of National Society for the Study of Education, Part I, 1969.

Payne, David. *Curriculum Evaluation: Commentary on Purpose, Process, Product.* Lexington, Massachusetts: D.C. Heath and Company, 1974.

Selltiz, C. Wrightsman, L. and Cook, S. *Research Methods in Social Relations.* New York: Holt, Rinehart and Winston, Inc., 1976.

Storey, Arthur. *The Measurement of Classroom Learning.* Science Research Associates, 1970.

Thorndike, R. and Hagen, E. *Measurement and Evaluation in Psychology and Education.* New York: John Wiley & Sons, Inc., 1969.

Walker, H. and Lev, Joseph. *Elementary Statistical Methods.* New York: Holt, Rinehart, and Winston, 1969.

Wiles, David, *Changing Perspectives in Educational Research.* Worthington, Ohio: Charles A. Jones Publishing Company, 1972.

Worthen, Blaine and Sanders, James. *Educational Evaluation: Theory and Practice.* Worthington, Ohio: Charles A. Jones Publishing, 1973.

part two

Curriculum Procedures

12

The Basic Tasks of Curriculum Development

Until recently, curriculum development was interpreted to be the development and implementation of new courses of study. Curriculum development today involves much more. It is a process involving not only content change, but patterns of personal and group relationships between teachers and community. Curriculum development involves the personalities of students, parents, teachers, and the structure of the school system. It involves social change as well as content change.

WHO SHOULD BE INVOLVED IN CURRICULUM DEVELOPMENT?

Curriculum development is a cooperative endeavor. Perhaps Figure 12.1 best illustrates the results of cooperation. It has to involve many groups, agencies, and individuals from both the school and community. The teacher, who must carry out the curriculum, will largely determine the success of any curriculum change. The recipients of the curriculum, students, must be a part of the process of curriculum development. Parents and members of the community who must support curriculum change should be involved in curriculum development work from the very start.

Administrators, supervisors, and other curriculum workers in leadership roles have to be involved in curriculum improvement.

The more persons and groups who can identify themselves with a curriculum, the more likely that curriculum will be successful. All curriculum decisions have direct consequences for the students, school personnel, and community persons involved.

COOPERATION

Figure 12.1

LEADERSHIP FOR CURRICULUM DEVELOPMENT

Curriculum planning groups must have competent leaders to direct them in their work. The person in a leadership role must recognize the leadership talents of all group members and be sensitive to the needs of those persons. Some of the specific tasks of a group leader are to:

1. Maintain a comfortable environment.
2. Develop a relationship with group members to keep communication flowing.
3. Secure resource personnel for necessary consultant services.
4. Determine consensus when appropriate.
5. Define and clarify problem areas in a suitable form for research.
6. Help distinguish between data and inference, fact and assumption.
7. Convey the idea that curriculum is not a neatly wrapped educational package, but rather that which emerges when resources and individual perceptions are joined.
8. Recognize that genuine participation will result in "psychological ownership" of a resulting curriculum.

The reader should see chapter 6 for a thorough discussion of who should participate in curriculum development.

A SYSTEMATIC APPROACH TO CURRICULUM DEVELOPMENT

Curriculum development arises out of a particular need found in a school or school system. It cannot begin with everything at once, but must begin with a specific situation that requires attention because a need is perceived by students, parents, community, or professional personnel. The learner is the focal point of all curriculum development, but it is the teacher who must recognize the need for curriculum change to benefit the learner.

Smith, Stanley, and Shores identified four principles that give the reasons teachers are the keys to effective curriculum development:[1]

1. The curriculum will improve only when the professional competence of teachers improves.
2. The competence of teachers will be improved only when teachers become personally involved in curriculum revision.
3. Teachers will be involved only when they share in the shaping of goals, in selecting, defining, and solving the problems to be encountered, and in judging their results.
4. As people encounter each other face to face, they will be able to understand one another better and reach a consensus on basic goals, principles, and plans.

Diagnosis

Diagnosis in curriculum development or revision means determining the facts that need to be considered in making curriculum decisions.

The first step in a diagnostic study of curriculum problems is the identification of problems that are of concern to the classroom teacher. If we assume that the functioning curriculum is in the hands of teachers who must translate objectives and plans into an operating curriculum, then we must start with problems that come from them. Whether it is getting help on dealing with slow learners, managing time and materials more efficiently to teach basic skills, or learning how to handle social problems of students, the classroom teacher wants curriculum development to provide them with the content or methods to deal with those problems.

Analysis

After a problem has been identified, the next step is an analysis of the problem. The analysis may be simple or complicated. For instance, teachers may simply share in workshop sessions their perceptions of the problem or participate in an extensive study to determine the dimensions of the problem. Thus, teachers may say that students are unable to read the materials in their classes and ask for materials at various reading levels. That action might lead to a complete analysis of all content materials to determine readability levels and a testing program to pinpoint reading deficiencies in students.

Formulating Hypotheses

The problem analysis is followed by the formulating of hypotheses to focus on the problem and narrow the task of data gathering to the most promising leads. The reading problem in the content area might be caused by a number of factors, including:

1. The readability level of the materials used in the classroom.
2. The mental abilities of students.
3. The cultural and social environments that influence the use of leisure time for reading or materials available for students to read at home.
4. Emotional problems brought out by fears and anxieties caused by an unstable or broken home.
5. Behavior at school such as restlessness or inattentiveness.

Teachers will then gather as much information as possible about each of the factors. They may use intelligence tests, reading tests, and surveys of parents to learn of the home atmosphere of the students.

Immediate action does not always follow the diagnostic process. There may be some interim steps that can be taken to solve particular problems. Teachers may learn that a child's school problems in one area, such as reading, may necessitate a number of curriculum changes. Multiple causes of reading problems may dictate multiple solutions that go beyond the individual teacher or classroom. The result of the analysis of a problem of concern to several classroom teachers often leads to a school or district curriculum council and the beginning of a curriculum development or revision process of considerable magnitude.

CURRICULUM PLANNING

Curriculum planning must begin with a needs assessment. *Needs assessment* is a process of defining the desired end (or outcome, result, or product) of a given sequence of curriculum development.[2] Needs assessment is a tool that allows curriculum planners to determine the steps necessary for curriculum development and provides for assessment of a curriculum in terms of what it was shaped to accomplish.

Steps of a Needs Assessment

1. **Planning to Plan.**   Much planning must precede a needs assessment. Most school districts take six months to a year to complete the full cycle of a needs assessment. Deciding on who should become involved, determining resources, and determining which needs are most critical are all time consuming.
2. **Determining Goals.**   There are several ways of determining goals. One way is simply to list goals on the basis of "felt needs." This is followed by an assessment of what is currently the state. A simple discrepancy list then is prepared. For instance, if some members of the planning group list an activity program as a felt need, that is followed by an assessment of what activities are being offered in schools. If just a few schools have activity programs, then a goal of establishing activity programs may be derived. The last step is called validating goals.
3. **Prioritizing Goals.**   Prioritizing goals most often is accomplished by surveys or questionnaires. Respondents are asked to rank order goals. Ranking the goals allows school boards to budget funds to attain the most important goals of the system.
4. **Translating Goals.**   After goals have been ranked, they must be translated into measurable terms. This involves construction of behavioral objectives or performance standards (see chapter 13). Much has been written about developing behav-

ioral objectives both pro and con, but such performance objectives do allow the translation of lofty goals into measurable
outcomes.

5. **Reassessing Goals.** As time passes, a district might
want to reassess goals and reorder certain goals. One district
committee, for instance, had listed bilingual education as a
low priority until there was a sudden influx of Vietnamese children into the district. The establishment of a bilingual program
then became the number one goal in that district.

After a plan has been developed and goals have been established
and ranked, a budget must be adopted for implementation strategies.
Each gap that has been identified between what exists and what is desired has to be closed. Strategies must be developed to close the gaps
and must be costed and placed within the appropriate budget program. A timetable must also be established and responsible agents
identified for carrying out the strategies. Curriculum must be developed and finally implemented. The curriculum development process
ends with an evaluation to see if goals are reached. The evaluation
process should also include assessment of data to indicate unex-
pected results (goal-free evaluation).

Development of a District Curriculum Plan: A Case Study

The following Comprehensive Plan was developed as a result of the
"felt need" of many parents, teachers, and students for a better program for pre- and early adolescent learners in a school district. Although the plan is not a complete plan (specific objectives are not
listed), it does illustrate a process that resulted in the development of
a dynamic new middle school program.

COMPREHENSIVE PLAN FOR MIDDLE SCHOOL DEVELOPMENT

Preface:

In 1969, the Board of Education accepted a document entitled *"A
Master Plan for Implementation of the Middle School in Stamford."*
This Master Plan was the result of committee work involving profes-
sional individuals from the school system.

During the intervening six years, the middle schools of Stamford
have made steady progress in implementing the organizational patterns detailed in the Master Plan. Also, at the direction of the Board
of Education, a middle school committee composed of lay and professional individuals was formed to study the middle school program.
The report of this committee has been submitted to the Board of Education.

In the spring of 1975, at the conclusion of a workshop, the middle school principals decided to assume the responsibility themselves of forming a central committee to further the implementation of the middle school concept in Stamford. Subsequently, a workshop was held during early summer 1975 to review the initial Master Plan. What follows is the report of that review in a form of philosophy, recommendations and time frames for the accomplishment of specific objectives as established by the Middle School Coordinating Committee.

Philosophy:

The middle school in Stamford shall be organized to provide an educational environment suited to the unique needs, interests and abilities of the early adolescents as it helps them develop to their maximum potential.

In an effort to promote quality education, each student should be accepted as an individual. The middle school should provide a unique program for the diverse age group which it serves—youngsters who are in the transition from childhood to adolescence. Each student shall have the opportunity to grow in self-awareness, in personal discipline, in citizenship, and in academic and social skills through diversified educational experiences.

This middle school program is presented as a dynamic, humanistic approach capable of utilizing the findings of ongoing research and educational innovation.

Goals:

The middle school must:

1. Meet the wide range of needs and abilities of the early adolescent.
2. Emphasize the learning process and the joy of learning.
3. Focus attention on the unique development stage of each child, the need for personal responsibility and independence, the identification of a positive self-image and the necessity of experiencing success.
4. Be staffed with personnel who respond to the unique needs of the middle school child.
5. Be a place in which students develop positive relationships with and among the school community.

Needs Identification:

The following needs have been identified:

1. Better communication lines to be established between district personnel, principals and staffs of the middle schools concerning goals and purposes of the middle school in Stamford.

2. A comprehensive plan developed to fully implement the middle school as originally proposed in 1969 and revised in 1975.
3. Teachers to become more aware of the unique needs of the middle school child.
4. Better ways of diagnosing and monitoring skills in the subject areas, especially the 3 Rs, must be established.
5. The middle school program be better articulated in the subject areas to provide more continuity between grade levels.
6. Classroom instruction to be reviewed and updated as appropriate in all subject areas. Teachers to make use of varied and current methods of instruction for middle school youngsters.
7. An expanded program (including special interest courses) to be fully implemented in all schools in balance with a strong academic program including the basics and the unified arts.
8. The interrelationship of subject matter to be emphasized.
9. Students to have close identification with teachers, a more flexible schedule and program.
10. Better continuity of programs, sharing of materials, and curriculum articulation to be developed between the middle schools.
11. The middle school program to be better articulated with the elementary and senior high school programs.
12. Long range goals to be set for middle schools in Stamford and a system developed to sustain positive curriculum changes in the middle school.

Recommendations:

1. The establishment of a Middle School Coordinating Committee.
2. The development of a comprehensive plan for middle school development in Stamford.
3. Preparation of a district plan for full implementation of the middle school concept in Stamford.
4. Conduct workshop sessions dealing with the characteristics of pre- and early adolescent children for all teachers in the middle schools.
5. Provide for vertical articulation, scope, and sequence in all subject areas.
6. District-wide workshop sessions conducted by coordinators with teachers from the four middle schools in all subject areas leading toward a better defined and articulated program in the middle grades.
7. To provide an expanded program (including special interest courses) in balance with a strong academic program.
8. Provide for better correlation of applied sciences, physical education, foreign languages, fine arts and music programs.

9. Workshop sessions conducted during released time and planning periods for the teachers of various disciplines to identify and plan for implementation of interdisciplinary units-objectives and activities, as well as content.
10. A comprehensive evaluation procedure be established to assess the ongoing efforts and programs of the middle school plan.
11. Develop objectives that will clearly define the strategies to be employed.

Evaluation:

A detailed plan for evaluating the middle school program for Stamford will be prepared by the Research Office. The plan will provide for the following:

1. developing specific, measurable objectives by those persons responsible for project activities.
2. measuring the extent to which project objectives are met.

Attention will be given to measuring intermediate and long-range objectives, as well as short-range objectives. Thus, for example, we will attempt to determine whether increases in teacher knowledge about the characteristics of pre-adolescents, gained through workshops, result in expected improvements in the teaching process and the student outcomes.

The timetable and continuum for development shown in Table 12.1 and Table 12.2 (pp. 204–9) are part of the comprehensive plan.

Curriculum Planning at the School Level

The curriculum of a school is encompassed within the following aspects of an educational program:

1. The class program of a school which utilizes bodies of content selected and organized in some predetermined manner.
2. Extra classroom activities.
3. Services provided by the school such as guidance, library, health, food, and transportation, and special services for exceptional children.
4. The social life of the school and the interpersonal relationship among students and teachers.
5. Organizational procedures and policies for providing the instructional program.[3]

A curriculum plan at the school level, as at the district level, has to be comprehensive. It should take into consideration all aspects of

Table 12.1
Timetable for a Comprehensive Plan

PERT Chart

Task	Responsible Agent	1975 June	July	Aug.	Sept.	Oct.	Nov.	Dec.	1976 Jan.	Feb.	March	April	May	June
Middle School Design Review Workshop	MSCC**	6/30 – 7/2												
Middle School Coordinating Committee: Sub Groups—														
1. PERT Chart	G. Roman			8/27										
2. Philosophy	C. Robinson				9/10									
3. Design	J. Markiewicz				9/14									
Comprehensive Middle School Plan: final review	MSCC				9/24									
					2:30pm									
Comprehensive Middle School Plan: to Superintendent	C. Robinson				9/30									
Middle School Project Inservice Workshop	SDC & Dr. Bondi			8/26 –29										
1. Awareness of middle school child														
2. Orientation of staff														
3. Curriculum develop.														
4. Team building														
Middle School Project Workshop (1–3 p.m.)*	SDC & Dr. Bondi					10/14 10/15								
1. Awareness of middle school child														
2. Orientation of remaining staff														
3. Curriculum needs														
4. Team building														

Curricular Assessment
by Principals, Coordinators
  a. Lang. Arts e. Art
  b. Soc. Stud. f. Math
  c. Science   g. Guid.
  d. Music   h. Phys. Ed.

Footnote dates: a 9/18 b 9/16 c 9/23 d 9/25 e 9/30 f 10/1 g 10/2 h 10/7

Activity	Responsibility	Sept	Oct	Nov	Dec	Jan	Feb	Mar	Apr	May	Jun
In-School Staff Development 1. Team building 2. Instruct. strategies 3. Block time scheduling	SDC, Dr. Bondi, et al.	9/8 –11	10/14 –15	11/10 –14	12/2 –5	1/12 –16	2/2 –5	3/1 –4	4/12 –15	5/10 –13 →	
Project Assessment and Planning (Mon., 9 a.m.)	MSCC		10/15	11/10	12/8	1/12	2/2	3/1	4/12	5/10	6/21 →
Up-date Information Sessions with M.S. Study Committee	MSCC chairman		10/1		12/10		2/3		4/7		
Staff Development Workshops (1 Wed./month)* a. Instruct. strategies b. Team building c. Expanded program refinement d. Interrelating unified arts program	SDC, Dr. Bondi, et al.			11/12	12/10	1/14	2/4	3/3	4/14	5/12	
Departmental Workshops (1 Wed./month 1–3 p.m.)* a. Curriculum assessment b. Skills continuum c. Profile charts d. Vertical articulation	Coordinators			11/19	12/17	1/28	2/25	3/24	4/28	5/26	
Middle School Project Workshop	SCD & Dr. Bondi										
Middle School Instructional Associates (4)	SDC										
1976–77 Schedules: block time for all COGS	Principals										Due 6/10

Table 12.1
Timetable for a Comprehensive Plan—continued

	Responsible Agent	1975 June	July	Aug.	Sept.	Oct.	Nov.	Dec.	1976 Jan.	Feb.	March	April	May	June
1976–77 Physical Plan: clustering all COG rooms	Principals													Due 6/10
Family Group COGS: fully functioning	Principals													
District Ad Hoc Committees (for articulation in each curriculum area) Elem.-Middle School Middle-High School	Coordinators													
Buildings: modify and/or replace as dictated by program)	Central Adm. & MSCC													
Planning for inclusion of 6th grade students	Central Adm. & MSCC													
Continuation of a. Team building b. Instructional strategies, etc.	SDC, et al.													
Building Curriculum Bank— materials, units, strategies for working with middle school students	SDC, Dr. Bondi, et al.								Start 1/76 →					
Refined Expanded Program: full implementation	Principals													
6th Grade Students included in middle schools	Central Adm. & Principals													

*released time
**Middle School Coordinating Com.

Table 12.2
Continuum for Development

Components	→	→	→	→
Organization for Instruction	COGS—four academic disciplines per 100 students. Other disciplines—independent units serving all students. Individual teacher in self-contained classroom.	COGS—four academic disciplines per 100 students. Other disciplines—independent units serving all students. Teams representing at least two disciplines* responsible for planning for common group of students (CORE).	COGS—related arts teams & special service teams. Four COGS teachers responsible for planning and teaching common group of students and/or related arts teams or LSP (special service teams)* working to plan for common group of students.	Teams representing all disciplines (COGS, related arts, special service)—working together to plan for common group of students.*
Learning Support Programs	Evaluation Crisis Referrals	Evaluation Crisis Referrals Diagnostic Counseling-Therapy Planning	Evaluation Crisis Referrals Diagnostic Counseling-Therapy Planning Preventive	Evaluation Crisis Referrals Diagnostic Counseling-Therapy Planning Preventive Consulting Developmental Therapeutic
Curriculum	Following one text with system continuum. Teacher—directed group instruction.	Interrelating scope & sequence in at least 2 content areas.* Teacher-directed group instruction. Small group organization.	Interrelating 4 content areas. Include special services for areas of self-awareness (values, study skills, career education)—interdisciplinary instruction. Teacher-directed group instruction—small groups, some teacher-pupil negotiation—individualized & independent work.	Interdisciplinary planning including all areas of curriculum.* Some teacher-directed group work. Some small group work. Independent work. Some pupil-directed work.

Table 12.2
Continuum for Development—continued

	→	→	→
Materials	One adopted text at grade level.	Multi-level texts. Media Center as Resource Center.	Supplemental texts, kits, and manipulatives. Media Center as an extension of classroom (teaming center). Production of media.	Manipulative, audio-visual, programmed kits. Community as classroom. Media Center as Learning Center.
Grouping	Programmed by guidance counselors for entire year.	Proficiency & interest groups formed by evaluation & diagnosis.	Formation of sub-groups through more complete diagnosis.	Program planned cooperatively by students & teacher. Small group work. Individualization
Scheduling	Set time periods on an administrative developed schedule.	Block of time scheduled to provide common instructional and team planning time.	Larger blocks of time to provide common instruction & planning for 4 disciplines. Flexible size of groups. Flexible time blocks.	Larger blocks of time to provide common instruction & planning for all content areas. Flexible size of groups. Flexible time blocks.
Physical Plant Organization	Separate self-contained classrooms Library	COG classrooms clustered together. Media Center	Flexible use of clustered space. Media Production Area	Flexible working space which may be adapted by teams to fit specific needs.
Articulation	Permanent records transfer Textbook & guide hierarchy	Permanent records ———— Text hierarchy ———— Communication at building level	↑ ↑	Totally integrated, articulated program.

Parent Communication	Individual report cards sent home. Open house	Parent conference with teachers Report cards Newsletters Open house Progress reports	Communication between elementary, middle, and high schools. Profile sheets K-12 Group activities for parents (seminars, parents' night, open house) COG meeting attendance All previous involvement & participation in school.
Staff Development	Optional workshops & inservice courses offered for credit. Half days & optional inservice courses.	Mandatory workshops directed by Staff Development Center.	Workshops requested by staff & supported by Staff Development Center. Optional inservice courses Mandatory workshops Teachers structure activities according to their own needs—assume responsibility for constructing plans for professional growth. Mandatory workshops & inservice

*While maintaining the integrity of individual disciplines.

schooling and give insights and assistance to the staffs in providing learning experiences for students toward the attainment of plan goals.

Most school plans are far from comprehensive. They are often reflected in curriculum guides, handbooks, or official policy manuals. An examination of many of these documents reveals that few schools systematically and adequately develop plans that result in a balanced program for students.

There are many reasons why curriculum development has lagged in schools. Perhaps the main reason is that most schools and school districts have experienced a rapid growth of enrollment over the last twenty years. Curriculum development was simply shunted aside by teachers who had all they could do to teach large numbers of students in overcrowded facilities. Curriculum development in our schools was in many cases the adopting of commercial, packaged programs. The blending of those programs with traditional textbook programs and teacher-designed programs resulted in a "hodgepodge" of courses with little continuity within grade levels, much less across grade levels. Although teachers were trained in new programs, teacher turnover, because of an easy job market and low salaries, resulted in programs still in existence after a few years, but few trained teachers left to teach those programs. Many times, after three years, only twenty to thirty percent of a faculty originally trained in the programs remained. Teachers, in many instances, felt no ownership in those programs because they never had a hand in developing them.

The growth in enrollment has today become a decline in enrollment for most schools and school districts and this phenomenon is having a pronounced effect on curriculum development. We see faculties with less turnover and some "breathing room" beginning to review and update curriculum. Curriculum committees are being established at the school and district levels to develop articulated programs in the subject areas. Other functions of schools are being examined in light of social changes such as the breakdown of the family.

Even though teachers are still utilizing commercially designed programs, they are using these programs as a part of a larger, teacher-designed curriculum. Teachers are beginning to communicate within grade levels, across grade levels, and across disciplines. Most important in this exciting process of revising curriculum is the positive attitude of teachers toward a curriculum *they* have developed. Participation by teachers in the curriculum development process is bringing on a feeling of ownership. Members of school faculties that are involved in curriculum revision and updating will often share feelings of closeness to one another and a feeling that something is being accomplished.

Development of a School
Curriculum Plan: A Case Study

The following curriculum study was developed to assist an elementary faculty in updating and revising their school curriculum. It is similar to one used with middle school faculties by the authors. The process of total involvement and development of a written plan that can be implemented are critical to the success of any school plan. For Lakeshore school teachers, the school study followed a lengthy district inservice program involving development of subject area skills continuums and resource guides.

LAKESHORE ELEMENTARY SCHOOL STUDY

I. **Purpose**

The purpose of the Lakeshore Elementary School Study is to explore the organization, curriculum and instruction within the elementary school with special emphasis on:

A. Rationale of the elementary school
B. Nature of the elementary school child
C. Elementary school teacher
D. Program of the elementary school
E. Organization of the elementary school
F. Implementing and evaluating the elementary school

This study is designed to meet the specific needs of Lakeshore Elementary School teachers, children and the community the elementary school serves. It will provide time to develop a total elementary school program by participants.

II. **Objectives**

Major objectives of the study are:
1. To examine the rationale of the elementary school and to identify its goals and purpose.
2. To study the nature of the elementary school child and in particular the characteristics of Lakeshore children.
3. To establish a program that includes:
   A. An emphasis on diagnosis and prescription in the skills areas building towards a continuous progress plan for students.
   B. A broad enrichment program.
   C. Wide use of media other than textbooks.
   D. A scope and sequence in each subject area.

4. To study organizational plans that have been identified with the concept of the open elementary school.
   A. Cooperative teaching.
   B. Flexible use of time and space.
   C. Schools within a school concept.
   D. Better utilization of administrative and service personnel
5. To develop strategies for implementing and evaluating a revised program.

III. **Evaluation**

A. As the study will concentrate on innovative use of human resources, self-evaluation to measure change will be a significant part of the evaluation.
B. Informal evaluations will take place on a continuous basis throughout the study.
C. A subjective study will be made of comments and summarizations of the participating teachers before, during, and at the close of the study.

IV. **Expectations**

A. A written Lakeshore Elementary School Guide will result from the study that will outline in detail a program that can be implemented at Lakeshore Elementary School. Major sections of the Guide will be the six areas listed under A-F, Section I. Staff members will be expected to work on one or more committees in addition to participating in horizontal and vertical team planning.

V. **Tentative Meeting Dates**

January 4	A. Vertical planning in math and communication skills with district consultants.
	B. Six major committees organized and assigned responsibilities.
January 16	A. Afternoon meeting—meet in vertical math and communication skills groups.
	B. During the day meet with Dr. Bondi on procedures to use in six major committees.
January 23	A. Afternoon meeting.
	B. Meet with Dr. Bondi during the day.
February 8	Major committees meet, vertical groups meet —morning session.
February 18	Status report major committees, final reports Math and LA's groups.

February 25	Afternoon session—science and social studies vertical planning.
March 4	Final reports A, B, C major committees.
March 18	Final report D (program committee including science and social studies reports, enrichment committee program).
March 25	Final reports E—organization committee and F—implementing and evaluation committee.
April 1	A. Visitations to other elementary schools. B. Editing and printing final report. C. Presentation of final report to superintendent.
June 1	D. Implementation of selected areas.

The Individual Within the Curriculum

All curriculum development has to be viewed in terms of its impact on the individual learner within the curriculum. A model of human behavior for curriculum development is presented in Figure 12.2 to help persons directly involved in curriculum planning and development examine the behavior of students in schools. The human behavior heading of the model is misleading unless one makes the assumption, as the writers have, that the human behavior we educators are concerned with is the behavior of the individual within the curriculum.

Although the model may seem quite complex, it is in reality very simple. The model is a dynamic, multi-dimensional system that is in constant interaction. The central or focal point of the model is neither the curriculum nor the individual, but the individual within the curriculum. The writers believe that the two cannot be separated.

Major variables exist within the model including society and culture, knowledge and cognition, personality theories, learning theories, and human development.

The individual within the curriculum is pictured as being bombarded by various subsystems (see arrows) which are part of larger systems or variables. But note that the arrows are two-way arrows. The individual within the curriculum is providing constant feedback through the various subsystems to the larger systems. The subsystems and larger systems are constantly changing in structure because of the feedback. The feedback forces a continual antithesis and synthesis on the part of the subsystems and larger systems.

The interaction within the model does not stop with the two-way interaction between the systems (or variables) and the individual within the curriculum. There is a constant interaction between the subsystems themselves and interaction among the larger systems (note the two-way arrows).

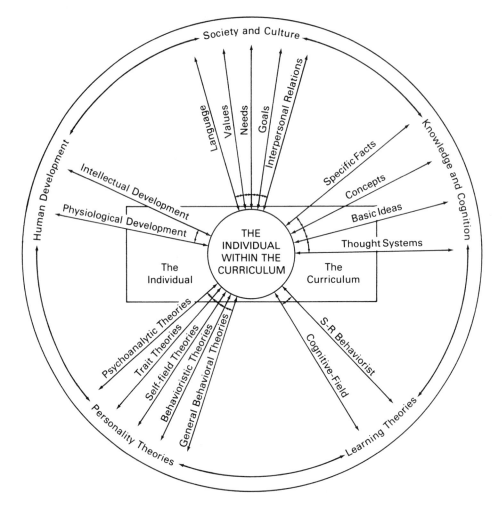

Figure 12.2
A Model of Human Behavior for Curriculum Development

Because of the feedback and other factors resulting from the inter-action of the systems, certain of the subsystems within the larger sys-tem, e.g., concepts within knowledge and cognition, become stronger and tend to dominate thinking. However, none of the subsystems under the variables is strong enough, according to present available research, to so completely dominate as to obliterate the other sub-systems.

Since there is so much discussion and little agreement as to the relative importance of the subsystems or larger systems themselves, the writers have included those systems and subsystems that have the most meaning to them in consideration of the individual within the curriculum. A greater or lesser number of subsystems or larger systems might be included by others.

Each of the subsystems has merit based on reliable research and it would be most difficult to select a subsystem for each of the variables (or larger systems).

For instance, when we look at learning theories, we find two major schools of thought (subsystems), behaviorist theory and cognitive-field theory. As the pendulum has swung in education, one of these two theories has dominated the thinking. Through the 1920s, the S-R behaviorists controlled the actions of educators. During the 1930s the cognitive-field theories came into their own and heavily influenced thinking about how individuals learned. The two have been competing ever since for the loyalties of educators. We could draw a heavier line for either one or the other in our model, denoting greater strength, depending on whom we are talking with.

Both of the theories have merit and it is impossible to select one at the expense of the other. This has been one of the major difficulties in curriculum development, the either-or syndrome on the part of educators and psychologists who think there always has to be a complete rejection of the other school of thought.

If teachers would understand that they don't have to be disciples of either of the schools, they would do a much better job of working with the individual learner. Perhaps, if one utilized this model, he could, in time, eliminate both of these subsystems (erase the arrows if you may) and add a third subsystem (new arrow) which would utilize the best from each of the systems. We need learning theorists in education who can overcome the either-or syndrome and give us a learning theory based on feedback from the individual within the curriculum. These theorists would synthesize both of the present theories into a theory that would be meaningful for all those engaged in helping youngsters learn.

Looking at society and culture as a system or variable affecting the individual within the curriculum, the reader will see the inclusion of five subsystems including language, values, needs, goals, and interpersonal relations. The two-way arrows are especially appropriate here because the individual within the curriculum is doing much to influence the subsystems and the general system (society and culture). For instance, society and culture help determine the goals of the individual within the curriculum, but that individual is helping determine those goals of society. The individual within the curriculum, through interpersonal relations, helps shape and is shaped by society. Language is included as a subsystem because culture and society give language to the individual and make it a part of his curriculum. But again, the individual within the curriculum, through feedback, is affecting language which is in turn affecting society and culture.

Human development is divided into two subsystems, physiological and intellectual. Our knowledge of human development helps us look at both the physical and mental development of the individual within the curriculum. The study of the individual within the curriculum furnishes valuable feedback that increases knowledge of human development. There is exciting research being conducted today in the area of human development that has great implications for educators. The value of early experiences and the acceptance of stages of development have greatly influenced recent thinking.

Personality theories are numerous, hence the large number of subsystems found in the model. Most personality theories incorporate the works of Freud, so psychoanalytic theory is included. Self or field theories and behaviorist theories are included, as well as trait theories and general behavior theories. No personality theory is right or wrong, but each should be useful. Each of the personality theories contains part of the truth. There is a wide variety to choose from in the model. As long as we can utilize all of these theories in looking at the individual within the curriculum, we can better predict and understand human behavior. Educators should never get trapped into choosing a particular school of personality theory which then becomes a set of blinders.

Knowledge and cognition as a major variable is divided into specific facts, concepts, basic ideas, and thought systems. We organize knowledge in terms of concepts. Concepts are influenced by the age, experience, social, and economic status of learners. The individual learner furnishes continual feedback to the field of knowledge. Behavior is a function of the concepts held by the learner.

Cognition, as contrasted with knowledge, is the process of thinking, so thought systems are included as a subsystem. Basic ideas are an important part of knowledge. Jerome Bruner and others have said that certain key ideas can be taught to the learner within the curriculum at any age.

Specific facts include those ideas at a low level of abstraction which are universally accepted. These basic facts should be used to support concepts. Ideas about the nature of knowledge are increasingly utilized in curriculum planning. Today's curriculum must utilize knowledge to make informal decision makers of learners so they can interpret the world around them.

In conclusion, the writers have attempted to develop a model of human behavior that would help one gain a better understanding of the process of curriculum development. Variables have been identified that should be considered in developing a model of human behavior. The central focus of the model is the individual within the curriculum. It is the behavior of this individual that we are concerned with in curriculum planning.

There is a constant interaction between individuals and the major variables affecting them. The model illustrates a system which is not static, but dynamic and moving. No one component of the system can be altered without some effect on the other components. The circle can be penetrated at any time by new variables or by new systems under the variables. The value of utilizing a model lies in the fact that one is not forced into an either/or trap since all systems are considered. If we utilize a model and make the individual the focal point within the curriculum, we can examine any number of variables affecting the learner and not get lost in our thinking.

If we look at all of the variables within the system and look at all facets of the model, it will help us understand a highly complex process of human behavior within a school context. In our model, we have centered on the individual within the curriculum, which is as it should always be in curriculum development.

PROVIDING THE LEADERSHIP
FOR CURRICULUM DEVELOPMENT

The Role of the Curriculum Worker/Leader

The term *curriculum worker* applies to most educators-teachers, central office administrators, or principals. The term *curriculum leader* applies to those persons in leadership roles who have the primary responsibility for planning, coordinating, and/or managing curriculum activity in a school district. Curriculum leaders may be teachers chairing departments or committees, supervisors, and/or school administrators.[4]

There is a growing emphasis on curriculum development at the school or district level. The identification of curriculum leaders who can facilitate curriculum development is essential to the success of any change process. Many competencies have been compiled for the curriculum leader. Since the success of a curriculum leader depends on good human relations, the following competencies have been identified that will help the curriculum leader coordinate the activities of an educational staff related to curriculum planning and development. The curriculum leader should be able to:

- Produce and implement a year-long plan focused upon curriculum planning and the development of problems involving staff, parents, students, and support personnel, indicate their specific assignments and responsibilities, and provide a schedule of steps toward completion.
- Coordinate at a variety of levels and areas (locally as well as regionally) programming for instructional development.
- Define, with staff, common problems and help staff with the solution of these problems.

- Develop, with staff, behavioral objectives, which will be measurable and compatible with the content area.
- Schedule periodic interdepartmental meetings within a school or a school system to define common curricular problems and to seek solutions.
- Help and encourage teachers to be innovative and to accept different methods as long as they produce the desired outcomes.
- Develop a program for continuous curriculum development.
- Accept the individual differences of adults in conducting workshops for the development of curriculum.
- Be a primary resource person.
- Help determine integration of subject areas into total overall curriculum.
- Evaluate the current educational trends and know the philosophical basis for these trends.
- Recognize the dangers to educational development inherent in each of these trends.
- Assist the group to pursue various possible solutions to a problem.
- Summarize clearly and concisely various solutions.
- Assist the group in coming to decisions based on the alternative choices.
- Follow through on a course of action decided.
- Evaluate the effects of a course of action may have on those affected by the program change.
- Disseminate information on current innovations to staff members directly involved in a specific area of innovation.
- Promote and encourage the direct involvement and participation of teachers in planning, implementing, and evaluating curricular innovations and adjustments.
- Describe the various points of view and the proper relationships of different subject areas to each other.
- Coordinate curriculum planning and development for the local district, K-12.
- Open channels of communication within professional staff that will allow crossing grade levels, ability levels, and individual discipline structures.
- Develop an attitude of commitment to local, district, state and national curriculum development and improvement programs.
- Determine the needs of the community and of individual pupils in planning and developing programs at all levels of instruction to fulfill these needs.
- Plan budgetary allocations to ensure that curriculum plans can be inaugurated.
- Improve his ability to communicate positively and influentially with many different personalities.

- Offer, by example, his own philosophy of education.
- Provide vision for long-range plannings.
- Seek help and cooperation from staff members in setting up programs of curriculum development and/or improvement.
- Use research on child development and learning in selecting and sequencing concepts for curriculum development.
- Communicate progress, plans, and problems between staff members and curriculum-making bodies.
- Speak competently before faculty and critically appraise their efforts.
- Understand both elementary and secondary education (with a strong background in one of the levels).
- Establish a philosophy or a frame of reference (from which he operates and acts in a manner consistent with such a philosophy or frame of reference).
- Appoint cross sectional committees (K-12) to establish in writing common goals for all levels.
- Approach all curriculum change with a concern for communication, both horizontal and vertical.
- Produce, printed form, a description of the district's organization for curriculum improvement (which accounts for both human and material resources).
- Identify, accept and anticipate the needs of teachers (who are engaged in planning for curriculum innovation).
- Identify, and accept the needs of teachers in planning and development.
- Set up a system for the exchange of information among teachers.
- Provide a means for continuous evaluation of existing programs.
- Identify and solve instructional problems which hinder improvement of teaching-learning situations in the classroom.[5]

SUMMARY

Curriculum development in recent years has shifted from primarily developing and implementing new courses of study to a complicated process of determining total programs for learners. Curriculum development is a cooperative endeavor with many groups involved including teachers, students, parents, and consultants. Curriculum planning groups must have competent leaders to direct them.

Curriculum development usually evolves from a particular need found in a school system. Teachers must recognize a need for curriculum change and must play a key part in finding solutions to curriculum problems.

Curriculum planning occurs at all levels. Needs assessment is a process used in curriculum planning. It is a process of defining desired outcomes of a given sequence of curriculum development.

Curriculum development is occurring more at the district and school levels rather than through national curriculum projects or by textbook writers. A comprehensive plan from an actual school district is presented in this chapter to illustrate processes used at the district level. Curriculum planning at the school level is also illustrated by an outline of a school study.

All curriculum development has to be viewed in terms of its impact on the individual learner. A Model of Human Behavior for Curriculum Development is presented in this chapter to help those persons directly involved in curriculum planning and development to examine the behavior of students in schools.

Curriculum development at the school or district level demands competent leadership. Competencies for curriculum leaders are identified that focus on good human relations since much of the success of curriculum development depends on leaders getting people to work together.

During the last ten years, considerable knowledge has been accumulated about the change process. It is now possible to develop the strategies necessary to develop and implement new programs—programs where a pride of ownership will be felt by all those taking part in developing them.

Notes

1. B.O. Smith, William Stanley, and J. Harlan Shores, *Curriculum Development: Theory and Practice,* rev. ed. (New York: Harcourt Brace Jovanovich, 1957), p. 429.
2. Fenwick English and Roger Kaufman, *Needs Assessment: A Focus for Curriculum Development* (Washington: Association for Supervision and Curriculum Development, 1974), p. 3.
3. J. Galen Saylor and William M. Alexander, *Curriculum Planning for Modern Schools* (New York: Holt, Rinehart, and Winston, Inc., 1966), p. 269.
4. Working Group on Role, Function, and Preparation of the Curriculum Worker, Donald Christensen, Chairperson, *Curriculum Leaders: Improving Their Influence* (Washington, D.C.: Association for Supervision and Curriculum Development, 1976), p. 5.
5. Francis Ciurczak, ed., "The Future Role of the Curriculum Worker," *IMPACT on Instructional Improvement* 9, No. 1 (1973), pp. 13, 14, 15.

Suggested Learning Activities

1. Study the assumptions proposed in "A Model of Human Behavior for Curriculum Development." Do you agree with the principles stated by the authors? What other variables or subsystems would you include in the model?

2. Your superintendent has asked you to chair a curriculum committee to develop new programs for slow learners. Who would you involve in the work of the committee? Outline the steps you would take in developing and implementing the new programs.

3. Construct a needs assessment questionnaire that would help prioritize goals found in your school or school district.

4. Develop your own list of competencies for curriculum leaders. How does your list differ from the list found in this chapter?

5. Outline the steps you would take to get a total faculty involved in curriculum planning. How would you organize the group to make use of the talents of every faculty member?

Books to Review

Christensen, Donald, et. al. *Curriculum Leaders: Improving Their Influence.* Washington: Association for Supervision and Curriculum Development, 1976.

DeNovellis, Richard and Lewis, Arthur. *Schools Become Accountable—A PACT Approach.* Washington: Association for Supervision and Curriculum Development, 1974.

Firth, Gerald and Kimpston, Richard. *The Curriculum Continuum in Perspective.* Itasca, Illinois: F.E. Peacock Publishers, 1973.

Hass, Glen; Bondi, Joseph; and Wiles, Jon. *Curriculum Planning: A New Approach.* Boston: Allyn and Bacon, Inc., 1974.

Oliver, Albert. *Curriculum Improvement,* 2nd ed. New York: Harper and Row Publishers, 1977.

Saylor, Galen and Alexander, William. *Curriculum Planning for Modern Schools.* New York: Holt, Rinehart and Winston, Inc., 1966.

Saylor, Galen and Alexander, William. *Planning Curriculum for Schools.* New York: Holt, Rinehart and Winston, Inc., 1974.

Smith, B. Othanel; Stanley, William; and Shores, J. Harlan. *Fundamentals of Curriculum Development,* rev. ed. New York: World Book Company, 1957.

Taba, Hilda. *Curriculum Development: Theory and Practice.* New York: Harcourt, Brace and World, Inc., 1962.

Zais, Robert S. *Curriculum, Principles and Foundations.* New York: Thomas Crowell Company, 1976.

13

Procedures for Clarifying Values and Goals

Values and goals not only influence the shape of the curriculum, but provide direction and focus for the entire educational process. The importance of curricular purposes is reflected in the fact that no other aspect of education has received more attention and provided as much controversy as has the question of aims or goals. This chapter will provide procedures for clarifying values and goals and relate goals and objectives to curriculum development. Major purposes of public schools will be examined. To understand schools and school systems, one must relate them to the social environment in which they are found. We must not forget that schools are both tools of society and tools for society.

SOURCES OF GOALS AND OBJECTIVES

All educational programs are built upon three bases: (1) learners and how they learn, (2) society and its forces, and (3) organized knowledge.

The Learner as a Data Source

Empirical studies of how children and adolescents learn have long been a source for determining curriculum purposes.

Two major learning theories have emerged over the years that have given direction to the curriculum planner. The first learning theory stresses a *stimulus-response (S-R) association.* This theory includes all the conditioning and reinforcement theories of learning. Transfer and rewarded response are essential elements of S-R theories. Transfer is defined as "an ability to perform a general act as a result of having performed another related act." Reward may occur through a variety of means and simply implies a recognition by an observer of a response made by the learner.

The second of the learning theory families important to the curriculum planner is the *perceptual-field* group of learning theories. In these theories, the important factor is an understanding that the learner starts with wholeness (the total aspect of a learning situation) and moves toward particulars in light of the whole. The perceptual psychology, or phenomenological theory, emphasizes that the self-concept of the learner is central. What affects the learner is what has meaning for the learner. Behavior and learning are functions of perception.

Studies of the learner today have resulted in the development of major programs in American education. Recent studies of the importance of early childhood experiences have led to the development of preschool programs and the mandating by many states of kindergarten programs. Research into the nature of the transition from childhood to adolescence has been the basis for the emergence of the middle school.

Society as a Data Source

To understand schools, one must relate them to the surrounding cultural, philosophical, economic, and political circumstances. The social environment today reflects the breakdown of many of the established institutions such as the family, church, and home. Descriptions of society of the 1950s or 1960s no longer suffice for giving us understanding of the social forces affecting our schools. The breakdown of the family and other problems in society have resulted in disaffected youth. News magazines carry startling statistics of the number of divorces, drug problems, violence in the home and in the school, and parents who can't cope with themselves, much less their children. *Time Magazine,* in a cover story, cited problem areas such as declining performance, rising violence, spreading shutdowns of schools, teacher troubles, and mounting absenteeism as symptoms of deep problems in our high schools.[1]

Lined up like so many planes on a runway are major contemporary problems of American society such as equal rights for women, the handicapped, and minority groups. The environment, changing values and morality, the family, and the urban crisis are all directly affecting our schools. With the breakdown of other institutions, the school stands alone as the hope for nurturing and shaping future generations.

Understanding the close relationship between the social environment and the development of appropriate educational programs is essential. Whether it is the teacher in the classroom or a group looking at national goals for education, the inescapable conclusion is that our schools are the products of the very society that schools are trying to improve.

Knowledge as a Data Source

Probably the most common source of goals and objectives is subject matter. In spite of the recent thrust towards "the basics," subject matter is open to serious criticism by those who believe the objectives generated from this source are rather narrow or specialized. Recent competency-based testing programs in a number of states have come under fire because the content being tested was so narrow. States such as Florida have designed testing programs to measure those competencies, or skills, that are essential to everyday life. They include such areas as figuring out interest rates, purchasing groceries, writing checks, and filling out applications for employment.

What knowledge is important and how that knowledge is structured remains a question under debate by educational leaders. What is important to education is what a particular subject can contribute to the education of youth *not* desiring to be specialists in that field. That is, what can the particular discipline or subject contribute to the general education of the lay citizen?

A major responsibility of the curriculum worker is to determine the validity and acceptability of desired outcomes of schooling. In curriculum planning, we must consider the sources of goals and objectives before we can discuss the goals and objectives themselves.

People who teach believe they can and do change student behavior. With that belief, teachers establish the curriculum they think will bring about those changes. They set the goals (ends) and then determine the means (curriculum) to reach them. This approach is used in other professions such as government, medicine, and the military. In setting goals, the basic data sources are the students to be educated and the society that establishes and operates our schools.

The means-ends approach to curriculum, where educators establish goals and objectives as ends to be reached, is best set forth in the classic "Tyler rationale" first published in a syllabus he prepared in the late 1930s for a course at the University of Chicago. Tyler identified four fundamental questions that must be answered in developing any curriculum and plan for instruction. They are:

1. What educational purposes should the school seek to attain?
2. What educational experiences can be provided that are likely to attain those purposes?
3. How can these educational experiences be effectively organized?
4. How can we determine whether these purposes are being attained?[2]

Tyler's model is still widely used as a guide for modern curriculum planning. Tyler identified the following three data sources from which the basic information needed for stating objectives should be obtained:

1. Studies of the learners themselves.
2. Studies of contemporary society outside the school.
3. Suggestions about objectives from subject matter specialists.

The data gathered from the above sources is then passed through "screens" of (a) Philosophy of Education, and (b) Psychology of Learning. From this refinement process come precise or measurable instructional objectives.

Although the Tyler rationale has risen to the position of near dogma, there are criticisms of his approach to curriculum development. Some consider the stating of specific objectives in behavioral terms to change student behavior as approaching brainwashing. Thomas Green states that the aim of teaching is not to change people's behavior, but to transform behavior into action.[3]

Taba[4] expresses the need for not only identifying the kind of behavior to be developed in the student, but the content or area of life in which the behavior is to operate.

Herbert Kliebard has pointed out that in Tyler's scheme "the last of the three data sources is not a source at all but a means of achieving objectives from the other two."[5]

Finally, John Goodlad, a highly regarded curriculum theorist and student of Tyler, chided Tyler, in an article written with Richter, for Tyler's failure to start with values.[6] Goodlad and Richter propose turning to values as the primary data source for selecting purposes for a school and as a data source for all curriculum decisions.

The only difficulty with the Goodlad-Richter model is a question of whose values should be used in selecting purposes for a school.

VALIDATING GOALS AND OBJECTIVES

The curriculum worker engaged in defining goals must continually check on the validity of those goals against basic data obtained from a study of students and the needs of society. Some goals must necessarily be discarded because of changing legal requirements, court decisions, or district or state regulations. Other goals must be reexamined in light of research on learning and changing societal needs. A curriculum worker has to realize that curriculum planning is an ever-continuing cycle of obtaining data, stating objectives, selecting teaching experiences, and evaluating learning outcomes.

FORMULATING GOALS

Educational goals are statements of the outcomes of education. The scope of the entire educational program of a school can be found in the goals of that school. Goals are the basic elements in educational planning. The reflection of societal needs in educational goals usually results in statements describing categories of human behavior. Goals relating to "maintaining health," and "carrying out the activities of a citizen in a democratic society" are examples of societal needs.

Goals may be stated at several levels of generality or specificity. Goals that are general or broad reflect a philosophical base and are not concerned with a particular achievement within a period of time.

Perhaps the most familiar goals were defined by the Commission on Reorganization of Secondary Education in 1918. Those goals were: (1) health, (2) command of fundamental processes, (3) worthy home membership, (4) vocation, (5) citizenship, (6) worthy use of leisure time, and (7) ethical character. These became widely known as the Seven Cardinal Principles of Secondary Education.

The second attempt at defining the purposes of secondary education was expressed in 1938 by the Educational Policies Commission of the National Education Association and the American Association of School Administrators. The group developed a number of goals under the four headings of (1) self-realization, (2) human relationships, (3) economic efficiency, and (4) civic responsibility.

Most recently, the ASCD Working Group on Research and Theory identified a set of valued learning outcomes "that reflected the 'holistic' nature of individuals." Hundreds of organizations, including state departments of education and regional research and development centers, were requested to share their goals with the group. The group identified ten major goals for youth: [7]

1. Self-Conceptualizing (Self-Esteem)
2. Understanding Others
3. Basic Skills
4. Interest and Capability for Continuous Learning
5. Responsible Member of Society
6. Mental and Physical Health
7. Creativity
8. Informed Participation in the Economic World of Production and Consumption
9. Use of Accumulated Knowledge to Understand the World
10. Coping with Change

The scope of all of the above goals indicates that they are general goals aimed at an entire unit of organization such as the elementary school, middle school, or senior high school.

In the following sections we should consider steps and procedures involved in clarifying goals and objectives. A discussion of the processes involved in defining various levels of goals and objectives is designed to assist the curriculum planner whether in the classroom or at the school or district level.

CLARIFYING GOALS AND OBJECTIVES

The following news item illustrates the need for formulating goals and objectives in a clear manner.

READING CROSS-EYED MIGHT HELP

HOUSTON—The parent of a Houston high school pupil recieved a message from the principal about a special meeting on a proposed educational program. It read:

"Our school's cross-graded, multi-ethnic, individualized learning program is designed to enhance the concept of an open-ended learning program with emphasis on a continuum of multi-ethnic, academically enriched learning using the identified intellectually gifted child as the agent or director of his own learning. Major emphasis is on cross-graded, multi-ethnic learning with the main objective being to learn respect for the uniqueness of a person."

The parent wrote the principal:

"I have a college degree, speak two foreign languages and four Indian dialects, have been to a number of county fairs and three goat ropings, but I haven't the faintest idea as to what the hell you are talking about. Do you?"

Goals provide a philosophically unified structure that undergirds and relates all aspects of the learning situation from the development of an overall curriculum plan to lesson plans in the classroom.

There appears to be a lack of organized coherence in many of the goals and objectives found in curriculum plans. Often, goals are not clearly stated and there is confusion when various levels of goals and objectives are indiscriminately grouped together. Educators have been accused of using their own language in describing programs to the public. That language is not only confusing to the public, but to educators themselves. The following exercise illustrates this point:

Instant Educator

To play the Instant Educator game, select in any order one word from Column A, one from Column B, and one from Column C. Now copy them on scratch paper in the order they were selected.

A	B	C
1. social	1. involvement	1. objectives
2. perceptual	2. motivation	2. activity
3. developmental	3. accelerated	3. curriculum
4. professional	4. cognitive	4. concept
5. homogeneous	5. effectiveness	5. evaluation
6. interdependent	6. maturation	6. processes
7. exceptional	7. integration	7. approach
8. instructional	8. orientation	8. articulation
9. individual	9. guidance	9. utilization
10. sequential	10. creative	10. resources
11. environmental	11. culture	11. adjustment
12. incremental	12. relationship	12. capacity

Examples: (A-10) sequential; (B-1) involvement; (C-2 activity; (B-4) cognitive; (A-3) developmental; (C-7) approach.

Now that you have the hang of it, enjoy your new status by sprinkling a few common words between the phrases like this:

Social involvement objectives in today's schools are realized by combining an accelerated developmental curriculum with professional effectiveness utilization and creative instructional evaluation.

The motivation of interdependent activity in an environmental adjustment culture is not easy when one takes into account the perceptual maturation processes of the individual.

The utilization of instructional guidance resources will enable students to employ a sequential orientation approach to social integration.

After you have mastered this creative incremental approach to educationalese, you will realize that happiness is social effectiveness through concept articulation. Infectious, isn't it?

CLASSIFYING GOALS AND OBJECTIVES

Educational goals inherently reflect to some degree a philosophical position of the writer. Each objective reflects the philosophical, sociological, and cultural peculiarities of the writer and the immediate school community of which he or she is a part.

The statement of goals leads to general or broad objectives that are more specific than the goal statements, but still stated in broad terms. Finally, specific behaviorally stated objectives evolve from the goals and general objectives. Activities or strategies and a means of evaluation are included in statements of behavioral objectives. The process found in development of all school programs is illustrated as follows: Philosophy———►Goals———►Broad Objectives———►Specific Objectives.

Learning objectives should be designed at more than one single level of operation. Table 13.1 illustrates three different levels—Level I, Level II, and Level III.

Level I objectives are stated in very general terms. They are usually found at the system level. Those responsible for writing Level I objectives sometimes refer to them as purposes or goals. These statements are found in school board publications, district publications, and at state levels. An example of a goal statement is found in the following resolution of the West Virginia Board of Education:

RESOLUTION

Resolution Identifying the Teaching
of Reading as the Highest Curricular
and Instructional Priority in the
Schools of West Virginia

WHEREAS, The West Virginia Board of Education adopted seventeen (17) Education Goals for West Virginia on February 14, 1975, which give the highest priority to the mastery of skills needed for reading, writing, speaking, perceiving, and using numbers; and

WHEREAS, In order to eliminate functional illiteracy which stands at approximately 20% of the adult population over sixteen years of age; and

WHEREAS, Efficiency in reading and the communication skills is the basic prerequisite for school achievement and for becoming an informed, productive, and active participant in our culture and society; and

WHEREAS, There currently exists a strong interest among professional educators and parents in the State of West Virginia in increasing both time and resources that are devoted to the teaching of reading and the other basic communication skills;

Table 13.1
The Relationships Between Levels I, II, and III Learning Objectives

LEVEL I

(Generally and broadly stated; normally includes policy and general direction and general outcomes. Formulated at the extraclassroom (system) level. Includes two or more Level II objectives.)

Level III	Level III	Level III	Level III
1.	1.	1.	1.
2.	2.	2.	2.
3.	3.	3.	3.
4.	4.	4.	4.
5.	5.	5.	5.
6.	6.	6.	6.
—	—	—	—
—	—	—	—
X.	X.	X.	X.
Level II	Level II	Level II	Level II

(More specifically stated than Level I, but still in general terms; normally set forth by departments and at subject area levels; each includes two or more Level III (behaviorally stated objectives.)

BE IT THEREFORE RESOLVED THAT, Beginning January 1, 1976, the teaching of reading shall become the highest priority in the curriculum of the schools in West Virginia. The West Virginia Department of Education, working cooperatively with both local and regional education agencies, shall begin immediately to pursue a plan for implementing curricular and instructional practices which concentrate on reading and the other basic communication skills, for providing programs to be utilized by parents to become knowledgeable regarding the reading development of children, for enabling teachers and prospective teachers to improve their skills in the teaching of reading, and for providing for the assessment and evaluation of reading achievement in the schools of West Virginia.

BE IT FURTHER RESOLVED THAT, County boards of education be encouraged to adopt this or similar resolutions declaring the teaching of reading and the other basic communication skills to be the highest curricular and instructional priority beginning January 1, 1976, and that the necessary resources be committed to a plan to implement this resolution.

Level I objectives should be accompanied by a related and complimentary policy statement. The West Virginia statement describes how the teaching of reading is to be met and upon whom the various responsibilities fall. Generally, a statement about how the educational program is to be evaluated is included.

Level II objectives are stated in broad or general terms, but are somewhat more specific than Level I statements. They are, however, not behaviorally stated as in the case of Level III learning objectives. Level II objectives support Level I objectives. They reflect the same philosophy and are directed toward the realization of the Level I goals or purposes.

Level III objectives are found at the classroom level and are behaviorally stated. These specific objectives support Level II and Level I objectives.

Behavioral objectives are statements describing what the learner is doing when he or she is learning. Teachers need to describe the desired behaviors well enough to preclude misinterpretation. Thus the key to writing successful objectives is to use action verbs to describe specific behaviors. Words such as "knowing" and "understanding" are not explicit enough to describe what the learner is doing to demonstrate learning.

An acceptable objective lets the student know what is expected of the learner. It also enables the teacher to measure the effectiveness of his or her own work.

Behaviorally stated objectives contain three essential elements:

1. The terminal behavior must be identified by name. An observable action must be named that shows that learning has taken place.
2. The important conditions under which the behavior is expected to occur should be described.
3. The criteria of acceptable performance should be specified.

The advocacy of behavioral objectives by those seeking to clarify educational purposes has met resistance from those who believe describing learner outcomes in this fashion is too simplistic and ignores the interrelatedness of human activity.

In the rush to write clear, precise statements, teachers often chose simple objectives that required little thinking on the part of their students. Those teachers actually were writing objectives in the lowest levels of cognitive behavior. Through inservice training, teachers can master the skill of writing objectives requiring higher forms of thinking on the part of their students. In addition, teachers should write objectives leading to affective and psychomotor behaviors.

The three taxonomies of educational objectives are best illustrated in Tables 13.2, 13.3, and 13.4.

Table 13.2
Levels of Cognitive Behavior

	Comprehension (ability to comprehend what is being communicated and make use of the idea without relating it to other ideas or material or seeing fullest meaning)	Application (ability to use ideas, principles, theories in new particular and concentrated situations)	Analysis (ability to break down a communication into constituent parts in order to make organization of the whole clear)	Synthesis (ability to put together parts and elements into a unified organization or whole)	Evaluation (ability to judge the value of ideas, procedures, methods, using appropriate criteria)
Knowledge (ability to recall; to bring to mind the appropriate material)	Requires knowledge	Requires knowledge	Requires knowledge	Requires knowledge	Requires knowledge
Comprehension		Requires comprehension	Requires comprehension	Requires comprehension	Requires comprehension
Application			Requires application	Requires application	Requires application
Analysis				Requires analysis	Requires analysis
Synthesis					Requires synthesis

Source: From *Taxonomy of Educational Objectives: The Classification of Educational Goals: Handbook 1: Cognitive Domain* edited by Benjamin S. Bloom et al. Copyright © 1956 by Longman Inc. Reprinted with permission of Longman.

Table 13.3
Levels of Affective Behavior

Receiving	Responding	Valuing	Organization	Characterization
(attending; becomes aware of an idea, process, or thing; is willing to notice a particular phenomenon)	(makes response at first with compliance, later willingly and with satisfaction)	(accepts worth of a thing, an idea or a behavior; prefers it; consistent in responding; develops a commitment to it)	(organizes values; determines interrelationships; adapts behavior to value system)	(generalizes certain values into controlling tendencies; emphasis on internal consistency; later integrates these into a total philosophy of life or world view)
				Requires organization of values
			Requires development of values	Requires development of values
		Requires a response	Requires a response	Requires a response
	Requires a response	Begins with attending	Begins with attending	Begins with attending
Begins with attending	Begins with attending			

Source: From *Taxonomy of Educational Objectives: The Classification of Educational Goals: Handbook 2: Affective Domain* by David R. Krathwohl et al. Copyright © 1964 by Longman Inc. Reprinted with permission of Longman.

Table 13.4
Levels of Psychomotor Behavior

Observing	Imitating	Practicing	Adapting
(watches process; pays attention to steps or techniques and to finished product or behavior; may read directions)	(follows directions; carries out steps with conscious awareness of efforts, performs hesitantly)	(repeats steps until some or all aspects of process become habitual, requiring little conscious effort, performs smoothly)	(makes individual modifications and adaptations in the process to suit the worker and/or the situation)
	Requires observation, or reading of directions	Requires imitation	Requires practice
		Requires observation, or reading of directions	Requires imitation
			Requires observation, or reading of directions

Source: From *A Taxonomy of the Psychomotor Domain: A Guide for Developing Behavioral Objectives* by Anita J. Harrow. Copyright © 1972 by Longman Inc. Reprinted with permission of Longman.

Taxonomies are classification schemes developed by educators to define educational goals. The reader is especially encouraged to review the following three sources for a detailed discussion of the three taxonomy schemes illustrated in Tables 13.2, 13.3, and 13.4:

Benjamin S. Bloom, ed., *Taxonomy of Educational Objectives, The Classification of Educational Goals—Handbook I: Cognitive Domain* (New York: David McKay Company, Inc., 1956).

David Krathwohl, Benjamin Bloom, and Bertram Masia, *Taxonomy of Educational Objectives, The Classification of Educational Goals—Handbook II: Affective Domain* (New York: David McKay Company, Inc., 1964).

Anita J. Harrow, *A Taxonomy of the Psychomotor Domain— A Guide for Developing Behavioral Objectives* (New York: David McKay Company, Inc., 1972).

If we are committed to identifying valued learning outcomes that reflect the "holistic" nature of individuals, then we must insist that goal statements, whether found in state departments or classrooms, reflect a balance of objectives in all three domains of behavior.

RELATING GOALS AND OBJECTIVES TO CURRICULUM DEVELOPMENT

Anyone familiar with curriculum documents is probably aware that there is a discrepancy between curriculum planned and curriculum implemented. Curriculum workers using curriculum materials know that statements of goals and objectives accompanying those materials are not always reflected in the curriculum as it becomes operative in the classroom. Since most curriculum development projects are cooperative endeavors involving people, it is sad that goals and objectives of curriculum documents are not reflected in classroom practice.

The authors are concerned about a general reluctance on the part of curriculum leaders to come to grips with the various existing processes and influences that shape and decidedly determine the final curriculum programs in our schools. It is the position of the authors that until these variables in the political realm of education are acknowledged and confronted openly, curriculum theory will continue to be superfluous to practice and curriculum development will continue to be a largely unpredictable phenomenon characterized by an ever-present gap between theory and practice.

COMPETENCY–BASED EDUCATION

The accountability movement of the late 1970s has resulted in a number of state legislatures passing laws establishing minimum competency requirements for promotion or graduation.[8] The terms of "coping skills," "survival skills," and "adult literacy" are finding a place in laws and in the literature. Criterion-referenced measures are used to determine progress of students. This process is designed to compare achievement with specific content coverage. The goals of the content are usually expressed in the form of specific behavioral objectives constructed to measure specific achievement of well-defined skills.

There is and will be controversy about the virtues of minimum competency programs. The authors believe those persons who would be instructional leaders need to argue persuasively for a balanced educational program that will have minimum standards, but not result in an elitist form of education that cuts off the disadvantaged or low-income student from the mainstream of our society. Our democratic ideal of public schools still holds that our schools are responsible to all of the children of all the people.

EXAMPLES OF GOAL STATEMENTS

There are many sources of goals and objectives available in the literature. School systems, state departments, schools, and national commissions are all sources of goals. The previously cited Cardinal Principles of Secondary Education and the goals stated by the ASCD Working Group on Research and Theory are excellent sources for those "timeless" goals. "Timely" goals can be found in publications of interpreting public laws at state and national levels. The stated goal of Public Law 94–142, for instance, stipulates that "all handicapped children aged three to twenty-one may enjoy special education and related services provided through this measure." Title Nine regulations express not only the law relating to prohibiting sex discrimination, but goals relating to the participation of women in all facets of American life.

Examples of goal statements include the following:

> "The School Board and Staff of the Pinellas County School System are committed to create and maintain an educational atmosphere that promotes the attainment of intellectual competencies, moral and ethical values, and marketable skills with an environment best calculated to meet individual differences."
>
> Pinellas County, Florida School Board

"Develop a program to identify the major needs of the overall community."

"Improve the extent and availability of community health services."

"Offer programs designed to increase understanding of political procedures and processes."

Three Community Education Goals

"The course of instruction in all public schools of Tennessee should include at some appropriate level or levels as determined by the local board of education, courses and content designed to educate children in Negro history . . . ."

Senate Bill No. 1394
State of Tennessee

"Highest priority and major emphasis shall be given to the production of sensitive, autonomous, thinking human beings."

Metropolitan Nashville School District

"The schools of University City exist primarily to serve the youths of this community and the society in which they live by aiding them to become responsible, perceiving, self-directing, self-educating individuals who are capable of making decisions and value judgments."

School District of University City

In concluding this chapter, we wish to recommend that the reader examine not only the sources recommended earlier in the chapter for general goals, but carefully review documents you are using in your curriculum work whether at a school, school district, state department, university, or other agency.

SUMMARY

This chapter has demonstrated that the defining of goals for education is a complex task. The formulation of goals and objectives is a time-consuming and demanding activity, yet it is an essential aspect of curriculum development. In developing goals and objectives, the curriculum worker must examine sources for goals and objectives. The authors have identified major sources of goals as society, the learner, and organized knowledge.

An analysis of major stated goals, such as the Cardinal Principles of Secondary Education and the recent goals defined by the Association for Supervision and Curriculum Development Working Group on Research and Theory, reveals a series of "timeless" goals that will stand the test of time.

Goals and objectives may range from global or general goals to specific behavioral objectives, yet they all constitute the building blocks of the total program. One source of complexity in stating goals arises from the need to translate general goals to very specific objectives.

The use of taxonomies assists the curriculum worker in writing objectives at varying levels of behavior. Taxonomies also can assist in determining sequence of segments of a course of study and provide for affective and psychomotor as well as cognitive experiences.

Finally, goals and objectives found in curriculum documents must be reflected in the classroom and the gap between theory and practice narrowed.

Notes

1. "High Schools Under Fire," *Time. Magazine* 110, No. 20 (November 14, 1977), pp. 62–4.
2. Ralph W. Tyler, *Basic Principles of Curriculum and Instruction* (Chicago: University of Chicago Press, 1949), p. 1.
3. Thomas F. Greene, "Teaching, Acting and Behaving," *Harvard Educational Review* 34, (Fall, 1964), p. 517.
4. Hilda Taba, *Curriculum Development: Theory and Practice* (New York: Harcourt, Brace and World, 1962), p. 200.
5. Herbert M. Kleibard, "Reappraisal: The Tyler Rationale," *School Review* Vol. 78, 269 (February, 1970), pp. 268–69.
6. John Goodlad and Maurice Richter, Jr., *The Development of a Conceptual System for Dealing with Problems of Curriculum and Instruction* (U.S. Office of Education, Cooperative Research Program, Project No. 454), p. i.
7. "Report to the Executive Council of A.S.C.D.," mimeo., Research and Theory Working Group, October 15, 1977.
8. Gordon Cawelti, "Requiring Competencies for Graduation—Some Curricular Issues," *Educational Leadership* 35, No. 2 (November, 1977), p. 86.

Suggested Learning Activities

1. Identify some ways educators are attempting to reach a goal consensus in the United States at this time.

2. Take any single major goal and derive a set of instructional objectives for a school or classroom.

3. Practice formulating behavioral objectives using the criteria suggested in the chapter.

4. Select some stated beliefs in your school or district and match practices with those beliefs. Where are the discrepancies?

5. "Balance in the curriculum" is a term used by the authors. When we are talking about a broad goal, such as "understanding others," persons holding different values can interpret that goal in different ways. Using goals in your school or district, analyze the meaning from several different positions. How would you obtain group consensus on the meaning of a particular goal?

Books to Review

Benjamin, Harold. *The Saber Tooth Curriculum.* New York: McGraw-Hill, 1972.

Bloom, Benjamin, ed. *Taxonomy of Educational Objectives—Handbook I: Cognitive Domain.* New York: McKay, 1956.

Harrow, Anita J. *A Taxonomy of the Psychomotor Domain.* New York: McKay, 1972.

Krathwohl, D.R.; Bloom, Benjamin; and Masia, Bertram. *Taxonomy of Educational Objectives—Handbook II: Affective Domain.* New York: McKay, 1964.

Mager, Robert. *Preparing Instructional Objectives.* Palo Alto, California: Fearon Publishers, 1962.

McAshon, H.H. *The Goals Approach to Performance Objectives.* Philadelphia: W.B. Saunders Company, 1974.

Oliver, Albert I. *Curriculum Improvement,* 2nd ed. New York: Harper and Row, 1971.

Saylor, J. Galen and Alexander, William. *Planning Curriculum for Schools.* New York: Holt, Rinehart, and Winston, 1974.

Smith, B. Othanel; Stanley, William; and Shores, J. Harlan. *Fundamentals of Curriculum Development,* rev. ed. New York: World Book Company, 1957.

14

Assessing Characteristics and Needs of Learners

Basic to all curriculum development efforts is an assessment of present conditions and goals. Without such assessment, individual development activities will lack purpose. School districts generally approach such an assessment through three formats: an accreditation review, a comprehensive survey, or a needs assessment. While all three of these mediums provide valuable planning data to schools, the review and survey techniques tend to have a quantitative focus and assume a traditional curriculum pattern. The needs assessment technique, by contrast, makes no assumption about the form of school organization and looks at the school district in terms of its avowed goals. For this reason, it is believed that the needs assessment is a more valuable assessment device for a school district serious about curriculum development.

A needs assessment represents a comprehensive inquiry into the educational status of a school district. It provides school leaders with the data necessary for completing the "status check stage" of a comprehensive educational plan. The major intent of a needs assessment is to determine to what degree the school district is implementing a stated philosophy of education and to what degree goals are being met by existing programs.

Where possible, the needs assessment utilizes the most objective methods possible of data collection and analysis. The type and quality of data available, and the time available for collecting and processing data, will place limits on the scope of the study, the number and types of instruments used, and the statistical procedures applied. Unlike the accreditation review and the school survey, a needs assessment will always be somewhat subjective in nature, incorporating in a purposeful manner the perceptions of students, parents and educators.

Needs assessments presuppose a commitment to maximum involvement of the school community. The plan provides for the collection of data from parents, students, and school personnel, and for the review of data by representatives from each group. This involvement process utilizes an important factor in the educational validity of needs assessment data—an attitude of "ownership" on the part of the school community.

The needs assessment represents a critical step toward the development of a comprehensive educational plan (see chapter 18) for curriculum development. The willingness of a school district to identify its deficiencies and select its goals in full view of public scrutiny paves the way for rational and orderly future planning in program development.*

THE NEEDS ASSESSMENT FRAMEWORK

The conduct of a needs assessment in a school district is flexible. The dimensions of school operations considered and the data to be gathered are dependent on the mandate for change in the district and the openness and honesty of those initiating such assessment. In general, however, it is possible to identify the primary needs assessment framework that supplies critical planning data to a school district. The following outline represents a typical needs assessment approach:

    I.   General Information
        a. Location of school district
        b. Demographic characteristics of immediate area
        c. Natural resources of region
        d. Commercial—industrial data

---

* The authors wish to thank Mr. William Nallia, Executive Secretary of the Kentucky Association of School Administrators, for many of the ideas contained in this chapter.

      e. Income levels of area residents

      f. Special social-economic considerations

  II. General Population Characteristics

      a. Population growth patterns

      b. Age, race of population

      c. Educational levels of population

      d. Projected population

  III. School Population Characteristis (Ages 3–19)

      a. School enrollment by grade level

      b. Birth rate trends in school district

      c. In-migration, out-migration patterns

      d. Race/sex/religious composition of school district

      e. Years of school completed by persons over 25 years of age

      f. Studies of school dropouts

  IV. Programs and Course Offerings in District

      a. Organization of school programs

      b. Programs' concept and rationale

      c. Course offerings

      d. Special program needs

  V. Professional Staff

      a. Training and experience

      b. Awareness of trends and developments

      c. Attitudes toward change

  VI. Instructional Patterns and Strategies

      a. Philosophical focus of instructional program

      b. Observational and perceptual instructional data

      c. Assessment of instructional strategies in use

      d. Instructional materials in use

      e. Decision making and planning processes

      f. Grouping for instruction

      g. Classroom management techniques

      h. Grading and placement of pupils

      i. Student independence

      j. Evaluation of instructional effectiveness

  VII. Student data

      a. Student experiences

      b. Student self-esteem

      c. Student achievement

  VIII. Facilities

      a. Assessment of existing facilities and sites

      b. Special facilities

      c. Utilization of facilities

      d. Projected facility needs

  IX. Summary of Data

CONDUCTING THE NEEDS ASSESSMENT

Using a needs assessment pattern to gather data essential to curriculum planning is advantageous in that most of the process is carried out by the people closest to the subject of study. While accreditation studies and formal school surveys usually use "expert" opinion to judge or evaluate the school district, a needs assessment format enables such districts to use parents, teachers, and students in the same process. The key to understanding this distinction is to be found in the idea that needs assessments address relative progress toward goals rather than absolute conditions. The emphasis in a needs assessment is not so much on what presently exists, but rather on what the present condition is compared to identified goals and objectives.

Usually, needs assessments are initiated because it is believed that present conditions in a school district can be improved upon. Such a position sees curriculum development as a continuum, and the needs assessment is begun to gain clarity of direction.

The first step of a needs assessment is to decide what data are needed for decision making, and to develop a strategy for data gathering. A typical needs assessment in a school district will utilize citizen's groups or study teams comprised of a mixture of persons from the school community. Sometimes such teams are formed by schools or according to school level, but it is often of benefit to have the teams study areas such as student achievement or facilities vertically through all grade levels. The following are some guidelines for teams organized according to the outline presented earlier.

General Information

It is important that any needs assessment be put in perspective so that findings of such a study will have meaning to the particular community under review. Each of the more than 18,000 school districts in the United States have different and significant variables that affect the type of schools which can be planned. Failure to understand these situational variables or to put findings into an appropriate context can lead to misunderstanding and, sometimes, false aspirations.

A needs assessment should include an accurate but brief description of the school district setting. The size of the district, its population, and the natural resources that might affect school operation should be included. So, too, should information about local commerce and industry which may indicate the tax support for schools in the area as well as the relative wealth of the parents of school children.

Special social or economic conditions in an area should also be noted. If, for instance, a military base nearby is served by the district or if there is a seasonal migrant population to plan for, it is important that these variables be acknowledged.

General data about the community, regardless of location, is available in public libraries in standard census reports. Current information dating from the last census data can generally be gained from the local chamber of commerce.

General Population Characteristics

In gathering information about the people who inhabit the area served by the school district, there is an attempt to understand the educational and cultural levels of the community, general attitudes about schools, and expectations for education in the area.

Some of the most important data to be gathered about the people who are served by the school district is that which indicates the cultural heritage and set of traditions in the community. In areas where populations are stable, both in terms of turnover and composition, there is usually mimimal social or cultural change. Because schools tend to reflect the communities they serve, one would expect to find a comparable stability in school data. In communities that have experienced considerable growth or turnover of population, however, school planning data tends to be more varied and expectations for change in the schools increased.

Along with information about population changes, data about economic development in the community will often indicate anticipated population changes which will affect schools. The closing of key industries, declining farm populations, closing of military bases, or seasonal industries can signal new patterns for school districts. Out-migration of urban population, regional economic prosperity, or the development of new industries based on natural resources can equally affect school planning.

In looking at the composition of the population to be served, a number of variables are important indicators for school planners. Birth rate projections, population stability patterns, racial and economic composition, and special social and cultural characteristics such as languages spoken or national origin of parents all have planning implications for school leaders.

Another influential variable to assess in a formal needs assessment is the educational level of parents and persons in the community over twenty-five years of age. Data about the educational achievement levels of the community will often indicate the amount of belief in, and support for, education. Knowledge of such a factor can also help planners to develop strategies for a school bond election, elect school officials, or initiate a new school program in the community.

Information about the social and economic composition of a community, with specific data about items such as the labor force, birth rates, housing construction, composition of population, and social characteristics of the community are public records gathered every ten years in national census reports.

School Population Characteristics

While it is important for educational planners to be knowledgeable about the general population of the community served by a school district, it is absolutely essential that characteristics of the school population be known before a comprehensive educational program can be developed. In most cases, data from the past ten years are utilized to enable planners to make a reasonable five year projection for school program development. Table 14.1 is an example of such a projection. Such linear projections, of course, assume stability in population, economy, and technologically induced events.

Among the most stable and useful data available to school planners are birth rate trends in the district and school enrollment patterns by grade level. With high consistency, school planners can anticipate enrollment in schools and within grade levels in schools. Closer analysis of population increases and declines within schools can even provide information about dropout and retention patterns, as well as alert school planners to new populations of students who must be accommodated by the curriculum. Up-to-date information about birth rates is usually available through county records, while data about grade level enrollment are readily available through school attendance records in most districts.

Table 14.1
Projected Grade Level Enrollment for 1975–1976

Age	3	4	5	6	7	8
Enrollment	98	106	110	103	110	123
Age	9	10	11	12	13	14
Enrollment	119	129	125	117	109	109
Age	15	16	17	18	19	TOTAL
Enrollment	96	98	85	70	10	1,717

These projections by age are based on the 1970 U.S. Census Data and School Enrollment Data from 1965 to 1975. These enrollment data are projection only.

The racial, ethnic, religious, and sexual composition of a school district is also important to school planners. Due to the mobility of populations within the United States today, primary characteristics of communities can change rapidly, and with such change, cause an alteration in the purpose of education in the district. Often, school districts will offer curriculum programs for the populations who lived in the community twenty-five years earlier.

Perhaps the most important planning data that can be gained from an assessment of the school age population is the information that deals with dropouts. Most school districts in the United States have an alarming number of students who, for a variety of reasons, terminate their schooling. The community and the school system should be particularly concerned by students who walk out of school never to return by personal choice. Not only can such an exodus indicate that something is lacking in the general school program, but dropouts present the community with a social problem rarely understood.

Table 14.2
Sample Dropout Grid

Year	Number of Dropouts	Number 16 Years and Older	Dropout Percentage
1971–72	34	258	13%
1972–73	38	253	15
1973–74	44	239	18
1974–75	30	234	13
1975–76	48	277	17
TOTAL	194	1,261	15

Students who quit school prior to graduation are usually faced with employment difficulties, limited job opportunities, low earning power, lessened opportunity for promotions, and emotional stress from social and cultural pressures. These realities for the dropout often translate into social problems for the community which find form in greater need for law enforcement, mental health services, welfare assistance, and public works projects. To accept a high dropout rate as a normal occurrence in schooling is shortsighted, indeed.

Studies of dropouts often provide school planners with a profile of students not benefitting from existing school programs. Causation factors such as the need to work, home problems, pregnancy, or poor scholarship can indicate to planners those areas of the curriculum in need of review and renewal.

Without question, the single leading cause of school dropouts is academic failure.* Included in this broad category are students who lack interest in school, students who rebel against failure and are expelled, students who choose less threatening environments in which to interact, and students who are incapable of competing with other students. School districts that have a substantial number of dropouts must decide where the fine balance between academic excellence and social conscience resides.

Data about dropouts are often available through school attendance records, while follow-up data are easily obtained from social agencies in the community. A valuable technique in assessing the school dropout is the interview.

Programs and Course Offerings

The general scope and depth of an educational program can be best identified by reviewing the number and types of courses and special activities offered by individual schools. Of importance in understanding the programs of a school district are the organization of school programs, the rationale for such organization, the breadth and scope of course offerings, and the degree to which special education needs are met.

Many school districts conceptualize schooling according to levels of attainment and reference programs such as primary school, elementary school, middle school, and high school. In such an organization, students advance through the program by grades rather than by age, maturation, achievement, readiness, or interest.

In such programs, content and skill development are dominant organizers; there is little consideration for individual differences, and curriculum planning focuses on the sequencing of experiences. Such programs are usually organized in quantitative units with teachers, students, classrooms, and textbooks assigned by a predetermined formula. Supplemental activities, enrichment experiences, and student services are added to the core program as resources allow.

---

* While school records show academic failure to be the leading cause of school dropouts, the relationship is considerably more complex. The cause of dropping out of school may vary with age, sex, race, social background, etc.

Some school districts perceive schooling as an evolution of development (as shown in Table 14.3) with school organization acting to facilitate passage through a predetermined development profile. In such districts, grade lines are not as clearly drawn, and district resources are applied as necessary for successful completion of the pattern.

Still other school districts focus on the individual learner and provide experiences thought beneficial to all learners. In such educational programs, expectations for performance are less uniform and structure is less rigid.

Perhaps less important than the actual organization in a needs assessment is the rationale of the school district for the schooling pattern that exists. Needs assessments analyze school programs in nonjudgmental ways according to how well they are accomplishing their stated objectives. Such objectives can often be found in formal philosophies or statements of purpose. Where such official documents are absent, the purpose of schooling can be inferred by those assessing the district with opportunity for reaction from school leaders.

Regardless of the avowed purpose of schooling and the primary organization of the educational program, the heart of the assessment process should address the course offerings and experiences had by the students. Most school districts in the United States, because of history and state and local requirements, arrange school into subject areas. Nearly all schools provide a core of activities that includes mathematics, science, English, and social studies. Most districts also provide supplemental programs in physical education, art, music, and vocational arts. Beyond such basic programs, courses and experiences are offered that reflect the capacity of the district to address individual differences. Often, the degree to which a school district "tailors" such offerings is an indication of the awareness of school leaders of the needs of students.

In recent years, due to research and legislation, school districts in the United States have become sensitive to the needs of special groups of students found in the school. While a list of all such special students would be lengthy, addressing programs to serve special education, career education, and adult education can illuminate course offerings outside of the general curriculum.

In every community there are children and youth who have special educational needs that cannot be met within the operation of the general program of instruction. There are many definitions of students with special needs in existence, and most include those children with emotional, physical, communicative, or intellectual deviations which interfere with school adjustment or prevent full attainment of academic achievement. Included in such a broad classification would be

Table 14.3
Developmental Profile

DEVELOPMENTAL PROFILE

Santa Clara Inventory
of
Developmental Tasks

Name _____ Birthdate _____

School _____ Teacher _____ Grade ____

Testing Dates: ____	Scoring:
C.D. _____	0 — Almost never
L.D. _____	1 — Some of the time
A.M. _____	2 — Most of the time
A.P. _____	
V.M. _____	
V.P. _____	
V.M.P. _____	
M.C. _____	

	Auditory Memory
	0 1 2
Auditory Perception	discriminate between com. sounds 5-5

Visual Memory	0 1 2 recall animal pictures 4-4	0 1 2 name objects from memory 4-5

Visual Perception	0 1 2 match color objects 3-3	0 1 2 match form objects 3-4	0 1 2 match size objects 3-5

Visual Motor Performance	0 1 2 follow target with eyes 2-2	0 1 2 string beads 2-3	0 1 2 copy a circle 2-4	0 1 2 copy a cross 2-5

Motor Coordination	0 1 2 creep 1-1	0 1 2 walk 1-2	0 1 2 run 1-3	0 1 2 jump 1-4	0 1 2 hop 1-5

PRE-SCHOOL

DIRECTIONS TO THE TEACHER: This is the record form on which each child's performance is recorded. The column for Testing Dates allows the teacher to measure each category up to three times; however, if the student exhibits mastery when first observed, only one date is entered. The abbreviations mean: M.C. — Motor Coordination, V.M.P. — Visual Motor Performance, V.P. — Visual Perception, V.M. — Visual Motor, A.P. — Auditory Perception, A.M. — Auditory Memory, L.D. — Language Development, C.D. — Conceptual Development. The scoring criteria for each task are listed in the Observation Guide.

(Each task is scored on a 0 1 2 scale.)

Conceptual Development		assign number value (8-8)	identify first, last, top, middle, bottom (8-9)	tell how 2 items are alike (8-10)	sort objects 2 ways (8-11)	
Language Development	give personal information (7-7)	describe simple objects (7-8)	relate words and pictures (7-9)	define words (7-10)	language usage (7-11)	
	perform 3 commands (6-6)	repeat a sentence (6-7)	repeat a tapping sequence (6-8)	repeat 4 numbers (6-9)	recall story facts (6-10)	repeat 5 numbers (6-11)
	identify common sounds (5-6)	locate source of sound (5-7)	match beginning sounds (5-8)	hear fine diff. between similiar words (5-9)	match rhyming sounds (5-10)	match ending sounds (5-11)
	recall a 3-color sequence (4-6)	recall 2 items in a sequence (4-7)	reproduce design from memory (4-8)	recall 3 items in a sequence (4-9)	recall 3-part design (4-10)	recall word forms (4-11)
	match size and form on paper (3-6)	match numbers (3-7)	match letters (3-8)	match direction on design (3-9)	isolate visual images (3-10)	match words (3-11)
	copy a square (2-6)	cut with scissors (2-7)	tie shoes (2-8)	copy letters (2-9)	copy a sentence (2-10)	copy a diamond (2-11)
	balance on one foot (1-6)	use of hands and arms (1-7)	skip (1-8)	balance on walking beam (1-9)	jump rope assisted (1-10)	jump rope unassisted (1-11)
	5 - 5½ YRS.		**6 - 6½ YRS.**		**7 YRS.**	

the intellectually gifted, the mentally retarded, physically handi-capped, speech handicapped, behaviorally disordered, multi-handi-capped, homebound, autistic, hospitalized, and visually or hearing impaired.

School districts vary in how they organize themselves to serve these special learners. In recent years, legislation has been erratic in provid-ing guidelines for the inclusion or exclusion of such students from regular classrooms. Districts do, however, recognize and monitor the presence of such students as shown in Table 14.4.

Career and vocational education is fast becoming a major curricu-lum component of many school districts in the nation. While the im-petus for this trend comes from many sources, career and vocational education still represents the major alternative for secondary school students who choose a non-college preparatory program.

Student interest in vocational programs is generally high among all types of students. The mandate for school districts to provide quality vocational experiences is heightened when it is recognized that the majority of all students graduating from secondary schools do not go on as full-time students in postsecondary institutions.

A valuable resource for those assessing student vocational interests is the *Directory of Occupational Titles* produced by the United States Department of Labor.[1] This directory identifies over 21,000 job titles which may be of interest to students. Using instruments such as the *Ohio Vocational Interest Survey,* areas in which vocational experi-ences might be developed can be identified. Student questionnaires which seek to pinpoint plans for following graduation can also provide school leaders with rough indicators of need (Table 14.5).

A third type of special education program provided by some school districts is adult education. A program for adults will depend on their level of educational attainment, the skills and knowledge needed by adults in the community, and whether interests are occupational or for personal development. School districts can effectively use adult edu-cation programs to increase community involvement as well as to build bridges to parents of school children.

For adults in the community who have less than a high school edu-cation, offerings may be geared to meet basic education needs. Such programs often lead to completion of a high school equivalency test. Other adults may be interested in education for job opportunities. Still other adults in the community may participate in education for personal improvement. Popular items are such topics as family-oriented courses, household mechanics, child development courses, and rec-ord keeping.

Schools providing educational experiences for adults in the com-munity can effectively use questionnaires to assess interests. Sam-ples of job-oriented and personal development courses are shown on p. 255.

Table 14.4
Students with Special Education Needs

Year	Elementary School			Middle School			High School			Total		
	73/74	74/75	75/76	73/74	74/75	75/76	73/74	74/75	75/76	73/74	74/75	75/76
Educable mentally retarded	24	26	28	26	28	31	20	23	25	70	77	84
Trainable mentally retarded	4	5	7	2	3	4	1	2	3	7	10	14
Behavioral disorders	4	7	8	9	10	12	2	5	6	15	22	26
Visually impaired	0	4	5	0	1	2	0	2	3	0	7	10
Hearing impaired	2	4	5	0	1	2	0	0	1	2	5	8
Speech impaired	18	20	21	16	19	20	0	2	3	34	41	44
Multi-handicapped	1	2	2	1	1	1	0	0	0	2	3	3
Hospital/homebound	5	6	6	3	4	4	2	2	2	10	12	12
Gifted	14	15	15	13	13	13	14	14	14	41	42	42
Learning Disability	15	18	20	30	34	35	31	31	31	76	83	86
TOTAL										257	302	329

Table 14.5
Sample Vocational Program Choices

PLAN	8TH GRADE		9TH GRADE		10TH GRADE		11TH GRADE		12TH GRADE		TOTAL	
	M	F	M	F	M	F	M	F	M	F	M	F
1. Gen. Agriculture	3		3			1			1		7	1
2. Forestry, Landscaping or Horticulture	4		2		5		1				12	0
3. Gen. Office Practice Clerical	1			2		3		5	2	6	3	16
4. Secretarial Practice Stenography		5		4		5				4	0	18
5. Business Data Processing				1	1				1	3	2	4
6. Bookkeeping	1	6						2	1	3	2	11
7. Distributive Education Sales–Retail, Wholesale	1		1					1	2		4	1
8. Food Preparation of Food Services	2			2		2					2	4
9. Practical Nursing and Child Care		3		3		2		2	1	2	1	12
10. Dental or Medical Assistant	1	1	3	2	2	2		1			6	6

M = Male
F = Female   Numerals represent combined first and second choices.

Job-Oriented	**Personal Development**
a. Typing	a. Reading improvement
b. Bookkeeping	b. Arts crafts
c. Shorthand	c. Horticulture
d. Office machines	d. Slimnastics
e. Income tax	e. Self-protection
f. Electrical wiring	f. Home improvement
g. Brick masonry	g. Photography
h. Cosmetology	h. Interior decorating
i. Sales clerking	i. Leisure activities
j. Carpentry	j. Basic sewing

The Professional Staff

A thorough needs assessment also reviews the professional staff in the school district. Among primary concerns are the training and experience of teachers, supervisors and administrators, the balance among the various teaching positions, and anticipated staff needs. Also subject to analysis is the awareness of the staff to recent trends and developments in the field as well as attitudes toward change.

A review of staff training often will indicate a dominance of age, race, or sex among school faculties. These patterns are important in terms of the goals of the district and the specific programs being promoted in the buildings. Such an assessment will sometimes reveal an excessive number of graduates from a single university or a pattern of inbreeding among teachers. While the latter situation is sometimes unavoidable in remote regions, a diversity among teaching backgrounds is desirable in terms of the experiences teachers bring to the classroom.

A district-wide assessment of allocated teaching positions will often reveal over-staffing in particular subject areas at the expense of other equally important areas. Such a district-wide review will also indicate trends in staffing that can assist planners in projecting future staffing needs.

An analysis of faculty familiarity with new trends and developments in subject areas, and new innovative concepts, is important if the district anticipates new programs. Such a review can often pinpoint staff development needs that can be addressed in inservice sessions.

Finally, school districts can find extremely useful the analysis of professional staff attitudes toward change in general and toward specific curriculum alterations in particular. Such attitudes are the result of many factors, and experience has shown that age and experience of teachers are poor predictors of readiness to change.

Instructional Patterns and Strategies

By far the most important segment of a needs assessment in schools is the part that focuses on instructional patterns and strategies. Such teacher behaviors should reflect uniformly the intentions of the district to deliver quality programs to students. The types of instruction found in classrooms should result from an understanding of the goals of the district, and an assessment of strategies and techniques can occur only following a clarification of the district philosophy.

In some districts, the predominant goal of instruction is to have all students master the essential data that will distinguish them as an educated person. Other school districts place greatest emphasis on the needs, interests, and abilities of students. A key distinction in these two extreme positions is the role of the student in the learning process. Since needs assessments tend to utilize subjective perceptual data about schools, they are most useful in districts favoring a student-centered curriculum.

Two major techniques can be used to assess instructional patterns and strategies: the observation technique and the administering of perceptual instruments. Since chapter 17 of this book deals with observational techniques in detail, coverage here will be restricted to perceptual instruments.

The perceptual data technique, commonly referred to as the opinionnaire, requires the administration of instruments to teachers and, in some cases, students and parents. This perceptual survey is based on findings of phenomenological psychology which holds that people behave in terms of personal meanings which exist for them at a given moment. In short, behavior is based on perception because we behave and react to that which we believe to be real. A personal perception may or may not be supported by facts, but such perceptions serve as facts to each of us.

Perceptual instruments are useful in needs assessments because they possess several distinct advantages. First, they are quick to administer and tally. Second, they are easily managed and are less time-consuming than interviews or quantitative measures. Most important, however, is the fact that such perceptual techniques allow all teachers in the district to participate in the data-gathering stage. Such involvement is critical if programmatic responses to such findings are to be credible and supported.

One such perceptual instrument currently in use is the experimental *Sims-Nallia Inventory of Instructional Strategies.* This instrument is comprised of sixty-five strategies commonly found in school classrooms (such as individualizing instruction or grouping students by achievement level). The Sims-Nallia feeds back to teachers a composite profile of instructional practices in use by all teachers in a percentage form. Such a "mirror" serves to alert classroom teachers to the practices of others in the district and does so without judgment about the meaning of the heavily-used practices.

Another instructional pattern worthy of assessment is the use of materials in the classroom. While most schools utilize textbooks as a medium for learning, others use a variety of instructional materials, and still others attempt to individualize the instructional materials used by students.

Needs assessments also regularly look at the type of planning and decision making that occurs in classrooms and schools. Are students (and teachers) involved in decisions that affect their learning and related experiences? Are students (and teachers) involved in the assignment of activities and tasks? The selection of content? The construction of courses?

Needs assessments generally gather data on the types of grouping patterns found in the school district. Are students grouped for instruction by interest or needs? Are they grouped in classroom settings by ability or age? Are students' contents grouped with each subject being taught separately? How are decisions about student grouping arrived at?

Classroom management is usually reviewed by a needs assessment. Although all teachers use some system of classroom management, formal or informal, some patterns are more common than others. Student prescriptions, contracts, tutors, furniture arrangement, classroom rules, and communication patterns are all valuable indicators of the prevailing management system. Sometimes such analysis will reveal problem areas common to many teachers and fertile ground for staff development activities.

Grading practices and grade-level placement of students is also an area addressed by a needs assessment. In particular, analyses of grade distribution by level, in schools and across the district, can indicate strengths and weaknesses. The construction of tables of overagedness in the school district can also be helpful to school planners.

In some needs assessments, student independence is an area that is analyzed. Particularly in districts where goals indicate a desire to foster independence, measures of how much students are dependent on teachers for direction and decisions can prove insightful. Student responsibility, for instance, is essential for the successful operation of an individualized curriculum.

A final measure of instructional strategy is the method by which instructional effectiveness is evaluated. Do teachers and building faculties make programmatic assessments on a regular basis and use such findings to "adjust" the curriculum? Is classroom supervision perceived as an assisting behavior that upgrades instructional practices or is it an irregular and feared activity?

Student Data

In school districts where there is an attempt to serve the individual needs of learners, as opposed to giving all students the same academic treatment, it is important to gather student data. Data relating to student experiences is valuable for preplanning input, while information about student feelings and achievement can assist school planners in making adjustments to the existing curriculum.

In reviewing student experiences, a number of variables are useful indicators of both the breadth and depth of the student's world. A questionnaire that assesses student travel, recreational, aesthetic, and cultural backgrounds can provide teachers with invaluable points of reference for instruction. Examples of such questions might be:

1. Have you ever seen an ocean?
2. Have you ever flown on an airplane?
3. Have you ever been to a band concert?
4. Have you ever been in a public library?
5. Have you ever visited a foreign country?

Questionnaires that deal with assessments of experiences, at the secondary as well as the elementary levels, give teachers insights into students' backgrounds and levels of sophistication. When tallied as a percentage, the general level of experience for entire schools can be developed. Another equally valuable assessment device that might provide the same type of experience is a projection technique that would ask students how to spend extra money, or to plan travel trips.

Information about student attitudes, particularly those relating to self-esteem, can assist school planners in personalizing the instructional program. Beyond learning of student interest, motivation, and attitudes toward learning itself, such assessments often give clear portraits of student confidence in the instructional setting. Research over the past twenty years has shown consistently that individuals who feel capable, significant, successful, and worthy tend to have positive school experiences. In contrast, students who have low self-esteem rarely experience success in school settings.[2]

Measures of self-esteem, a personal judgment of worthiness the individual holds toward himself, are plentiful. Two measures used regularly in needs assessments are the *When Do I Smile* instrument (grades K-3) and the *Coopersmith Self-Esteem Inventory* (grades 4–12). *When Do I Smile* is a twenty-eight item instrument that can be administered to nonreaders. Students respond by marking faces that are happy, blank, or sad. By this means, school planners can gain insight into attitudes about school, peers, and general self.

The Coopersmith Self-Esteem Inventory, a fifty item instrument, assesses student attitudes about themselves, their lives at home, and school life. Students respond to statements such as "I can make up my mind without too much trouble" or "I'm pretty happy" with either a "like me" or "unlike me" response. Such instruments can tell school planners a great deal about student confidence, support from home, and attitudes toward the existing curriculum.

Assessments of student achievement can be either broad or narrow in focus. The measure of this essential category is really a reflection of the school district's definition of education. When an educational program is perceived as primarily the mastery of skills and cognitive data, standardized achievement tests can be used exclusively to determine progress. When *education* is defined more broadly, measures of achievement become personal and more affective in nature.

Standardized achievement testing is carried out in most school districts in the United States on a scheduled basis. Tests such as the *California Achievement Test* can provide computer-scored analyses in areas such as math, language arts, and reading. Such standardized tests give school districts an assessment of relative progress in terms of validated national norms. Achievement tests compare a student's progress with what is considered to be normal progress for students in the nation of approximately the same age and/or grade level. These tests do *not* address a student's ability to perform.

It is useful for school planners to know if students in a district or particular school are achieving above or below grade level, for such information might suggest the retention or elimination of a specific curriculum program. More important, however, are general trends revealed by such tests. A continuing decline in reading scores, for instance, may pinpoint a level of schooling where curriculum review is needed. In Table 14.6, students in a district are displayed according to whether they are achieving above or below grade level in reading according to three commonly used standardized tests: *Gates McGinitie* (lower elementary), *Iowa Test of Basic Skills* (middle grades), and *Test of Academic Progress* (secondary grades).

In school districts where education is defined in terms of comprehensive criteria, assessments of student achievement are generally multiple. Sometimes such assessments have multiple dimensions, such as achievement in knowledge utilization, skill acquisition, and personal development. Sometimes such assessments are criterion-referenced, matching student achievement against goals rather than norms. Almost always the evidence of student achievement is multidimensional, supplementing standardized tests with samples of student work, teacher observations, and other such measures of growth.

Facilities

A final area considered by most needs assessments are the educational facilities used by the district to accomplish its program goals.

Table 14.6

Summary of Reading Achievement in One School District

▨ Indicates Below Grade Placement

GRADE LEVEL	NUMBER OF STUDENTS BY GRADE							TOTAL
	2	3	4	5	6	8	11	
14.0-14.9								
13.0-13.9							6	6
12.0-12.9							6	6
11.0-11.9						1	8	9
10.0-10.9						5	16	21
9.0-9.9						6	21	27
8.0-8.9					1	14	16	31
7.0-7.9				1	7	9	9	26
6.0-6.9				2	16	29	7	54
5.0-5.9		3	7	9	29	27		75
4.0-4.9		5	27	25	43	13		113
3.0-3.9	3	14	28	55	26	2		128
2.0-2.9	16	40	30	21	9			116
1.0-1.9	75	41	3	11	0			130
0.0-0.9								
TOTAL	94	103	95	124	131	106	89	742

Ideally, such facilities should be designed on the basis of program concepts.

An indepth study of facilities seeks to answer the following critical questions:

1. What is the overall pattern of facilities in the district?
2. How adequate is each plant and site for educational use?
3. How are the facilities currently being utilized?
4. What is the net operating capacity of each facility?

Since chapter 19 of this book will address the analysis of buildings and classrooms from an instructional perspective, facilities in this section will be discussed in terms of four criteria: facilities and sites, special facilities, the overall utilization of facilities, and projected facility needs.

Assessments of facilities and sites attempt to analyze the adequacy and capacity ratings of all plants and grounds for maximum benefit to the educational program. A basic principle of most such studies is that flexible, multi-use facilities are more beneficial than those that limit programs to a single instructional pattern. A facility (school building) is considered adequate and modern if it provides for a variety of grouping patterns, the utilization of educational media, guidance, health and food services, special interest instruction (music, art, home economics, science, horticulture, etc.), large group assembly, and administrative functions.

One commonly used criteria for assessing school facilities is the *Linn-McCormick Rating Form for School Facilities* developed by the Institute of Field Studies, Teachers College, Columbia University. The Linn-McCormick scale uses a point system that systematically evaluates school buildings from classrooms through custodial facilities. Facilities are then rated on a scale from "excellent" to "poor." Such a scale does not consider the financial capability of the district to provide such facilities.

The value of such a building-by-building analysis, for educational planning, is that it allows school planners to see facilities in terms of the desired educational program. School plants can be compared and priorities for new building programs identified. If additional school sites are projected, lead time is available for survey and acquisition. Remodeling, where needed, can be scheduled.

In the assessment of facilities, an important phase is the identification and analysis of special facilities. In most school districts, special facilities are perceived as supplemental to regular instructional spaces and thus are a luxury. School districts must choose among a host of special rooms and spaces such as gymnasiums, art rooms, teacher offices, and so forth. Additionally, many schools have had to plan special rooms to deal with special students such as the physically handicapped. The decision as to which kinds of special rooms and spaces are present should be based on school planning rather than convenience or familiarity.

When school facilities are assessed, considerable attention should be directed to the utilization of such facilities. Detailed study of plant utilization can often lead to more efficient use of existing buildings and sites. Such study also will often reveal multi-use spaces in areas where only single use is presently in operation, i.e., the "cafetorium."

The assessment of school facilities and sites, including special areas and utilization patterns, should assist school planners in developing long-range facilities planning. Such planning can eliminate an undesirable pattern of building schools and acquiring sites after housing needs are in a critical state. Under such conditions, educational facilities are rarely adequate or appropriate to the needs of the instructional program.

SUMMARY

Basic to all educational planning is an assessment of what exists. From such an assessment should come an understanding of the strengths and weaknesses of the educational program, as well as goals for development.

School districts approach the assessment of learners who experience school programs in a number of ways. Of the comprehensive reviews of school programs, the needs assessment approach seems to provide the broadest profile to school planners. Using generic categories such as general information, population characteristics, school population characteristics, programs and course offerings, instructional patterns and strategies, student data, professional staff, and facilities, the needs assessment thoroughly analyzes the school program. Such analyses provide school planners with a comprehensive set of data for future school development.

The needs assessment provides school planners with a vehicle for involving the public in the development of school programs. Such an inclusion strategy is thought by the authors to have maximum payoff in the long-range development of public school programs.

Notes

1. *Directory of Occupational Titles,* 3rd ed., United States Department of Labor, Bureau of Employment Security, (Washington, D.C., 1965).
2. Wallace LaBenne and Bert Greene, *Educational Implications of Self Concept Theory* (Pacific Palisades: Goodyear Publishing, 1969).

Suggested Learning Activities

1. Outline major steps necessary to conduct a comprehensive needs survey in a school. At what points can professional staff members be involved?
2. Describe the relationship of demographic data to school planning.

Books to Review

Calton, E.B., et al. *Education For Relevance: The Schools and Social Change.* Boston: Houghton-Mifflin Company, 1968.

Saylor, Galen. *The Schools of the Future—Now.* Washington, D.C.: Association for Supervision and Curriculum Development, 1972.

15

Identifying and Securing Instructional Materials

Instructional materials play a central role in the instructional process. In this chapter we will look at sources, types, and evaluation of instructional materials. From the most traditional kinds of instruction, such as textbooks and films, to the most innovative types of materials, such as the computer and video-recorder, modern technology has produced creative and attractive media for learners.

The skillful use of instructional materials by teachers is a long-sought goal of teacher educators. Having the most modern materials available does not guarantee their use in the classroom. Also, any method or material is susceptible to abuse. The textbook method of teaching is often abused, but sometimes the overly extensive use of educational films to carry the teaching load is a greater abuse of instructional materials.

In the hands of professionally competent teachers, instructional materials, whether teacher-made or commercial, can make instruction come alive for students.

SOURCES OF INSTRUCTIONAL–CENTER MATERIALS

A. **Teachers** are a prime source of instructional materials. Knowing his or her own students and their capabilities and interests, teachers can develop individualized materials with which to reach their students.

B. **Schools** are centers of materials development. Often curriculum guides, guidance materials, and other useful materials are produced by curriculum committees established at the school level. Again, the closeness to students makes these materials especially relevant for the students using materials developed at the school level.

C. **School districts** produce numerous materials that are often disseminated across district lines. Curriculum guides in the subject areas, interdisciplinary booklets, skill continuums, and total curriculum packages that include sources of materials, suggested activities, and skill checklists are found at the district level. The *Savvy Curriculum Project* of the Memphis City Schools is an excellent example of the latter. Many of the inservice activities conducted at the district level include the development of instructional materials.

D. **State departments of education** make use of the services of school personnel, consultants, and staff persons to develop numerous instructional materials. State guides for the elementary, middle, or high school are produced as well as guides in the subject areas. Topics such as team teaching and learning centers often are the source of booklets published by departments of education.

E. **Regional agencies** funded by private and government grants turn out many instructional materials. Often, several school districts will fund a regional agency for purposes of evaluation, research, or to foster innovations. Materials generated by such agencies become the property of the member districts. The development of Leagues of Middle Schools in the past ten years has resulted in the sharing of instructional materials. The Florida League of Middle Schools, established in 1973 as an association for mutual aid, had as one of its stated purposes, "To serve as a clearinghouse for the exchange of ideas, materials, and personnel needed for middle school development."

F. **National networks,** such as the Kettering Foundation, IGE, and the National Middle School Resource Center, are funded by government or foundation grants and provide materials, programs, and consultants. Materials development is usually contracted out to state departments, school systems, and universities. The ERIC network, housed at different universities and other educational agencies, provides for wide dissemination of instructional materials. A similar agency that produced instructional materials for teacher education was the Protocol Center, housed at the University of South Florida in Tampa.

G. **Professional associations** produce numerous instructional materials. Some of the national organizations that produce materials are:
   1. The Association for Supervision and Curriculum Development (ASCD)
   2. The National Education Association (NEA)

3. Phi Delta Kappan (PDK)
4. The National Elementary Principals Association (NAESP)
5. The National Association of Secondary School Principals (NASSP)
6. The American Educational Research Association (AERA)
7. The National Middle School Association (NMSA)

State affiliates of these organizations also produce instructional materials. Annual meetings of state and national organizations usually feature extensive displays of instructional materials.

H. **Commercial publishers and other businesses** produce textbooks that represent the major source through which students gain formal knowledge about the subjects studied at school. Commercial publishers also produce audio and visual materials. Big business has not ignored the education market and such giants as IBM, Westinghouse, and RCA are actively engaged in producing "software" and "hardware" for schools.

I. **Professional journals** usually have a listing of materials that can be obtained free or at nominal costs. Many materials are found on the pages of such journals. Two journals that contain a wealth of such information are *The Instructor* and *Teacher.*

TYPES OF INSTRUCTIONAL MATERIALS

In this section we shall examine several of the traditional kinds of instructional materials found in most classrooms. We will also discuss some of the newer kinds of instructional materials that are finding their way into our schools.

Textbooks certainly represent the traditional and possibly the major source of formal knowledge acquired by students. Although the use of textbooks has come under increasing attack, teachers have refused to discard them in the classroom. Textbooks are useful and provide a way of organizing information into a meaningful structure. "Base textbook series" in reading are still adopted by school districts although numerous other reading materials and systems are in use. The "back to the basics" movement has strengthened the use of "base" textbooks in schools.

Today's textbooks are well written and more attractive than they were in the past, but with emphasis on individualized instruction, they can only be a part of the repertoire of the classroom teacher. Many textbooks, when examined for readability level, reveal that they seldom are geared for the age or grade group they are intended for in schools. That, coupled with the fact that age or grade level is a poor indicator of mastery of skills, mandates the use of flexible materials of varying difficulty in the classroom. Textbooks are just one of the resources a teacher should use in carrying out instruction.

Other printed materials used in instruction are aimed at individualizing instruction. One form of textual material is called *programmed instruction.* The concept of programmed instruction has fared better than the "teaching machine" advocated by Skinner although many of the same operant conditioning principles are found in programmed instruction.

Self-pacing materials such as "Uni-Pacs," Learning Activity Packages (LAPS), and curriculum units are becoming a part of the vocabulary of students and teachers. Self-pacing materials are materials developed to individualize instruction and are usually found in school settings where the following features are typically found:

> Concept-centered curriculum
> Some type of provision for flexible scheduling
> Continuous progress
> Team teaching
> Independent study

Self-pacing materials are designed to teach a single idea or concept and are structured for use in a continuous progress school program.[1] Such materials generally include a statement of a major concept, subconcepts, behavioral objectives, a pretest, sequential and diversified learning activities, multi-level content, quest study, posttest, evaluation of materials, teaching suggestions, and identifying information. Behavioral objectives are written at all levels of the cognitive, affective, and psychomotor domains.

Curriculum units can best be illustrated through the model illustrated in Figure 15.1.

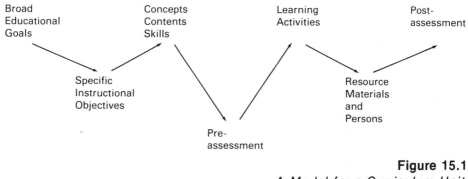

Figure 15.1
A Model for a Curriculum Unit

The following is an explanation of the model in Figure 15.1:

a. The relationship of the curriculum unit to the broad goals of society and to the school's total curriculum must be clearly defined.

b. Instructional objectives must be delineated in unambiguous behavioral terms.

c. The curriculum unit must include the concepts to be developed, the content to be assimilated and the skills to be mastered. A continous progress prescription is essential.

d. Performance criteria must be established in order to preassess the learner's degree of success in understanding of concepts or proficiency in skills.

e. The learning activities must be tailored to several levels of difficulty in order to challenge each individual learner. Most learning will occur independently or in small groups.

f. Resource materials and persons (teachers and aides) are needed to facilitate learning.

g. Post-assessment is administered in order to measure the degree of proficiency to which the learner can perform the skills, understand the content and demonstrate observable changes in behavior.

The Nature of the Learner
1. Sets his own pace.
2. Has unique abilities, variegated interests, and unfulfilled needs.
3. Is assiduously striving to improve his image.
4. Is inextricably entangled in "self" (self-esteem, self-direction, self-fulfillment, and self-actualization).

The Imperatives of the School
1. Nurture sequential concept development (spiral learning rather than fragmented learning).
2. Maintain a balance between convergent and divergent thinking.
3. Maintain a balance between the cognitive and affective domains.
4. Cultivate critical judgment.
5. Imbue values.
6. Inculcate the spirit of inquiry.

The Curriculum Unit
1. It must be purposeful to each learner.
2. It must be at the learner's level of understanding, that is, his expectancy level and not his frustration level.
3. It must remove hurdles that stultify the learner's progress in moving from concept to concept.
4. It must be sequential in order to be effective.
5. It must have a salutary effect upon the learner.

Figure 15.2
Aspects of a Curriculum Unit

Games and Simulation. Classrooms are becoming areas where not only teacher-made, but commercial materials are being innovatively employed. Games and simulation devices have been used to stimulate interest in students in all subject areas.

Games are grounded in the belief that learning ought to be fun—and a conviction that allowing youngsters to find joy in learning bears fruit throughout the rest of their lives.

The attitude of learners toward an activity is important because it so crucially affects how well they will learn that activity.

The use of gaming and simulation devices provides students with an opportunity to learn by doing, and emphasizes the maximum of discovery through activity.

The following list of academic games and simulations are examples of those used at all levels of schooling:

Academic Games and Simulations

Name of Game	Description
Napoli	Students act as legislators in a fictional House of Representatives, and each represents a region and a party. Each student exercises one vote after each of 11 issues have been discussed and debated. The student's reelection depends upon satisfactorily representing both the *region* and the party.
Plans	The student acts as a member of an Interest Group which uses its influence to produce changes in American society. Each group has specific goals.
A Simulation of American Government	This game utilizes the roles played by national government officials such as President, Cabinet, Senate, and the pressures exerted by interest groups and news media.
Simsoc	Students participate as citizens in a simulated society, in which each person's goals depend on other people in the society for their achievement.
Life Career Game	Designed to simulate the kinds of choices and decisions each of us must make throughout life. Each player is given various basic facts about the hypothetical person and must then make decisions relative to education, employment, marriage, etc. Each round of the game represents a year in the person's life.

Name of game—*continued*	Description—*continued*
Galapagos	Focuses on the evolution of Darwin's finches on the Galapagos Islands. It aids in teaching the concepts of speciation and adaptive evolution.
Structural Linguistics	Game of English.
Emergency Preparedness Simulation Game	Game of health and physical education.
Equations	This game of creative mathematics provides a situation for learning some of the elementary operations of mathematics—addition, subtraction, multiplication, division, and exponentiation.

AUDIOVISUAL MATERIALS OF INSTRUCTION

The term *audiovisual materials* includes a broad range of materials, but typically excludes textbooks and other printed materials. The distinction becomes less clear when audiovisual materials are accompanied by written materials.

Computer-Assisted Instruction (CAI) has been an entrant into the field of instructional materials for several decades, but is just now reaching its potential as a learning tool. The development of a home computer that can be purchased at a reasonable cost and can be used in conjunction with a television set raises the possibility of a dramatic breakthrough in the teaching-learning process.

Educational films can be projected in the classroom or over educational television channels. Films today are produced by government agencies, private companies specializing in educational materials, corporations, and by school districts. An exciting trend of schools today finds students producing films. Availability of cameras and other film equipment in schools today opens up this dimension of instruction for many students.

Educational television became the subject of criticism in its infancy because it was used as a total instruction program by some educators. Educational television stations, as a part of the public television network, are now producing both in-school programs and out-of-school programs. Government support of public television has resulted in a vast improvement in the quality of programs.

Cassettes, slides, and tapes are a part of the audiovisual equipment in today's schools. Slide-tape productions are used in learning centers and students are using and producing audiovisual materials. Peer-produced materials are adding to the quality of instruction in many classrooms.

The impact of television on curriculum content has drawn increasing attention from educators who view television as both a threat and a promise. Research indicating that school age youth view television an average of twenty-five hours a week has caused concern about the quality of television programming. A number of groups over the last decade have been organized to aid in the development of television as a medium for positive learning experiences.

1. The AIT (Agency for Instructional Television) is a nonprofit American-Canadian organization formed in 1973 from the parent organization, National Instructional Television. The stated purpose of AIT is to strengthen education through television and other technologies. The AIT, in a joint effort with state agencies, develops and distributes program projects. Schools may write to the main office to request their being placed on the AIT mail list to receive the quarterly newsletter and program information:

   Agency for Instructional Television
   Box A
   Bloomington, Indiana 47401
   (812) 339-2203

2. PTST (Prime Time School Television) is a nonprofit organization dedicated to "making television work for teachers and teachers work for television." Teachers are encouraged to recommend and use the evening television as part of their classroom resources. Guides and program materials produced throught PTST are made available through the programs' commercial sponsors. PTST is funded in part by the Harris Foundation of Chicago and the Bush Foundation of St. Paul. PTST's advisory board includes parents, educators, and representatives of ACT, AASL and television networks. The PTST guides include a self-contained booklet with single and series program listings, the Creative Handbook (every other month), units of study concerned with television, special interest subjects, and a monthly PTST calendar listing important programs for the coming months.

   Each guide has a poster with art work or photograph, title, date, time and network of the program, a synopsis, background information, suggested activities and resources for further exploration of the subject.

   To receive PTST materials you must make application for membership and contribute $10.00 to the organization:

   PTST
   120 South LaSalle Street
   Chicago, Illinois 60603

3. Periodicals such as *Media and Methods,* which is published September-May; *Instructor,* published September-May; and *Senior Scholastic,* published biweekly during the school year, have sections providing teachers with guides to television. *Media and Methods,* as well as *Instructor,* provides "TV News," which describes one or more programs with suggestions for class discussion and follow-up.

4. *Teachers' Guides to Television* is a subscription booklet published in the fall and spring with the cooperation of the Television Information Office of the National Association of Broadcasters. The guides cost only $3.50 per year. The guides state the objectives of the program, give a synopsis, teaching suggestions before viewing, and ideas for further exploration. Time, date, network and subject area are given.

5. Action for Children's Television (ACT) began in 1968 in Newtonville, Massachusetts. It is a "national organization of parents and professionals dedicated to child-oriented quality television without commercialism." A *Newsweek* article ("What TV Does to Kids" (Feb. 21, 1977), pp. 63–70) credits this group of activist parents with achieving more reform in television programming than any other group. ACT is responsible for reducing the time of commercials on children's programs from 16 to 9½ minutes per hour. ACT provides information in its pamphlets concerning advertising, violence, and exploitation of children. ACT wants to use television positively. They urge parents to preview and recommend programs of value, watch and discuss television with their children, changing passive to active.

   Their quality newsletter includes articles on commercials, programming, a book review, materials available for order from ACT, and a list of contact people in every area:

   Action for Children's Television
   46 Austin Street
   Newtonville, Massachusetts 02160

6. Potter, Rosemary. *New Season: The Positive Use of Commercial Television with Children.* Charles E. Merrill Publishing Co., Columbus, Ohio, 1976.

   A Florida educator shows how to utilize commercial TV constructively in the classroom, with many learning exercises based on programming popular with children. All grade levels included. Available in paperback—cost $3.95:

   Charles E. Merrill Publishing Company
   1300 Alum Creek Drive
   Columbus, Ohio 43216

7. Florida Instructional Technology Services. Instructional television and radio programming and services available from the Florida Department of Education to tax-supported educational institutions:

Office of Special Programs
Instructional Television and Radio
Educational Products Division
Florida Department of Education
Tallahassee, Florida 32304
(904) 488-7101

EVALUATION OF INSTRUCTIONAL MATERIALS

Although new instructional materials are continually being developed, there is little evidence that many have been formally evaluated before they reach the classroom. Some materials are field-tested in a few classrooms while others don't get much evaluation. Ideally, all teachers should have some training and competence in evaluation. In most schools, there is generally a department head or curriculum director who can assist teachers in evaluating new materials. Their task is to ascertain what kinds of evidence can be used by teachers to determine the adequacy of materials in general and also to determine what materials need revision.

Some of the criteria that could be established for reviewing instructional materials are:[2]

1. From the viewpoint of the subject area, how accurate are the curriculum materials? Are there errors in the materials? How sound is the subject matter with regard to current views of the field?
2. How are parts of the curriculum materials related to one another? Do the sequence of the parts appear to be appropriate? Are there proposals for improving the internal relations among the elements and parts of the curriculum procedures?
3. Are the materials feasible and practical for use by teachers in the classroom?

SAMPLES AND SOURCES OF
INNOVATIVE LEARNING MATERIALS

Druthers

Druthers is a publication of the Optional Education Programs Project, Title III, New York State Department of Education. This fascinating document is a compilation of innovative practices and materials found in rural schools in New York State.

*Suggested Activities for Teaching
the Sixty Basic Reading Skills*

This document demonstrates the use of everyday references such as the television guide, newspaper, telephone book, and merchandise catalogs in teaching, in a meaningful way, many of the basic reading skills. Table 15.1 illustrates some of these activities.

Free Educational Materials Lists

These lists are found in the back of such journals as *The Instructor,* or are available through professional associations, state departments, or federal government offices.

Sample of a Mathematical Game

MORE OR LESS

PURPOSE: Ordering numerals 0–10. Subtraction of whole numbers 0–10.

PROCEDURE: Duet card game. Each child turns up a card. The child with the larger number on his card is to tell how much larger it is than the other. If he is correct, he scores a point. The first player to score 10 points wins. Each player may display as many counters as is named by the numeral on his card. Correct answer by providing one-to-one matching by the child claiming the point.

MATERIALS: One set of ten numeral cards, 1–10.

Materials for Elementary Learning Stations

1. **Reading Station**
   A wide variety of supplementary books on many levels
   Newspapers & *Weekly Readers* (on many levels)
   Dictionaries on many levels
   Sear's and Penney's catalogues
   Telephone directory
   Book jackets showing Caldecott and Newberry Award Winners
   A bulletin board nearby to show favorite authors, books, stories, poems, etc.
   A box containing comic books labeled "Enjoy a Classic"
   A rocking chair
   Chairs of different heights
   Many types of magazines, *Time, Newsweek,* etc.
   Atlas
   Pilot library
   Developing Reading Skills

Table 15.1
Teaching Basic Reading Skills

Material	Activity	Skill
Look at the area code map of the U.S.	What state would you live in if your area code was 208, 913, 703, etc. What time zone would you live in if your area code was 808, 303, 913, 304, 506	Decoding Word recognition of the various states Map reading Number recognition
Advertisements Select similar ads from different stores	You want to purchase a stereo radio and record player. Where will you get the most for your money? There are five grocery stores near you. (Select five ads.) Plan a meal for five people. You have $10 to spend. What will you purchase? Where will you purchase it? Why? List your items. Where can you buy one dozen oranges for the lowest price?	Comprehension Reading for detail Compare and contrast Compare and contrast Math skill Nutritional ability
Sports section	On what days could you see "Duckpins and Dollars"? How many football games are on television on Sunday? At what time do the Redskins play football on Monday? What day could you see wrestling?	Word recognition Reading for detail
Sears catalog	Fill out an order form. Print your name, address and phone number. Order the following items: 　2 pairs boys slacks 　1 ski parka 　1 shower curtain rod 　3 records Indicate on the order form the page you found each item on, the price of each item, the combined price, and the catalog number of each.	Decoding Using the table of contents Math skills Number sequence

Paperbacks
Almanacs
Steno books—cook books
Mystery stories, fairy tales
Manuals for operating equipment in classroom

2. **Listening and Viewing Station**

Tape recorder and tapes from all curriculum areas
Record player and records from all curriculum areas (headphones too)
Filmstrip machine and filmstrips:

Viewlex	Graphlex
Ducane	Miniloop

Overhead projector and transparencies

3. **Math Station**

A variety of supplementary texts
Tapes and records (sometimes they are at station 2 and other times at station 3)
Games—The Winning Touch, Math Quizno
Crossword kits—whole numbers, fractions, and problem solving
Cuisenaire rods
Geometric blocks
Play money
Compass
Protractor
Different sizes of cylinders, squares, rectangles, graph paper, etc.

4. **Writing Station**

Handwriting books
Paper, pencils, pens, paper clips
Scratch and scribble box containing ideas for creative writing
Picture box
Dictionaries on all levels
Thesaurus
Area to publish finished work
Typewriter
Poetry Box

5. **Social Studies Station**

A state variety box containing pictures, articles, brochures, maps, travel posters about state, etc.
A map box containing road maps, land forms, information about population
Biography box listing famous people who have contributed to our culture
A variety of materials such as magazine articles, pictures, books
Map and globe skill lab
Assortment of charts and graphs
Globe

Atlas
Variety of maps—cover a box with a map to house these
Historical study prints
Games

6. **Personal Attention Station**
Mirror
Soap and towels
Large assortment of different colors of paper (students stand in front of mirror, hold colored paper in front of them to discover which colors compliment them best). Two or three children share this experience at one time.

7. **Current Events Station**
Newspaper
Weekly Readers—many levels
Magazines
Space for clippings
Weather study (daily reports may be a part of this)
News items on local, state, and world level

Materials to Foster Oral Expression in Children

1. **Policeman, Policeman, My Child Is Lost:**   Using walkie-talkies, (real or made of two cans and a string), a student-mother calls the police and describes her "child." The policeman tries to guess which student in the room she is describing.

2. **Story Starter:**   Give the students a card with the beginning of a story and let the students develop their story orally.

3. **Picture on Book Jacket:**   The child studies a book jacket carefully, and then tells what he thinks the story is. He gets the book, reads, and compares his first impression and presentation. He presents the story once again to the class noting his comparisons.

4. **Comic Strip Pictures:**   Cut comic strips into puzzles, leave out conversations. Children are given sets of these strips to arrange in sequential order. The children are divided into small groups so that they may share orally the stories they have composed.

5. **Object Talk:**   Each child should select an object in the room and make a short, one-minute talk about the usefulness of the object.

6. **Impromptu Skits:**   On slips of paper write conversational sentences, one per paper. The sentences may or may not relate to each other. Pass the slips out to each group of children in the classroom. After a brief time limit, each group is to perform a skit acted around the sentences on their paper. Each person must say his sentence somewhere in the context of the skit.

7. **Space Talk:**   In conjunction with science, social studies or just for fun, construct a space station and rocket ship in the classroom.

The children, in any size group, can then conduct simulated dramas and conversations between astronauts and "Mission Control."

8. **TV Show:**   Produce your own TV show in conjunction with any subject. A group can develop the skit, (a basic show, and several commercials), and act out all parts. An example is the CNC evening news with Walter Cronkite for a study of Florida history. The commercials could advertise Florida products. Reporters could be Dan Rabbit and Roger Mudpuddle. They interview great figures and events in Florida history.

Using the Typewriter as a Teaching Machine

1. Type spelling words.
2. Type a sentence using your troublesome spelling word.
3. Type a poem from the board.
4. Type the language arts story of the day.
5. Type all the two-letter words pupils can think of. (Teach or review vowels with these lists.)
6. Find your favorite words in books and type them.
7. Type the names of your friends.
8. Make a picture by typing x's.
9. Type a square or a triangle.
10. Type your address (teach use of comma).
11. Type your telephone number.
12. Type all the three syllable words you can find within ten minutes.

Diversifying Learning Materials Through the Structuring of Creative Activities

By structuring creative activities for students, a variety of audio and visual materials can be brought into play. Note the materials suggested in the following activities suggested for student projects:

1. Write and produce a radio script entitled "On the Nature of the Good Life." Select readings from the great philosophers of the present and past. Write narrative bridges between these passages and record appropriate musical background. Record on tape for later presentation.
2. Make an 8mm sound movie illustrating a consistent theme. Select a subject that can be handled in a relatively short segment—film is expensive. This project would require extremely careful preparatory planning.
3. Study the lyrics of the fifty most popular recordings of the past year. What do these lyrics reflect about our culture and our times? Write your own lyrics which you think have the same ingredients of the popular songs.

4. Make a historical study of American automotive design for the past thirty years. What does our taste in cars reveal about us? Predict what design changes will take place in the next ten years and design a car for the present year.
5. By using primary sources—interviews, minutes books, original documents, local materials—write a history of your community or school.
6. Create, select, and arrange a series of paintings and photographs in an essay format to reveal the effects of the machine in American culture.

Sample of Individualized Task Sheet

1. Use a soft voice.
2. Select a partner.
3. Do your work without disturbing others.
4. Finish one task, go on to another.

Name _____ Section _____ Week _____

Check the correct space when the task is finished.

	Mon.	Tues.	Wed.	Thurs.	Fri.
1. Read a story (small books)					
2. Write the title					
3. Draw a picture about the story					
4. Do four lessons (practice readers)					
5. Practice instant words or phrases (filmstrip)					
6. Study phonics lesson (record player and filmstrip)					
7. Read a story (controlled reader)					
8. Listen to record or tape					
9. Study ten new words (Language Master)®					

Samples of Individualized Task Sheet — *continued*

10. Read a poem

---

11. Study a skill (overhead
    projector)

---

12. Play a skill game

---

13. Talk to me

Partial List of Teaching Activities and Materials

Learning centers	Role playing
Collages	Resource people
Models	Field trips
Films	Interviews
Bulletin boards	Debates
Small group discussion	Newspaper articles (want ads)
Exhibits or displays	Brainstorming
Games	Research projects
Scrapbooks	Simulated work activities
Notebooks	Writing letters
Speeches	VTR (Video taping)
Plays or skits	Unipacs or LAPS
Large group discussion	Committee work
Filmstrips	Overhead and/or opaque projectors
Observations	Demonstrations
Panel discussions	Problem solving
Assigned readings	Decision making problems
Slides	Radio and television programs
Puppets	

SUMMARY

Instructional materials play a central role in the instructional process. There are many sources of instructional materials from the teacher to regional agencies and professional associations. National networks are a particularly valuable source of dissemination of materials.

Textbooks remain the mainstay of classroom materials, but supplementary materials, both written and audiovisual, are used more and more in today's schools. Such materials as films and curriculum units have been around for a time in schools, but newer materials such as computers, cassettes, and self-pacing materials show promise as generators of learning.

The impact of television is receiving increased attention and organizations are at work to improve television programming and to assist in the development of television as a medium for positive learning experiences.

There is little evidence that instructional materials are evaluated either before or after use in the classroom. Criteria can be established for reviewing instructional materials.

In conclusion, the authors have presented in the last section of the chapter a number of samples and sources of innovative learning materials.

Notes

1. Joseph C. Bondi, *Developing Middle Schools: A Guidebook* (Wheeling, Illinois: Whitehall Company Publishers, 1977), p. 72.
2. Arieh Lewy, *Handbook of Curriculum Evaluation* (New York: UNESCO, 1977), pp. 90–91.

Suggested Learning Activities

1. Compile a list of sources of instructional materials for your school.

2. Write for lists of free materials and share those with your colleagues.

3. You have been appointed chairperson of a committee to review all new instructional materials for your school. What criteria would you suggest for the evaluation of new materials?

4. Write several of your colleagues, develop several educational games and try them out with your students.

5. Your PTA has offered to purchase a video recorder for your school, but wants you to identify ways the equipment would receive full use in your school. What ways would you identify?

6. You have received an appointment to a commission studying the impact of television on youth. What would you expect that commission to accomplish?

Books to Review

Bondi, Joseph. *Developing Middle Schools: A Guidebook.* Wheeling, Illinois: Whitehall Company Publishers, 1972.

Hudgins, Bryce B. *The Instructional Process.* Chicago: Rand McNally and Company, 1971.

Lewy, Arieh. *Handbook of Curriculum Evaluation.* New York: UNESCO, 1977.

Oliver, Albert I. *Curriculum Improvement,* 2nd edition. New York: Harper and Row Publishers, 1977.

Tanner, Daniel and Tanner, Laurel. *Curriculum Development: Theory into Practice.* New York: MacMillan Publishing Co., Inc., 1975.

Taylor, Peter A. and Cowley, Doris. *Readings in Curriculum Evaluation.* Dubuque, Iowa: W.B. Brown Company, 1972.

16

Selecting and Evaluating Instructional Programs

In any educational system decisions have to be made daily on how and when children will learn. On the basis of these decisions, learning materials and activities are generated to assist that learning. What is to be taught may be formally stated by governments or legislative acts in countries where such formal acts exist. They are explicit in the values of the society that produces them.

As stated in chapter 13, general goals are of political significance. These goals are stated in broad terms in order to be approved by the majority of the society expressing them. Many societies mandate that the culture of that country must be taught or that certain languages of that country must become the media of that country. The legislating of the use of English and French languages in Canada is an example of the latter.

In the United States, education is delegated to the states. Programs, textbooks, materials, and policies are dictated at the state or district level. We have no national curriculum or national policy on education. However, the schools have been viewed as institutions for changing social patterns by the national government. Both the executive and judicial branches have used the schools as instruments of social change. The Equal Rights Amendment to the Constitution has resulted in programs that foster racial integration, rights for women, and rights for the handicapped. The poor and minority groups have been assisted by federal programs, and federal participation in the funding of public school education has increased dramatically in the past twenty years. Guidelines for participating in federal programs dictate the types of instructional programs, kinds of teachers, and materials to be used as well as the students eligible to participate in such programs.

Within the existing social structure, curriculum workers have a major professional responsibility in selecting the kinds of instructional programs appropriate for learners.

LEVELS OF DECISION MAKING REGARDING INSTRUCTIONAL PROGRAMS

Planning an instructional program requires a decision about what learning outcomes are desired and how best to achieve those learning outcomes. Decisions about learning outcomes occur at four levels of education:

1. *Societal*—Decisions are made by legislators and other policy-makers of local, state, and federal governments.
2. *Institutional*—Decisions about the objectives for a particular school are made by teachers and administrators.
3. *Instructional*—A teacher or teacher team makes decisions about objectives for a specific learner or group of learners.
4. *The learner*—The learner has a say about what he or she is to learn.

Decisions at the general level usually influence what occurs at more specific levels. The societal, institutional, and instructional levels are where Level I, II, and III goals and objectives originate. The reader should review chapter 13 for a discussion of this process.

AVOIDING THE DICHOTOMY OF THE CHILD-CENTERED CURRICULUM AND THE SUBJECT-CENTERED CURRICULUM

A distinction in curriculum planning is often made between the child-centered curriculum and the subject-centered curriculum. Frequently, the distinction is made to describe a certain level of schooling such as the elementary school being child-centered and the secondary school being subject-centered. If an instructional program is based solely on what a child chooses, then the results of such a program are likely to be disappointing. If the subject-centered curriculum means that content is selected without reference to the needs, abilities, and interests of students, again the results will be disappointing to say the least. If all the relevant characteristics of learners are taken into account in the selection of objectives and later in the organization of content and methods of learning, then the distinction between child- and subject-centered curricula would not exist.

CRITERIA FOR SELECTING INSTRUCTIONAL PROGRAMS

1. The first consideration in the selection of instructional programs has to be the purposes for which the instructional program is being planned. Whether it is the objectives stated for a particular lesson in a classroom or the general educational goals for a school or district, planning occurs on the basis of the purposes defined. As stated early in this text, the authors believe a good instructional program must adequately reflect the aims of the school or agency from which they come. At the school level, the faculty, students, and parents need to define comprehensive educational goals and all curriculum opportunities offered at the school should be planned with reference to one or more of those goals.
2. A good instructional program must provide for continuity of learning experiences. Students should progress through a particular program on the basis of their achievement, not on the basis of how much time they have spent in the program. Instructional programs in a school that are planned over several years lend themselves to better vertical progress. Continuity of learning experiences within a program dictates that a relationship between disciplines be established. Core or interdisciplinary programs allow students to see purpose and meaning in their total instructional program.
3. All principles of learning need to be drawn upon in selecting an instructional program. Programs that rely solely on operant conditioning as a psychological base for teaching neglect the important theories of Combs, Piaget, and others. All those associated in education understand the difficulty of putting psychological principles into practice. A careful analysis of new programs can reveal the psychological bases of those programs.
4. Programs selected should make maximum provision for the development of each learner. Any program selected should include a wide range of opportunities for individuals of varying abilities, interests, and needs. Each child is characterized by his or her own pattern of development. Youngsters are curious, explorative, and interested in many things. An instructional program must promote individual development in students rather than making them conform to a hypothetical standard.[1]

5. An instructional program must provide for clear focus. Whether a program is organized around separate subjects such as history or science, or around related subjects such as social studies, it is important that the one selecting the program know which dimensions to pursue, which relationships of facts and ideas should stand out, and which should be submerged.[2] The problem for those who are reviewing programs is to decide which element of the program is the center of organization. Instructional programs may be organized around life problems, content topics, interests, or experiences. In selecting instructional programs, however, the organizing focus must also be examined to see which topics are emphasized, which details are relevant, and which relaships are significant.

6. A good instructional program should be well planned and must include a built-in process for evaluation. Steps need to be defined that would include a periodic assessment of the success of the program and a continuous process for reviewing and updating the program.

EVALUATING A SCHOOL PROGRAM

There are many facets of a school program that can be evaluated including its objectives, its scope, the achievement of students, quality of teaching, and equipment and materials used in the program. Evaluation of an instructional program may be informal or formal. Informal evaluations may be accomplished by simply talking to students, teachers, and parents about the program or through written opinion surveys. Formal evaluations may include examining achievement of students, checking whether stated objectives were met, or through the use of other criteria such a number of students gaining employment or number of students exceeding national norms on college entrance tests.

Purposes of Evaluation

The general purpose of evaluation is to improve the educational program by facilitating judgments about its effectiveness based on evidence.[3] Specific purposes include:

1. To make explicit the rationale of the instructional program as a basis for deciding which aspects of the program should be evaluated for effectiveness and what types of data should be gathered.

2. To collect data upon which judgments about effectiveness can be formulated.
3. To analyze data and draw conclusions.
4. To make decisions which are based on the data.
5. To implement the decisions to improve the instructional program.

Many of the curriculum innovations introduced in the 1960s and 1970s brought about little improvement in the curriculum. Innovations introduced for a limited purpose, such as the improvement of reading, often produced limited results. There are hundreds of reading programs available, yet we still find large numbers of our students who are poor readers. The failure to assess the effects of innovations against their total outcomes has probably been the reason why curriculum revision in American education appears to proceed by replacing one scheme with another. Figure 16.1 lists some questions useful for studying curriculum changes.

1. *Background of the curriculum change*
   Where did the impetus come from for change?
   Who spearheaded the effort?
   When did it get underway?
   What specific events or activities were involved?
2. *Process of the curriculum change*
   Who was involved?
   How many participated?
   Who coordinated the efforts?
   Who sponsored the efforts?
   How long a period of time was involved?
   What kinds of activities did participants engage in?
3. *Nature of the curriculum change*
   What are the objectives of the new curriculum?
   What was changed?
   Who decided what changes should be made?
   What criteria were employed in deciding to make the changes?
   What kind of learning theory underlies the changes?
4. *Results of the change*
   How widespread is change today?
   What is the present direction of the change today?
   How is the change being evaluated?
   What plans are presently available regarding the future of the change?
5. *What research has been done on the change* (Study of studies: include abstracts)
   How much research has been done?
   Where was the research done?
   Who did the research?
   How available and how trustworthy are the data?
   What does the research show?
   What problems have been identified in the research thus far?
   What conclusions are apparent from the research done?

Figure 16.1
Questions Useful in Studying Curriculum Changes

Programs are not scrapped because they have failed, but because another innovation has gained more attention.

There are many sources of data for evaluating an instructional program. Figure 16.2 illustrates some of these sources.

A. Pupil performance
   1. Standardized tests—teacher-made tests
   2. Pupil grades
   3. Dropout data
   4. Pupil attendance
   5. Observation of pupil performance
   6. Inventories—skill continuums
   7. Observations of teaching-learning situations in the classroom
   8. Degree of student attention and involvement
B. Questionnaires—polls of opinions of pupils, teachers, parents
   1. Polls of parents regarding the success of certain school programs
   2. Group interviews with students, parents, teachers about the success of curriculum innovations
   3. Attitude surveys of students about certain programs
   4. Comparison of attitudes of pupils and teachers toward contrasting programs
   5. Systematic questionnaires, rating sheets, and interviews with small random samples of students
C. Follow-up studies of learners
   1. Success at the next grade level
   2. Continuation of schooling
   3. College success
   4. Success in work
   5. Application of skills learned, interests generated in school—e.g., participation in lifetime sports, the arts
D. Examination of learning materials
   1. Examining learning materials to see if they are feasible and practical for use by teachers in the schools—accuracy and soundness of materials
   2. Determining if costs of materials are too great
   3. Checking materials to see if they are at the right level for students
   4. Determining whether teachers get special retraining in order to understand and use new materials
   5. Matching materials to students' interests, needs, and aspirations—relevancy of materials

Figure 16.2
Sources of Data for Evaluating an Instructional Program

Some Things to Consider When
Evaluating Instructional Programs

1. *Specify the desired outcomes of instructional programs.* More than forty years ago, Ralph Tyler and his colleagues urged educators to use precise, rather than vague, language in describing instructional goals. Recently, others have endorsed that position.
2. *Describe in operational terms the planned classroom transactions*

for a given instructional program. An evaluator must specify appropriate independent and dependent variables to be measured. When examining innovations, there is frequently little agreement among experienced educators as to the effectiveness of those programs and they are commonly adopted with little supporting evidence for their use. The use of such terms as "a problem-solving approach" sounds good, but until we describe what procedures are involved, it is difficult to measure the success of the approach.

3. *Select the most valid and practical design for investigating the specified relationships.* Avoid errors in the planning of comparative studies. Educators tend to stay away from experimental research and objective evaluation; however, they are always designing new instructional materials and methods. Whether experimental research is thought to require a level of mathematical and statistical sophistication that is beyond the reach of most educators, or whether it is thought to be disruptive of the classroom, such research seldom is used to determine the effectiveness of programs. When experimental research is attempted, it is usually under the banner of "action research," which leads to much enthusiasm, but little else of value. Doctoral students in curriculum and instruction tend to avoid experimental studies, preferring to determine by questionnaire procedures or subjective judgment what current practices exist or should not exist in a school or school district.

4. *Identify the essential components of a sound evaluation program and describe operationally the specific conditions each must meet.* The evaluator should be sure that all of the known cause-and-effect relationships are identified. Be specific about a given instructional factor (a process) and a given learner factor (a product) that are known to be related. For instance, the level of student achievement should be specified so that a given process factor can be determined to be acceptable. Without the identification of specific relationships and their associated levels of acceptability, evaluators are in danger of making value judgments that are based on subjective or unempirical evidence.

5. *Specify the inferences that can be made from the results of a specific study.* Educational studies are filled with statements of conclusions that are not warranted by the procedures and data from the reported studies.

6. *"Contingency management" procedures must be specified and described operationally for a given evaluation project to determine whether the requirements of the operational procedures are met.* Even though an evaluator might specify the exact operational procedures for an evaluation project, that evaluator has little assurance that the procedures will be carried out correctly in the classroom. Too frequently, data are collected that give inadequate attention to the transactions that occur in the classroom. Thus, the instruc-

tional program is evaluated on the basis of intended transactions rather than on the basis of observed transactions.

ACCOUNTABILITY

Much has already been written and said about accountability. Competency-based education was discussed in the previous chapter and is a product of the "accountability movement." Legislators in all our states have rushed to enact some sort of competency requirement. Some states have established minimum competencies for promotion and/or graduation. Whether professional educators like competency-based education or not, they are going to have to learn to cope with it.

Education accountability acts have done much more than just establish minimum competency requirements. The Florida Educational Accountability Act of 1976, for instance, is a very detailed act that is designed to establish the framework for a totally integrated system of accountability for the public schools in Florida. The stated intent of the act is to:

1. Provide information for educational decision makers at the state, district and school levels in order to appropriately allocate resources and meet the need of the system in a timely manner.
2. Provide public information on the costs of educational programs and the differential effectiveness of various types of instructional activities.
3. Guarantee to each student the availability of instructional programs which meet minimum performance standards consistent with the state plan for education.
4. Provide thorough analyses of various programs costs and the degree to which school districts meet the state-established minimum performance standards.
5. Provide information to the public about the performance of the state system in meeting established goals, and in providing effective, meaningful, and relevant educational experiences designed to give students at least the minimum skills necessary to function and survive in today's society.

Under provisions of the act, the Department of Education was directed to identify all functions that contribute to or comprise a part of the State System of Accountability, and to establish the necessary organizational structure, policies, and procedures for effectively coordinating such functions.

The following functions or activities are specifically identified and treated in the act as elements of the State System of Accountability:

1. Educational planning
2. Management information systems
3. Educational research and development
4. Educational evaluation procedures
5. Student assessment testing programs
6. Public reporting procedures
7. District and school advisory committees
8. Secondary level examination program
9. Pupil progression
10. Cost accounting and reporting

An example of the Accountability Act as it relates to one school in Florida is found in the following Principal's Annual Report of School Progress:

Report to Parents

Dear Parents,

This document was produced in compliance with Chapter 73–338, Law of Florida. We hope that the following report will assist our parents and school community to be informed of the progress at Riviera Middle School during the 1975/76 school year.

Achievement of This Year's Goals

The implementation of the Academic Centers Concept was our major goal for this school year. This has been successfully accomplished through the establishing of three centers which are actually three schools within a school. The fourth group, the teachers of Related Arts classes, supported all three teams.

The state-wide Attitude and Opinion Poll supports the success of the new program by showing that Riviera students are proud of their school, and that Riviera out ranked the county and state scores by a large percentage in almost all areas.

Absenteeism was very low and the number of suspensions was reduced. This can be attributed to the success within the teams of averting discipline problems and helping students with their social and emotional as well as academic growth.

Teacher Education Center: Staff Development

This year emphasis has been placed upon Middle School certification. Many teachers attended the pre-school workshop held here at Riviera and, during the year, completed other required courses. Others met the requirements through Staff Development courses. At this time it appears that all the staff have met, or are very close to meeting, the requirements for Middle School certification.

Use of School Facilities

The building was used by the community for the following activities:

Jr. Raiders—Youth Association monthly board meeting, practice and ball games on our fields.

Northeast Little League—Practice on our fields.

Adult Education—Various night classes were offered.

P.T.A.—4 night meetings

Advisory Committee—4 meetings with the P.T.A. Executive Board

School System, County Wide—Meetings, workshops, inservice classes

Guidance

Riviera's Guidance Department has performed such guidance activities as counseling, orientation, registration, scheduling, dissemination and interpretation of information concerning student progress, parent/teacher consultation, and identification and referral of specific learning or adjustment problems. Testing for the 1975–76 year included two state assessment programs: one in the sixth grade and one in the eighth grade. In the seventh grade, the county testing program was administered. Occupational information activities and field trips have been an integral part of the year's program. Maintenance and updating of student records has also been a guidance responsibility. The Riviera Guidance Department has been staffed this year with two counselors, one occupational specialist and one records clerk.

Student Advisory Committee

In the various meetings chaired by Mrs. Antoinette Rambo, the Riviera Advisory Committee this year reviewed plans for the building program, viewed a slide presentation explaining the three academic centers program, and previewed the new middle school grade reporting form. In addition the members also discussed a variety of topics including: parent and student concerns with stolen and lost personal items, repair and restoration needs in the school building, effects of zone changes, changes to the Raider Football Field, proposal to form a comprehensive middle school in lower Pinellas County. The communication between the committee and the school staff has greatly aided all persons to understand the concepts of the school's program.

Curriculum Organization for 1976/77

Riviera Middle School will continue the 1976/77 school year with three cross-grade level centers. The three interdisciplinary teams within each center will provide learning experiences in Math, Language Arts, Reading, Social Studies and Science. There also is a Related Arts Team which covers courses in Humanities and Vocations. In addition, all students will participate in a Physical Education Program. The Exploratory Program, which we call RED period, includes Research, Enrichment, and Developmental classes, which are based on the abilities, needs, and interests of the students.

Accomplishments and Items of Interest

Open House in August.

Bicentennial Year Book published.

Band and Chorus presented Christmas and Spring Concert.

Candy Sales netted the school $5,456.47.

Student Council supported many school projects.

Orientation was provided for outgoing 8th graders and for incoming 5th and 6th graders.

Two school-wide field trips were conducted involving 320 students.

2,816 students went on 56 other field trips sponsored by the teams.

16 activities other than field trips were conducted.

Honors were won in the Optimist Speech Contents, Spelling Bee, and Math Competition.

Varsity Teams won Division Honors in Volleyball, Basketball, and Track.

Bicentennial Celebration—April 9 was an all day Field Day honoring the spirit of the Bicentennial.

The Florida State-Wide Eighth Grade Testing Program was administered in February of this year. Results were expressed as percentages of students who have reached mastery level in certain essential reading skills and essential math skills. Riviera's percentages of eighth graders who have achieved mastery is greater than the county percentages and the state-wide percentages in a majority of the skills sub-tests. The opinions expressed by these students in the Opinion Poll section of this program indicate an extremely high regard for their school experiences, as do the results of the Student/Parent/Teacher Attitude Survey. Such enthusiasm and support of their school is due to a great extent to the attitudes and regard with which parents view the educational institution. With that thought in mind, I would like to close this school year by expressing my heartfelt appreciation to you and your community for the time, effort, backing, and support without which no school can be successful.

Chalmers Coe
Principal

Examples of other data provided parents of Riviera Middle School are found in Tables 16.1, 16.2, 16.3, and 16.4.

NATIONAL ASSESSMENT

National Assessment is a major project designed to gather and make public information describing what groups of Americans know and can do in a number of subject areas. The idea for National Assessment originated with the Carnegie Foundation in 1964. Under the direction of Ralph Tyler, a committee called the Committee on Assessing the Progress of Education developed a plan for assessing both the cognitive and affective realms for ten subject areas. The subject areas included reading, writing, science, citizenship, literature, mathematics, music, social studies, art, and career and occupational development. Four age groups were identified for assessment: nine-year-olds, thirteen-year-olds, seventeen-year-olds, and young adults between the ages of twenty-six and thirty-five. A sample of dropouts was also to be assessed.

A number of procedures are used in National Assessment that are unique for an educational study. Samples of age groups are tested rather than all the youngsters in that age group. *Testing* is a term avoided in the project. The aim of the project is to describe what groups of people know and how they feel about certain subjects. No norms against which to compare individuals and no individual scores are published. In the literature section, for instance, the percentages of students who can read and understand a certain passage are shown, but there is no reporting that a particular student scored at the 80th percentile.

Table 16.1
*Pinellas County School Attitude Survey
1975/76 for Riviera Middle School*

Below are the results of this year's School Attitude Survey of students (S), parents (P), and teachers (T).

Percent Response	Strongly Agree			Agree			Uncertain			Disagree			Strongly Disagree		
	S	P	T	S	P	T	S	P	T	S	P	T	S	P	T
1. Enough time is available in this school for teachers to meet with parents.	8	17	35	40	67	45	44	8	5	6	5	15	2	3	0
2. Learning materials available to students in this school meet their instructional needs.	19	20	0	54	44	50	9	11	15	15	15	35	3	10	0
3. This school offers instruction which prepares students for daily living.	18	20	10	55	52	65	14	15	20	10	11	5	3	2	0
4. The guidance services offered in this school meet the needs of students.	30	15	0	42	60	20	19	10	20	8	13	45	1	2	15

5.	The range of extra curricular activities offered at this school (clubs, sports, etc.) is wide enough to interest most students.	35	25	50	41	57	40	8	10	5	13	8	0	3	0	5
6.	Students have a good feeling about attending this school.	20	26	70	43	64	30	24	10	0	9	0	0	4	0	0
7.	Enough money is spent on this school's instructional programs.	17	16	5	27	36	30	38	25	15	14	18	45	4	5	5
8.	The lunch program in this school serves good tasting food.	8	10	0	33	36	25	16	37	35	22	17	25	21	0	15
9.	In this school, rules are enforced with fairness to all.	20	10	10	32	65	70	15	15	15	19	8	10	14	2	0
10.	This school is kept in good repair.	29	31	15	47	'57	55	12	10	10	9	0	20	3	2	0
11.	This school communicates well with parents.	15	22	20	32	61	75	38	8	5	11	7	0	4	2	0

PRINCIPAL'S SUMMARY: The survey was completed by over 300 parents and students selected randomly and classroom teachers. Results show that approximately 95% of those participating do not strongly disagree with the school's overall position on the eleven items. This is a 6% improvement over the previous year. The lowest rated items are: by students, those dealing with lunches and school rules; by parents, those dealing with finances; by teachers, those dealing with availability of materials and services. However, the overall results are high and with gains in most areas. Student spirit is very high and students have a good feeling about attending this school. Teachers and parents feel there is a high degree of cooperation between home and school. The majority feel that the school is maintained well and communications and relations between community and school are excellent.

Table 16.2

Grades: 6–8
Program Capacity: 1229*
Number Other Instructional Staff: 10.3
Acreage: 16
Percent Air Conditioned: 100%

Enrollment (October 11, 1975): 1125
Number of Teachers: 62
Supporting Staff: 28.1
Original Construction Date: 1965

*Not including 4 portables

COMPARISON INFORMATION

Category	This School	All Pinellas Middle Schools
Pupil Absentee Rate	5.8%	7.7%
Pupil Mobility Rate	24.3%	30.5%
Pupil Non-Promotion Rate	0.6%	1.8%
Pupil Drop-Out Rate	1.3%	2.6%

All data in the above four categories are from the 1974–75 school year; all data below are from the current year (1975–76).

	This School	All Pinellas Middle Schools
Percent Non-White Pupils	16.0%	16.3%
Percent Non-White Faculty	5.8%	10.3%
Percent Male Faculty	42.0%	44.2%
Percent Faculty Holding:		
Bachelor's Degree	73.9%	66.4%
Master's Degree or Higher	26.1%	33.6%
Percent Faculty Teaching Experiences: Less than 1 Year	2.9%	2.1%
1–3 Years	17.4%	17.3%
4–9 Years	37.7%	30.2%
10 or More Years	42.0%	50.4%
Pupil/Teacher Ratio	18.1	19.8
Pupil/Other Instructional Staff Ratio	109.2	118.4
Pupil/Total Instructional Staff Ratio	15.6	17.0
Per Pupil Expenditures:		
Instruction	$ 789.35	$ 735.19
Instructional Support Services	87.82	76.63
General Support Services	209.43	199.99
TOTAL	$1,086.60	$1,011.81
Remodeling and Construction	$ 0.00	

Table 16.3
Riviera Middle School
Florida Statewide Eighth Grade Testing Program
February, 1976

Objective	% Reaching Mastery Florida	% Reaching Mastery Pinellas County	% Reaching Mastery This School
Essential Reading Skills			
1a. Labels—Caution	95.1	96.2	96.8
1b. Labels—Vocabulary	63.1	67.2	66.1
1c. Ingredients	88.3	91.8	90.7
1d. Medical Instructions	96.2	97.3	98.0
1e. Preparation Directions	89.9	92.4	94.1
2a. Driver's Handbook	89.9	92.6	93.9
2b. Transportation Schedules	54.1	60.8	61.5
3a. Job Want Ads	81.5	84.2	85.4
3b. Job Applications	90.5	92.7	93.9
3c. Tax Forms	66.5	73.5	76.3
4. Newspaper Reporting (Fact vs Opinion)	88.4	90.6	90.0
5. Store Directions	89.3	92.1	92.9
6. Outdoor Signs	83.8	87.5	90.0
7. Telephone Directories	89.8	92.2	92.7
8. Abbreviation Meanings	72.7	76.5	79.3
Essential Math Skills			
1. Rate of Interest	59.9	63.5	61.7
2. Discount Rate	40.9	47.1	43.5
3. Cost Comparison	86.7	90.2	89.1
4. Travel Time	75.0	79.5	76.5
5. Time Calculations	72.6	77.2	74.8
6. Spending Behavior	82.3	85.5	84.5
7. Sales Tax	56.1	63.4	56.9
8. Currency	93.7	95.4	95.1
9. Income Tax Calculations	45.4	49.7	49.6

Table 16.4
School Board of Pinellas County

FINANCIAL STATEMENT
May 31, 1976
RIVIERA MIDDLE SCHOOL

	Year to Date			
	Beginning Balance	Receipts	Expendi- tures	Balance
INSTRUCTIONAL AIDS FUND				
Total	$ 1,265.30	$ 2,037.49	$ 2,441.65	$ 861.14
GENERAL FUND				
Total	2,200.48	2,128.79	2,802.22	1,527.05
CLASS, CLUB, TRUST FUND				
Total	8,020.03	30,971.46	27,851.40	11,140.09
COUNTY BUDGET TRUST FUND				
Total	0	4,982.00	3,851.55	1,130.45
MUSIC ACTIVITIES				
Total	1,805.52	350.10	1,081.90	1,073.72
ATHLETIC ACTIVITIES				
Total	49.15	153.45	120.95	81.65
TOTAL	$13,340.48	$40,623.29	$38,149.67	$15,814.10
			Outstanding orders yet to arrive and be paid for	2,004.27
			Projected Balance	$13,809.83

Educational objectives were determined for each subject area before questions were designed to assess whether the objectives were being met. Subject matter experts, other educators, and lay persons helped define the objectives.

The National Assessment policy has continued to be to report the results, but not attempt to interpret them. Although this policy is soundly based, some critics want the National Assessment staff to tell them what the results mean. Some members of Congress have joined the chorus of critics about lack of information and propose a national testing program. The implications of such a program would be profound.

National Assessment results can contribute to educational planning and provide guidelines for improving instructional programs. National Assessment information should be used as just that—information. As with testing, assessment results should be used as information, not judgment.

NATIONAL STUDY OF SCHOOL EVALUATION

In 1933, the Cooperative Study of Secondary School Standards was formed to provide effective instruments and procedures for evaluating secondary schools. In 1959, the name was changed to the National Study of Secondary Evaluation. A decade later, because attention was given to evaluation of elementary schools, the name of the organization was changed to the National Study of School Evaluation. The organization provides evaluative criteria for regional accrediting associations and guidelines for evaluating school programs. The evaluation process of a school using the guidelines includes a self-study, the services of a visiting committee, and a report of the visiting committee.

GLOSSARY OF TERMS

This glossary contains brief descriptions of terms that are commonly used in connection with curricular, instructional, and evaluative considerations.

CURRICULUM

AFFECTIVE: A term that describes behavior or objectives of an attitudinal, emotional, or interest nature; discussed in the *Taxonomy of Educational Objectives: Handbook II, The Affective Domain* by David Krathwohl and others.

BEHAVIOR OBJECTIVES: This term describes what the learner should be able to do at the conclusion of an instructional sequence.

COGNITIVE: An adjective referring to learner activities or instructional objectives concerned with *intellectual* activities; discussed in *The Taxonomy of Educational Objectives: Handbook I, The Cognitive Domain* by Benjamin S. Bloom and others.

COURSE OF STUDY: A guide prepared by a professional group of a particular school or school system as a prescriptive guide to teaching a subject or area of study for a given grade or other instruction group.

CRITERION: The measure used to judge the adequacy of an instructional program. Ordinarily, it would be a test, broadly conceived, of the program's objectives.

CURRICULUM: A structured series of intended learning outcomes.

LESSON PLAN: A teaching outline of the important points of a lesson for a single class period arranged in the order in which they are to be presented. It may include objectives, points to be made, questions to ask, references to materials, and assignments.

PSYCHOMOTOR: This refers to learner activities or instructional objectives relating to physical skills of the learner, such as typing or swimming.

RESOURCE UNIT: A collection of suggested learning and teaching activities, procedures, materials, and references organized around a unifying topic or learner problem; it is designed to be helpful to teachers in developing their own teaching units.

SCOPE: The extent of content or objectives (or both) covered by a course or curriculum.

SEQUENCE: The order in which content or objectives are arranged in the curriculum.

SUBJECT: A division or field of organized knowledge, such as English or mathematics.

SYLLABUS: A condensed outline or statement of the main points of a course of study.

TEACHING UNIT: The plan developed with respect to a particular classroom by an individual teacher to guide the instruction of a unit of work to be carried out by a particular class or group of learners for a period longer than a single class session.

INSTRUCTION

ANALOGOUS PRACTICE: This term describes the responses made by the learner during the instructional sequence which are comparable, but not identical, to those called for in the instructional objective.

APPROPRIATE PRACTICE: This expression refers to opportunities provided the learner during the instructional sequence to respond in a fashion consistent with that described in the instructional objective. (See ANALOGOUS PRACTICE and EQUIVALENT PRACTICE.)

CONSTRUCTED RESPONSE: This refers to a learner's response, either to criterion test items or to material in the instructional product, wherein he is obliged to make a response which he must generate, as opposed to choosing between responses that have been generated for him. For instance, when a student is obliged to construct a short essay, this would be an instance of constructed response. Short "fill-in" answers to questions are also classified as constructed responses.

CONTINGENCY MANAGEMENT: This generally refers to classroom schemes that are based on the learner's receiving some kind of positive reinforcement for particular learning attainments. For example, in some cases the child can secure coupons for achieving certain instructional objectives, the coupons later being redeemable for rewards the child wishes to receive.

DISCIPLINE: This term can be used in a variety of ways, but for most teachers it refers to the procedures by which classroom control and order are maintained.

EN ROUTE BEHAVIOR: The behavior(s) that the learner acquires as he moves through an instructional program from his original entry behavior to the desired terminal behavior.

ENTRY BEHAVIOR: Sometimes referred to as prerequisite behavior, this describes the learner's behavioral repertoire as he commences the instructional program.

EQUIVALENT PRACTICE: Responses made by the learner during the instructional program which are *identical* to those called for in the instructional objectives.

KNOWLEDGE OF RESULTS: A scheme by which a learner is provided with information regarding the adequacy of his responses. Sometimes called *feedback* or *corrective feedback*, knowledge of results is provided whenever the learner can find out whether his responses are appropriate or inappropriate.

NEGATIVE REINFORCER: A stimulus which, when *removed* from a situation, increases the probability of the response that it follows. For example, a teacher might find that releasing a child from some aversive situation (staying after school) would increase the likelihood of a particular response of the child. (Negative reinforcement is not to be confused with punishment.)

PERCEIVED PURPOSE: Promoting the child's realization of the worth of a particular subject he is studying or an objective he is attempting to accomplish.

POSITIVE REINFORCER: A stimulus which, when *added* to a situation, increases the probability of the response it follows. For example, a teacher might find that verbal praise would increase the student's tendency to perform a particular classroom action.

PUNISHMENT: An aversive act that occurs after a particular response and is designed to diminish the frequency of the response it follows.

SELECTED RESPONSE: In selected responses, the learner chooses among alternatives presented to him, as when he selects multiple-choice responses, discriminates between true and false statements, and so on.

TASK ANALYSIS: The ordering of instructional objectives or en route behaviors to facilitate the attainment of instructional goals.

TERMINAL BEHAVIOR: The behavior that the learner is to demonstrate at the conclusion of the instructional program. What is terminal behavior in one program may, of course, be the initial behavior for a subsequent program.

EVALUATION

CONTENT VALIDITY: The degree to which a measuring device is *judged* to be appropriate for its purpose; for example, the degree to which it is congruent with a set of instructional objectives.

CORRELATION: The tendency for corresponding observations in two or more series to have similar positions.

CRITERION-REFERENCED MEASUREMENT: A measurement designed to assess an individual's status with respect to a particular standard of performance, irrespective of the relationship of his performance to that of others.

CRITERION VALIDITY: Characteristically, the degree to which a particular measure, such as a test of intellectual ability, correlates with an external criterion such as subsequent scholastic performance in college.

DISTRACTORS: These are the alternatives, or wrong answers, in a multiple-choice or comparable test item.

FORMATIVE EVALUATION: The evaluation of an instructional program before it is finally completed—that is, the attempt to evaluate a program in order to improve it.

ITEM ANALYSIS: Any one of several methods used in revising a test to determine how well a given item discriminates among individuals or different degrees of ability or among individuals differing in some other characteristic.

ITEM SAMPLING: The procedure of administering different forms of a test (characteristically, shorter forms), to different individuals, thereby reducing the time required for testing.

NORM-REFERENCED MEASUREMENT: A measurement designed to assess an individual's standing with respect to other individuals on the same measuring device.

PERCENTILE (CENTILE): The point in distribution of scores below which a certain proportion of the scores fall. For example, a student scoring at the seventieth percentile on a test would have exceeded the scores of 70 percent of those taking the test.

RELIABILITY: The accuracy with which a measuring device measures something; the degree to which a test measures consistently whatever it measures.

STANDARDIZED TEST: A test for which content has been selected and checked empirically, for which norms have been established, for which uniform methods of administering and scoring have been developed, and which may be scored with a relatively high degree of objectivity.

SUMMATIVE EVALUATION: The final evaluation of a program in which the results of the program are characteristically compared with results of comparable programs in order for selection to be made among competing instructional programs.

VALIDITY: The extent to which a test or other measuring instrument fulfills the purpose for which it is used.

SUMMARY

Selecting and evaluating instructional programs is a major task of educators. In the United States, education is delegated to the states, yet the national government, through regulations and financing of programs, has a profound influence on the direction of American education. Levels of decision making regarding instructional programs include societal, institutional, instructional, and the learner. Decisions at the general level usually influence decisions at the more specific levels. The learner, for instance, is certainly influenced by decisions made at the school level. Criteria for selecting instructional programs are also listed in the chapter.

Evaluation of instructional programs includes many dimensions. Suggestions for studying curriculum changes and sources of data for evaluating instructional programs are presented in Figures 16.1 and 16.2. Evaluation today is mandated by legislative acts in many states. The Florida Accountability Act provides for a comprehensive evaluation design.

National Assessment is a project designed to provide the public with information about what groups of Americans know and can do in ten subject areas. The procedures used in the National Assessment Project include just reporting results, not interpreting them.

The National Study of School Evaluation is an organization dedicated to developing effective means of evaluating schools.

In conclusion, a glossary of terms is included to provide the reader with brief descriptions of terms commonly used in curricular, instructional, and evaluative considerations.

Notes

1. Galen Saylor and William Alexander, *Curriculum Planning for Modern Schools* (New York: Holt, Rinehart and Winston, Inc., 1966), p. 256.
2. Hilda Taba, *Curriculum Development: Theory and Practice* (New York: Harcourt, Brace and World, Inc., 1962), pp. 304–5.
3. Alan B. Knox, "Continuous Program Evaluation" in Peter Taylor and Doris Cowly, *Readings in Curriculum Evaluation* (Dubuque, Iowa: W.C. Brown Company, 1972), p. 199.

Suggested Learning Activities

1. Develop a checklist for selecting new instructional programs in your school.
2. What sources of data would you use for a follow-up study of students leaving an elementary school? middle school? high school?
3. You are chairing a committee to suggest an evaluation design for a new science program at your school. What things would you consider in the design?
4. What is the role of an accrediting agency? Which association of colleges and secondary schools represents your area?
5. You have been asked by your PTA to explain the accountability movement. Outline in detail what you would say.
6. Develop a program for the continuing evaluation of your school.

Books to Review

Gagne, Robert and Briggs, Leslie. *Principles of Instructional Design.* New York: Holt, Rinehart and Winston, Inc., 1974.

Hall, Gene and Jones, Howard. *Competency-Based Education.* Englewood Cliffs, N.J.: Prentice-Hall, Inc., 1976.

Lewy, Arieh, editor. *Handbook of Curriculum Evaluation.* New York: UNESCO, 1977.

McNeil, John D. *Designing Curriculum.* Boston: Little, Brown and Company, 1976.

Popham, W. James. *Educational Evaluation.* Englewood Cliffs, N.J.: Prentice-Hall, Inc., 1975.

Popham, W. James and Baker, Eva. *Systematic Instruction.* Englewood Cliffs, N.J.: Prentice-Hall, Inc., 1970.

Saylor, J. Galen and Alexander, William M. *Curriculum Planning for Modern Schools.* New York: Holt, Rinehart and Winston, Inc., 1966.

Taba, Hilda. *Curriculum Development: Theory and Practice.* New York: Harcourt, Brace and World, Inc., 1962.

Taylor, Peter A. and Cowley, Doris M. *Readings in Curriculum Evaluation.* Dubuque, Iowa: W.C. Brown Company, 1972.

17

Analyzing Classrooms and Supervising Instructional Personnel

While instructional supervision is not normally considered a function of those responsible for curriculum development, the authors believe that it should be. The truth is that any curriculum program is only as good as the instructor who delivers it. By any logic, the classroom teacher is a part of the curriculum and therefore should be a concern of curriculum planners. In this chapter, the reader is introduced to research and techniques which will allow a program planner to analyze and supervise instructional personnel.

NEW WAYS OF LOOKING AT CLASSROOM INSTRUCTION

Until recently, educational researchers have had a fairly long history of not being of much help to educational practitioners. Other than a general checklist of teacher competencies, a supervisor was armed with little else to judge the effectiveness of a particular teacher. Since about 1960, however, systems and instruments have been developed to help us look at classroom instruction in a more systematic way.

Observational systems that measure classroom interaction probably show the most promise as learning devices for both preservice and in-service teachers.[1] An observational system is defined here as any systematic technique for identifying, examining, classifying, and/or quantifying specific teaching activities. Of the observational systems available, Flanders' System of Interaction Analysis of verbal behavior is probably the most widely known and used.[2]

Interaction Analysis

During the past ten years, a number of innovations have been developed and implemented in teacher education programs in attempts to improve the ultimate effectiveness of the teachers who come out of these programs. The concept of systematic observation is certainly one of the more widely publicized of these recent innovations. By its very nature and basic construct, an observational system represents an effective means for providing objective empirical data describing specific teacher and student variables that are found to interact in a given teaching-learning situation. Data of this kind have been found to be quite helpful in helping teachers analyze and improve their individual teaching effectiveness.

Currently, several manageable observational systems are available for teacher use. Each is specifically designed to assess a different and particular dimension of the classroom situation. Originally developed by Flanders, interaction analysis is designed to assess the verbal dimension of the teacher-pupil interaction in the classroom.[3]

Flanders developed a category system that takes into account the verbal interaction between teachers and pupils in the classroom. The system enables one to determine whether the teacher controls students in such a way as to increase or decrease freedom or action. Through the use of observers or by using audio or video tape equipment, a teacher can review the results of a teaching lesson. Every three seconds an observer writes down the category number of the interaction he or she has just observed. The numbers are recorded in sequence in a column. Whether the observer is using a live classroom or tape recording for his or her observations, it is best for the observer to spend ten to fifteen minutes getting oriented to the situation before categorizing. The observer stops classifying whenever the classroom activity is inappropriate as, for instance, when there is silent reading or when various groups are working in the classroom, or when children are working in their workbooks.

A modification of the Flanders system of ten categories is a system developed by Hough and used by Bondi and Ober in research studies.[4,5] That system provides three more categories of behavior than the Flanders system. In the thirteen category system, teacher statements are classified as either indirect or direct. This classification gives central attention to the amount of freedom a teacher gives to the student. In a given situation, the teacher can choose to be indirect, that is, maximizing freedom of a student to respond, or she or he can be direct, that is, minimizing the freedom of a student to respond. Teacher response is classified under the first nine categories.

Student talk is classified under three categories and a fourth category provides for silence or confusion where neither a student nor the teacher can be heard. All categories are mutually exclusive, yet totally inclusive of all verbal interaction occurring in the classroom. Figure 17.1 describes the categories in the thirteen category modification of the Flanders System of Interaction Analysis.

Verbal Patterns of Teachers in the Classroom

Utilizing the Flanders system and other modifications of that system, teachers and supervisors can begin to isolate the essential elements of effective teaching by analyzing and categorizing the verbal behavioral patterns of teachers and students.

Four classroom patterns that particularly affect pupil learning are thrown into sharp relief when verbal patterns are identified and revealed by these techniques.

The first pattern can be labeled "the excessive teacher-talk pattern." This occurs when teachers talk two-thirds or more of the time in the classroom. Obviously, if teachers are talking that much, there is very little time for students to get in the act. In classrooms where teachers talk at least two-thirds of the time, pity the curriculum approaches that emphasize extensive student participation in learning. Yet the two-thirds percentage of teacher talk is found in many classrooms today. Teachers can become aware of and able to control the amount of time they spend in the classroom through the use of feedback from interaction analysis.[6] This finding alone makes interaction analysis an effective teaching and supervisory tool.

A second verbal pattern is recitation. Arno Bellack, a pioneer in describing verbal behavior of teachers and pupils, has noted that despite differences in ability or background, teachers acted very much like one another.[7] They talked between two-thirds and three-quarters of the time. The majority of their activity was asking and reacting to questions that called for factual answers from students. Bellack and others presented an elaborate description of the verbal behavior of teachers and students during a study of fifteen New York City area high school social studies classrooms.[8] They summarized the results of their analysis in a set of descriptive "rules of the language game of teaching." Among their observations were the following:

1. The teacher-pupil ratio of activity in lines of typescript is 3 to 1. Therefore, teachers are considerably more active in amount of verbal activity.

Figure 17.1

Description of Categories for a Thirteen-Category
Modification of the Flanders System of Interaction Analysis

	Category Number	Description of Verbal Behavior
	1	ACCEPTS FEELING: Accepts and clarifies the feeling tone of students in a friendly manner. Student feelings may be of a positive or negative nature. Prediting and recalling student feelings are also included.
T E A C H E R — I N D I R E C T	2	PRAISES OR ENCOURAGES: Praises or encourages student action, behavior, recitation, comments, ideas, etc. Jokes that release tension not at the expense of another individual. Teacher nodding head or saying "uh-huh" or "go on" are included.
	3	ACCEPTS OR USES IDEAS OF STUDENT: Clarifying, building on, developing, and accepting the action, behavior, and ideas of the student.
	4	ASKS QUESTIONS: Asking a question about the content (subject matter) or procedure with the intent that the student should answer.
	5	ANSWERS STUDENT QUESTIONS (STUDENT-INITIATED TEACHER TALK): Giving direct answers to student questions regarding content or procedures.
T A L K — D I R E C T	6	LECTURE (TEACHER-INITIATED TEACHER TALK): Giving facts, information, or opinions about content or procedure. Teacher expressing his or her own ideas. Asking rhetorical questions (not intended to be answered).
	7	GIVES DIRECTIONS: Directions, commands, or orders to which the student is expected to comply.
	8	CORRECTIVE FEEDBACK: Telling a student that his answer is wrong when the correctness of his answer can be established by other than opinions (i.e., empirical validation, definition, or custom).
	9	CRITICIZES STUDENT(S) OR JUSTIFIES AUTHORITY: Statements intended to change student behavior from a nonacceptable to an acceptable pattern; scolding someone; stating why the teacher is doing what he is doing so as to gain or maintain control; rejecting or criticizing a student's opinion or judgment.
	10	TEACHER-INITIATED STUDENT TALK: Talk by students in response to requests or narrow teacher questions. The teacher initiates the contact or solicits student's statements.

Figure 17.1—*continued*

S
T   T
U   A
D   L
E   K
N
T

11   STUDENT QUESTIONS: Student questions concerning content or procedure that are directed to the teacher.

12   STUDENT-INITIATED STUDENT TALK: Talk by students in response to broad teacher questions which require judgment or opinion. Voluntary declarative statements offered by the student, but not called for by the teacher.

13   SILENCE OR CONFUSION: Pauses, short periods of silence, and periods of confusion in which communication cannot be understood by an observer.

Indirect-Direct Ratio = $\dfrac{\text{categories } 1, 2, 3, 4, 5}{\text{categories } 6, 7, 8, 9}$

Revised Indirect-Direct Ratio = $\dfrac{\text{categories } 1, 2, 3}{\text{categories } 7, 8, 9}$

Student-Teacher Ratio = $\dfrac{\text{categories } 10, 11, 12}{\text{categories } 1, 2, 3, 4, 5, 6, 7, 8, 9}$

2. The pedagogical roles of the classroom are clearly delineated for pupils and teachers. Teachers are responsible for structuring the lesson and soliciting responses. The primary task of the pupil is to respond to the teacher's solicitations.
3. In most cases, structuring accounts for about ten lines spoken; soliciting, responding, and reacting each account for twenty to thirty percent of the lines.
4. The basic verbal interchange in the classroom is the solicitation-response. Classes differ in the rate at which verbal interchanges take place.
5. By far, the largest proportion of the discourse involved empirical (factual) meanings. Most of the units studied were devoted to stating facts and explaining principles while much less of the discourse involved defining terms or expressing or justifying opinions. The core of the teaching sequence found in the classrooms studied was a teacher question, a pupil response, and more often than not, a teacher's reaction to that response.[9]

William Hoetker studied junior high English classes in 1967 and his findings were much the same as Bellack's.[10]

Hoetker compared his findings in a report found in the *American Educational Research Journal.* Those comparisons are found in Table 17.1.

The findings of Bellack and Hoetker hardly seem earth-shaking to those who have observed teaching over the years. As a pedagogical method, the question-answer sequence was fully recognized fifty years ago when teacher education consisted of considerable training in the skill of asking questions. Unfortunately, it is still with us, despite the fact that successive generations of otherwise quite disparate educational leaders have condemned the rapid-fire question-answer pattern of instruction. This leads us to question the efficiency, or, in this case, the inefficiency of teacher training institutions in affecting the classroom behavior of teachers. If recitation is indeed a poor pedagogical method, why have teacher educators not been able to deter teachers from using it? Is recitation of textbook facts still to be the representative method of teaching pupils in American schools?

A classroom where recitation predominates suggests not only that a teacher is doing most of the work, but is giving little attention to individual needs of students. Moreover, the educational assets of role recitation are only verbal memory and superficial judgment.[11]

A third verbal pattern of teachers that affects student learning is teacher acceptance of student ideas. There is ample evidence that teachers who accept the ideas and feelings of students enhance learning in the classroom. A number of observational systems have been used to identify teacher acceptance. In a large-scale study, Flanders isolated junior high school teachers whose students learned the most and the least in social studies and mathematics. He found teachers of higher achieving classes used five to six times as much acceptance and encouragement of student ideas than teachers in lower achieving classes. Teachers in higher achieving classes were also less directive and critical of student behavior.[12] Findings similar to Flanders were found by Amidon and Giammatteo when they compared thirty superior teachers with one hundred fifty randomly selected teachers in elementary schools.[13]

The fourth pattern of teachers that affects pupil learning uncovers a teacher's flexibility—or inflexibility. Arno Bellack, in his "Rules of the Classroom Game," dramatically points up the power of the teacher. The teacher structures the game, asks the questions, evaluates the responses, and speaks "the truth" while students don't structure the game, respond to questions, keep their own questions to a minimum, and depend upon the teacher to decide whether or not they have spoken the truth.[14]

Hughes, in a study of classroom behavior, found the most frequent teaching acts were controlling ones.[15] Teachers in her study who were considered "good teachers" were those well-organized and generally attentive. Control meant goal-setting and directing children to the precise thing to which they gave attention. Not only is content identified

Table 17.1

Comparisons Between Selected Mean Measures of
Classroom Verbal Behavior in Bellack (1966) and Hoetker (1967)

Measure	Bellack	Hoetker
A. Percentage of teacher talk, moves	61.7	65.7
B. Percentage of teacher talk, lines of typescript	72.1	74.5
C. Distribution of teacher moves, as percentage of all moves		
STRUCTURING	4.8	3.6
SOLICITING	28.8	32.3
RESPONDING	3.5	1.8
REACTING	24.3	27.0
D. Distribution of pupil moves, as percentage of all moves		
STRUCTURING	0.4	0.3
SOLICITING	4.4	2.0
RESPONDING	25.0	30.4
REACTING	5.7	1.1
E. Distribution of teacher moves, as percentage of total lines of typescript		
STRUCTURING	14.5	22.4
SOLICITING	20.3	20.6
RESPONDING	5.0	4.3
REACTING	24.8	31.4
F. Distribution of pupil moves, as percentage of total lines of typescript		
STRUCTURING	3.0	3.4
SOLICITING	2.5	1.2
RESPONDING	15.6	13.1
REACTING	5.1	0.6
G. Percentage of teacher questions calling for memory processes	80.8*	87.9

*Estimated from data on pages 74–75, Bellack (1966)

Source: From James Hoetker and William Ahlbrand, "The Persistence of the Recitation," *American Educational Research Journal* 6, no. 2 (March, 1969): 147. Copyright © 1969, American Educational Research Association, Washington, D.C.

for pupils, but they are held to a specific answer and process of working. The teacher wants one answer. As long as the question or statement that structures the class requires but one answer, the teacher is in absolute control.

Implications for Training

Can teachers recognize these patterns and change them? Will supervisors be able to assist teachers in changing patterns of teaching that inhibit student learning? The answer is *yes*—but more must be done in preservice and inservice teacher training programs to help teachers identify and change verbal behavior. Educators in teacher training institutions must not just provide instruction when students read about verbal behavior, but help students to learn to "read" behavior itself. When teachers learn to "read" behavior, they will be able to identify and modify the behavioral patterns that facilitate or inhibit pupil learning in the classroom.

If we are to sensitize people to the importance of verbal patterns, we must provide training in the use of a variety of language patterns. Training requires practice in the acquisition of new behaviors. With ample evidence that children learn more effective social, cognitive, and affective behavior if adults learn to modify and expand their verbal behavior as they interact with children, a means for providing this practice should be sought. Materials and systems for training teachers to widen their verbal behavior are available and should be put to use in universities and school districts.

Classroom Questions

In the Flanders or Modified Flanders System of Interaction Analysis, only one category of behavior deals with questions. That category concerns a teacher asking questions about content or procedure in order to elicit a student response. For a teacher to obtain greater understanding of her or his questions, other types of feedback instruments must be used.

Questioning is probably the most ancient pedagogical method. The dialogues of Socrates and dialectics of Plato have been used throughout history as models for teachers. As pointed out earlier in the section on recitation, unfortunately most of the questions asked by teachers require little thinking on the part of students. A number of reports in recent years have confirmed the high frequency of questions asked by teachers that require little more than the recall of memorized material.[16]

Perhaps these reports of the low level of teachers' questioning are the result of a tradition of teachers asking set questions requiring memorized answers. In improving classroom instruction, we must examine ways teachers' questioning ability can be developed. One of the most frequently used guides to the cognitive level of teachers' questions has been Bloom's *Taxonomy of Educational Objectives,* 1956.[17] A report of studies conducted by Farley and Clegg indicated that training in the knowledge and use of Bloom's taxonomy helps teachers increase their use of questions at higher cognitive levels.[18]

Figure 17.2 illustrates how Bloom's taxonomy can be used in classifying teacher questions.

Another guide to cognitive level of teachers' questions has been Norris Sanders' taxonomy of questions.[19] Sanders has classified questions into the following seven categories:

Memory Questions—These are questions that ask students to recall or recognize ideas previously presented to them.

Translation Question—This occurs when students are presented with an idea and asked to restate the same idea in a different way.

Interpretation Questions—Students are asked to compare certain ideas or use ideas studied previously to solve problems that are new to them.

Application Questions—Application questions are similar to interpretation questions in that a student has to use an idea learned previously to solve a new problem. However, in application a student has to use an idea when not told to do so, but when the problem demands it. This involves transfer of training to a new situation.

Analysis Questions—Analysis questions ask students to solve problems through logical processes such as induction, deduction, cause and effect.

Synthesis Questions—Students put ideas together to create something. This could be a physical object, a communication, or even a set of abstract relations.

Evaluation Questions—Students must make a value judgment based on certain considerations such as usefulness, effectiveness, etc.

Inquiry or discovery methods of teaching have focused attention on questioning techniques. Richard Suchman has reported on a system of inquiry training to help teachers ask the appropriate "why" questions to get students to hypothesize about the relationship of events to explain phenomena.[20] Suchman's studies suggest that children can learn to develop a questioning style that will lead them to form testable hypotheses and procedures for verifying hypotheses.

Another approach to questioning has been developed in Taba's system of cognitive processes or tasks.[21] Taba developed a set of eliciting questions for use with each of the cognitive tasks of concept formation, development of generalizations, and application of principles to new situations. The teacher questions were formulated to elicit

Category	**Key Word**	**Typical Question Words**
1. KNOWLEDGE (Any question, regardless of complexity, that can be answered through simple recall of previously learned material.) e.g., "What reasons did Columbus give for wanting to sail west to find a new world?"	Remember	1. Name 2. List; Tell 3. Define 4. Who? When? What? 5. Yes or No questions: e.g., "Did . . . ?" "Was . . . ?" "Is . . . ?" 6. How many? How much? 7. Recall or identify terminology. 8. What did the book say . . . ?
2. COMPREHENSION Questions that can be answered by merely restating or reorganizing material in a rather literal manner to show that the student understands the essential meaning.) e.g., "Give the ideas in your own words."	Understand	1. Give an example . . . 2. What is the most important idea? 3. What will probably happen? 4. What caused this? 5. Compare. (What things are the same?) 6. Contrast. (What things are different?) 7. Why did you say that? 8. Give the idea in your own words.
3. APPLICATION (Questions that involve problem solving in new situations with minimal identification or prompting of the appropriate rules, principles, or concepts.) e.g., "How big an air conditioner?"	Solve the problem	1. Solve 2. How could you find an answer to . . . ? 3. Apply the generalization to . . .
4. ANALYSIS Questions that require the student to break an idea into its component parts for logical analysis: assumptions, facts, opinions, logical conclusions, etc.) e.g., "Are the conclusions supported by facts or opinion?"	Logical Order	1. What reason does he give for his conclusions? 2. What method is he using to convince you? 3. What does the author seem to believe? 4. What words indicate bias or emotion? 5. Does the evidence given support the conclusion?
5. SYNTHESIS (Questions that require the student to combine his	Create	1. Create a plan . . . 2. Develop a model . . . 3. Combine those parts . . .

Category	Key Word	Typical Question Words
ideas into a statement, plan, product, etc., that is new for him.)		
e.g., "Can you develop a program that includes the best parts of each of those ideas?"		
6. EVALUATION (Questions that require the student to make a judgement about something using some criteria or standard for making his judgment.)	Judge	1. Evaluate that idea in terms of . . . 2. For what reasons do you favor . . . 3. Which policy do you think would result in the greatest good for the greatest number? [22]

Figure 17.2

Classifying Classroom Questions

certain essential behaviors by students that are necessary to the accomplishment of cognitive tasks. Teachers in preservice or inservice programs might apply this approach to gain experience in a particular learning process before she or he begins to analyze it as a teaching process.

The Gallagher-Aschner system of analyzing and controlling classroom questioning behavior has been widely used in preservice and inservice teacher training programs.[23]

This system is derived from intensive analyses of human mental abilities done by J.P. Guilford and his associates. Although there are many subcategories in the system, the use of just four of the major categories of classifying levels of questions can give a teacher strong clues as to the level of thinking demanded of students by that teacher.

Figure 17.3 lists four of the major categories of the Gallagher-Aschner system with examples of types of questions used in each of the categories.

In their work with their system, Gallagher and Aschner found that a majority of teacher behavior falls in the first level, cognitive memory, but that even a slight increase in divergent questions leads to a major increase in divergent ideas produced by students. Sanders' work indicated that for teachers not acquainted with a system of looking at questioning, very few questions asked by those teachers fell above category one. The Florida Taxonomy of Cognitive Behavior, used at the University of Florida and the University of South Florida, parallels the Gallagher-Aschner system. It is based on Bloom's Taxonomy of Educational Objectives and the Sanders system. Use of the Florida taxonomy with teachers has produced findings that indicate extensive teacher use of low levels of questioning.

1. *Cognitive-Memory:* calls for a specific memorized answer or response; anything which can be retrieved from the memory bank.

   1a. What is 2 X 3?
   1b. When did Florida become a state?
   1c. What is a noun?
   1d. At what temperature Centigrade does water boil?

2. *Convergent:* calls for a specific (single) correct answer which may be obtained by the application of a rule or procedure; normally requires the consideration of more than a single quantity of information and/or knowledge.

   2a. What is 30.5 X 62.7?
   2b. How many years was the U.S. under the Prohibition Law?
   2c. Diagram this sentence.
   2d. How many calories are required to melt 160 grams of ice at 0 C?

3. *Divergent:* allows the student a choice between more than one alternative or to create ideas of his own; more than a single answer is appropriate and acceptable.

   3a. What is 10 to three other bases?
   3b. What might have been the effects on the growth of the United States had there not been a Civil War?
   3c. Write a short story about Halloween.
   3d. Design an apparatus that will demonstrate the Law of Conservation of Matter.

4. *Evaluative:* the development and/or establishment of relevant standard of criteria of acceptability involving considerations as usefulness, desirability, social and cultural appropriateness, and moral and ethical propriety, then comparing the issue at hand to these; involves the making of value judgments.

   4a. Is 10 the best base for a number system?
   4b. Was the Civil War defensible?
   4c. Is English the best choice for a universal language?
   4d. Should we continue our space program now that we have landed on the moon?

Figure 17.3

*The Gallagher-Aschner System
A Technique for Analyzing and Controlling
Classroom Questioning Behavior*

The need for helping teachers analyze classroom questions and developing appropriate strategies of questioning indicates that systematic training in the use of questions be made available to teachers. A number of systems of analyzing and controlling classroom questioning behavior has been presented in this chapter. These and other systems should be used in helping train teachers to stimulate productive thought processes in the classroom.

Nonverbal Communication in the Classroom

The importance of analyzing and controlling verbal behavior of teachers has been well documented. Another dimension of teaching that has drawn the attention of researchers is nonverbal communication. Nonverbal communication is often referred to as a silent language. Individuals send messages through a variety of conventional and nonconventional means. Facial expressions, bodily movements, and vocal tones all convey feelings to students. A student may be hearing a teacher verbally praise her work while the teacher's facial expression is communicating disapproval of that work. If a teacher fails to understand the nonverbal message being conveyed to his pupils, he may not be able to comprehend their responses to him. In analyzing a classroom then, it is just as important to examine *how* the teacher says what she has to say, how she behaves and expresses feelings, as *what* the teacher says, does, and feels. How teachers communicate their perceptions, feelings, and motivations can be identified with facial expressions, gestures, and vocal tones. Such expressions determine in large measure how pupils perceive those teachers.

In examining the significance of nonverbal communication, it is important to understand that teaching is a highly personal matter and prospective and inservice teachers need to face themselves as well as to acquire pedagogical skills. Teachers need to become more aware of the connection between the messages they communicate and the consequences that follow. Teachers also need to capitalize on the nonverbal cues expressed by students as keys to their clarity and understanding. While nonverbal interaction in the classroom is less amenable to systematic objective inquiry than verbal interaction, the meanings pupils give to a teacher's nonverbal message have significance for learning and teaching.

Through continued study of nonverbal behavior, teachers can sharpen, alter, and modify their nonverbal messages they transmit to students. The advantage of adding nonverbal analysis in a study of teaching is that teachers can look at their behavior in two ways—what their behavior means to pupils, and how their behavior is being interpreted by their pupils.

Classroom Management

Another aspect of teaching, and one that is becoming increasingly important in today's classrooms, is classroom management. The changing family structure and increased conflict found in all elements of our society have led to concern about a general breakdown of school discipline and the need for better classroom management. There are a number of techniques to help a teacher maintain an effective learning environment in the classroom.

Kounin* has developed a system for analyzing classroom management that deals with transitions from one unit to another. The following are examples:

Group alerting. The teacher notifies pupils of an imminent change in activity, watches to see that pupils are finishing the previous activity, and initiates the new one only when all of the class members are ready. In contrast, *thrusting* is represented when the teacher "bursts" in on pupil acitivity with no warning and no awareness, apparently, of anything but his own internal needs.

Stimulus boundedness is represented by behavior in which the teacher is apparently trapped by some stimulus as a moth by a flame. For example, a piece of paper on the floor leads to interruption of the on-going activities of the classroom while the teacher berates the class members for the presence of the paper on the floor or tries to find out how it got there.

Overlappingness is the teacher's ability to carry on two operations at once. For example, while the teacher is working with a reading group, a pupil comes to ask a question about arithmetic. The teacher handles the situation in a way which keeps the reading group at work while he simultaneously helps the child with his arithmetic.

A dangle occurs when the teacher calls for the end of one activity, initiates another one, then returns to the previous activity. For example, "Now pupils, put away your arithmetic books and papers and get out your spelling books; we're going to have spelling." After the pupils have put away their arithmetic materials and gotten out their spelling materials the teacher asks, "Oh, by the way, did everybody get problem four right?"

If the teacher never gets back to the new activity which he initiated (for example, if he had never returned to the spelling in the previous example) this would be a *truncation*.

With-itness is the teacher's demonstration of his awareness of deviant behavior. It is scored both for timing and for target ac-

* From notes of presentation by Dr. Robert Soar at conference, "The Planning and Analysis of Classroom Instruction," The University of Florida, November, 1975, pp. 7–8. For a detailed report of Kounin's work, see Jacob S. Kounin, *Discipline and Group Management in Classrooms* (New York: Holt, Rinehart and Winston, Inc., 1970).

curacy. Timing involves stopping the deviant behavior before it spreads, and target accuracy involves identifying the responsible pupil. If, for example, an occurrence of whispering in the back of the room spread to several other children, and at this point the teacher criticizes one of the later class members who joined in, this would be scored negatively both for timing and for target accuracy.

The Kounin examples illustrate the ways teachers can maintain the group and not hinder learning in the classroom. In analyzing classrooms, we must not ignore the techniques of group management teachers must utilize daily. Teachers must be provided feedback of their own behavior if they are to improve instruction.

Young teachers enter the classroom filled with such pedagogical terms as social control, group dynamics, behavior patterns, and democratic procedures. These terms mean little to the worried teacher who must get Johnny to sit down and keep quiet—at least long enough for the teacher to get the day started.

What is good discipline? Certainly not a classroom in which no one speaks but the teacher. A classroom where students respond willingly and quickly to routine requests of the teacher is a well-controlled class. A teacher who can maintain good working conditions and controls noise when necessary, without pressure, makes it possible for children to learn.

The 1977 Gallup Poll of the public's attitudes toward public schools indicated, as it had in eight of the last nine years, that discipline was the major problem facing public schools in the nation. Parents still blamed themselves for the problems of discipline, motivation, and drug and alcohol addiction that normally have their origin in the home.

In spite of the breakdown of the family and parent acceptance of blame for many student problems, teachers must still cope with the day-by-day discipline problems in the classroom. The literature is filled with the dos and don'ts of good teaching. School districts provide numerous materials for teachers to read about discipline and have procedures for helping teachers with discipline problems in the classroom. Suggesting any practical approach in dealing with classroom discipline will appear to be an oversimplification. Everything the teacher does in the classroom or does not do improves or destroys discipline. Diagnosing the problem(s) in a classroom where a teacher has trouble maintaining good discipline and providing the teacher with help are two major tasks of supervisors and administrators in today's schools.

SUPERVISING INSTRUCTIONAL PERSONNEL

The Role of the Supervisor

The field of instructional supervision has changed dramatically in the past ten years. Supervisors are faced with an upsurge of governmental regulations, mandates, assessments, competency tests and other accountability measures from state and national levels that are attempting to control the quality of instruction. Other pressures are coming from needed attention to culturally diverse youth, mature, tenured, and unionized faculties that are scornful of persons in supervisory roles, and public apathy toward providing increased financing for public schools.

Supervisors are unsure as to their role in supervising instructional personnel. Modern, sophisticated faculties are often distrustful of persons in supervisory roles. Improvement of instruction is oftentimes secondary to that of reacting to teacher complaints about sizes of classes, extra duties, etc.

These and other problems are not likely to go away in the future. Supervisors must provide leadership for improving the quality of instruction. They must provide leadership for joint planning and vigorous participation by all those engaged in inservice and curriculum development programs.

Peer Supervision

Peer supervision as a system for improving teaching has been the subject of considerable discussion in recent years. Defining the concept of peer supervision is not an easy task. The literature might describe peer supervision as an informal situation of teachers assisting other teachers, an advisory system where special groups of personnel are available to help teachers,[24] or a system where teachers have the total responsibility for improvement of instruction.

If supervision is primarily a process of observation, analysis, and feedback, then perhaps teachers may well be their own best supervisors.[25] Teachers have always exerted an influence on other teachers. The older, experienced teacher always takes the inexperienced teachers under his or her arm to guide them through the first weeks of school. Often, the experienced teachers just share information on what to do or not to do to stay out of trouble with the administration. Growing unionism has resulted in strong group norms that influence the supervising efforts.

In the face of teachers attempting to influence peers, there is very little direct knowledge on the part of most teachers as to what goes on in adjoining classrooms. The advent of team teaching, microteaching, interaction analysis, and teachers becoming part of supervisory teams has resulted in teachers having more knowledge about what goes on in peers' classrooms. That knowledge is still limited, however. Until teachers open their classroom doors totally to peers and share practices and problems, there will be little influence that peers can exert on the improvement of instruction.

With its limitations, peer supervision does show promise as a supplement to self-evaluation and formal evaluation by an administrator or supervisor. Peer supervision implies an atmosphere of trust and cooperation in which teachers share their ideas and successes as well as their frustrations and failures. That sort of school atmosphere will result in a new sense of professionalism and will result in teachers who have greater competence.

Improving the Skills of Teaching

Teachers are almost universally expected to evaluate, revise, and improve the methods they follow in their teaching. The improvement of teaching involves a behavioral change on the part of teachers. That change comes after careful analysis and feedback of information. Feedback may come from any number of sources including observational systems such as the Flanders system, the analysis of a microteaching lesson, or simply from peer comments.

Evaluation of teaching performance has numerous meanings and connotations ranging from a rating or grading to a gathering of information to assess the effects of program and teaching.

In the first section of this chapter, a number of different instruments and systems were identified that look at classroom instruction and provide teachers with feedback about teaching performance. The use of evaluation instruments involves appropriate procedures and techniques. The following guideline should be used by professional personnel in using evaluation instruments:

1. Evaluation instruments should be as objective as possible.
2. Evaluation instruments should be relatively simple, understandable, and convenient to use.
3. Evaluation criteria should focus on performance.
4. All personnel should be familiar with the instruments used and procedures followed in evaluating effectiveness.
5. Personnel should be encouraged to make self-evaluations prior to formal evaluations by others.

The accountability movement with its emphasis on student performance has resulted in increased data from researches linking pupil performance to a number of variables, most of which are not directly controlled by the teacher. Changing social patterns have resulted in increased numbers of school children coming from broken homes. The trauma of a breakdown in the family structure has placed an additional burden on the schools which must provide additional instruction in the "basics" and still provide an atmosphere of attention, affection, and stability so needed by school-age youngsters. The human quality of teaching then becomes an important dimension in today's schools.

A feedback model that attempts to assess the unique human quality of teaching is the Tuckman Teacher Feedback Form.[26]

The Tuckman Form shown in Figure 17.4 involves an observer rating a teacher in each of twenty-eight categories of behavior describing a human element in teaching.

Teacher Observed ＿＿＿＿＿＿ Observer ＿＿＿＿＿＿ Date ＿＿＿＿＿＿

Place an X in that one space of the seven between each adjective pair that best indicates your perception of the teacher's behavior. The closer you place your X toward one adjective or the other, the better you think that adjective describes the teacher.

1.	original ＿ : ＿ : ＿ : ＿ : ＿ : ＿ : ＿	conventional
2.	patient ＿ : ＿ : ＿ : ＿ : ＿ : ＿ : ＿	impatient
3.	cold ＿ : ＿ : ＿ : ＿ : ＿ : ＿ : ＿	warm
4.	hostile ＿ : ＿ : ＿ : ＿ : ＿ : ＿ : ＿	amiable
5.	creative ＿ : ＿ : ＿ : ＿ : ＿ : ＿ : ＿	routinized
6.	inhibited ＿ : ＿ : ＿ : ＿ : ＿ : ＿ : ＿	uninhibited
7.	iconoclastic ＿ : ＿ : ＿ : ＿ : ＿ : ＿ : ＿	ritualistic
8.	gentle ＿ : ＿ : ＿ : ＿ : ＿ : ＿ : ＿	harsh
9.	unfair ＿ : ＿ : ＿ : ＿ : ＿ : ＿ : ＿	fair
10.	capricious ＿ : ＿ : ＿ : ＿ : ＿ : ＿ : ＿	purposeful
11.	cautious ＿ : ＿ : ＿ : ＿ : ＿ : ＿ : ＿	experimenting
12.	disorganized ＿ : ＿ : ＿ : ＿ : ＿ : ＿ : ＿	organized
13.	unfriendly ＿ : ＿ : ＿ : ＿ : ＿ : ＿ : ＿	sociable
14.	resourceful ＿ : ＿ : ＿ : ＿ : ＿ : ＿ : ＿	uncertain
15.	reserved ＿ : ＿ : ＿ : ＿ : ＿ : ＿ : ＿	outspoken
16.	imaginative ＿ : ＿ : ＿ : ＿ : ＿ : ＿ : ＿	exacting
17.	erratic ＿ : ＿ : ＿ : ＿ : ＿ : ＿ : ＿	systematic
18.	aggressive ＿ : ＿ : ＿ : ＿ : ＿ : ＿ : ＿	passive
19.	accepting (people) ＿ : ＿ : ＿ : ＿ : ＿ : ＿ : ＿	critical
20.	quiet ＿ : ＿ : ＿ : ＿ : ＿ : ＿ : ＿	bubbly
21.	outgoing ＿ : ＿ : ＿ : ＿ : ＿ : ＿ : ＿	withdrawn
22.	in control ＿ : ＿ : ＿ : ＿ : ＿ : ＿ : ＿	on the run
23.	flighty ＿ : ＿ : ＿ : ＿ : ＿ : ＿ : ＿	conscientious
24.	dominant ＿ : ＿ : ＿ : ＿ : ＿ : ＿ : ＿	submissive
25.	observant ＿ : ＿ : ＿ : ＿ : ＿ : ＿ : ＿	preoccupied
26.	introverted ＿ : ＿ : ＿ : ＿ : ＿ : ＿ : ＿	extroverted
27.	assertive ＿ : ＿ : ＿ : ＿ : ＿ : ＿ : ＿	soft-spoken
28.	timid ＿ : ＿ : ＿ : ＿ : ＿ : ＿ : ＿	adventurous

Figure 17.4

Tuckman Teacher Feedback Form (TTFF)

A scoring system for the twenty-eight items is shown in Figure 17.5.

Person observed _____   Observer _____   Date _____

A. Item Scoring

    I. Under the last set of dashes on the sheet of 28 items, write the numbers 7–6–5–4–3–2–1. This will give a number value to each of the seven spaces between the 28 pairs of adjectives.

    II. Determine the number value for the first pair, Original-Conventional. Write it into the formula given below on the appropriate line under Item 1. For example, if you place an X on the first dash next to "Original" in Item 1, then write the number 7 on the dash under Item 1 in the summary formula below.

    III. Do the same for each of the 28 items. Plug each value into the formula.

    IV. Compute the score for each of the four dimensions in the summary formula.

B. Summary Formula and Score for the Four Dimensions

    I. Creativity

        Item $(1 + 5 + 7 + 16)–(6 + 11 + 28) + 18$

        $(_ + _ + _ + _)–(_ + _ + _) + 18 = $ _____

    II. Dynamism (dominance and energy)

        Item $(18 + 21 + 24 + 27)–(15 + 20 + 26) + 18$

        $(_ + _ + _ +)–(_ + _ + _) + 18 = $ ____

    III. Organized Demeanor (organization and control)

        Item $(14 + 22 + 25)–(10 + 12 + 17 + 23) + 26$

        $(_ + _ + _)–(_ + _ + _ + _) + 26 = $ _____

    IV. Warmth and Acceptance

        Item $(2 + 8 + 19)–(3 + 4 + 9 + 13) + 26$

        $(_ + _ + _)–(_ + _ + _ + _) + 26 = $ ____

Figure 17.5
Tuckman Teacher Feedback Form Summary Sheet

The Tuckman Form is a system for providing feedback in the affective domain. Teaching can be improved by an efficient program of supervision and through the use of systems such as the Tuckman Form that provide effective feedback to teachers. Modern teachers must make use of the feedback provided them whether that feedback comes from formal observations of outside observers or from instruments used by teachers themselves in the classroom.

SUMMARY

There have been a number of systems and instruments developed in the past ten years that have given us ways of looking at classroom instruction in a more systematic manner. Observational systems that examine verbal, nonverbal, and other dimensions of teaching are providing professional educators with effective means of analyzing classrooms.

Supervisory practices are also changing in today's schools. The role of the supervisor has changed dramatically in recent years as the result of government regulations, budget cutbacks, and accountability measures that are designed to improve the quality of instruction. The field of supervision itself is threatened with being taken over by agencies outside the school system.

The challenge ahead for both teachers and supervisors is to maintain an atmosphere of trust and openness in schools where teachers can constantly obtain feedback from a number of sources and utilize that feedback to improve learning opportunities in the classroom.

Notes

1. Joseph C. Bondi, Jr. "The Effects of Interaction Analysis Feedback on the Verbal Behavior of Student Teachers," *Educational Leadership* (May, 1969): 794–99.
2. Ned A. Flanders, *Teacher Influence—Pupil Attitudes and Achievement,* (Washington: Research Monograph 12, H.E.W., 1965).
3. Ibid.
4. John B. Hough, "A Thirteen Category Modification of Flanders' System of Interaction Analysis," mimeographed (Columbus, Ohio: The Ohio State University, 1965).
5. Joseph Bondi and Richard Ober, "The Effects of Interaction Analysis Feedback on the Verbal Behavior of Student Teachers." A paper presented at the annual meeting of the American Educational Research Association, Los Angeles, Feb., 1969.
6. Joseph C. Bondi, Jr., "Feedback in the Form of Printed Interaction Analysis Matrices as a Technique for Training Student Teachers." A paper read at the annual meeting of the American Educational Research Association, Los Angeles, Feb., 1969.
7. Arnold A. Bellack et al., *The Language of the Classroom* (New York: Teachers College Press, 1966).
8. Ibid.
9. Ibid., p. 84–6.
10. William J. Hoetker, "An Analysis of the Subject Matter Related Verbal Behavior in Nine Junior High English Classes." (ed. D. diss., Washington University, 1967.)
11. Joseph C. Bondi, Jr., "Verbal Patterns of Teachers in the Classroom," *National Elementary Principal* 50, 5 (Washington, D.C., April, 1971): 90–91.
12. Flanders, *Teacher Influence—Pupil Attitudes and Achievement*, p. 97.

13. E. Amidon and M. Giammatteo, "The Verbal Behavior of Superior Teachers," *Elementary School Journal* 65 (February, 1965): 283–85.
14. Bellack, *The Language of the Classroom*, p. 13.
15. Marie Hughes, "What is Teaching? One Viewpoint," *Educational Leadership* 19, no. 4 (January, 1962): 37.
16. Ambrose A. Clegg, Jr., et al., "Teacher Strategies of Questioning for Eliciting Selected Cognitive Student Responses," (A Report of the Tri-University Project, University of Washington, 1970), p. 1.
17. Benjamin S. Bloom, ed., *Taxonomy of Educational Objectives: Handbook I—Cognitive Domain* (New York: David McKay, Inc., 1956).
18. George Farley and Ambrose Clegg, Jr., "Increasing the Cognitive Level of Classroom Questions in Social Studies." (A paper read at the annual meeting of the American Educational Research Association, Los Angeles, February, 1969).
19. Norris Sanders, "Synopsis of Taxonomy of Questions" mimeographed, n.p., n.d. See also Sanders' excellent text, *Classroom Questions, What Kinds* (New York: Harper and Row, 1966) 176 pages.
20. J. Richard Suchman, "Inquiry Training: Building Skills for Autonomous Discovery," *Merrill-Palmer Quarterly of Behavior and Development* 7 (1961): 154–55.
21. Hilda Taba, *Teaching Strategies and Cognitive Functioning in Elementary School Children*. (Washington, D.C.: H.E.W., U.S. Office of Education, Cooperative Research Project No. 2404, 1965).
22. Rosemarie McCartin, "Raising the Level of Teacher Questions by Systematic Reinforcement" (A paper read at the annual meeting of the American Educational Research Association, Los Angeles, February, 1969).
23. J.J. Gallagher and Mary Jane Aschner, "A Preliminary Report: Analyses of Classroom Interaction," *Merrill-Palmer Quarterly of Behavior and Development* 9 (1963): 183–94.
24. Theodore Manolakes, "The Advising System and Supervision," In Thomas J. Sergiovanni, ed., *Professional Supervision for Professional Teachers* (Washington D.C.: Association for Supervision and Curriculum Development, 1975), pp. 51–64.
25. Robert J. Alfonso, "Will Peer Supervision Work?" *Educational Leadership* 34, no. 8 (May, 1977), p. 595.
26. Bruce Wayne Tuckman, "Feedback and the Change Process," *Kappan* 57, No. 5 (January, 1976), pp. 341–44.

Suggested Learning Activities

1. Prepare a checklist of the teaching skills you think are most important. Try to identify instruments or systems available that would provide you with feedback on how those skills are being demonstrated in the classroom.

2. After instruction in the Flanders System of Interaction Analysis, audio- or videotape a fifteen-minute teaching lesson. Determine the percentage of use of each category of behavior as well as the indirect-direct ratio and student-teacher ratio of talking.

3. Utilizing the Gallagher-Aschner system of analyzing questions, determine the use of each of the four types of questions during an hour of teaching.

4. Review Traver's *The Second Handbook of Research on Teaching.* Read especially chapter 5, "The Use of Direct Observation to Study Teaching," pp. 122–83.

5. Develop an instrument that students could use in the evaluation of teaching.

6. Arrange a panel discussion of subject area and general supervisors in a school district, teacher union officials, classroom teachers, and district administrators to discuss evaluation procedures.

7. With a colleague, develop a set of "ground rules" for peer supervision in a school.

Books to Review

Bellon, Jerry J., et al. *Classroom Supervision and Instructional Improvement: A Synergetic Process.* Dubuque, Iowa: Kendall-Hunt Publishing Co., 1976.

Henning, Dorothy Grant. *Mastering Classroom Communication—What Interaction Analysis Tells the Teacher.* Pacific Palisades, California: Goodyear Publishing Co., Inc., 1975.

Hunkins, Francis P. *Questioning Strategies and Techniques.* Boston: Allyn and Bacon, Inc., 1972.

Kounin, Jacob S. *Discipline and Group Management in Classrooms.* New York: Holt, Rinehart and Winston, Inc., 1970.

Leeper, Robert R., ed. *Supervision: Emerging Profession.* Washington, D.C.: Association for Supervision and Curriculum Development, 1969.

Ober, Richard L.; Bentley, Ernest; and Miller, Edith. *Systematic Observation of Teaching.* Englewood Cliffs, New Jersey: Prentice-Hall, Inc., 1971.

Sanders, Norris M. *Classroom Questions: What Kinds?* New York: Harper and Row Publishers, 1966.

Sergiovanni, Thomas J., ed. *Professional Supervision for Professional Teachers.* Washington, D.C.: Association for Supervision and Curriculum Development, 1975.

Travers, Robert M.W., ed. *Second Handbook of Research on Teaching.* Chicago: Rand McNally and Company, 1973.

18

Developing Comprehensive School Planning

School planning is a critical area which often fails to incorporate the essential purpose of the institution. It is common for school planning to be neither long-range nor comprehensive, resulting in short-run responses to environmental pressures and conditions. Such a reactive "administrative" perspective to planning fails to focus on the target of all school arrangements—the students. As Goodwin Watson has so simply stated this condition: Probably the only essential feature of any elementary or secondary school is that it is a social arrangement which exists for the purpose of bringing about desirable change in children.[1]

To be effective, school planning must be both purposeful and comprehensive. Changes in existing programs must be derived from conscious decisions to effect improvement in the educational system. Such a planned mobilization of resources is in stark contrast to natural or evolutionary change which is ever-present in school environments.

Planned change is the linkage between conceptual systems and areas of applied problems. It consists of a clarification and assessment of the system, the establishment of goals and intentions, the translation of such intentions into efforts, and the stabilization of the aforementioned process. As Sarason has observed, to be successful planned change must "introduce into the schools some regularity, behavioral or programmatic."[2]

It is worth noting that long-range planning in schools is somewhat unique and unlike long-range planning in other institutions of our society. Schools are "open" systems, constantly buffeted by social trends and pressures. As Miles has concluded, schools, unlike industrial organizations, are "domesticated" organizations that are especially vulnerable to short-run demands from the environment.[3]

In this chapter there is an attempt to observe the process by which schools can introduce order in change by utilizing comprehensive planning techniques. Such planning includes both the identification and systematizing of efforts but does not reference strategies and tactics of changing. Such logistical manuevers are addressed in chapter 7 of this book.

COMPREHENSIVE CURRICULUM PLANNING

The development of a comprehensive plan for school development represents the culminating activity of a series of events. Such a plan is developed only after the philosophy and goals of the district have been clarified, student and program needs have been assessed, program concepts have been agreed upon, and activities to achieve the above have been delineated. It is at that point that a comprehensive plan can be drawn to manage and evaluate progress toward desired ends.

Comprehensive school plans serve two major functions: they enhance the possibility of involvement by persons from the school and community and they expedite the completion of planned activities. Comprehensive plans can be thought of as having two basic steps which lead to action. First, goals and objectives are identified which define the educational program of the school district. Such directives are rationalized by supportive data drawn from needs assessments or other similar surveys. Second, a program of action and the resources required to implement the various components are identified.

The result of such comprehensive planning is an overall management system that accomplishes the following:

1. What is to be accomplished is clearly spelled out.
2. Communication among all interested parties, especially between the school and the community, is encouraged.
3. There is a maximum utilization of resources within the school district.
4. Information needed for decision making is coordinated.
5. Problems are identified that prevent the accomplishment of activities.
6. Progress leading to the accomplishment of the plan is monitored.

The comprehensive educational plan begins with the formalization of a statement of philosophy (see chapter 5). Such a philosophy, to be useful to planners, is generally presented in the form of belief statements which later become the basis for educational programs and more specifically, teaching and organizational strategies. The development of belief statements by a school district rests on a simple premise: each time a person acts, there is a rationale for action. Without a formalization of such rationales, it is impossible to coordinate or manage individual activities.

Belief statements can be organized in numerous ways, and the correct way for any individual district is dependent upon the planning format. Below are listed examples of belief statements organized around students, learning, teaching roles, grouping of students, and educational programs in general. The generic philosophy from which these are drawn is that the school exists to meet the needs and interests of students:

STUDENTS
1. WE BELIEVE that students are individuals with unique characteristics and interests.
2. WE BELIEVE that each student should have an equal opportunity to learn, based on his/her needs, interests, and abilities.

LEARNING
1. WE BELIEVE that students learn best when content is relevant to their own lives.
2. WE BELIEVE that students learn best in an environment that is pleasant and one in which the democratic process is modeled.

TEACHING
1. WE BELIEVE that the role of the teacher in the classroom is primarily that of a facilitator of learning.
2. WE BELIEVE that student learning may be affected more by what teachers do than by what they say.

GROUPING
1. WE BELIEVE that a more effective program of instruction can be provided for students if they are grouped according to maturation level and similar interest.
2. WE BELIEVE that a high school should include those students who are mature enough to participate in a program that is more specialized than the middle school and those students beyond the age of 18 who have a need to complete the requirements for a high school diploma.

THE EDUCATIONAL PROGRAM

1. WE BELIEVE that all special programs should incorporate specific educational objectives that complement the total school program.
2. WE BELIEVE that evaluating and changing programs to more effectively meet the needs and interests of students should be a continuous process.

Once the school district or school has identified its philosophy and stated such a philosophy in easy-to-understand belief statements, it is ready to develop goals that will serve to guide development. Such goals are drawn from the philosophic orientation of the district, the needs of the school population, and the unique characteristics of the community.

The derivation of a philosophy and the assessment of community needs have been dealt with in earlier chapters (chapters 5 and 14) and the reader is encouraged to review those sections to ascertain the type of planning data available to those who are setting goals. Knowledge about students and their needs can be drawn from two major sources: school records and studies of school-age children.

School records about students generally contain a considerable amount of useful data for planning purposes. Records of student achievement, information about home life, teacher annotation, health records, and similar data present profiles of the general student body as well as indicating special populations. Such records do not, however, speak to the particular educational needs of students either as individuals or as a group.

Studies of school-age children can be extremely useful to school planners in setting goals and developing programs. The studies done on school-age children in the United States are voluminous, and summaries or conceptualizations of growth and development can prove most valuable to planners in the goal-setting stage. At a later time, specific research can be reviewed to answer questions of instructional effectiveness.

An example of a conceptualization which is of use to school planners in terms of student needs is the idea of the *developmental task*. This term, coined by sociologist Robert Havighurst in the 1950s, refers to recurring needs and interests of young people as they strive to become adult.[4] A list of regular concerns by developmental level is shown in Figure 18.1.

Using input about human growth and development, school planners can gain rough indications about the optimum school role at certain ages and stages of development. Such guidelines, as those shown in Figure 18.2 for a secondary school, are important planning considerations along with the district philosophy and community preferences.

Adolescence
Emancipation from parent-
dependency
Occupational projection-selection
Completion of value structure
Acceptance of self

Preadolescence
Handling major body changes
Asserting independence from family
Establishing sex role identity
Dealing with peer group relationships
Controlling emotions
Constructing a values foundation
Pursuing interest expression
Utilizing new reasoning capacities
Developing acceptable self-concept

Late Childhood
Mastering communication skill
Building meaningful peer relations
Thinking independently
Acceptance of self
Finding constructive expression outlets
Role projection

Middle Childhood
Structuring the physical world
Refining language and thought patterns
Establishing relationships with others
Understanding sex roles

Early Childhood
Developing motor control
Emerging self-awareness
Mapping out surroundings
Assigning meaning to events
Exploring relationships with others
Developing language and thought patterns

Figure 18.1
Examples of Developmental Tasks

The formal drafting of goal statements is an important step in the transformation of intentions into efforts. Goal statements are general indications of intent and are characterized by being timeless and not concerned with particular achievements. By identifying goals, a school system can more clearly define the specifics expected of students, teachers, and administrators. For greater clarity and ease of management, general goals can be further broken down into subgoals which express specific directions for development.

Goal statements are divided into two categories: product goals and process goals. Product goals express the desired outcomes relating to student behavior and attitudes. Process goals refer to programs, systems, and strategies to be used by the school district in reaching product goals. An example of a product goal with subgoals might be:

Goal: Acquire the knowledge, skills, and attitudes for effective citizenship.

Subgoals: 1. Develop an awareness of civic rights and responsibilities
2. Develop an attitude of respect for personal and public property
3. Acquire knowledge and skills relevant to the citizen's role in the decision-making process of government
4. Develop a desire to improve the quality of life in the community

Tasks

Late Childhood

Mastery of communication
Building peer relationships
Thinking as an individual

Acceptance of self
Finding means of expression
Role projection

Preadolescence

Handling physical change
Asserting independence
Establishing sex role identity
Refining peer relationships
Controlling emotions
Constructing a values foundation
Pursuing interest
Use of reasoning capacity
Developing self-concept

School Roles

1. *Social development and refinement*
Acceptance of responsibility
Interdependence of individuals
Exploration of social values

Human relations
Communications skills

2. *Promotion of physical and mental health*
Conditioning and coordination
Understanding of hygiene
Sex education
Understanding nutrition
3. *Develop self-concept and self-acceptance*
Accentuate strengths
Self-analysis
Increased responsibility
Values exploration
Interest expansion

4. *Academic adequacy*
Basic literacy
Org. for academic achievement
Skills for continued learning
Introduce knowledge areas
Explore career potential
Develop learning autonomy
Critical thinking

5. *Aesthetic stimulation*
Develop latent talents
Promote aesthetic appreciation
Develop leisure time activities

Figure 18.2
Developmental Tasks and School Roles

An example of a process goal with subgoals might be:

Goal: Provide instructional content which is relevant to the needs and interests of students.

Subgoals: 1. Provide for vocational / career education
2. Provide for the general education of all students
3. Provide for health and safety education
4. Provide programs that focus on the special needs of students

A useful instrument for goal-setting by educational planners has been developed and marketed by Phi Delta Kappa, a professional education fraternity.[5] The Phi Delta Kappa instrument lists eighty-five subgoals encompassing a wide range of desired outcomes in education. Planners rate each subgoal as important (agree with) or unimportant (disagree with) in a "sorting" fashion until all eighty-five subgoals are in order of importance for the planner. Then, using a frequency of response criterion as a quantifier, goals for all planners are prioritized. The resulting composite of desired outcomes represent the general goals of the planners. School districts can easily use the same procedure for ranking their goals by all persons involved in planning.

Once goals have been formalized, clearly identifying the desired outcomes for education in terms of both products and process, it is useful to compare those ends with present conditions. This intermediate step between the isolation of goals and the development of specific program objectives is needed to insure that district resources are directed toward areas of greatest need. Such a step also reduces the possibility of resources being directed toward areas where satisfactory conditions already exist.

A practical step for clearly communicating to teachers and parents the flow of goals at this point is to construct a description of the desired outcomes in their ideal state. When such descriptions are contrasted with existing conditions, planning as a "construct" can move from absolutes to continuums. Thus a thread is established that ties the present to the future. In the example below, a faculty desiring to establish a middle school outlined the present and the future in fourteen areas of school planning:

Continuums of Progress

Moving From	Moving Toward
1. *Philosophy*	
A written document on file in the school office, defining the school in terms of knowledge areas and administrative concerns.	An active, working philosophy which is known by all teachers and which serves as the basis of day-to-day decision making. Defines the school in terms of expected learner growth.

Moving From   **Moving Toward**

2. *School Plant*
   Using only standard classroom spaces for instructional purposes.

   Encompassing varied learning environments, using all available building spaces for instructional purposes (school yard, corridors).

3. *Staffing Patterns*
   Isolated teachers in self-contained classes.

   Teachers grouped in cooperative arrangements, dealing with large numbers of learners collectively. Planning time and home-base teaching function built in organizationally.

4. *Instructional Materials.*
   Classrooms dominated by a basic grade-level text. Libraries are usually study halls for large class groups.

   Diversified learning materials within any given classroom setting: "something for everybody." Multiple texts, supplemental software, integrated and cross-subject materials. Heavy use of multimedia learning resource centers for independent exploration.

5. *Organization of Students*
   Basic pattern of one teacher and thirty students in standardized room spaces. Students in same sized groups all day.

   Greater variability in the sizes of learning groups ranging from individualized study to large group (120 students) instruction. Grouped according to the objective of the instruction.

6. *Teaching Strategies*
   Variety of approaches found but most classes dominated by lecture, single text, question-answer format.

   Greater variety of patterns of teacher-pupil interchange. Teaming when advantageous, greater use of media, possible peer teaching, counseling, more hands-on experience.

7. *Role of the Teacher*
   Defined in terms of subject(s) taught. Teacher perceived as source of of knowledge and responsible for order.

   Greater concern with students. A planned teacher-counselor role. More group work (projects, issues). Teacher role an organizer-facilitator of learning experiences.

Moving From	**Moving Toward**
	Teacher monitoring "contracts" with students. Shared responsibility for order.
8. *Role of Student* Passive recipient of knowledge. Most instruction paced to group. A reactive posture.	Greater input and chance for expression. Involved in planning. Goal to become self-directed. Emphasis on self-conduct and "success." Use of contracts for student goal setting.
9. *Role of Parents* Limited access to the schools. Few parents involved at meaningful level.	Greater involvement of all parents in school activities. Opportunities for more direct involvement in instructional roles in classroom and curriculum planning. Greater flow of information to parents about school objectives and program.
Involvement in only administrative concerns.	
10. *Role of Community* Limited interface with schools. Some strong foundational ties with social services in the city.	School becoming more outwardly oriented; seeing the community as a learning environment and source of instructional resources. Systematizing the connections with social services in the community.
11. *School Rules and Regulations* High degree of regimentation through rules and regulation. Little student input into process. High degree of student dependence on adults for direction.	Greater involvement of students in the design of regulatory policies. Identifying the real essential rules; aiming toward minimum acceptable level of control. Goal to foster increased student independence and self-control.
12. *Discipline* Reactive pattern of discipline, ranging from admonishment and parent conferences to paddling and expulsion.	Design an active program to deter potential disciplinary problems. Greater involvement of pupils in process. Insured degrees or success for all students, seeking to curtail frustration and boredom.

Moving From	**Moving Toward**
13. *Reporting of Student Progress* Letter grades assigned, concern with only narrowly defined academic progress.	Striving for varied student evaluation using a more descriptive medium (conferences, student folders, etc.). Focused on all dimensions of student growth.
14. *Staff Development* Global, not closely tied to building level needs of teachers and students.	Designed to attack building level problems identified by teachers and students. Development of a monitoring process to measure achievement of predetermined goals.

Following the development of goals and general descriptors of direction, long-range planning requires the specification of objectives that will guide the creation of school programs. Objectives are written operational statements which describe the desired outcome of an educational program. Without such objectives, the translation of general goals into programs is likely to be haphazard.

The objectives developed by a school district should be derived from existing goal statements. If objectives are developed that do not directly relate to a goal area, they may suggest goals which need to be addressed by the district. The major purpose of identifying objectives, from a planning perspective, is so that the population to be served, timing, and expected outcomes can be managed and evaluated.

Many school districts become "bogged down" in an attempt to translate goals into objectives due to the behavioral aspect of stating objectives. In general, objectives attempt to communicate to a specific group the expected outcomes of some unit of instruction. When such objectives are stated in behavioral terms, identifying both the capability learned and the performance the capability makes possible, the process can become mechanical and sometimes threatens individualized programs. If the emphasis of the school program is on experiencing, rather than being able to exhibit behaviors, such specificity may be altogether inappropriate for curriculum planning. Advantages of using behavioral objectives:

1. Helps to identify the specific behaviors to be changed.
2. Increases inter-school and intra-school communication.
3. Directs instructional activities in the classroom.
4. Provides a meaningful basis for evaluation.

Disadvantages of using behavioral objectives:

1. Is sometimes simplistic; human behavior is more than the sum of the parts.

2. Behavioral objectives disregard the interrelatedness of human activity.
3. Often will limit choice, remove or prohibit alternatives.
4. In the classroom can limit concommitant learning.

In terms of working through understandings about a desired educational program, it is believed that general or conceptual descriptors can serve as planning objectives. School districts may, however, wish to pursue instructional objectives which are behaviorally stated, and many guides are available to assist such a task.* An example of a planning objective is as follows:

Understand the nature and purpose of science:

1. Understand the investigative nature of science
2. Know the history and development of science
3. Know the relationship between scientific progress, technical achievements, and economic development
4. Realize the impact of science on our lives

Once such objectives or conceptual descriptors are developed by educational planners and related to goal areas, it is possible to order them in hierarchical form so that they are tied to both a population and a time in school. Thus, it may be that science for children in kindergarten may be concerned with distinguishing between plant and animal life, while seniors in high school may be focusing on applying scientific information in new and wider contexts. The following is a *science continuum* for senior high school developed by a group of classroom teachers participating in curriculum planning:

1. *Understand the scientific approach*
   a. Understand the distinction between pure science and its application.
   b. Understand the stages of scientific inquiry.
   c. Understand the creative nature of the scientist's work.
2. *Apply scientific methods to life*
   a. Have an exploratory, speculating, questioning attitude.
   b. Base solutions to problems on logic and empirical evidence.
   c. Apply scientific processes and skills to solve practical problems.
3. *Have scientific experimentation skills*
   a. Plan a simple experimental design and carry it to completion.
   b. Demonstrate skillful use of laboratory tools and equipment.
   c. Select from several experimental procedures the one most appropriate for testing a given hypothesis.

---

* For example see Robert Mager's *Preparing Instructional Objectives,* (Belmont, California: Fearon Publishers, Inc., 1962).

4. *Have scientific observation and description skills*
    a. Observe and identify phenomena, objects, and their proper-
    ties.
    b. Observe and identify changes in physical and biological ob-
    jects.
    c. Order a series of observations.
5. *Have scientific hypothesis formation skills*
    a. Distinguish among hypothesis, prediction, inference, and
    opinion.
    b. Formulate a simple hypothesis, and give explanations for
    various phenomena on the basis of known information and
    observations.
6. *Understand the content and concepts of advanced science*
    a. Understand concepts about the life of man.
    b. Understand the concepts relating to physical science.
    c. Understand the concepts relating to ecology.*

A final step in mapping out objectives for the school program is to
order objectives according to grade level or schooling level, and to
identify objectives with subject areas. In performing this step, school
planners are able to gain an overview of what is intended in each
subject area at each level of schooling.

There are two major benefits in this mapping process which con-
nects goals and objectives to programs. First, by viewing the intentions for students in totality, school planners can often identify re-
dundancy in both the scope (breadth) and the sequence (order) of the
general curriculum. Second, such an overview can help planners see
commonality among parts of the curriculum. Understanding the interrelatedness of the curriculum can have payoff in both instructional
coordination and in a maximum utilization of district resources.

Once objectives have been generated for each desired goal and
placed in a format that allows a review of the total blueprint for educating students in the district, it is necessary to identify program concepts which will give form to instruction. Program concepts are, in
essence, sets of instructional and organizational strategies that are
philosophically based.

The program concept phase of curriculum development is perhaps
the most difficult step in building school programs. Although the
need is to develop programs that are compatible with the district
philosophy, there is always a tendency to return to what is familiar to
us. Hence, the conceptual objectives often end up being translated
into school programs with standard characteristics such as a text-
book-dominated six-period day. At this stage, the educational philosophy adopted before specific objectives were developed can assist

---

* Science continuum developed by teachers in Lanier County, Georgia, public schools.

in answering the question of how to best teach to achieve the desired ends.

Schools and school districts differ tremendously in how they interact with students to accomplish desired goals and objectives. The subtlety of this condition is fully developed in chapter 19. Generally speaking, however, schools vary according to how much structure they demand in the instructional program. Structure, as opposed to flexibility in instructional organization, is a reflection of the anticipated conciseness of the desired outcomes. School districts that desire highly predictable outcomes for all students who experience their program should not encourage instructional flexibility, for each variable encourages diversity of outcome.

In schools where there is a philosophy focusing on the student as an individual, there is a wider choice for instructional patterns. The program concept, when translated into instructional arrangements, indicates to school planners how desired outcomes should be approached. In the following example, a school district identifies seven concepts that are felt to reinforce their desire to develop a program focused on the individual child.

Philosophy Statement—We desire in each school, kindergarten through adult education, a program that will focus on the individual student to provide learning experiences in the affective, cognitive, and psychomotor areas.

Program Concepts
1. A program of individualized instruction will be implemented.
2. A basic diagnostic-prescriptive approach to teaching will be utilized.
3. A variety of materials, both commercial and teacher-made, will be used.
4. A flexible schedule will be implemented.
5. Instructional assistants will perform teaching, planning, and clerical tasks.
6. Instructional leaders (teachers) will serve as facilitators of program planning and implementation.
7. A facility that provides as much flexibility in programming as possible will be promoted.

At this point in the sequence of events, the comprehensive school plan shifts its focus from one of *what* to one of *how*. School planners now possess a philosophy, goal statements, related instructional objectives, a blueprint of the overall program, and some program concepts which sketch the instructional delivery system at the school and classroom level. What must now be accomplished is to take all such input and place it into a long-range plan that will enable the district to accomplish its desired program. Such a long-range plan serves as an architectural design for schooling in the district, a management system for monitoring progress toward goals, and the rudimentary framework of an evaluation/accountability instrument. Such a plan should identify necessary resources, actions to be taken, and deadlines for accomplishment. The plan should also present the entire operation in a form understandable by all involved.

One of the primary tasks to be accomplished by long-range planners is to develop a complete listing of needs for each segment of the program. This would include a brief description of the program itself, the areas of learning to be addressed, the organization of the program, the organization of staff, staffing requirements, teaching strategies, and resources needed. In the following example, a complete plan for the establishment of a kindergarten is outlined:

PLAN FOR ESTABLISHING A KINDERGARTEN

Population—Approximately 300 students, ages 3–5, and 6-year-olds who do not have the readiness for the first grade.

Program Concept—The kindergarten program will be divided into two distinct components. An A.M. program will be provided with a basic instructional format that will match the individualized and continuous progress concepts. The major focus of the A.M. program will be readiness for the more formal education program to follow, while the specific objectives will be to develop social skills, motor skills, self-direction, self-esteem, and communication. During the P.M. program, a child care service will be provided for those students who need the service because both parents work away from the home. The program will follow an action format that will have little structure. Focus will be primarily on socialization.

Areas of Learning—Socialization, school readiness, independence, motor skills, communication.

Program organization—The student population will be divided into instructional units of thirty students each and will be comprised of students of varying ages, but with similar maturation characteristics. The formal program will be scheduled from 8:00 A.M. to 12:00 noon, with a breakfast and lunch program provided. Students that are eligible for the child care program will remain at school until 3:00 P.M. The kindergarten program will operate five days a week, twelve months of the year when school is in session.

Staff Organization—The staff will be organized to complement the instructional unit approach. For each unit, there will be one teacher and three instructional aides who will work as a team.

Staff Requirements—The kindergarten school staff will consist of one program coordinator, ten teachers, thirty instructional aides, one school nurse, and one secretary/bookkeeper.

Teaching strategies—Some examples of teaching strategies to be used by the kindergarten staff are: role playing, field trips, working with educational games, regular planned rest, rhythmical activities, positive reinforcement, creative expression, peer teaching, exploration of self, school, and community.

Facilities—The kindergarten school will utilize the cafetorium and the auditorium located on the current high school site. Both buildings need remodeling in order to be adequate for an early childhood program. Floors and restrooms of the auditorium need remodeling, and lighting, controlled air, and carpeting should be updated.

Using such a complete plan, curriculum development teams can assess the scope and cost of desired programs and make decisions about priorities based on factual information. In Table 18.1 and Table 18.2, the cost of the proposed kindergarten program is computed, and district-wide staffing requirements have been plotted.

Table 18.1
Cost of Proposed Kindergarten

	Cost	
Item	**Start Up**	**Continuing**
1. PERSONNEL		
a. 10 Regular Teachers		$102,790
b. 30 Instructional Aides		135,000
c. 1 Program Coordinator		12,000
d. 1 Secretary/Bookkeeper		5,000
2. FIXED CHARGES		
Social Security and Teacher Retirement @15% of $254,790		38,218
3. MATERIALS		
Continuous Cost—10 teachers @$260/teacher	$10,000	2,600
4. EQUIPMENT		
Cots, chairs, tables, learning center equipment, playground equipment	10,000	1,500
5. FACILITIES		
Renovation of the cafeteria and auditorium on the present high school site	48,750	
6. MAINTENANCE AND OPERATION OF PLANT		
10 Teachers @$1,500/teacher		15,000
7. STAFF DEVELOPMENT		
a. Consultant honorarium and travel	800	1,200
b. Materials		300
TOTAL	$69,550	$313,608

TOTAL COST OF KINDERGARTEN SCHOOL PROGRAM $383,158

Table 18.2
Staff Requirements

	KINDERGARTEN	ELEMENTARY SCHOOL	MIDDLE SCHOOL	HIGH SCHOOL	ADULT SCHOOL	SYSTEM-WIDE SPECIAL SERVICES	TOTALS
Driver Education				1			1
Vocational/Occupational				6			6
Reading				2			2
Special Education		2	4	2			8
Music Teacher		1	1	1			3
Art Teacher		1	1	1			3
Physical Education Teacher		1	2	3			6
Regular Teachers	10	25	24	11			70
Part-time Teachers					6		6
Instructional Aides	30	27	26	18			101
Secretary/Bookkeeper	1	1	1	1			4
Bookkeeper						1	1
Secretary						1	1
Program Coordinators	1	1	4	1	1		8
Counselors		½	1	2			3½
Media Specialists		1	1	1			3
Career Awareness Coordinators		½	1				1½
Vocational/Occupational Coord.				1			1
Language Arts Coordinator						1	1
Registered Nurse						1	1
Social Worker						1	1
Curriculum Director						1	1
Director Pupil Services						1	1
Principals		1	1	1			3
Superintendent						1	1

Following the selection of priority programs which can be accomplished within the scope of district resources, it is necessary to conceptualize and order the desired changes in terms of events or activities. Such events might include renovating or constructing school sites, acquiring instructional materials, retraining instructional personnel, pursuing community/public relations, and the development of specific program syllabi. A first step in this process is to develop activity packages which include the task to be accomplished, the participants, the group responsible for the accomplishment of the task, the resources required, and a target date for completion. Such an activity package is generally presented in chart form as shown in Figure 18.3

Activity/Task	Participants	Groups	Respon.	Resources	Target	Date

Figure 18.3
Activity Chart

Once activity packages have been completed, and program development assignments made, it is possible to develop displays of long-range planning which communicate to all participants the district-wide progress toward goals. Such displays generally take one of three format: a milestone chart, a flow chart, or a PERT chart.

A milestone chart is really a schedule of major events which are sequenced according to calendar dates. The purpose of milestones is to ensure that each task is accomplished on time and to aid in monitoring the progress of the overall plan. In Table 18.3, a milestone chart is used to begin a major needs assessment in the district.

A flow chart is a similar display of development activity over a period of time. Unlike the milestone chart, a flow chart displays the entire time frame of the development project. It is possible, using the flow chart, to survey the entire project at one glance as in the twenty-four-month example shown in Table 18.4.

A final display commonly found in long-range planning in schools is the PERT chart, or Program Evaluation and Review Technique display.*   PERT, a management system originally used by the Depart-

---

* For more information see *A Programmed Introduction to PERT,* Federal Electric Corporation, ITT, (London: John Wiley & Sons, 1963).

Table 18.3
Milestone Chart

Milestones	Completion Date						
	1979				1980		
	Sept.	Oct.	Nov.	Dec.	Jan.	Feb.	Mar.
1. Review guidelines with State Department of Education June 7							
2. Identify the criteria for selecting a representative group of the school, community to serve as a task force	△13						
3. Identify the Education Task Force	△20						
4. Orientation for Education Task Force to guidelines and intent		△4					
5. Design a management system for processing the development of a plan		△6					
6. Identify special groups representing the school and community for involvement		△7					
7. Describe the scope and depth of the plan		△7					
8. Plan task for completing the philosophy stage		△7					
9. Appoint Task Force committees		△7					
10. Orientation for all special groups to guidelines, intent and management system		△11					
11. Collect data for the philosophy stage		△18					

Table 18.4

Middle Years Implementation Flow Chart

By Theme   Months
_____

1. **DATA GATHERING**
   1.1 Set up research group and establish terms of reference (1) _____
   1.2 Instrument selection and development for data gathering (2–6) _____
   1.3 Collate, publish, and disseminate data (7–8)
   _____

2. **ADVISORY GROUPS**
   2.1 Create demand for advisory groups (1–7) _____
   2.2 Use existing grants for advisory groups (1–36) _____
   2.3 Encourage school community contact (1–36) _____
   2.4 Facilitate two-way school/community communication (1–36) _____
   2.5 Facilitate community involvement in the school (1–36) _____
   2.6 Facilitate school involvement in the community (1–36) _____
   2.7 Prepare how-to manuals on school/community contact (1–36) _____
   2.8 Facilitate school climate open to community (1–36) _____
   2.9 Contact with CDSS (1–36) _____
   2.10 Provide stirrer to set up advisory groups (7–18) _____
   2.11 Provide training information for advisory groups (7–18) _____
   2.12 Follow up support to advisory groups (7–36)
   _____

3. **FACILITIES**
   3.1 Establish working party re: middle years facilities design (6)_____
   3.2 Review materials re: types of facilities (6–9) _____
   3.3 Write paper re: middle years facilities (9–10)_____
   3.4 Seek approval for paper from outside groups (10–11) _____
   3.5 Seek approval for paper from minister (12)_____
   3.6 Disseminate (12–36)
   _____

4. **MATERIALS PRODUCTION**
   4.1 Survey topic needs for materials production (1–6 and 12–18) _____
   4.2 Evaluation and validation of middle years units (2–36) _____
   4.3 Produce "how-to" materials to meet PD needs (2–36) _____
   4.4 Design workshop series for program development (4–10) _____
   4.5 Evaluate materials acquired (5–36) _____
   4.6 Send bibliographies to schools (5–36) _____
   4.7 Plan and offer one day in-services (5–8) _____
   4.8 Get incentive money for teacher produced materials (5) _____
   4.9 Establish criteria for distribution of incentives (5) _____
   4.10 Monitor incentive contracts re: materials production (5–36) _____
   4.11 Hold workshops on how to develop sample units for middle years
        (6–36) _____
   4.12 Build new units for middle years (6–36) _____
   4.13 Disseminate new middle years units (6–36) _____
   4.14 Negotiate with commercial publishers to publish materials (8–36) ____
   4.15 Assessments by participants of workshops and in-services (1–36)
   _____

5. **FACULTIES**
   5.1 Meet faculties to discuss middle years needs and role (1–6) _____
   5.2 Negotiate with faculties re: preservice courses (1–6) _____
   5.3 Negotiate with faculties re: in-service (1–6) _____
   5.4 Meet Graduate Studies Committee, Faculty of Education re: research
        and program development (3–36) _____
   5.5 Meet faculties re: student production of materials (10–36) _____
   5.6 Check if faculties offering courses (11) _____

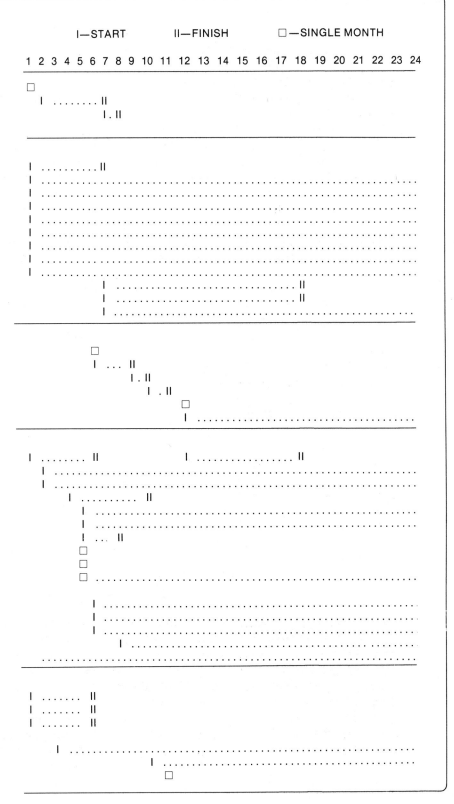

I—START   II—FINISH   □—SINGLE MONTH

1 2 3 4 5 6 7 8 9 10 11 12 13 14 15 16 17 18 19 20 21 22 23 24

ment of Defense to accelerate the development of Polaris submarines, is widely used outside of education and holds promise for assisting educators with planning complex changes in schools. It does two major things: PERT is a manager's tool for defining and coordinating what must be done, and it is a method for focusing attention on problems which require decisions.

PERT charts have an advantage over milestone charts and flow charts in that they assist the planner in arriving at the optimum order for events. By forcing planners to make time estimates for short-duration activities, PERT charts can show the time dependence of one event on another. For example, in refurbishing a kindergarten classroom, there must first be a program concept if the classroom is to be functional to the teachers.

PERT charts employ symbols and formulas for assisting planners in establishing a long-range plan. Some of those symbols are as follows:

DEFINITION	SYMBOL
Event—the start or completion of a task. There is always a sequential relationship between events.	①
Flow—the order of events is indicated by arrows, not event numbers.	
Activity—the performance of a task. The time-consuming portion of the PERT network. An activity always requires resources.	*a, b, c*
Time—the estimated performance time is an average of "optimistic," "most likely," and "pessimistic" estimates in weeks or months.	$Te = \dfrac{a + 4m + b}{6}$

a = optimistic time
m = most likely time
b = pessimistic time

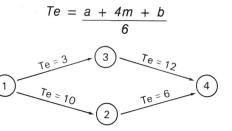

In the example, event 4 shows a dependence on both events 2 and 3. Since the largest time-consuming path (in this case 1–2–4) represents the earliest possible time to begin event 4, Te for event 4 is 16 weeks. If this example were translated to the kindergarten refurbishment, it might mean that carpeting could not be laid until painting (1–3–4) and electrical wiring (1–2–4) were completed.

Any of the three long-range displays serves a secondary function for the school district; they set up an evaluation system for district-wide activities. By identifying goals, translating those goals into objectives

Figure 18.4
Management System

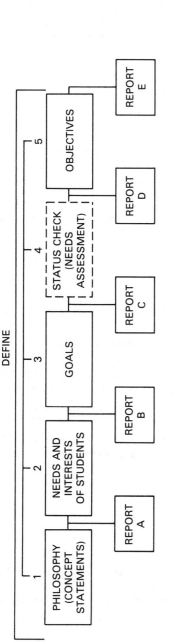

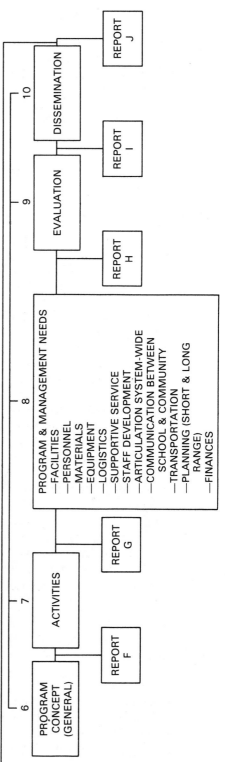

and activities, and placing completion of those activities in a time frame, school leaders establish an accountability criterion for their efforts. As activities and events are completed they can be checked off as an accomplishment. Such activities can also be assessed according to cost-effectiveness and personnel management.

Finally, it is possible for school planners to develop a record of progress in curriculum development by requiring that reports be issued at the completion of every phase of the process. In Figure 18.4, ten reports would outline progress in comprehensive school planning.

SUMMARY

The development of school programs, to be meaningful, requires comprehensive planning. Comprehensive plans aid in critical decision-making and in resource management. Such plans communicate to all concerned where curriculum development is directed and what is considered desirable. Comprehensive planned change presents an alternative to ever-present evolutionary change in schools.

A comprehensive school plan consists of an assessment of the system, the establishment of goals and intentions, the translation of goals into objectives and program concepts, and the implementation sets to achieve those desired conditions. Comprehensive plans introduce regularity into ongoing events, and serve to involve people and expedite the completion of activities.

The translation of intentions into a long-range plan requires that activities be identified with philosophically-based program concepts. Such activities can be constructed in packages that identify participants, resources, and target dates for action.

The summary of all activities to accomplish the desired programs in schools are generally displayed on one of three common formats for long-range planning: the milestone chart, the flow chart, and the PERT chart. Each of these can aid the district in developing an evaluation/accountability system and, when accompanied by a series of reports, a record of curriculum development progress.

Notes

1. Goodwin Watson, *Change in School Systems* (Cooperative Project For Educational Development, NTL-NEA, 1967), p. 3.
2. Seymour B. Sarason, *The Culture of the School and the Problem of Change,* (Boston, Mass.: Allyn and Bacon, 1971), p. 3.

3. Matthew Miles, "Some Properties of Schools as a Social System" in G. Watson, ed., *Change in School Systems,* (National Training Laboratory, National Education Association, 1967).
4. Robert J. Havighurst, Developmental Tasks and Education (New York: Longmans, Greene, 1952).
5. Commission on Educational Planning, Phi Delta Kappa, Incorporated, Bloomington, Indiana.

Suggested Learning Activities

1. Describe the stages by which a school philosophy becomes a school program.
2. Using a packet of Phi Delta Kappan goal cards, sort possible goals until you have prioritized the eighty-five items.
3. Starting with a program concept, attempt to develop K-12 goals for any subject area found in the public schools.
4. Construct a five-step PERT network for a hypothetical curriculum project that will occur during the next year.

Books to Review

Havighurst, Robert. *Developmental Tasks and Education.* New York: Longsman, Greene, 1952.

Mager, Robert. *Goal Analysis.* Belmont, California: Fearon Publishers, 1964.

A Programmed Introduction to PERT. Federal Electric Corporation, ITT, London: John Wiley and Sons, 1963.

part three

Curriculum Practice

19

Dimensions of a School Setting

During the past century American schools have evolved from highly standardized content-focused institutions to more flexible and diverse forms of education. More than other factors, an increase in the volume of accumulated knowledge and a growing understanding of the learning process account for these changes in the school. Still, it is common to speak of and perceive schools as a monolithic body. Such an orientation detracts from our ability to develop better schools.

This chapter will help the reader see schools as they really are. The underlying thesis is simple: schools are not alike. By design or by default, schools represent a blueprint to promote learning. If we can begin to view schools analytically, from a design perspective, we can begin to understand the relationship among the parts of the school. Being able to compare, contrast, and categorize schools by design is an important skill in curriculum development. Such a skill is a necessity for effective decision making and evaluation in education.

All schools are created to promote education, but it is the definition of what constitutes an education that differentiates schools. Even though many variables might be used to illustrate the differences in school programs, the authors believe that the long view of what schools are trying to achieve with students represents the most useful analytic tool.

In this respect, the intentions of schooling might be thought of as a continuum of choices. On one end of such a continuum is the belief that education is the process of shaping raw human talent into something definitive and useful to society. This classic view of education sees schools shaping and refining human thought and behavior through an increasingly controlled program of study. Such control, in the legitimate sense of the word, is accomplished by structuring the learning environment to facilitate highly predictable ends.

On the other end of that same choice continuum is the belief that human talents are best managed by allowing the natural capacities of individuals to develop through the removal of growth barriers. This definition of education would have schools acting to release the student from behaviors and perceptions which limit personal development. Thus, the institution of the school would formally seek the expansion of human potential in the process of learning.

Strong arguments can be made for either of these positions, as well as for the many intermediate stances on such a continuum. The crucial concept to be understood is that schools are institutions created by society to accomplish certain ends. Since there are many possible goals for the institution of the school, there are many legitimate forms of schooling. To the degree that the organization of the school corresponds with the objectives of the school, the school can effectively educate students.

In this chapter, the range of possible intentions for a school program, bordered on one end by a school seeking maximum control and on the other by a school promoting maximum freedom, has been translated into the universal variables of structure versus flexibility. These two variables, structure and flexibility, are used to facilitate the analysis of fifteen major dimensions of schooling. These fifteen dimensions are all ones that can be readily observed by a visitor to a school:

1. Community involvement
2. School buildings and grounds
3. Classroom spaces
4. Organization of knowledge
5. Uses of learning materials
6. Philosophy of education
7. Teaching strategies
8. Staffing patterns
9. Organization of students
10. Rules and regulations
11. Discipline measures
12. Student progress reporting
13. Administrative postures
14. Teacher roles
15. Student roles

Examining the school by such criteria, in a systematic manner, will help the reader see a school in its totality. The underlying beliefs about educating will become more obvious and the program congruence or inconsistencies will be more visible. In short, the reader will be able to analyze the dimensions of a school setting in a selective and regular way.

THE LEARNING ENVIRONMENT

It is clear that environments, both real and perceived, set a tone for learning. What people feel about the spaces they occupy or interact with causes them to behave in certain ways. Churches, for instance, call for discrete behavior while stadiums elicit a different behavior.

Traditionally, schools have been solitary, sedate, and ordered environments. This atmosphere was the result of many forces: a narrow definition of formal education, a limited public access to knowledge, a didactic (telling-listening) format for learning.

In contrast, many innovative schools seem to be the organizational opposite of the traditional, structured school. They are often open, noisy, and sometimes seemingly chaotic activity centers. These changes in schools are the result of both a changing definition of education and a new understanding of the environmental conditions that enhance learning.

Three measures of the learning environments of schools are the relationship of the school and the surrounding community, the construction and utilization of buildings and grounds, and the organization of learning spaces within buildings. Within each of these three areas, selected dimensions have been identified which may assist in understanding the learning environment of the school.

Community Involvement

Individual schools differ according to the degree and type of interaction they enjoy with the immediate community. Schools that perceive their role as shaping the behavior and thoughts of students into acceptable patterns normally seek to limit community access and involvement in the school program. By limiting community access, the school also limits community influence on the school program and thus insures more predictable outcomes for students.

Conversely, schools intent on expanding student responses to the educational process generally encourage community access and involvement in school activities. By encouraging community access the school encourages community influence, thus insuring the divergent input characteristic of most communities.

Measures of community access and involvement with a school are plentiful. A simple measure readily available to the observer is to note how many and what kinds of nonschool personnel are in a school building on a given day. Perhaps a more analytic approach to the assessment of involvement, however, is to observe the school operation in terms of physical, legal, participatory, and intellectual access.

In a physical sense, community involvement can be measured by the amount of quasi-school related activity occurring in the school building. Activities such as school-sponsored visits to the building, community-sponsored functions in the building, parental participation in school-sponsored activities, and school programs being conducted in the community are indicative of interchange and involvement.

On the other hand, schools where the public is never invited to visit, where classes never leave the building, where the public is fenced out or locked out, held at the office when visiting, not welcome after school hours, or discouraged from mobility within the spaces of the school indicate limited access and involvement.

Legally, the community is allowed to become involved with the school at varying levels. In a tightly structured or closed school, legal access is normally restricted to setting limits and voting on school bonds. Increasing participation is measured by electing school officials and the chief administrative officer of the school district. Further access is indicated by school-building-level committees (such as a textbook selection committee) which allow community members to play an active role in policy formation. The ultimate access, not surprisingly called "community schools" in educational literature, has parents and the community-at-large serving in governance roles over school operation and activity.

In terms of participation in the daily operation of the school program, the community can be ignored, informed, included at an advisory level, or asked to participate wholly. Whether a school chooses to include the community in the type of school program that is being experienced by the students depends on whether such participation is seen as contributing to or detracting from the mission of the school.

Finally, there is an intellectual dimension to community involvement with the school that is indicated by access to goal setting, resource allocation, and program development. To the degree that the community is excluded from thinking about the substance of what is taught and the method of instruction, the school is characterized by limited intellectual access or high structure. If the school encourages programmatic and instructional participation from parents and members of the community, then access or high flexibility is evidenced.

There are great differences in the degree of access and community involvement with individual school buildings. As such, community involvement represents one salient dimension of the learning environment. The following descriptive continuums suggest the potential range of alternatives present in schools:

1.1 Access-Physical

No contact	Community functions in the school buildings	Scheduled community visits to the school	Regular community participation in school building activities	School learning activities in the community

S- —|— — — — — — — —|— — — — — — — +— — — — — — — — +— — — — — — — — |— — F

1.2 Access-Legal

Voting for bonds	Electing school officials	Serving on official committees	Policy boards at school building level	Operational control over school programs

S-+ — — — — — — —|— — — — — — — +— — — — — — — — — |— — — — — — — — — +— — ·F

1.3 Access-Participatory

Ignored	Informed	Advisory	Planning	Participatory

S-+ — — — — — — — —|— — — — — — — — |— — — — — — — +— — — — — — — —|— —·F

1.4 Access-Intellectual

Never consulted about program content	Advisory in goal-setting	Set goals and parameters of school programs	Involved in planning implementation	Actively involved in implementing at classroom level

S- — — +— — — — — — — |— — — — — — — —|— — — — — — — —|— — — — — — +— —·F

1.5 Access-General

Media access (the news)	Legal access (voting bonds)	Physical access (visitations)	Participatory access (school programs)	Intellectual access (goal-setting)

S- ·— —|— — — — — — —|— — — — — — — — +— — — — — — — — +— — — — — — — |— —·F

School Buildings and Grounds

The physical nature of school buildings and school grounds may be subtle indicators of the school's perceived mission and therefore useful measures for a visitor or interested observer. Features such as access points, building warmth, traffic control inside the building, and space priorities may reflect the intended program of the school.

Architects have observed that buildings are a physical expression of content. A dull, drab, unexciting building may reflect a dull, drab, unexciting educational process. An exciting, stimulating, dynamic building may reflect an active, creative learning center. A building not only expresses its interior activity, but may also reflect, and even control, the success of these functions. If school corridors, for example, are colorful, well lighted, and visually expansive, then this excitement and stimulation directs the individual in such a space. It is for this reason that most new airports have extremely wide and brightly colored corridors. The environment "sets up" the participant dispositionally.

School buildings have changed a great deal during this century, and those changes in architecture and construction reflect more subtle changes in the programs of schools. A stereotypic evolution of school buildings in the United States would show a progression from a cellular lecture hall (many one-room school houses together) to an open and largely unstructured space as illustrated in Figure 19.1.

While many of these changes might be explained by evolutions in architecture and cost effectiveness demands, it can be observed that a primary force behind the diminishing structure in school buildings has been the dissemination of knowledge through other mediums. As the "essential" curriculum of the turn of the century gave way to a more broadly-focused academic preparation, buildings were designed to incorporate diversity. Because spaces had multiple uses, the construction was necessarily flexible in design.

Just because a school building is traditional or open-space in design, however, tells the visitor little about the current philosophy of the school. Many flexible programs are found in old "egg crate" buildings and, equally, highly structured programs are sometimes found in modern open-space schools. Returning to our analytic tools, the degree of access, the warmth of the building, traffic control patterns inside the building, and space priorities, we can approach knowing the real program in the building.

Degree of Access

Many schools, because of genuine danger in the immediate neighborhood, limit the number of access points to the school building. Other

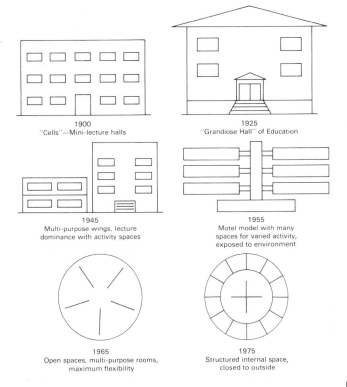

1900
"Cells"—Mini-lecture halls

1925
"Grandiose Hall" of Education

1945
Multi-purpose wings, lecture
dominance with activity spaces

1955
Motel model with many
spaces for varied activity,
exposed to environment

1965
Open spaces, multi-purpose rooms,
maximum flexibility

1975
Structured internal space,
closed to outside

Figure 19.1

schools deliberately limit public access as a means of controlling the environment and personnel in the building. Signs of extreme control in school buildings are a single entrance for all entering the building, constantly locked spaces such as bathrooms and auxiliary spaces, and purposeful physical barriers to movement such as long unbroken counters in school offices.

Cues such as these tell visitors, students, and even teachers in the building that there are acceptable and unacceptable ways to enter the building and move in the building. Highly controlled access and mobility in school buildings indicate a belief that only certain types of movement in a building is conducive to successful education.

Building Warmth

Related to physical access is the concept of building warmth. The size of spaces, shape of space, scale of the environment (relationship between size of the people and objects in the environment), coloration, and use of lighting all affect the warmth of a school building. Generally speaking, a combination of extreme space (large or small), extreme light (bright or dim), extreme coloration (too drab or too bright), repelling shapes, (not geometrical or too geometrical), or disproportionate scale (too big or too little) can cause discomfort to the occupant.

In the past, small classrooms with oversized furniture, drab coloration, and square walls have been used purposefully to control environmental stimulation and direct attention to the teacher. Such a discomforting setting presupposed that teacher behavior was the significant action in the learning environment.

More recently, schools have used bright colors, curved walls, large expansive spaces, and acoustical treatments to encourage student mobility and mental freedom. Such an environment presupposes that education is an act which is highly individual and conducted through exploration. Control under such environmental conditions is often difficult.

While few school buildings are constructed to promote an identifiable pattern of instruction, the effect of environmental warmth is great on instructional procedure. Failure to consider this factor has led to many unsuccessful and inefficient teaching episodes.

Traffic Control Patterns

Traffic control within a school building, made famous by Kaufman's book *Up The Down Staircase,*[1] is also a reflection of the school's belief about the nature of education. Many schools go to great lengths to communicate *order* to inhabitants of the building. Adhesive strips dividing hallways into acceptable paths, turnstiles, fences, and children marching single file along walls are indicative of such structure in a building.

In buildings where flexibility is encouraged, the observer will see curved sidewalks, entrances to learning spaces without doors, seating spaces where occupants can stop and rest enroute to their destination, and multiple patterns of individual progression from point to point in the building.

Space Priorities

Finally, space usage and priorities reflect the learning environment in school buildings. Priorities are indicated by both the size of spaces in the building and the location of spaces in the building. In some schools, old and new, a significant portion of total available space is dominated by single-event spaces such as auditoriums, gymnasiums, swimming pools, and central office suites. In terms of construction costs and utilization, these spaces speak subtly of the priorities of the resident educators.

The number, kind, and quality of spaces can be a measure of the definition of educational priority in a school building.

A second, and perhaps more accurate, measure of space priority in a school building is the location of various areas. Studies of school buildings have indicated that the longer a teacher is in a building, the better his or her resource base becomes relative to other teachers. How much space, for instance, does the English department have? Where is the fine arts complex located? What new additions have been made to the building and which program do they serve?

Beyond the structural walls of the school building lie the school grounds. Sometimes these spaces will reveal the attitude of the school toward learning. One interesting measure of the school yard is whether it is being utilized at all. Some schools are located on ten-acre sites and never plant a bush or add a piece of equipment to make the grounds useful to the school. Other schools, by contrast, use the grounds extensively and perceive them as an extension of the formal learning spaces.

Another question to be asked about the school grounds is whether they are generally used for student loitering, casual recreation, physical education, or comprehensive educational purposes. Equipment and student behavior will indicate which, if any, uses are made of this valuable resource.

There are great differences in the way individual schools utilize their buildings and grounds. As such, the use of these resources represents another relevant dimension of the school environment. The following descriptive continuums suggest the potential range of alternatives present in schools.

2.1   Building-Access

High visible control of access exterior building	Access control visible interior only-high regimentation	Access control visible exterior only	Order visible but not excessive	Access not controlled exterior or interior

S — — —⊢— — — — — — — — —+— — — — — — — —+— — — — — — —+— — — — —⊣— -F

2.2   Building-Warmth

Spaces drab, overwhelming, repulsive, cold	Spaces ordered and monotonous	Spaces neutral, neither pleasant or unpleasant	Spaces pleasant, light, clean, attractive	Spaces inviting, cheery, colorful

S— — +— — — — — — — — —⊢— — — — — — — — —⊢— — — — — — —⊣— — — — — — —⊣—F

2.3   Building-Traffic control

Movement in building highly controlled	Movement patterns structured by arrangement	Traffic patterns established	Traffic patterns not specified; options available to individuals	Movement patterns not discernable

S— — +— — — — — — —+— — — — — — — —+— — — — — — —⊢— — — — — —⊣—-F

2.4   Building-Space priorities

Space allocation grossly distorted	Space allocation highly disproportioned in building	Some priorities via space allocation obvious	Space equally allocated to various components, location key	No space priority observable by size or locale

S — —+— — — — — — — —+— — — — — — — — —+— — — — — — —+— — — — — — —+— — —F

2.5   Building-Grounds

Grounds not in active use	Grounds used for informal activity	Grounds used for specific activity	Grounds use variable	Grounds use extensively for multiple activity

S— —+— — — — — — —+— — — — — — —+— — — — — — —+— — — — — — —+— —F

Classroom Spaces

Just as the school learning environment may be revealed in school dimensions such as community involvement and building use, the organization, movement, and ownership of physical space in the classroom is often indicative of the intentions of the school. In viewing these characteristics of the classroom, it is again obvious that all schools are not alike.

One way of viewing the classroom spaces is in terms of the organization for instructional effectiveness. A traditional pattern would be to order the room in such a way that all vision and attention is on the teacher. Figure 19.2 shows that there is little opportunity for lateral communication. Activity is "fixed" by the arrangement of furniture. The conditions are perfect for teacher lecture but little else.

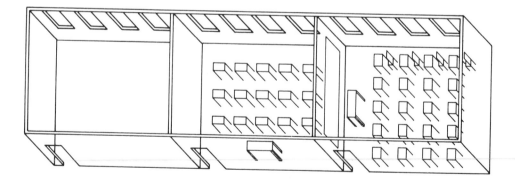

Figure 19.2

Another possibility in organization of classroom spaces is to create multi-purpose spaces with the focus of attention generally in the center of the classroom. This style permits increased student involvement, mobility, and varied learning activities simultaneously. It does not focus attention solely on the teacher and cannot easily be controlled in terms of noise or lateral communication among students.

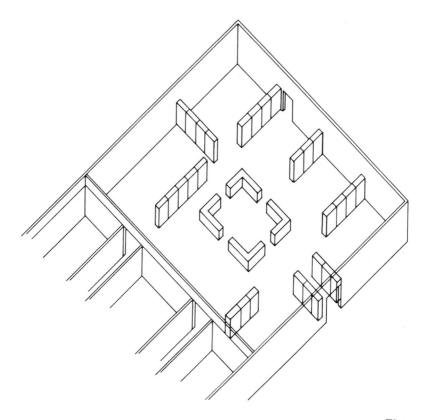

Figure 19.3

The extreme degree of flexibility in organization of classroom spaces is, of course, to perceive the classroom as simply a place where learners meet to prepare for educational experiences both in the school building and in the community. Several noted educational programs during the 1960s utilized this approach.*

Pupil movement within the classroom may be another subtle indicator of the structure or flexibility present in the learning environment. Movement in some classrooms is totally dependent upon the teacher. Students in such a classroom must request permission to talk, go to the washroom, or approach the teacher. Such structure usually minimizes noise and confusion but restricts activity to only verbal ex-

---

* In particular, the Parkway Schools of Philadelphia, Pennsylvania, demonstrated the possibilities of "schools without walls."

change. Movement in such classrooms, when it occurs, is generally to and from the teacher's desk.

In a less stationary classroom, movement is possible within controlled patterns monitored by the teacher. Movement is usually contextual depending upon the activity being engaged in. During teacher talk, for instance, movement may not be allowed, while at other times students may be able to sharpen pencils, get supplies, or leave the room for water without complete dependence on teacher approval.

Pupil movement is sometimes left to the complete discretion of the student. Even during a lesson or a teacher explanation a student may leave to use the washroom. In open-space buildings with high degrees of program flexibility, students are often seen moving unsupervised from one learning area to the next. Parents who have attended more structured, traditional programs often view such movement as questionable since it is believed that the teacher must be in direct contact with students for learning to occur. Yet, self-directed unsupervised movement is an integral part of any open, activity-centered curriculum.

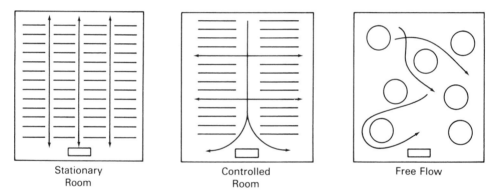

| Stationary Room | Controlled Room | Free Flow |

Figure 19.4

A third consideration in viewing classroom spaces is what might be considered *ownership* or *territoriality* of the area. In most classrooms this dimension can be seen by both the spaces the teacher and student occupy, and by items that belong to those persons inhabiting the classroom.

At the most structured end of an ownership continuum in a classroom is the situation where the teacher has total access to any area or space in the room while the student "owns" no space. In some classrooms, particularly in elementary schools, teacher ownership of space can even extend into the desks, pockets, and thoughts of students.

In somewhat less structured environments, students have zones where they can locate without being inspected or violating the teacher's territoriality. The average classroom is divided about two-thirds for students and one-third for the teacher.

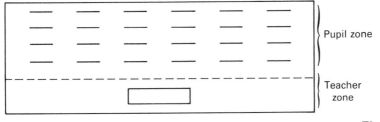

Pupil zone

Teacher zone

Figure 19.5

The most flexible pattern of ownership is the classroom where no overt symbols of territoriality exist. Either the teacher's desk is accessible for all purposes or, in newer schools, the teacher has a private place somewhere else in the building. Furniture in such classrooms is uniform for students and teachers alike.

Another measure of ownership available to the observer are personal items on display in the room. In particular, the display of student work or student art is a useful indicator. When student work is displayed, for example, are samples drawn from the work of all students, or simply a few? Are the samples on display uniform (everyone colors the same picture the same color) or diverse?

Other questions related to ownership would be concerned with the kind of teaching visuals on display (standard or tailored), the presence or absence of living objects, and any signs of reward for creative or divergent thinking. A highly structured classroom will generally be bland and uniform, while a highly flexible room will be nearly chaotic in appearance.

There are great differences in school classrooms, and these differences reflect the intentions of the school in educating students. As such, classroom spaces represent another important dimension of the learning environment. The following descriptive continuums suggest the potential range of alternatives present in schools:

3.1   Classroom Organization

Uniform seating arrangement dominates room	Classroom furniture uniform but not symmetrical	Furniture arranged for each activity	Multi-purpose spaces in room	Space out of classroom used for instruction.

S— —⊣ — — — — — — — —+ — — — — — — — —⊦ — — — — — —+ — — — — — —⊣ — —F

3.2   Classroom Movement

Movement totally restricted by teacher	Total teacher control with noted exception	Pupil movement contextual	Pupil has freedom of movement within limit	Pupil movement at pupil discretion

S— — —├— — — — — — — — —├— — — — — — — —+— — — — — — —├— — — — — — —├— —F

3.3   Classroom Ownership

Classroom space is dominated by teacher	Teacher dominates— some student zones	Classroom has areas of mutual free access	Territory only at symbolic level—open to all	All classroom spaces totally accessible to all persons

S— —+— — — — — — — —+— — — — — — — —┤— — — — — — —+— — — — — — —+— —F

PROGRAMS OF STUDY

Schools differ to a great extent in the way in which they organize and utilize knowledge in the programs of study. In highly structured schools knowledge is, for all practical purposes, the curriculum and ordering knowledge represents the major activity of curriculum development. In highly flexible schools, by contrast, knowledge can be a simple medium through which processes are taught.

The Organization of Knowledge

The organization of knowledge can best be understood by viewing it in several dimensions: the pattern of its presentation, the way it is constructed and ordered, its cognitive focus, and the time orientation of the content.

In most schools, knowledge is presented as an essential body or set of interrelated data (1 in Figure 19.6). In some schools, however, this essential knowledge is supplemented by other useful learnings which may appear as unequal satellites around the main body of information (2 in Figure 19.6).

To the degree that student needs and interests are considered in planning the program of study, the satellites, or electives are expanded and become a more important part of the program. In some schools, electives are equal in importance to essential knowledge areas and consume up to one-half of school time (3 in Figure 19.6). Once the school acknowledges the value of student-related content, it may find that it can teach the "essential" content in a form that accounts for student needs and interests (4 in Figure 19.6).

As the interrelatedness of essential "subcourses" is verified, cross-referencing of coursework may occur (5 in Figure 19.6). Finally, a maximum of flexibility in the ordering and utilization of knowledge may occur when a problem-oriented activity is the common denominator for organizing knowledge (6 in Figure 19.6).

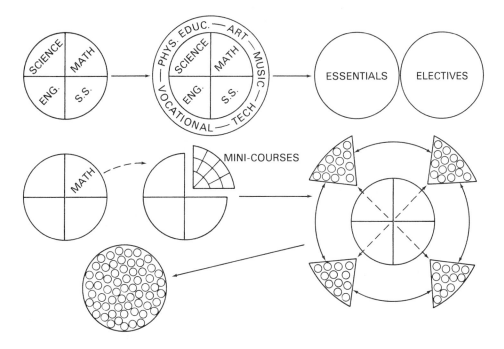

Figure 19.6

Another distinguishing dimension of the organization of knowledge is to be found in the way it is constructed or ordered. Most programs of study employ one of three standard curriculum designs: the building blocks design, branching designs, or spiral designs. It is also possible, however, to order knowledge in school programs in terms of task accomplishment or simple learning processes.

The building blocks design takes a clearly defined body of knowledge and orders it into a pyramid-like arrangement. Students are taught foundational material which leads to more complex and specialized knowledge. Deviations from the prescribed order are not allowed because the end product of the learning design (mastery) is known in advance. Also, activities that do not contribute to this directed path are not allowed due to the efficiency of this model. Building blocks designs are the most structured of curriculum organizations.

Another common learning design found in schools is a branching pattern. Branching is a variation of the building blocks design but incorporates limited choice in the knowledge to be mastered. Branching

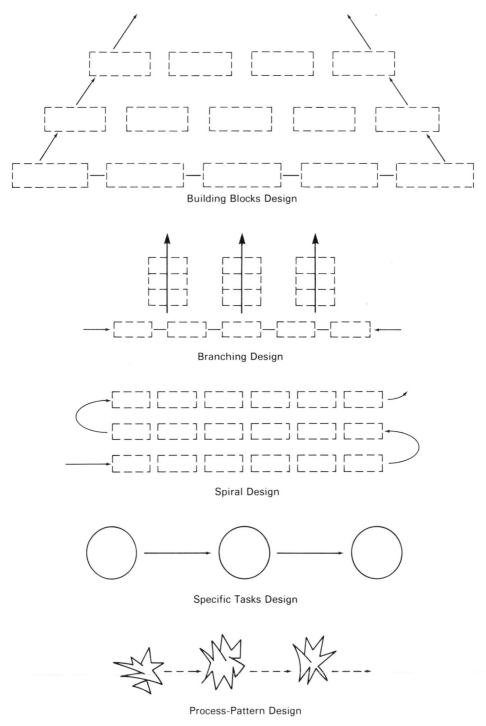

Building Blocks Design

Branching Design

Spiral Design

Specific Tasks Design

Process-Pattern Design

Figure 19.7

designs recognize the value of foundational knowledge in learning, but allow choice within prescribed areas beyond the common experience. Like the building blocks, branching prescribes the eventual outcomes of the learning program, although the prescription is multiple rather than uniform. The branching design allows for some variability in learning but only within tightly defined boundaries of acceptance.

A third common organization of knowledge in programs of study is the spiral curriculum. In this design, knowledge areas are continually visited and revisited at higher levels of complexity. While this design does have some flexibility, it still controls what it taught and learned, and even predetermines the time it is to be received by the student.

A fourth possible organization of knowledge could occur if knowledge were organized to accomplish specified tasks. In such a case, the purpose of the learning experience would be predetermined, but the student interaction with data in terms of both content and order of content would be flexible.

A final organization of knowledge in a school program of studies might use knowledge as simply a medium for teaching processes. Thus, reading could be taught regardless of the particular material used by the student. Such a process pattern would feature great flexibility in terms of the knowledge utilized, its order in learning experiences, and the expected outcomes for its selection and use.

The five patterns of knowledge construction are symbolized in Figure 19.7.

Still another dimension of the treatment of knowledge is the cognitive focus of instruction. In addition to a focus on factual material, such as learning important dates in history, is an organization of knowledge that teaches generalizations. Sometimes conceptual treatments of information are related to the lives of students. Maximum flexibility in the treatment of knowledge is gained by focusing on the personal world of the students, drawing concepts and facts from their experiences.

A final area related to knowledge in school settings is the time orientation of the instructional material. In some classrooms, all information is drawn from past experiences of mankind. In other rooms, information from the past is mixed with that from the present. Some classrooms will be strictly contemporary and deal only with the here-and-now. Beyond the present-oriented instructional space are those that mix current knowledge with projected knowledge, and some that deal only in probabilities. With each step from the known (past) to the speculative (future) content flexibility increases.

The following descriptive continuums suggest the potential range of alternatives found in schools:

4.1 Pattern of Presentation

Essential courses only	Essentials plus some satellite courses	Essentials and co-equal elective courses	Cross-referenced courses	Integrated courses

S—┝————————┥————————————┝———————————+———————┝–F

4.2 Constitution of Knowledge

Building blocks	Branching	Spiral	Task focused	Process pattern

S—┝————————+————————┝————————+———————————┝——–F

4.3 Cognitive Focus

Related facts	Series/set of facts	Conceptual organization	Concepts via world of the students	Concepts via personal life of individual

S—┝————————┥————————————┝———————————+————————+——–F

4.4 Time-Focus of Curriculum

Past only	Past and present	Present only	Present and future	Future only

S—┝————————+————————┝————————+————————┤-F

Uses of Learning Materials

The ways in which learning materials are used or not used in classroom spaces varies tremendously from room to room. In some settings, no materials are visible to the observer except perhaps a single textbook. In other classroom spaces, the volume and variety of learning materials gives the impression of clutter. Three measures of the use of learning materials are the degree of sensory stimulation present, the diversity of learning mediums found, and the location of usable learning materials.

On the most structured end of a continuum, the stimulation from learning materials can be fixed and absolute, as when all material is written or programmed. Sometimes stimulation from learning materials is prescribed or controlled as during lectures. A slightly more flexible version of stimulation is available when the materials are interpreted, such as during an animated film or game playing. Still greater stimulation occurs when the learner is in physical proximity to the materials and has a tactile experience. Finally, stimulation that immerses the learner in multi-sense experiencing represents the greatest degree of stimulation to the learner.

Another measure of the effect of learning materials is found in the diversity of mediums present. While some classrooms have only textbooks, others have printed matter, audiovisual aids, games, displays, and interactive materials. An important question is, "How many types of learning mediums are interacting with the learner at any moment?"

Finally, the location of usable learning materials is a variable in classroom settings. In some schools, all learning materials are contained in standard classrooms. Still others have special purpose spaces where students may interact with materials. A third, and more flexible possibility, is that the school possesses areas (Instructional Materials Centers) where learning materials are clustered. An even more flexible pattern would be to identify and select learning materials both in the school and outside the school. Maximum flexibility, of course, would perceive all objects as being possible learning materials for instruction.

The following descriptive continuums suggest the potential range of alternatives found in schools:

5.1 Degree of Sensory Stimulation

Stimulation fixed	Stimulation prescribed	Stimulation interpreted	Stimulation experienced	Stimulation immersion

S— ⊣— — — — — — —+— — — — — — — —+— — — — — — — —⊦— — — — — — — —⊦— - F

5.2 Diversity of Learning Mediums

Single medium	Two mediums	More than two mediums	Multiple concerted mediums	Infinite learning mediums

S— —+— — — — — — — —⊦— — — — — — — —+— — — — — — —⊣— — — — — —+- F

5.3 Location of Usable Learning Mediums

Classroom contained	Special purpose spaces	Clustered in special spaces	Found in school and out-of-school	All objects perceived as materials

S—+— — — — — — —+— — — — — — —+— — — — — — —⊣— — — — — — —+— - F

INSTRUCTIONAL ORIENTATION

Philosophies of Education

Schools and classrooms within individual schools vary tremendously in how the role of the instructional process is perceived. Such perceptions, when formalized, constitute philosophies or belief systems about the educational process (see chapter 5). While a formal assessment of philosophies can be conducted, the basic philosophy of a teacher can be inferred by several behaviors. One such behavior relates to the instructional format of the learning process. Another teacher behavior is the acceptance of diversity among students.

In some classes, learning is absolutely structured. The teacher controls the flow of data, communication, and assessment. Such a condition is characterized by drill. Slightly more flexible is a pattern of didactic teaching whereby the teacher delivers information, controls the exchange of ideas, and enforces the correct conclusions through a question-answer session. A balance between complete structure and flexibility in the learning process is for the teacher to allow the free exchange of ideas in the classroom, but to enforce a standardized summation of the process. Even more flexible would be a pattern where students are allowed to experience a learning process and then draw their own conclusions about meaning. Most flexible is an instructional process that is not uniformly structured for all students, allows an exchange of ideas, and leaves the process open-ended.

Yet another measure of philosophy in the classroom is the acceptance of diversity among students. Sometimes this is observable in norms relating to dress or speech enforced by the teacher. Sometimes such a measure can be assessed by the appearance of the learning space. The key to this variable is whether students are made to act in standardized ways, or whether differences are allowed. On the most extreme end of structure would be a classroom where no individuality is allowed. In a classroom with maximum flexibility, diversity among students in appearance and behavior would be significant.

The following descriptive continuums suggest the potential range of alternatives found in schools:

6.1 Instructional Format

Teacher drills	Didactic format with cloture	Free exchange with summation	Experience learning with individual summation	Non-structured learning with no summation

S — — ├ — — — — — — — — ├ — — — — — — — — + — — — — — — — + — — — — — — — + — — F

6.2 Acceptance of Diversity Among Students

Teacher enforces conformity	Teacher communicates expectations for conformity	Teacher tolerates limited diversity	Teacher accepts student diversity	Teacher encourages student diversity

S — ┤ — — — — — — — — ├ — — — — — — — — + — — — — — — — + — — — — — — — ┤ — — F

Like the actions that suggest educational philosophies, the teaching strategies found in classrooms often give clues regarding the degree of structure in the learning program. Such strategies can often be inferred from teacher behaviors and organizational patterns. For instance, some teachers behave in ways that allow only a single learning interface with students as in the case of the didactic method. Other times, teachers will provide multiple ways for students to interact and communicate during instruction.

Two behaviors that speak louder than words about the learning strategy employed in the classroom are the motivational techniques being used and the interactive distances between the teacher and student. By watching these phenomena, the observer can anticipate a pattern of structure or flexibility in other instructional areas.

There are a range of motivational techniques available to classroom teachers, and all are situationally legitimate. Some techniques, however, seek to control and structure learning while others encourage flexibility. Teachers using threats or fear as a motivator generally seek maximum structure in the classroom. Coercion, as a rule, arrests behavior and encourages conformity to previous patterns of behavior. Extrinsic rewards, immediate or deferred, also encourage structure by linking desired behavior with reward. Intrinsic rewards, whether immediate or deferred, have an opposite effect. Intrinsic rewards encourage student participation in the reward system and thereby a wider range of acceptable behaviors. If the motivational technique is observable, the overall learning strategy to constrict or expand student behavior is also understood.

Another dimension of the learning strategy in a classroom setting is the interactive distance between the teacher and students. To the degree that it is important to have two-way communication in the classroom, and to the degree that the instructional strategy values multiple learning styles among students, the teacher will make adjustments for differences.

In his book, *The Silent Language,* Edward Hall made observations about the appropriateness of certain distances between persons for certain activities.[2] Some distances (25 feet and beyond) were appropriate for broadcasting, while other distances (6 inches and under) were reserved for intimate moments. In a classroom setting, it is possible to observe if the teacher makes adjustments in interactive distances during instruction or chooses to treat all situations alike.

The following descriptive continuums suggest the potential range of alternatives found in schools:

7.1 Motivational Techniques Used

| Teacher threatens students, forces conformity | Teacher reinforces immediate conformity | Teacher reinforces eventual conformity | Teacher allows student to decide to conform | Teacher hopes student will eventually conform |

S — — —|— — — — — — — — —|— — — — — — — — —|— — — — — — — — —|— — — — — — — —|— - F

7.2 Interactive Distances

| Teacher operates at constant inter- active distance | Teacher uses varied interactive distances | Teacher interacts at multiple distances | Teacher tailors distance to needs | Teacher uses full range of interactive distances effectively |

S — — —|— — — — — — — — —+— — — — — — — —+— — — — — — — —|— — — — — — — +— --F

Staffing Patterns

A final indicator of structure versus flexibility in schools, in terms of instruction, is found in the staffing patterns observed. Two staffing indicators are the role of teachers in staffing, and the organization of teachers in the school building.

In some school buildings, all teachers are hired and assigned on the basis of subject-matter preparation. Such teachers are perceived as solitary craftsmen with the highly structured task of teaching a subject to students. In other schools, a teacher might be hired as a subject specialist, but assigned to a team which is interdisciplinary in nature. A more flexible pattern would be to staff a school with teachers having two or more subject specialties. It might even be possible to have one teacher (as in the elementary grades) responsible for all subjects. Or, a teacher could be hired to teach students at a certain level, rather than subjects.

Another staffing pattern is the organization of teachers in the building. Are all teachers isolated in self-contained classrooms? Do the isolated teachers have instructional aides? Do the classroom teachers meet together to plan activities? Are there ever combined teaching units? Do the teachers teach in teams or other cooperative arrangements?

The following descriptive continuums suggest the potential range of alternatives found in schools:

8.1 The Role of the Teacher

| Solitary subject specialist | Subject specialist on team | Subject specialist in multiple areas | Subject specialist all areas | Specialist in teaching at a level |

S — +— — — — — — —+— — — — — — — —|— — — — — — — —+— — — — — — —|--F

8.2 Organization of Teachers

Teachers isolated in self-contained classrooms	Teacher and aide isolated	Teacher isolated except for planning	Two or more teachers work cooperatively	Teachers in formal teams for instruction

S— —+— — — — — — — — —|— — — — — — — —|— — — — — — — —|— — — — — — — —|— —F

ADMINISTRATIVE CONDITIONS

Organization of Students

The way in which a school organizes students can give an observer some measure of the degree of structure in the school. Two different measures of student organization are the criteria for organization and the actual grouping patterns found in the school.

Most schools in the United States group students according to their age since most schools in the United States admit children into schools according to age. Schools use a more flexible criterion when students are organized by subject taught. Still greater flexibility is evidenced in schools that group students within grades and subjects according to capacity. Even greater organizational flexibility is found in schools that group students by needs and by student interests.

Beside criteria for grouping, the actual organization pattern of students can indicate the degree of structure or flexibility in the school. Perhaps the most structured situation exists when the size of the room determines the number of students present. A uniform number of students for all activities is also a highly structured condition. When a school begins to recognize that some activities should have large or small classes, a degree of flexibility is in evidence. Assignment of students based on the tasks to be accomplished and the individualization of instruction wherever possible represent the most flexibility in organization of students.

The following descriptive continuums suggest the potential range of alternatives found in schools:

9.1 Criteria for Organizing Students

By age/grade	By subject taken	By student capacity	By student needs	By student interest

S— —+— — — — — — — — —+— — — — — — — —|— — — — — — — —+— — — — — — — —|— —F

9.2 Grouping Pattern of Students

By room size	By uniform number	By large and small designation	By task to be performed	Stressing individualization where possible

S—|— — — — — — —+— — — — — — — —|— — — — — — — —|— — — — — — —+— —F

Rules and Regulations

Within schools and within individual classrooms, rules and regulations vary. Perhaps the most structured situations are those in which an excessive number of regulations exist based on historical precedent. Slightly less structured is the school with numerous and absolute regulations. A more flexible condition is when there are a few rules which are formal and enforced. When there are few rules and the rules are negotiable, or when no formal or informal regulations are stated, maximum flexibility is indicated. The following descriptive continuum suggests the potential range of alternatives in schools:

10.0   Rules and Regulations

Numerous rules with historical basis	Numerous and absolute rules	Few but absolute rules	Few and negotiable rules	No formal or informal rules

S − − ⊣ − − − − − − − − − + − − − − − − − −⊢ − − − − − −⊢ − − − − − − − ⊣ − − F

Disciplinary Measures

Discipline techniques used in schools to influence student behavior cover a wide range of actions. In some schools, all infractions are given the same treatment regardless of severity. In more flexible schools, there is a hierarchy of discipline measures to deal with differing discipline problems. Sometimes, the pattern found in schools will be to deal only with the severe or recurrent discipline problems. In schools where great flexibility is found, the pattern for discipline is sometimes unclear due to the uneven application of discipline measures. There are schools where no discipline measures are observable.

The following descriptive continuum suggests the potential range of alternatives for discipline in schools:

11.0   Disciplinary Measures

All infractions same treatment	Heirarchy of discipline actions	Discipline activity only in severe cases	Unpredictable pattern of discipline	No observable discipline measures

S − − ⊣ − − − − − − − + − − − − − − − −⊢ − − − − − − − + − − − − − − −⊢ − F

Reporting Student Progress

The reporting of student progress in the most structured schools and classrooms is a mechanical process whereby students are assessed in mathematical symbols such as "83" or "upper quartile." A generalization of such preciseness is a system whereby student progress in learning is summarized by a symbol such as a "B" or "U." Increased flexibility in reporting student progress is evidenced by narrative descriptions which actually describe student work, and by supplemental reporting by other interested parties such as the student or the parent. Maximum flexibility in reporting student progress is found when such reporting is informal, verbal, and continuous.

The following descriptive continuum suggests the potential range of alternatives for reporting student progress found in schools:

12.0   Reporting Student Progress

Numerical symbolism	General symbols	Descriptive narrative supplements	Descriptive supplements from several parties	Informal verbal evaluation

S — + — — — — — — — — — + — — — — — — — — + — — — — — — — — — + — — — — — — — + — F

ROLES OF PARTICIPANTS

Administrative Attitudes

Administrative style, more than any other single factor, determines the atmosphere of a school building. It is certain that the way others in the school building perceive the administrator affects both teacher and student behavior. For this reason, clues about the structure or flexibility of a school or classroom can be gained by observing the administrator.

Administrators often assume one of five attitudes that characterize their pattern of interaction with others. At the most structured end is a "warden" who rules by intimidation. Closely allied to this model is the "benevolent dictator" who maintains absolute control while giving the impression of involvement. A more flexible posture for the administrator is to act as the "program manager," reserving key decisions for the only person with the comprehensive viewpoint. Still more flexible is the "collegial" leader who shares all decision making with the teaching faculty. Finally, there is a leadership style which is nondirective, or "laissez faire."

A second interesting variable for studying administrative attitudes is the medium used to communicate with students. In some schools, the lead administrator is a phantom, known only by the presence of his portrait in the foyer. Such an administrator generally leaves communication with parents or students to an intermediary such as a vice-principal. Another impersonal medium is the intercom which is often used to communicate to students. Slightly more personal is a "live" address at assemblies. Finally, some administrators communicate with students by coming into the classrooms, and even sometimes by individual conferences.

The following descriptive continuums suggest the potential range of alternatives for administrative behavior found in schools:

13.1   Administrative Decision-Making Role

Makes all decisions unilaterally	Makes all key decisions unilaterally	Shares decision-making on specific items	Shares all decision-making on all items	Abdicates all key decision-making

S— —|— — — — — — — — —|— — —— — — — — — — +— — — — — — — —|— — — — — — — —|— - F

13.2   Administrative Communication With Students

Unknown to students	Communicates through an intermediary	Speaks through intercom or at assemblies	Visits classes for discussion	Holds individual conferences

S— —|— — — — — — — — +— — — — — — — — —|— — — — — — — — — +— — — — — —|— - F

Teacher Roles

The role of a classroom teacher in a school can vary from being an instructional unit who teaches a prescribed set of facts to students to a multi-dimensional adult who interacts with students and others in the building. For the most part, such perceptions are self-imposed. A key observation can be made from teacher responses to the question, "What do you teach?"

The following descriptive continuum suggests the potential range of responses to that question:

14.1   Teacher's Role Perception

Teacher deals with prescribed data only	Teacher deals with all knowledge in his field of expertise	Teacher deals with school knowledge and related matters	Teacher deals with both school and non-school items	Teacher teaches whatever he deems valuable

S— — —|— — — — — — — — +— — — — — — — — —|— — — — — — — +— — — — — —+— - F

Student Roles

Like teachers, students in schools hold a role perception of what they are and what they can do in a classroom setting. Sometimes such perceptions are self-imposed, but more often they are an accurate reflection of expected behavior for students. A question that usually receives a telling response for an observer in a school is, "How do students learn in this classroom?"

The following descriptive continuum suggests the potential range of responses to such a question:

15.1   How do Students Learn in Class

They recite and copy from board	They listen, take notes, take tests	They listen, read, question, take tests	They work on things, read	They do things that interest them

S— — —|— — — — — — — +— — — — — —|— — — — — — — — —|— — — — — — — +— — F

The value of an analytic approach that views school components on a continuum is that program congruence or inconsistencies ·can be identified once the school is plotted on a profile graph. Such a graph would be constructed with a scale from structured (1) to flexible (5) as continuums, and items of analysis as reference points as shown in Figure 19.8.

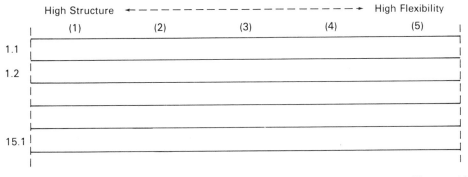

Figure 19.8

In schools where the program intentions are clear, the degree of structure or flexibility should be relatively constant. When graphed through all items of analysis, the profile of such schools should appear as reasonably vertical columns. An erratic zig-zag pattern in the profile shows inconsistency in the learning blueprint.

SUMMARY

Over the years the American public school has evolved from a highly structured institution to one that has considerable flexibility. The degree of structure and flexibility represents a useful tool for analyzing school plans for learning.

The learning plan in a school is a translation of a definition of education; a design organized around what the school is trying to accomplish with students. Such a design, to be effective and efficient, should be consistent in its efforts to educate students.

In this chapter, fifteen dimensions of a school setting were presented as samples of areas which can be observed and analyzed. The universals of structure and flexibility were presented in continuum form so that a profile of a school might be drawn through a simple graphing technique.

Developing a profile of a school will enable the curriculum developer to compare, contrast, and categorize schools thereby identifying areas worthy of review and renewal.

Notes

1. Bel Kaufman, *Up The Down Staircase* (Englewood Cliffs, New Jersey: Prentice-Hall, Inc. 1965).
2. Edward Hall, *The Silent Language* (New York: Doubleday and Company), 1959.

Suggested Learning Activities

1. Using the scales found in this chapter, visit a school with which you are familiar and analyze its profile. What observations can you make about this type of analysis of a school?

Books to Review

Cay, Donald, *Curriculum: Designs for Learning.* New York: Bobbs-Merrill Company, Inc., 1966.

Herman, Therese, *Creating Learning Environments.* Boston: Allyn and Bacon, Inc., 1977.

Joyce, Bruce and Morine, Greta, *Creating the School.* New York: Little, Brown and Company, 1976.

Rogers, Frederick A., *Curriculum and Instruction in the Elementary School.* New York: MacMillan Publishing Company, 1975.

20

Curriculum Designs of the Twentieth Century

During this century, differing opinions on fundamental questions concerning education have led to repeated efforts to change the form of the American school. Throughout this period, public schools have been able to sustain themselves despite challenges and criticism. Such stability, in the face of massive societal changes, is testimony to the soundness of the basic design of the public schools and to the ability of the American schools to accommodate change.

Differences of opinion are inevitable in an open and democratic society. Such variability in educational philosophy and programs is in stark contrast to the apparent consensus and purposefulness of educational opinion in totalitarian societies. Still, if history is an accurate indicator, the American school has benefited from the diversity of educational philosophy and attempts to reform public schools. An openness to ideas and a flexibility in meeting changing conditions have enriched our schools immeasurably. We live in a world which is constantly changing, and schools, to some extent, must change to maintain their utility.

In the early years of this century, attempts to introduce changes in our schools came from professional educators who were concerned with broad philosophical issues about the role of an education in society. Reform efforts, for the most part, had a philosophical base and evolved slowly over several decades. Only after considerable discussion and experimentation were educational reforms attempted.

Early attempts to reform the American school assumed a somewhat monolithic culture and aimed at developing programs that would serve the entire American society. In the latter half of this century, reform efforts have come more frequently, from more diverse sources, and without clear philosophical bases or records of controlled experimentation.

During the late 1950s and early 1960s, the American society experienced a cultural awakening. The diversity of the society, a pluralistic configuration of many subcultures, was revealed and the historic pattern of the public school was called into question. If the public school was to serve all members of the society, both the substance and the organization of the institution was open to review.

The frustrations and hopes of the numerous groups of the American public became linked to the schools, which are the social institutions for instilling values. The divergent norms and values of the subcultures suggested new ideas about what schools should be. Some of the ideas and concepts of these schools were incorporated by the public schools, but many were not.

Related to these attempts to reform the school, which came primarily from inside the ranks of education, were numerous reformation efforts by external groups. The importance of public education as an influence for social change led industry, foundations, and the federal agencies to introduce changes in the school. The sponsorship of such efforts continues today.

The implications of these trends for curriculum planners are multiple. First, it seems apparent that persons responsible for designing school programs should be able to view "forces of change" with some degree of perspective. Innovations and educational trends need to be seen in terms of some overriding framework and in light of historical precedence. An inability to categorize and order the multitude of curriculum changes found in today's public schools will result in short-range decisions and long-range chaos.

Second, it must be recognized that public sophistication concerning curriculum development has grown considerably during the past several decades. Seeing schools as purposeful agents of change has led to the development of many restricting designs with little or no concern for long-term social implications. Such educational focus has also led to the development of some relatively efficient public school programs.

Finally, recent changes in the design of school programs should suggest to curriculum leaders that schools are institutions with numerous possibilities. To be influential in the educational environment, curriculum designers must break away from the familiar and begin to be responsible to the changing needs and values of the society. The clients who support public schools must be responded to in imaginative ways.

This chapter looks at educational designs from a comprehensive vantage point, with the hope of leading the reader to see curriculum development as a means of working with young people in desired ways. Examples of school designs used in this chapter serve only as a reminder that such a role has been a consistent theme of curriculum development throughout the twentieth century.

MAJOR CURRICULUM DESIGNS

There are numerous ways in which the many forms of schooling in the United States might be classified. Each social science perspective would suggest a different set of variables and categorization. Perhaps the most useful existing classification available today is one developed by Lucas.[1] In this classification, school forms are separated by function. Six major types of school design, and their rationale, are presented:

1. Conservative liberal arts designs
2. Educational technology designs
3. Humanistic designs
4. Vocational designs
5. Social reconstruction designs
6. Deschooling designs

The pervasive educational design found in the United States and throughout most of the world is one that has roots leading back to Hellenistic Greece. It is based on a belief that a human being's unique and distinctive quality is intellect, and the quest for knowledge is the natural fulfillment of that intellect. In short, the highest purpose in life is to engage in the process of inquiry: to move from ignorance to truth, from confusion to enlightenment.

Historically, this quest for knowledge was seen as a reflection of a world whose laws and physical order were fixed properties. The process of education was concerned simply with the pursuit of objective knowledge for its own sake. A liberal education was suitable to free people who possessed the legal opportunity and means to devote themselves to cultural attainment.

In later times, after scientific revolutions and the loss of a shared culture had diminished the concept of *paideia* (the cultured man), the liberal arts approach to educating became a perspective. Liberal arts was not so much a mastery of subject matter as it was a way of looking at things. The human mind was trained so that the individual might live fully.

As this notion of education was translated into a public education format during the early American experience, such knowing was seen as a means of producing an enlightened citizenry. In the words of R. Freeman Butts: . . . the prime purpose of the public schools is to serve the general welfare of a democratic society by assuring the knowledge and understanding necessary to exercise the responsibilities of citizenship are not only made available but are inculcated.[2]

The curriculum design of the conservative liberal arts is familiar to most Americans as the program they experienced. Such a design was spelled out formally in a declaration of "permanent studies."[3]

1. Language and its uses (reading, writing, grammar, literature)
2. Mathematics
3. Sciences
4. History
5. Foreign languages

The program design of the liberal arts curriculum is also standard enough to warrant the omission of a descriptive program. Single resource texts, mastery learning, lecture format, and uniform blocks of time are dominant in most schools.

A second major curriculum design found in this century is one which is technological in nature, focusing on process and technique without equal regard for the goals or ends. Behavioristic in nature, this design has been used throughout the century to promote various school programs.

An early example of technological education was to be found in the much publicized Winnetka plan of the 1930s. In this program, students interacted with mimeographed assignment booklets to master essential skills and knowledge. Self-instructive practice exercises were monitored through a diagnostic-practice-remediation format that was the forerunner of much of today's programmed instruction. "Tests indicated whether the goal had been attained or whether further practice was necessary."[*]

Technological designs stress objectivity, precision, and efficiency. As a modern proponent B.F. Skinner has stated, "The traditional distinction comes down to this: when we know what we are doing we are training . . . any behavior which can be specified can be programmed."[4] Usually, goals and objectives of this design are described in terms of overt learner behaviors which may or may not last beyond the immediate treatment.

---

[*] As reported in J. Wayne Wrightstone's *Appraisal of Experimental High Schools,* Bureau of Publications, Teachers College, Columbia University, 1936.

Modern applications of the technological approach have come in the form of electronic hardware and communication mediums: first generation television, programmed instruction, films, cassettes, and other visuals; second generation technology in the form of automatizing devices, computer-assisted instruction, air-beamed programming, microwave relays, and satellite transmissions.

Modern applications of the technological design have also employed "systems" technology in the form of concepts such as "delivery systems," cost-benefit analyses, and accountability. Organizationally, planning has been in the form of sophisticated programs like the Program Planning and Budgeting System (PPBS), using basic strategic planning, delineated procedures, and decentralized management techniques. Students in technological designs are "hooked-up and plugged-in" to the program.

Perhaps the best developed public school program to date which emphasized educational technology as the ultimate delivery system was the Ford Foundation-sponsored Nova Schools in Fort Lauderdale, Florida. In this program, students from preschool to high school interacted with hardware of all kinds in the pursuit of education.

Technological curriculum designs are usually characterized by high degrees of structure, but with greater student interaction with materials or equipment. Students in the Nova Schools, for instance, could be found with headsets on in video carrels, playing electronic musical instruments, or manipulating interactive games on the computer.

A third curriculum design in the United States during the twentieth century has had as its main theme the "humanizing" of learning. Such designs generally feature student-centered curriculums and instructional patterns and a decentralization of authority and organization.

Humane curriculum designs have deep roots in American education and have taken numerous forms in this century. In such programs there is a shift in atmosphere toward understanding, compassion, encouragement, and trust. Physical settings usually encourage freedom in the form of student mobility, increased choice of curricular activities, and a learning-by-doing format.

An early example of this design in the United States was the Dalton Plan, which was implemented in the Dalton, Massachusetts schools in the 1920s. The program featured freedom of movement and choice of materials by students, cooperation and interaction of student group life through a "house plan," and subject matter laboratories in the classrooms.

Another early version of a humanistic curriculum design was the organic method of education developed at the Fairhope, Alabama school around 1910. This program held that children are best prepared for adult life by fully experiencing childhood. Children were led "naturally" into more traditional areas of schooling only after experiencing a curriculum of physical exercise, nature study, music, field geography, storytelling, fundamental conception of numbers, drama, and games. General development rather than the amount of information controlled the classification of students.*

Contemporary versions of the humanistic design are to be found in open elementary schools, emerging middle schools, and student-centered programs such as Outward Bound. In such programs, the instruction is humane, personalized, and individualized. Curricula is geared to the maturational levels of students, and teachers serve as guides to learning rather than authority figures or purveyors of knowledge. The problem-solving process of the instructional format borrows heavily from another humanistic design, the core curriculum.

The core curriculum, developed in the 1930s in schools such as the Denver public schools, attempted to present learning from a humane and holistic perspective. The following excerpt from an evaluation report outlines the program objectives:

> It is so named because it represents an attack upon those problems which are relatively common to the young people in the school and because it carries the chief responsibility for guidance, for general testing, and for record keeping. It is that part of the total school program which is planned for the development in boys and girls of the ability to solve common problems and of the power to think together and to carry on the democratic processes of discussion and group decisions.†

Core curriculums used a ten-point plan in organizing for instruction:

1. Continuity of teacher-pupil relationships
2. Greater teacher participation in formulating policies of the program.
3. Elimination of barriers to learning experiences through the attack on problems rather than through reliance upon the logical organization of subject matter in isolated courses.
4. Development of core courses based on student concerns.
5. Relating school activities to the community.
6. Pupil-teacher planning, emphasizing choice and responsibility.
7. Guidance by a teacher who knows the student in an intimate classroom setting.
8. Using a wide variety of sources of information.

---

* As reported in John and Evelyn Dewey's *Schools of Tomorrow* (New York: E.P. Dutton and Company, 1915).

† As reported in *Thirty Schools Tell Their Story*, vol. 5, (New York: Harper and Brothers, 1943) p. 166.

9. Using a wide variety of means of expression—words, art, music.
10. Teacher-to-teacher planning.

Humanistic designs generally are characterized by highly flexible instructional areas, high degrees of student involvement, and an emphasis on the process of learning as opposed to a product orientation or a "preparation for life" outlook.

A fourth curriculum design present in the United States in this century has been one concerned with vocational and economic aspects of life. For years such designs were referred to as vocational education, and more recently have been identified by the broad phrase *career education.*

In the early years of this century, vocational programs were perceived as separate and parallel curriculum designs in public schools. These programs served the non-college-bound populations and were strongest in highly industrialized and agricultural areas. The curriculum consisted of crafts and labor skills that had application in the immediate economic environment. More recently, there have been efforts to make work and the preparation for work a primary emphasis of the curriculum at all levels.

Sidney Marland Jr., former commissioner of the U.S. Office of Education, has stated the case for a vocational design in the following manner:

> It is flatly necessary to begin to construct a sound, systematic relationship between education and work. This system will make it a standard practice to teach every student about occupations and the economic enterprise. A system that will markedly increase career options open to each individual and enable us to do a better job than we have been doing of meeting the manpower needs of the country.[5]

Efforts to implement a comprehensive vocational design have been increased during the past decade by a number of factors. First, there has been a growing recognition that the schools are an essential piece of the national economic condition. Welfare, unemployment, large segments of the population without useful skills, and the fact that only 40–45% of all high school graduates attend college have been given as reasons for an increased vocational emphasis in the schools.

Second, the entire relevancy movement of the 1960s revealed a condition of students who are bored and listless in senior high school, resentful of the holding pattern of formal schooling.

Third, vocational/career education has been promoted as a means of assisting minority groups and other disenchanted members of the society in breaking out of the cycle of poverty. Students experiencing such programs can escape the containment of environments and family backgrounds.

Finally, the whole concept of a utilitarian education and no-frills curriculums has increased the awareness and demand for vocational designs. There is a growing opinion among the public that insufficient attention has been paid to the hard social reality that everyone must eventually seek gainful employment. Technological and political conditions demand a change in the basic definition of an education.

An interesting application of the vocational design is the number of large technical/vocational high schools being constructed in the United States such as McGavok High School in Nashville, Tennessee and Skyline High School in Dallas, Texas. The Skyline program features a 21.5 million dollar building, and over five million dollars worth of technological and scientific hardware. In the Center for Career Development complex, visitors will find airplane hangars, greenhouses, television studios, and computer terminals leading to careers in transportation services, horticulture, entertainment, and computer technology.

The Skyline curriculum takes the student through a series of steps enroute to employment: the development of a positive self-image, an understanding of economic structures, an expansion of occupational awareness, the development of occupational goals, perception of education as a means to goal attainment, and developing marketable skills.[6]

Proponents of vocational designs in the twentieth century have pictured them as a necessity: a means of serving all students in the public schools, a vehicle for making school useful and relevant, a contributor to the well-being of the American society. Vocational designs are practical. Critics of vocational designs, including career education, see them as static conceptions of life in the American society and insufficient preparation for life in an unknown future.

A fifth curriculum design found in the United States in this century has as its main theme social reconstruction. The conception of the school as a vehicle for social improvement is not new. Arguments for this type of school were made in the 1930s by members of the social reconstruction wing of the Progressive Education Association. Harold Rugg, for example, spoke of the changes portending in the American society and encouraged the schools to influence social changes. He outlined characteristics of a needed curriculum in the 26th National Society for the Study of Education Yearbook:

> A curriculum which will not only inform but will constantly have as its ideal the development of an attitude of sympathetic tolerance and critical open-mindedness . . . a curriculum which is constructed on a problem-solving organization providing constant practice in choosing between alternatives, in making decisions, in drawing generalizations . . . a curriculum in which children will be influenced to put their ideas sanely into action.[7]

The social reconstruction designs seek to equip students with tools to deal with the forces about them and to manage conditions as they meet them. They seek to alert students to social issues and choices and to equip them with attitudes and habits of action. Two recent educational programs approach a social reconstruction design in their curriculums as they work with students to become more self-sufficient in a rapidly changing society. These schools are Harlem Prep in New York City and the John Adams High School in Portland, Oregon.

Harlem Prep is a school started during the 1960s to assist students in a black ghetto to overcome social forces and succeed in a college preparatory program. The technique of the curriculum is to instill attitudes of racial pride which will allow the student to compete in academic circles. Using what Fantini and Weinstein refer to as a "contact curriculum," teachers start instruction where the student is and take him someplace else.[8] Ultimately, the goal of schools like Harlem Prep is to develop a cadre of educated inner-city leaders who can transform the Lower East Side of New York City.

The John Adams High School in Portland, Oregon, is an experiment in what has been termed a "clinical curriculum." School governance is carried out by the Adams Community Government which is modeled after the structure of the United States government. Students and teachers have control over such important areas as budget and the hiring and firing of teachers. The focus of study is on contemporary problems such as change in society, racial conflict, and street law. Working as a collective unit, "houses" within the school seek to design a more workable school and society.

The major assumption of social reconstruction designs is that the future is not fixed, but rather is amenable to modification and improvement. The school, as an institution, cannot remain neutral in a changing world and can influence and direct social change.

Recent applications of the social reconstruction design have used "futurism" to justify the necessity of social intervention. Since the future will not be like the present, it is necessary to be flexible and develop the ability to make value decisions. In the words of Kirschenbaum and Simon: Unless one believes that the future is inevitable—that we have absolutely no control over our private and public destinies—the study of the future must include not merely possible and probable futures but preferable futures. This is why the broad movement aimed at shifting education into the future tense also brings with it a heightened concern with values.[9]

Social reconstruction designs generally combine classroom learning with application in the outer world. Teachers and students are partners in inquiry, and instruction is usually carried on in a problem-solving or inquiry format.

The final curriculum design of the twentieth century in the United States is a rare and relatively new one. It seeks through its organization, or lack of, to de-emphasize or disestablish the formality of education, and the reliance on formal schooling. Most of the applications of this curriculum design have been found in alternative schools which, in a variety of ways, set the learner free to pursue knowledge and an education on his own.

According to its chief spokesman, Ivan Illich, schools are social tools which actually operate to deprive individuals of an education and real learning. Schools are not the panacea for social ills, but rather are rigid, authoritarian institutions which perpetuate the social order through a number of functions. Illich sees deschooling as an alternative design:

> Will people continue to treat learning as a commodity—a commodity that could be more efficiently produced and consumed by greater numbers of people if new institutional arrangements were established? Or shall we set up only those institutional arrangements that protect the autonomy of the learner—his private initiative to decide what he will learn and his inalienable right to learn what he likes rather than what is useful to somebody else? We must choose between more efficient education of people fit for an increasingly efficient society and a new society in which education ceases to be the task of some special agency.[10]

Problems of institutionalized education revolve around questions of power, leadership, and structure. Schools, by dominating the values and focus of organization, control the learner. Such control is often racist and sexist, and is always oppressive. Further, schools are undemocratic in their method of converting knowledge into power.

Reactions to formal schooling and its structure has been a continuous phenomenon of the twentieth century in the United States, but the free school movement of the late 1960s presents the best examples of the deschooling design. Glatthorn outlines the emergence of the free school movement during that period:

> The period of the late sixties, then, was a time ripe for radical change. The curriculum reform movement had run out of steam. The innovations in scheduling and staffing were proving to be only superficial tinkering. And there was acute dissatisfaction with all the public schools. This dissatisfaction was most keenly sensed by militant blacks and by radicals of the New Left. Each of these groups responded by opening their own schools, and these schools were the progenitors of the public alternatives that followed.[11]

Glatthorn identifies a number of ways in which free schools and alternative schools attempted to release the individual student from the institutional oppression of the school: travel-learn programs, work and apprenticeship programs, volunteer service, informal study in the community, and affective experiences. Collectively, these curriculum arrangements sought to define education as a personal act.

Efforts to break the monopoly of formal education and deschool learning continue today. They seek to downgrade the importance of accepting the functions of formal schooling, and to break the myth of a need for education. While on the decline, such curriculum designs are likely to emerge again in the future.

Together, these six curriculum designs outline the diversity of educational programs in the United States during the twentieth century. Curriculum leaders need to be aware that such diversity has always been present in American education and will continue to be present in the future.

We hope that these designs will suggest other possibilities to you. Curriculum leaders need to develop the intellectual freedom which will allow them to design the best possible school programs for children. As Lawrence Cremin has so eloquently stated in his *The Genius of American Education,* "Education is too significant and dynamic an enterprise to be left to mere technicians."[12]

SUMMARY

Throughout this century, divergent opinions about education have led to efforts to reform the American public school. Because these efforts continue today, curriculum leaders should be aware of the multiple curriculum designs in existence, and be open to new thinking about the way schools and educational programs are organized.

Six designs have been prominent in the American experience: educational conservatism, technological designs, humanistic designs, vocational designs, social reconstruction designs, and deschooling designs. Such diversity has unquestionably enriched the programs of the American public school.

Notes

1. Christopher J. Lucas, *Challenge and Choice in Contemporary Education* (New York: Macmillan Publishing Company, 1976).
2. R. Freeman Butts, "Assaults on a Great Idea," *The Nation,* (April 30, 1973): 553–60.
3. Robert M. Hutchins, *The Restoration of Learning* (New York: Alfred A. Knopf, 1955).
4. B.F. Skinner, *Beyond Freedom and Dignity* (New York: Alfred A. Knopf, 1971), p. 169.
5. Sidney Marland, Jr., Working paper, U.S. Office of Education, 1972.
6. S. Marland, H. Lichtenwald, and R. Burke, "Career Education Texas

Style: The Skyline Center in Dallas," *Phi Delta Kappan* (May, 1975): 616–20.

7. Harold Rugg in *The Foundation and Techniques of Curriculum Making*, 26th Yearbook of the National Society for the Study of Education (Bloomington, Indiana, 1927): 7–8.

8. Mario D. Fantini and Gerald Weinstein, *The Disadvantaged: Challenge to Education* (New York: Harper & Row, 1968).

9. Howard Kirschenbaum and Sidney Simon, "Values and the Futures Movement in Education," in *Learning for Tomorrow: The Role of the Future in Education,"* Alvin Toffler (ed.), (New York: Vintage Books, 1974), p. 257.

10. Ivan Illich, *After Deschooling, What?* in Alan Gartner, et al. (ed.) *After Deschooling, What?* (New York: Perennial Library, 1973), p. 1.

11. Allen A. Glatthorn, *Alternatives in Education: Schools and Programs* (New York: Dodd, Mead, and Company, 1975), pp. 117–36.

12. Lawrence A. Cremin, *The Genius of American Education* (Pittsburgh: The University of Pittsburgh Press, 1965), p. 75.

Suggested Learning Activities

1. State in three sentences or less what you believe to be the purpose of formal education in the United States.

2. React to each of the six designs suggested by Lucas by developing a list of pros and cons for each position.

Books to Review

Perspectives on Curriculum Development: 1776–1976. Washington, D.C. Association for Supervision and Curriculum Development, 1976.

Hyman, Donald. *Approaches in Curriculum.* Englewood Cliffs, New Jersey: Prentice-Hall, Inc., 1973.

Krug, Mark. *What Will be Taught—The Next Decade.* Itasca, Illinois: F.E. Peacock Publishers, Inc., 1972.

Lucas, Christopher. *Challenge and Choice in Contemporary Education.* New York: Macmillan Publishing Company, Inc., 1976.

Wilhelms, Fred. *What Should the Schools Teach?* PDK Fastback #13, Bloomington, Indiana: Phi Delta Kappa Educational Foundation, 1972.

21

Curriculum Development: Alternatives and Future

To attempt to assess the possibilities for the future of curriculum development in America is to enter an area of inquiry which has seen great activity in recent years. Futurism in education is a topic of concern to all educators, and has been the subject of numerous commissioned studies and investigations by "think tanks" such as RAND, Incorporated, and the Hudson Institute. You are encouraged to become familiar with resources such as those presented in the suggested readings section of this chapter.

In this chapter, we hope to stimulate thinking about the many possibilities for education which the future might hold, and present the process of curriculum development as the vehicle by which schools might arrive at that unknown future. Following a theme found throughout this book, the future of educational programs is presented in a format that suggests a trend toward either greater control in curriculum designs or greater flexibility in educational plans. It is entirely possible, of course, that other intellectual constructs may be more useful in addressing this highly complex topic.

A date of departure for this assessment is the year 1957, the date of the launch of Sputnik I. It was this event that jarred American education into a purposefulness which has been absent in the past and opened up fully the idea of using schools as an instrument of national policy. While the space race of the late 1950s has evaporated in scale to that of "just another federal program," the question of what role the schools shall play remains.

As we approach the twenty-first century, American education is faced with a bewildering array of alternatives concerning what it might become. The question that must be faced by all leaders in the field of curriculum is the primary question of all educational planning. What is the role of education in our society? Failure to consider this critical question is to abdicate a basic responsibility and decide by indecision.

Specifically, there are some questions that must be considered as we peer into the last years of the twentieth century. Among these are the following:

1. What directions seem to be most promising for the American society to pursue in planning for education?
2. Where and how do professional educators begin to assess educational alternatives?
3. Can the future be influenced by our actions or is it largely predetermined?
4. Where do we as planners gain the value structure to plan for the future?
5. How can we most effectively involve others in our society in planning for the future?

These questions present a challenge to all who are involved in developing educational programs.

THE FUTURE

In the final quarter of the twentieth century, the American society stands in awe of the possibilities of an unknown future. Developments during the third quarter of the century presented us with unprecedented changes in every aspect of social existence. Such changes were both substantive and superficial, and touched the lives of all citizens.

Harold Shane, well-known educational futurist, outlines some of the more substantial changes during the 1950–1975 period:

1. Human vision was extended a billion light years.
2. The molecule was made visible.
3. Low virus-like forms were created in the laboratory.
4. Men landed on the moon's surface.
5. The number of people on earth more than doubled.
6. Atomic and hydrogen bombs were exploded.

7. Biological cloning allowed the genetic reproduction of plants and animals.
8. Major organ transplants were made in human subjects.
9. Satellites internationalized television viewing on all continents.[1]

Shane's list could, of course, be multiplied ten-fold. The third quarter of the twentieth century provided numerous miracles and disrupted the traditional mode of linear thinking about the future. Observing the scale of such changes, economist Kenneth Boulding stated, "As far as any statistical series related to the activities of mankind are concerned the date that divides human history into two equal parts is well within the living memory."[2]

So pervasive and rapid was change during this period that prediction challenged projection as the most accurate indicator of future events. One writer in the mid-sixties went so far as to formulate this condition into the form of "Clark's Law" which read, "When a distinguished but elderly scientist states that something is possible, he is almost certainly right. When he states something is impossible, he is very probably wrong."[3]

The changes of the third quarter of the twentieth century had implications for all dimensions of the American society, introducing an element of "future shock" to all institutions. In his best-selling book by the same title, author Alvin Toffler cited numerous indicators of the scope of such change. A fact of great importance to an educational system still based on mastery of fundamental knowledge, for example, was that by the mid-1960s the output of books on a worldwide scale approached 1,000 titles per day or 30,000 titles per year in the United States alone.

Citing one study on the explosion of organized knowledge, Toffler stated, "At the rate at which knowledge is growing, by the time the child born today graduates from college the amount of knowledge in the world will be four times as great. By the time that same child is fifty years old, it will be 32 times as great and 97 percent of everything known in the world will have been learned since the time he was born."[4]

McDanield has identified seven factors that contribute to the type and scale of such changes:

1. *Demographic change*—sex and age patterns, death rates, life spans, etc.
2. *Technological innovation*—adaptive changes in machines and productivity
3. *Social innovation*—new arrangements, styles, and systems in education, politics, the economy, etc.
4. *Culture-value shifts*—changing preferences and ideas

5. *Ecological shifts*—scarcity of resources, catastrophic events, etc.
6. *Information-idea shifts*—the scope, quality, and manipulability of knowledge; new conceptions of how things work
7. *Cultural diffusion*—transfer of ideas, values and techniques from one culture to another via war, travel, advertising, etc.[5]

The changes experienced by the American society between 1950 and 1975 altered the social fabric of the society. Legal rulings, economic pressures, political intrigue, social upheaval, and information analysis and processing left basic institutions in a chaotic state. Schools, in particular, were beseiged by challenges of a social-economic-political nature. Such an experience greatly increased concern for the future and stimulated formal future planning in education.

PLANNING FOR THE FUTURE

One of the effects of too much change in too short a period of time in the United States has been the emergence of *transience.* Such transience, a mood or feelings of impermanence, is reflected in relationships among people, things, places, organizations, and information. Excessive transience threatens social stability by undercutting the framework of cultural preservation and transmission. The historic role of the school as the adaptive mechanism of the society is questioned in a culture where impermanence becomes a regular condition.

One of the roles of future planning in education, then, is to determine the exact purpose or purposes of the school as it relates to a changing society. This has proven to be difficult in the American culture due to the phenomenon of culture lag. The term culture lag refers to a condition where some sectors of the society exhibit different rates of change and therefore transform themselves more slowly. Since formal public school education represents the single largest institution in the United States, it has not kept pace with social and cultural evolution caused by technological and economic conditions. The result of culture lag in educational planning has been to have insufficient information with which to make critical decisions. Educational planners have regularly utilized linear thinking when necessary.

Futurists in education have recognized the problems of basic linear change. As Shane has observed:

> In all forms of planning, including educational planning, the assumption of linearity which leads to the passive, conformist policy of adaptting to an inferred series of coming future events is an erroneous one . . . Actually, the future may be construed to be a fan-shaped array of possibilities of alternative futures which can be powerfully influenced or 'created' by man.[6]

The response of educational planners to conditions of transience, cultural lag, and the need for nonlinear thinking has been to project educational goals and desired educational futures in a variety of ways. Early efforts at projection borrowed techniques from social science research including the use of scenario, think tanks, and Delphi technique.* One example, a study by Kahn and Wiener conducted in 1967, used "reasonable speculation" to identify conditions which might influence future educational planning. Among possible changes identified were:

1. Practical use of direct electronic communication with and stimulation of the brain
2. New and more reliable drugs for the control of personality and perceptions
3. Chemical methods for improving memory and learning
4. Home education via television and computerized learning
5. Genetic control over the "basic constitution" of the individual[7]

Such projective techniques, it was hoped, would provide educational planners in the public schools with preferences and options that would assist them in structuring decision making.

Another vehicle used by educators concerned with the future was the establishment of special commissions which would set standards and goals for long-range planning. An example of such a commission is the Commission on the Year 2000. Other similar groups of experts are to be found in the selected readings section of this chapter. By lending expert opinion to preferred futures in education, it was thought that education could be attracted to an improved state.

A third technique used by educational planners in moving toward the future is goal-reduction. In this procedure, agencies, professional groups, state departments of education, and others are asked to submit a list of their goals for the future of education. Then, through a ranking or sorting mechanism, the most desired goals are identified. These preferred goals will hopefully influence future decision making in schools.

It should be noted that, in spite of considerable activity in professional education, dealing with the future is a primitive art in school circles. There is a heavy dependence on social science research for ideas and basic structures. There is also a problem, stemming from the affluence of education in the 1960s, of undue optimism in projecting goals. As Toffler has stated:

> Today in techno-societies there is an almost iron-clad consensus about the future of freedom. Maximum individual choice is regarded as a democratic ideal. Yet most writers predict that we shall move further

---

* The Delphi technique, developed by Olaf Helmer, is a rounded questionnaire which uses reduction of opinion to gain consensus.

and further from this ideal. They conjure up a dark vision of the future in which people appear as mindless consumers, surrounded by standardized goods, educated in standardized schools, fed a diet of standardized mass culture, and forced to adopt standardized styles of life.[8]

Whether educational planners can meld the idealism of futurology with the realism of social conditions remains to be seen. For all the rhetoric about the future, school planning remains dominated by quantified projections stemming from present conditions.

ALTERNATIVES AND IDEAS

There are numberous conceptions in existence about what schools should be like in the future. They represent the best thinking of individuals and professional organizations and come from all points on a philosophical continuum. Rather than trying to be comprehensive in presenting these models, the authors have chosen samples that project very different futures for the American public school.

One example is drawn from a working paper of the Research and Theory Group of the Association for Supervision and Curriculum Development, the largest professional association of curriculum specialists in the United States. The task of this group was to develop and identify a set of valued learning outcomes that could guide curriculum development in the future. The result of their study was the development of a group of basic skills which would be attained by all students:

> Self-Conceptualization
> Understanding Others
> Learning Skills
> Capability for Continuous Learning
> Responsible Member of Society
> Mental and Physical Health
> Creativity
> Informed Participation in Economic World
> Use of Accumulated Knowledge
> Coping With Change[9]

The ASCD conception of the future of public education should be seen as an extension of previous global positions by the Educational Policy Commission of the National Education Association and other such groups. While each of the basic skills identified by the Research and Theory Work Group had accompanying subgoals, the projection is necessarily unfocused. Because ASCD represents curriculum leaders from all segments of public education, the vision of the future is necessarily broad-based and an extension of the present. Such a projected future illustrates the difficulty of melding theory with existing practice.

A second idea about the future of public education in the United States is presented by James S. Coleman who conducted a massive study of educational opportunity during the 1960s. Coleman's concern is with access to education and the question of who shall benefit from such a tax-based program:

> The relative intensity of the convergent school influences and the divergent out-of-school influences determines the proximity of the educational system in providing equality of educational opportunity. That is, equality of output is not so much determined by quality of the resource inputs, but by the power of those resources in bringing about achievement. The implication of the concept as I have described it here is that the responsibility to create achievement lies with the educational institution.
>
> I suggest that it may be realized through a change in the very concept of the school itself; from being an agency within which the child is taught to being the agent responsible for seeing that the child learns—a responsibility in which the school's own facilities may play only a part.[10]

Coleman's view that the school must be responsive to all learners represents the position of many minority groups in the United States. His definition of the responsibilities of the school would expand the operation of education into all walks of life, from cradle to grave.

A third conception of the future of public education is presented by psychologist B.F. Skinner. Skinner believes that we can no longer afford an educational system that does not control outcomes, and hopes for a school that contributes to "an improved society":

> We need to make vast changes in human behavior. . . . What we need is technology of behavior. . . . We can follow the path taken by physics and biology by turning directly to the relation between behavior and the environment and neglecting supposed mediating states of mind.
>
> We need to design contingencies under which students acquire behavior useful to them and their culture—contingencies that do not have troublesome byproducts. We must look to the contingencies that induce people to act to increase the chances that their culture will survive. We have the physical, biological, and behavioral technologies needed to save ourselves; the problem is how to get people to use them. The intentional design of a culture and the control of human behavior it implies are essential if the human species is to continue to develop.
>
> What is needed is more intentional control, not less, and this is an important engineering problem.[11]

The Skinner blueprint for schools of the future acknowledges the many social problems faced by our society as we enter the final quarter of the twentieth century, and is representative of a host of positions which seek to manage education toward greater efficiency.

A final conception of the school of the future is offered by Alvin Toffler who concluded, after an intensive study of change in the American society, that what is needed is an education system that serves individuals:

> Every society has its own characteristic attitude toward the past, present, and future. This time-bias, formed in response to the rate of change, is one of the least noticed, yet most powerful determinants of social behavior, and it is clearly reflected in the way the society prepares its young in childhood.
>
> One hundred and fifty years ago Americans needed to learn to survive in a thinly settled frontier in the face of often threatening natural environments. Today there is a need to educate children to survive in a world made increasingly dangerous for man by man.
>
> No educational institution today can set sensible goals or do an effective job until its members subject their own assumptions about tomorrow to critical analysis. For their shared or collective image of the future dominates the decisions made in the institution.
>
> What we do in teaching depends on what we think people are like and what they can become.
>
> Learning for tomorrow includes learning to know one's own mind, so to speak, to understand one's own values clearly enough to be able to make consistent and effective choices.[12]

These four conceptions of the future in education present planners with very different alternatives. Do we develop an education program that helps each individual become capable of adapting to a changing world as Toffler suggests? Do we provide all learners with a set of common adaptive skills and behaviors as the ASCD work group suggests? Do we construct an educational program that reaches out to serve all learners in society and guarantee, through whatever means necessary, that such learning occurs as Coleman recommends? Or do we begin to seriously engineer an educational program that will benefit the American society as Skinner suggests?

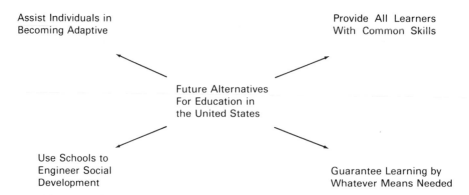

Assist Individuals in
Becoming Adaptive

Provide All Learners
With Common Skills

Future Alternatives
For Education in
the United States

Use Schools to
Engineer Social
Development

Guarantee Learning by
Whatever Means Needed

Even a cursory review of educational events in the United States since 1957 reveals that public schools are pursuing all of the above alternatives simultaneously.

Following the launching of Sputnik I there was a massive effort in the United States to "gear up" education so that our society might compete in a technological war with the Soviet Union. Heavy funding produced extensive curriculum renewal in the form of the so-called alphabet projects (BSCS, PSSC, etc.). The programs of the public schools were initially dominated by mathematics and hard sciences; curriculum improvement later spread to the social sciences and fine arts.

The reaction to this high pressure approach to curriculum development coincided with the awakening of cultural pluralism in the United States and the civil rights movements. Curriculum development efforts were sponsored to serve minority groups and divergent segments of the population.

As the American society entered the latter half of the 1960s, civil rights became individual rights. Numerous programs, in the public schools and outside the public schools, were developed to meet the needs of unique learners. Such alternatives raised important questions concerning the criteria for such program development, i.e., preparation for what?

Finally, into the 1970s the educational systems of the United States have attempted to define and refine the goals and objectives of programs. Diminishing levels of funding have created an accountability movement that seeks to maximize resources by engineering educational learning systems.

What the 1980s and beyond hold for public education in America is a matter of conjecture. History would suggest that economic prosperity and diminished social stress encourages increased flexibility and freedom in curriculum design. By the same token, social tension and economic problems have historically encouraged tight curriculum designs with greater degrees of control and structure.

Whatever the future holds for American public education in the remainder of the twentieth century, it is certain that the shape of education will be influenced by the thinking of those responsible for developing such programs: the curriculum development specialists. The challenge to all persons in the field of curriculum is to become aware of possibilities and develop models which present alternatives for the sponsoring public. To do so, we must overcome a historic reluctance to provide such leadership.

Charles Silberman, in his classic 1970 analysis of American education, posed the problem in the following manner:

> It simply never occurs to more than a handful (of educators) to ask why they are doing what they are doing . . . to think seriously about the purposes or consequences of education. This mindlessness—the failure or refusal to think seriously about educational purpose—is not the monopoly of the public school; it is diffused remarkably evenly throughout the entire educational system and indeed the entire society.[12]

To be aware of alternatives and to utilize opportunities to develop quality programs for our children is the mark of effective leadership in curriculum development.

SUMMARY

The future holds multiple possibilities for education in the United States of America. Curriculum development is the vehicle by which schools will approach the unknown future in planning education.

Studies of the future reveal that we have experienced enormous changes in the American society during the third quarter of the twentieth century. It is probable that the rate and scale of change in our society will continue into the twenty-first century.

Planning for the future of education is made difficult by impermanence in our society, by cultural lag in educational institutions, and by the inefficiency of traditional linear projections of the future. Educational futurists have responded to these conditions by using projection and prediction techniques to attempt to attract schools to preferred futures.

There are numerous conceptions of what education should be like in the future. Some educators favor decentralized programs focused on the individual or specific publics in the American society. Others favor highly centralized programs which serve the state. School districts throughout the United States have responded to these options during the past twenty years by pursuing diverse and multiple ends for education.

The exact nature of educational programs in the United States during the final quarter of the twentieth century will be heavily influenced by the thoughts and work of curriculum specialists. The challenge to all curriculum workers is to think about the meaning of education in our society and present viable alternatives to the sponsoring public.

Notes

1. Harold G. Shane, "Future-Planning as a Means of Shaping Educational Change," in *The Curriculum: Retrospect and Prospect,* 70th Yearbook, Part I, National Society for the Study of Education (Chicago: University of Chicago Press, 1970), p. 191.
2. Kenneth Boulding, *The Meaning of the Twentieth Century* (New York: Harper & Row Publishers, 1964).
3. Arthur C. Clark, *Profiles of the Future* (New York: Harper & Row Publishers, 1963), p. 14.
4. Alvin Toffler, *Future Shock* (New York: Random House, 1970), pp. 157–58.
5. Michael M. McDanield, "Tomorrow's Curriculum Today," in Alvin Toffler, ed., *Learning for Tomorrow: The Role of the Future in Education* (New York, Vintage Books, 1974), pp. 115–16.

6. Harold G. Shane, "Future Planning as a Means of Shaping Educational Change," p. 187.
7. Herman Kahn and Anthony Wiener, *The Year 2000: A Framework for Speculating on the Next Thirty-Three Years* (New York: Macmillan Publishing Company, 1967).
8. Alvin Toffler, *Future Shock*, p. 263.
9. Preliminary draft of a 1978 report, "Valued Learning Outcomes," to the Executive Council of ASCD by the Research and Theory Working Group. Forthcoming.
10. James S. Coleman, "The Responsibility of the School: A Sociologist's Perspective," in Charles Tesconi and Emanuel Hurwitz, eds., *Education for Whom* (New York: Dodd Mead & Company, 1974), pp. 106–7.
11. B.F. Skinner, *Beyond Freedom and Dignity* (New York: Alfred A. Knopf, Inc., 1971), pp. 12, 149, 150, 167, 169.
12. Alvin Toffler, *Learning for Tomorrow,* pp. 4, 5, 20, 107, 196, 399.
13. Charles E. Silberman, *Crisis in the Classroom* (New York: Random House, 1970), pp. 6, 11.

Suggested Learning Activities

1. Develop arguments for and against the types of educational futures envisioned by the ASCD work group, James Coleman, B.F. Skinner, and Alvin Toffler. If you were required to do so, how would you rank these proposals as preferred futures in education?

2. Imagine the design of a new society on the planet Mars. What values should be dominant? How might education function in such a new society? What would be the consequences of such an education system?

3. Try to brainstorm likely changes in our society during the coming decade. How will such changes affect public school education? Which of your identified changes will have the greatest impact on educational planning?

4. Develop a list of ways in which the public schools might incorporate future thinking into their daily operations. How might curriculum specialists in public schools become more aware of alternatives in education?

Books to Review

Bagdikian, Ben. *The Information Machines: Their Impact on Men and the Media.* New York: Harper & Row Publishers, 1971.

Bronwell, Alfred, ed. *Science and Technology in the World of the Future.* New York: John Wiley and Sons, Inc., 1970.

Commoner, Barry. *The Closing Circle: Nature, Man, Technology.* New York: Alfred A. Knopf, Inc., 1971.

Hipple, Theodore, ed. *The Future of Education 1975–2000.* Pacific Palisades, California: Goodyear Publishing Company, 1974.

Rubin, Louis, ed. *The Future of Education: Perspectives on Tomorrow's Schooling.* Research for Better Schools, Inc.: Boston, Allyn and Bacon, Inc., 1975.

Technological Change: Implications for Education. Eugene, Oregon: Center for Advanced Study of Educational Administration, 1970 Conferences and Commissions.

American Youth in the Mid-Seventies. Conference held in Washington, D.C., November, 1972, sponsored by NASSP, P.O. Box 17430, Washington, D.C. 22091

Youth: Transition to Adulthood. Report of the Panel on Youth of the President's Advisory Committee. U.S. Government Printing Office, 1973.

The Greening of the High School. Conference held in Dayton, Ohio, March, 1973, sponsored by Educational Facilities Laboratory and I/D/E/A. Box 628, Far Hills Branch, Dayton, Ohio 45419.

The Reform of Secondary Education. National Commission sponsored by Charles F. Kettering Foundation, 1973. New York: McGraw-Hill, 1973.

Appendix A

Training Paradigm for Curriculum Developers

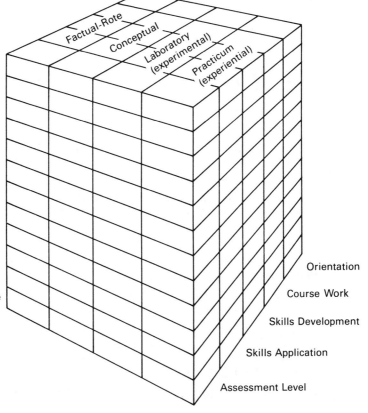

Learning
Human Development
Curriculum Theory
Psychology
Human Relations
Leadership
Change Theory
Instruction
Management
Systems/Commun.
Research Procedure
Evaluation Technique

Factual-Rote
Conceptual
Laboratory (experimental)
Practicum (experiential)

Orientation
Course Work
Skills Development
Skills Application
Assessment Level

Appendix B

Partial Listing of Organizations and Associations Affecting American Education

Citizens' Organizations

Council for Basic Education
725 15th Street, NW
Washington, D.C. 20005

National Coalition for Children
6542 Hitt Street
McLean, Virginia 22101

National Congress of Parents and Teachers
1715 25th Street
Rock Island, Illinois 61201

Educationally Related Organizations and Associations

American Association for Higher Education
One Dupont Circle, NW
Washington, D.C. 20036

American Association of School Administrators
1800 North Moore Street
Arlington, Virginia 22209

American Council on Education
One Dupont Circle, NW
Washington, D.C. 20036

American Educational Research Association
1126 16th Street, NW
Washington, D.C.

American Vocational Association, Inc.
1510 H Street, NW
Washington, D.C. 20005

Association for Supervision and Curriculum Development (ASCD)
1701 K Street, NW
Washington, D.C. 20006

Childrens Television Workshop
One Lincoln Plaza
New York, New York 10023

College Entrance Examination Board
888 7th Avenue
New York, New York 10019

Council for American Private Education
1625 I Street, NW
Washington, D.C.

Council of Chief State School Officers
1201 16th Street, NW
Washington, D.C. 20036

International Reading Association
800 Barksdale Road
Newark, Delaware

Joint Council on Economic Education
1212 Avenue of the Americas
New York, New York 10036

National Art Education Association
1916 Association Drive
Reston, Virginia 22091

National Association for Education of Young Children
1834 Connecticut Avenue
Washington, D.C.

National Association of Elementary School Principals
1801 North Moore Street
Arlington, Virginia 22209

National Association for Public Continuing Adult Education
1201 16th Street, NW
Washington, D.C. 20036

National Association of Secondary School Principals
1904 Association Drive
Reston, Virginia 22091

National Council of Teachers of English
1111 Kenyon Road
Urbana, Illinois 61801

National Council of Teachers of Mathematics
1906 Association Drive
Reston, Virginia 22091

National Education Association
1201 16th Street, NW
Washington, D.C. 20036

National Middle School Association
P.O. Box 968
Fairborn, Ohio 45324

National School Boards Association
800 State National Bank Plaza
P.O. Box 1496
Evanston, Illinois 60204

National Science Teachers Association
1742 Connecticut Avenue, NW
Washington, D.C. 20009

Ethnic and Minority Organizations

Bilingual Education Service Center
500 South Dwyer
Arlington Heights, Illinois 60005

National Council of Negro Women, Inc.
1346 Connecticut Avenue, NW
Washington, D.C. 20036

National Indian Education Association
3036 University Avenue, SE
Minneapolis, Minnesota 55419

National Organization for Women (NOW)
1424 16th Street, NW
Washington, D.C.

General Associations

Committee for Economic Development
477 Madison Avenue
New York, New York 10022

National Association of Manufacturers
Economic Development Department
1776 F Street, NW
Washington, D.C. 20006

National Urban League
New York, New York

Labor Organizations

American Federation of Teachers
11 Dupont Circle
Washington, D.C.

Publishers

American Association of Publishers
One Park Avenue
New York, New York 10016

Association of Media Producers
1221 Avenue of the Americas
New York, New York 10020

Federal Bodies

House of Representatives
130 Cannon House Office Building
Washington, D.C. 20510

National Institute of Education
1200 19th Street, NW
Washington, D.C. 20208

National Science Foundation
5225 Wisconsin Avenue, NW
Washington, D.C. 20015

Office of Education
Office of the Assistant Secretary
Room 3153
400 Maryland Avenue, SW
Washington, D.C. 20202

U.S. Senate
Senate Office Building
431 Russell
Washington, D.C. 20510

Jon Wiles received his Ed.D. in curriculum and instruction from The University of Florida. His present position is acting dean of the School of Education at The University of Montana. Dr. Wiles has served as a classroom teacher, curriculum director, professor of education, and educational consultant to school districts in over twenty states.

Dr. Wiles is the author of two additional books, *Curriculum Planning: A New Approach* (1974) and *Planning Guidelines for Middle School Education* (1976). He has also authored numerous articles in professional education journals.

Joseph Bondi, professor of education, The University of South Florida, received his doctorate in education from The University of Florida. Dr. Bondi has both teaching and administrative experience in public schools on elementary and secondary levels and has served as chairman of the Department of Curriculum and Instruction during his college teaching at The University of South Florida.

Dr. Bondi has authored or co-authored four texts in education and is the author of numerous articles in professional journals. He has served as president of the Florida Association for Supervision and Curriculum Development and as a member of the Board of Directors and Executive Council of ASCD. He is active in other professional associations and has been a consultant in curriculum development to school districts in forty states and Canada.

Name Index

Subject Index